REGIONAL DEVELOPMENT AND PLANNING:
INTERNATIONAL PERSPECTIVES

Editor
Antoni R. Kukliński

Editorial Board
D. Michael Ray
D. R. F. Taylor
Philip E. Uren

Editorial Assistant
Linda Göllner

1975
SIJTHOFF - LEYDEN

The Norman Paterson School of International Affairs at Carleton University, Ottawa was founded in 1966. The School was established to encourage and promote graduate study and professional research and publication in the field of international affairs. The program concentrates mainly on the following fields: political and economic integration, political and economic development, strategic studies, conflict analysis, Canadian foreign policy and the role of technology in international affairs.

Further information may be obtained by writing to:

The Director,
The Norman Paterson School of
International Affairs,
Carleton University,
Ottawa, Ontario,
Canada K1S 5B6.

The Department of Geography at Carleton University offers a program of graduate study which, since its inception in 1967, has evolved a focus of interest in rural and regional development. Several members of the department are closely associated with the Norman Paterson School of International Affairs, and have been involved in the preparation of this volume.

ISBN 90 286 0385 9

Printed in The Netherlands

6000297747

PREFACE

The idea for this book grew out of a series of seminars conducted by Professor Antoni Kukliński during his term as Visiting Professor in the Norman Paterson School of International Affairs, Carleton University, in 1974. These discussions brought together many of the contributors and underlined the value of assembling ideas and experiences related to regional planning from many parts of the world. The purpose of this volume is to present a global selection of these ideas in the hope that their juxtaposition will not only be of immediate use and interest but will also result in further debate and development.

The major credit for this imaginative notion must go to Professor Kukliński himself whose work in this field, particularly with the United Nations, is well known. We are also indebted to the Department of Geography at Carleton University, and to Professors Michael Ray and Fraser Taylor for their advice and assistance, as well as to Ms. Linda Göllner for her energetic and efficient assistance in preparing a complicated manuscript for the press. Finally, we must acknowledge our debt to the typists Mrs. Brenda Sutherland and Mrs. Iris Ward who worked so hard to meet our deadlines.

While we accept editorial responsibility for this endeavour, the views expressed are of course those of the individual contributors.

Philip E. Uren
Director
The Norman Paterson
School of International
Affairs

CONTENTS

7

8

I

THE WESTERN COUNTRIES

THE WESTERN COUNTRIES: INTRODUCTION

The nine papers that comprise this opening section on the Western countries focus individually on single countries or regions and on particular themes. But collectively, they include discussions of the heartland regions and resource hinterlands in both Western Europe and North America and of subjects ranging from theory, models and data needs, to specific regional problems, policy issues and the evolution of regional policies. Furthermore, these papers not only identify the lessons that have been learned from regional development efforts, but also illustrate the thinking and attitudes that are coming to guide decision makers in the developed world.

The most fundamental lessons that have been learned concern the need for comprehensive regional goals and an understanding of the inter-relationships among them. It is acknowledged in all developed countries that national policy objectives must go beyond maximizing economic development to include, among other goals, the quest for social and regional equity, a higher quality of life, and protection of the environment. It is clear from the papers that follow that attitudes to the relationships among these goals are changing. All the papers recognize that economic development by itself does not necessarily contribute to such goals and may indeed be responsible for increasing the difficulty in meeting them. Also evident is the belief that these other goals will have to be met even at some cost to economic growth, posing a conflict between national and regional objectives. Finally, the suspicion is expressed in some of the papers, notably Pedersen's and Koskiaho's, that economic development at the national level, measured so as to take account of all the economic costs involved, may suffer unless adequate attention is paid to social, economic, and environmental goals at the regional level. Implicit in these changes of attitudes is the recognition that separate goals are, in reality, interdependent elements of complex systems.

The section begins with papers by Pedersen and Jobert that focus on the economic and social consequences of economic development. Both papers identify innovation and the accompanying functional specialization as the engine of economic development. Pedersen argues that this development process, in turn, leads to a deterioration in the quality of life, greater regional disparities, congestion and environmental overload, and in-

11

creasing organizational difficulties. Moreover, it follows that the no-growth optimal-size city is an impossible dream. Indeed, even the postulated population size for the ideal city has grown exponentially since Ebenezer Howard's garden city of 35,000 described in 1898, because of the increasing population thresholds needed to support local services (Pedersen, Figure 2). Pedersen's answer to these problems is de-specialization and de-concentration. In contrast to Pedersen's stress on the incremental effect of individual innovations, Jobert emphasizes the cumulative effect of groups of innovations that together comprise new scientific and technical systems. The problem of social change is interpreted as the transition from one form of decision and power system to a new one involving antagonisms and lasting contradictions between groups and social classes. Similarly, changes to new scientific and technical systems involve problems of transition with respect to the physical structure and organization of the city. It is critical that research be focussed on the interrelationships between scientific and technical systems. Planners "risk being one step behind if they centre themselves exclusively on the problems of classical industrialization".

What are the consequences for information needs of this interpretation of industrialized society as a highly complex system? Thoss elaborates the answer to this question for three types of formal mathematical models: simple accounting models, impact models, and decision models. Actual examples and research activities are presented for West Germany, which serve to identify the specific data needs on environment impact, land use, social indicators, and economic activity.

The balance of the section provides documented examples of the range of regional problems evident in Western countries, and of the policy initiatives undertaken in response to them. Koskiaho examines the volume of migration flows, the severity of structural unemployment and of regional economic disparities, and the environmental impact of economic development in Finland. Richardson and Rodriguez, in an examination of the regional planning experience in Spain since the 1960's, find that in this case at least, dramatic improvements in the perception by policy makers of the problems faced have not been matched by corresponding improvements in the results of the plans and policies initiated. Key sectors such as education, agriculture, tourism, pollution control and land use still lack a policy cutting edge to make them viable instruments of regional policy. Ray and Villeneuve underline the need for comprehensive regional policies in Canada by taking account of external relations, particularly immigration and foreign investment, as well as internal factors. Regions are seen not as unique entities whose growth patterns can be separately manipulated, but as distinctive blendings of common social and economic ingredients— a concept which has important implications for how regions are designated

12

for development assistance or controls. But in Canada and in the United States, as in Spain, Brewis and Hansen show that a clearer understanding of the nature of regional problems has not yet been matched by success in dealing with them. The hope, as Cumberland and Fisher note in the final paper, is that the lessons learned and the experience gained will be successfully applied in Alaska, which offers the last great opportunity to develop a major region in a Western country not only for the resources that can be exploited, but with the goal of achieving a new balance between the claims of economic development, and social and environmental responsibility.

D. Michael Ray

ORGANIZATION STRUCTURE AND REGIONAL DEVELOPMENT

Poul Ove Pedersen

1. *Specialization and Scale Economies*

The first and foremost characteristic of economic development since the advent of industrialization has been a rapid innovation process which has primarily manifested itself in increased specialization. Goods production has been rationalized by dividing the production process into sequences of individual operations, either because it is easier to mechanize such simple operations or because it is easier to train people to carry them out. The conventional academic disciplines have also, as a result of the "explosion of knowledge", been sub-divided into a number of new specialities. So too many tasks which used to be performed by individual households have been taken over by "specialists".

Together with, and partly as a consequence of, such specialization, the optimum production level has also risen because of scale and agglomeration economies. These scale economies owe their existence, first of all, to the purely physical consideration that capital investment is often cheaper per unit produced when production is increased.

Another and more important reason for scale and agglomeration economies is the multiples of capital goods and persons involved. If the individual operations in a production process have different optimum sizes, the optimum size of the entire process will be equal to the smallest size which contains all the optimum sizes of the constituent processes. Such cases of multiples are frequent both in the production process itself and increasingly also in administration and research, so that it is often the size of the administrative units which now governs the optimum size of an undertaking.

The third cause of the scale and agglomeration economies is the stochastic phenomenon which is known as "pooled reserves". Examples of such "pooled reserves" are the stocks of goods in a sales organization or of spare parts in a factory which can be kept at proportionately lower

15

levels, the larger the operation concerned. Correspondingly, the rate of unemployment which, even with otherwise full employment, is unavoidable in a specialized labour market where the jobs disappear or appear at random, will be the lower the greater the labour market.[1]

The number of multiple capital goods and specialists as well as the significance of "pooled reserves" will increase as the specialization process advances. The optimum size of production and agglomeration will therefore also increase.

2. *The Negative Effects: Transport and Communications*

The increasing rate of specialization has, however, given rise to an increasing number of transport and communication problems, both internally within each different undertaking and externally between different undertakings and between them and their clients. These growing transport and communication problems are due partly to the difficulties in co-ordinating the various constituent operations in the divided production process, and partly to the fact that increasing specialization and large-scale operation often lead to an increasing geographical spread of the markets for the different products. If these problems become severe enough, they may have an important bearing on location decisions.

In the traditional location theory the main emphasis is placed on the transport costs. More recent location theories, however, are more concerned with communication problems. The decreased importance of transport costs is due partly to the innovations in the transport sector which have reduced transport costs per tonne-kilometre in relation to other costs, and partly to the intensified degree of processing in industry which has reduced the relative importance of goods transport.

The shift from transport to communication costs has, however, not led to a general reduction in the centralization tendencies. One of the reasons is that, whilst the curve indicating the geographical minimum of the transport costs for a production process is normally fairly flat, the location with optimum accessibility for face-to-face communications is very clearly defined (see Figure 1). As far as transport costs are concerned, the premises can therefore be located anywhere within a fairly large area without causing a drastic increase in transport costs although the area with high accessibility, on the other hand, is much smaller.

Growing communication problems can be mitigated partly with the help of purely technical aids such as telephones, data transmission plants, television telephones, etc., and partly through a restructuring of the organization. These two factors are obviously not independent of each other since the optimum structure of the organization must, at any time,

16

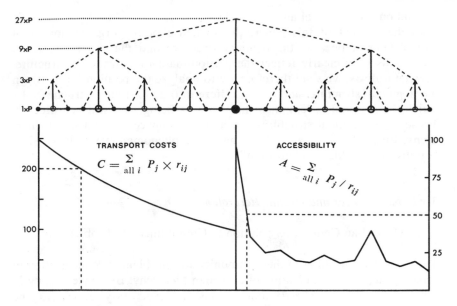

Figure 1.   Accessibility and transport costs in an urban system

In the hypothetical uni-dimensional and hierarchical urban system shown in the top part of the illustration we have calculated, for each town:

Firstly, the transport costs for distributing a commodity from each town to all the residents in the urban system, i.e.:

$$C = \sum_{\text{all } i} P_j \times r_{ij}$$

where P_j signifies the population in town j and where r_{ij} signifies the distance between the towns i and j; and

Secondly, the accessibility from the town to all the other towns on the assumption that the contacts in the urban system are functions of the distance, i.e.:

$$A = \sum_{\text{all } i} P_j / r_{ij}$$

The illustration shows that only in the three most peripheral towns are the transport costs more than twice the transport costs in the central city; on the other hand, the accessibility throughout the urban system is less than half as great as in the central city.

The charts showing the transport costs and accessibility indices in David S. Neft ("Statistical Analysis for Areal Distribution", *Regional Science Research Institute*, Philadelphia, 1966) show the same pattern.

17

depend on the technical aids available.

In the context of this paper, the structure of the organization is of special interest because the regional structure and the system of urban settlements very clearly reflect the predominant organizational structure. In what follows, we shall therefore try to analyze the relationship between the regional structure and three different organizational structures by which the regional development has been, is being, and will be, affected. These organizational structures are a) the urban centre and urban hierarchy, b) the large organizations, and c) a phenomenon which we shall tentatively call "de-specialization".

3. *Urban Centres and Urban Hierarchies*

3.1. The Urban Centre as a Solution to Communication Problems

The traditional solution to the communication problem is concentration in urban centres and the creation of an urban hierarchy. By concentrating in urban centres, specialized undertakings achieved easy access to the suppliers of raw materials and semi-finished products, to clients and service organizations, and to sources of information in general. They also had better possibilities for improving the long-distance communication and transport channels between different centres, since the expenses could be shared by many parties, who could, moreover, together exert political pressure on the authorities holding the purse.

The drawbacks in the growth of the urban centres were that it led to increasing land prices, difficulties in getting sufficient labour, increasing congestion of the transport and communication networks, and increasing pollution.

3.2. The Concept of the Optimum Size of a Town

The recognition that such drawbacks increase with the progress of specialization and the growth of the large cities, gave rise to concepts of an optimum town size. In its early days around the turn of the century, modern town planning was to a large extent based on such concepts. Thus in 1898, Ebenezer Howard [2], reacting against the growth of slums in the English cities, proposed the creation of garden cities that were to be self-contained units with a maximum population of 30-35,000.

During the inter-war period, it was mainly the American sociologists who worked with the idea of an optimum town size. Their idea was, as a rule, either based on a pure minimization of costs (which were often confined to public expenditures) or on analytical surveys which revealed a growing rate of criminality and ill health as the towns expanded. When, after the Second World War, London had to be rebuilt, the basic idea was to create a number of "new towns", this time with a maximum population of 60-80,000. Later, around 1960, when the second generation of "new towns" was due to be built, the concept of an optimum town size was still in vogue, but the population now envisaged was as high as 80-100,000.

This increase in what the British town planners have regarded as the optimum size of a town has simply kept pace with urban development in general. In Figure 2 this is demonstrated by plotting the trend of the

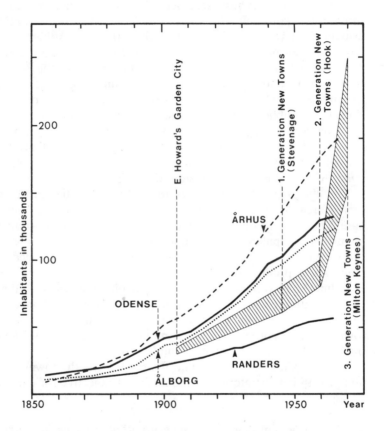

Figure 2. The development of the British town planners' concept of an optimum town size (shaded area) compared with the development of the four largest Danish provincial towns.

Source as regards the size of the "new towns": Ray Thomas, "Aycliffe to Cumbernauld", PEP Broadsheet, No. 516, London 1969.

19

"optimum town size" in England (shaded area) against the population growth in the four largest provincial towns in Denmark. The diagram shows that the "optimum town size" has kept pace with the urban development and has all the time (up to 1960) maintained its position between the third and fourth largest provincial towns in Denmark.

3.3. The Growth of the Optimum Town Size

The explanation of the increase in what the town planners have regarded as the optimum town size is that the population needed for maintaining a given local service has increased. This is because the rationalization through specialization which has continued without interruption over the last hundred years has mainly benefited the large urban areas where it has thus been possible to reduce prices. In the small town, on the other hand, where the population is too small to enable the town to benefit from specialization, prices had to remain unchanged (i.e., they increased in relative terms), or the service activities had to close down. Moreover, since many public or semi-public service activities are governed by charges fixed on a national basis—i.e. on the average for the country as a whole which is dominated by the large towns—any regional price differences can only be maintained to a minor extent. Service activities had, therefore, either to close down or be subsidized.

The charging of higher prices for service activities in the thinly populated areas would, however, for social reasons be unacceptable in any case. This is especially so as wages in those trades which export their goods from thinly populated areas would have to be lower than in the cities if those goods are to be able to compete with goods produced in the large cities where productivity is higher.

Bylund[3] has worked out that in the peripheral areas in northern Sweden, the population on which a service centre is based would have to grow at a rate of 2% per annum if the centre is to maintain its services. The British town planners' concept of the optimum town size has, coincidentally, also on average grown at a rate of about 2% per annum.

To maintain their position and their activities, the towns have to grow, and growth has therefore become a central objective for each centre.

4. *The Growth of Towns and the Formation of Large Organizations*

4.1. Self-Generated Growth

The increase in the optimum town size is linked with the fact that the town with its hinterland does not—as has been assumed in discussions

20

about the optimum town size—represent an immutable society isolated from the outside world. With increasing specialization, this assumption has become increasingly false, especially in the case of small towns that are wholly dependent on the exchange of goods and information with the outside world. If there is a change in production and consumption in the outside world, the activities of the town must follow suit. If there is such a thing as an optimum town size, it is therefore likely to vary as a function of time and of technological development.

In the course of time, many of the present activities in the town will become outdated and unprofitable, and it is only if new activities are introduced that the town will be able to maintain its size and income. New activities in a town can be introduced through local initiatives based on local inventions or ideas, through local initiatives based on ideas and inventions imported from outside, or through outside organizations, both public and private, that establish branches in the town.

However, results of much recent research indicate that entirely new ideas or inventions most frequently originate in the largest cities.

The probability of new ideas being initiated is highest in the larger cities since these normally have the greatest exchange of ideas, people and products with other cities both in the country and abroad. But even if ideas or inventions should not *arise* more frequently in the large cities than elsewhere, the probability that new ideas will be *used* for new activities is still greater in the large cities because new, small activities are much more dependent on external economies than are older established undertakings, or those with more routine functions. For small undertakings, easy access to customers, suppliers and service functions is very important as they have not developed any permanent purchasing and sales organization. In contrast, larger and older undertakings will, to a high degree, have developed such organizations internally so that they are less dependent on the metropolitan environment.

The large cities therefore form a self-generating growth mechanism:

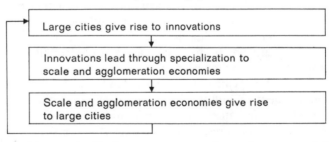

Finally, the large cities normally have a more variegated commercial life than the small towns, and are thus not as sensitive to stagnation in any individual sector.

21

4.2. The Formation of Business Concerns: "The Urban Field"

In practice, the increasing difficulties experienced in the large cities have therefore not led to a stagnation in their growth but rather to a re-organization of both private organizations and public authorities.

In the case of private undertakings, the increasing local problems of transport and communications led to attempts at converting external to internal problems, to which the undertakings could more easily find their own solutions. This was achieved by making the individual undertaking so large that it was able to build up a number of service and sub-contractor activities of its own, instead of having to rely on less accessible external contacts.

This, however, created its own problems since the large areas and manpower reserves needed for such large undertakings became more and more difficult to come by in, or in the vicinity of, the large centres.

The solution to this problem consisted in improving the means of communications and changing the structure of these large organizations. The conventional, hierarchically-designed linear organization was replaced by a staff organization. The traditional undertaking with a single factory was superseded by a loosely-constructed concern consisting of an administrative unit, possibly a research and development unit, and a number of production and service undertakings linked vertically as part of a production process, horizontally in a network of branches, or merely through a financial roof organization. As the telecommunications network has proved to be well suited to deal with internal data flows in such a combine, yet not effective enough to deal with external data flows between different concerns, the improved telecommunication network has, in conjunction with the modified organizational structure, permitted a physical decentralization of a number of productive activities.[4] The administrative and decision-making activities which need the high accessibility in the town centre have, however, not moved out. The town centre has assumed the function of making contacts, not between the different activities but between one concern and another, and between the concerns and the service facilities serving them.

The result has been an increasing spread of industrial production but also, at the same time, an increasing concentration of industrial administration and management in a smaller number of larger cities.[5] Since, however, employment in industrial production is stagnating while employment in the service activities and administration is growing, this development has not relieved the pressure on the cities. The outwards movement from the large cities has been selective: it is always the worst paid jobs that have moved out.

As the outward movement from the towns has, to a large extent, taken place within the framework of the large organizations as they establish branches or shift sub-contractors, the purely physical decentralization too has not resulted in a corresponding organizational decentralization. Indeed, the outlying districts have, on the contrary, become even more dependent on the large administrative centres than before because the small independent undertakings find it much more difficult to move away from the contact centres unless they work as sub-contractors for a small number of large companies.

Furthermore, the outwards movement is largely confined to areas within about 150 km of the largest cities. The formation of combines has thus not made any contribution towards aiding the more peripheral areas. This limitation of the areas which benefit from the outwards movement is due to the fact that although the curve indicating the minimum of the transport costs is flat, the transport costs nevertheless begin to increase more significantly if the distance from the cost minimum is fairly long (see Fig. 1). The distance of 150 km more or less corresponds to that over which commercial vehicles can carry out a return trip within a day if loading and unloading are taken into account.

It is this area with a radius of 150 km around the large cities which Friedman and Miller[6] have termed "the urban field".

As regards the pollution problems in the large cities, the decentralization of productive activities may well be imagined, in the short term, to have a positive influence on the metropolitan environment. To the extent, however, to which the pollution problem is not a local but a regional or global problem, decentralization does not in itself offer a solution.

4.3. The Public Organization: Sector Planning

The description given above has been mainly concerned with commercial undertakings. Increasing concentration has, however, also affected the public sector: here, too, increasing specialization has meant that the hinterland which can be served by an individual specialist has become larger and larger. In other spheres with high capital input, e.g. schools and hospitals, this has likewise contributed to a growing concentration. Finally, the democratic desire for equality of all citizens has led to a centralization of more and more decisions. This has, to a large extent, taken the form of laying down more and more extensive standards for the different sectors, with the result that local self-government is slowly being superseded by sector planning.

The argument for such centralization has been that an excessive degree of self-government in the local authorities could easily lead to a "ghetto formation", as has in fact happened, around the large cities. This is unfortunate as it can result in a rapidly deteriorating service level in these outlying areas.

Economic development, however, has resulted in increasing disparities in the size and growth rate of different local communities, and the migrations from the country to the towns have exacerbated the differences in demographic structure between one community and another. Centralized decision-making and the fixing of standards have thus failed to prevent the "ghetto-formation" that they were intended to prevent. Because, moreover, country-wide measures have been applied to local authorities with widely different structures, many spheres have experienced a distribution of resources which must be regarded as highly irrational from a local point of view.

4.4. Improvements in the Communications Network as a Tool of Regional Policy

The formation of business concerns and the adoption of sector planning have done a certain amount to solve the problems caused by increasing specialization: they have, to a certain extent, helped to relieve the pressure on our town centres and have, at least partly, tackled some of the problems connected with regional development in the areas close to the major centres. They have not, however, been able to solve the problems in the more remote outlying regions that have not benefited from the movement away from the large cities.

An often attempted solution to the problems of the outlying areas is to improve the accessibility of these areas by creating transport and communications networks. Past experience indicates, however, that this solution is not particularly effective, especially if this is the only kind of measure that is taken. The reason is that improving a link in the communications network improves accessibility at both ends of the link. When a peripheral region is thus linked to a large conurbation, the peripheral region will admittedly derive the greater benefit in terms of accessibility as it comes closer to the large population in the city, while the benefit to the large city will be confined to an improved accessibility to a thinly populated peripheral area. Since, however, *both* of the regions stand to gain, the improvements to the network will only in extreme cases affect the relative position (in terms of accessibility) of the regions within a regional system.[7]

4.5. The Growth Centre Theory

An alternative solution to the problems of peripheral areas that has been receiving an increasing amount of attention since 1960 is the creation of growth centres. This involves the determination not of the optimum size of the town but rather of the minimum size required to create self-generated growth. The figure most frequently quoted is that of a population of about 250,000 which is, in fact, the minimum size envisaged for Britain's latest "new town", Milton Keynes.

Such major growth centres are envisaged as being developed in peripheral areas by a relocation of public and private activities. According to the theory, the effect of such action should spread from the growth centre into its hinterland. Pedersen [8] describes three such diffusion processes, one based on trade (input-output process), one based on the diffusion of innovations, and one based on the diffusion of industrial investments to the "urban field" as described above.

Of these diffusion processes, the last-named will presumably be the most important in thinly populated areas, and this represents one of the weaknesses of the growth centre theory as it means that the growth of the centre will only begin to spread to the hinterland when the centre is overcrowded.

The usefulness of growth centres as a tool of regional policy is, moreover, confined to peripheral areas which are either relatively densely populated or are very large, as it is only in such areas that the creation of sufficiently large growth centres can be realistically envisaged.

5. De-Specialization

5.1. A Critique of the Growth Philosophy

The third solution to the problem arising from continued specialization is to cease to specialize, or to "de-specialize" which, for lack of a better word, is a term we shall use in what follows. The arguments in favour of a de-specialization policy have been advanced by two parties in particular: those who warn against the alienation resulting from the increased specialization and scale of production, and who instead propose a decentralization, both organizational and geographical; and those who warn against the negative by-products of production, the pollution, and who propose a change in organization and production such that by-products are reduced to a minimum, and such that the unavoidable by-products are recirculated into production. These two arguments, which partly coincide, have both been formulated as a critique of the growth philosophy. Some of the most important points of this critique are summarized below.

"The growth in material goods and services resulting from continuous rationalization through specialization only satisfies a limited part of human needs." Based on Maslow's *Hierarchy of Needs,* this statement of Wallin's [9] thus postulates that the different specialized jobs can be described accord-

25

ing to the extent to which they help the worker to satisfy:
— the need for survival and physical security
— the need for social security and recognition, and
— the need for self-realization.

He concludes that many specialized jobs hardly satisfy the first of these needs. "An increasing proportion of the growth in production does not satisfy real human needs but is rather the result of a demand inflation." One form of demand inflation is resulting from our attempts to alleviate the negative side-effects of production, for instance when we produce devices to clean the environment which we ourselves have polluted, or when we built hospitals to cure the victims of traffic and work accidents.

Another form of demand inflation is related to the use of time as a scarce resource. Burenstam Linder[10] argues that for the time budget of the individual to be in equilibrium, the marginal productivity of different time uses must be equal. Therefore, when it happens that the productivity of the work-time goes up then the productivity of the leisure time must also increase, or else the leisure time will have to be reduced. The productivity of some leisure activities can be increased by means of material goods such as cars, summer homes or pleasure-boats, while to produce such goods, the productivity of the work time must be increased further, etc. However, for some leisure activities, e.g. cultural activities, there are not the same possibilities of increasing productivity by means of material goods, and the leisure time will, therefore, tend less and less to be devoted to such activities.

According to Burenstam Linder, steadily increased work productivity will, therefore, when working time is kept constant, result both in a steadily increased material demand and in the development of leisure activities in a specific direction.

Demand inflation is perhaps not an evil per se; but it becomes problematic when we are no longer able to decide which production can satisfy demand and which merely compensates for the negative side-effects, because this makes it impossible for us to determine the price, in terms of resources and time, which we must pay in order to satisfy the real demands.

5.2. The Degree of Specialization:
A Conflict between National and Regional Objectives

The possibilities of de-specialization are linked with the reason for specialization, which is that it better allows the society and/or the individual to utilize limited resources either in the form of education and training or in the form of tools, machinery, or other capital equipment. The specialist becomes a specialist because he, either by virtue of his education or because he has other specific limited resources at his disposal, can carry out

26

his speciality more effectively than other people.

In our contemporary specialized society, however, specialization may also be due to lack of co-ordination, perhaps because co-ordination becomes so difficult that it no longer seems "worthwhile" to make the attempt.

Not all specialities become occupations. Wallin [11] mentions a number of conditions which must be met if a speciality is to become an occupation. The most important of these is that there must be work enough, in the local area, to fill a specialist's time and secure him a sufficient income. The degree of specialization in a local community, therefore, depends on the size of the community. When, moreover, the national government or a professional organization establishes national standards for local services, or national agreements for wages and work time, they thereby influence the level of specialization in the local community.

A specialization which may be regarded as reasonable from a national point of view may therefore well be irrational if applied to a peripheral area, and may lead to the cessation of activities or to the misuse of resources.

This conflict may be exemplified by the organization of school buses, by school planning and by the closing-down of commercial undertakings.

School buses are often organized independently of the licensed public transportation. In the densely populated areas where public transportation is relatively good and school bussing solves a marginal problem this might be reasonable; but in thinly populated areas where the demand for school buses is larger and the supply of licensed public transportation is very small, a separation of school buses and licensed buses in two independent systems constitutes a misuse of resources.

In densely populated areas it is reasonable that schools should provide a varied supply of specialized courses and educational facilities. In the thinly populated periphery the same level of specialization can only be provided if small local schools are shut down, and education is concentrated in a few schools that are far apart. This involves much increased transport time for a large number of students.

From a national viewpoint the shut-down of small, unprofitable production units might be desirable. For the local community, however, the main effect is unemployment and economic uncertainty, and it might very well be cheaper for society as well as more satisfactory for the people involved to subsidize the unprofitable production unit than to pay unemployment relief.

This schism between national and local viewpoints is reinforced by the fact that a misuse of resources that may be of considerable importance within the thinly populated areas is often negligible from a national viewpoint.

27

From the local point of view the situation is further aggravated in that every time one activity is shut down the possibility of retaining the rest is reduced. The only way to halt the process is to stop the specialization, i.e. to de-specialize.

5.3. Two Forms of De-Specialization

Specialization takes place partly through a division of existing jobs, and partly when specialists take over jobs which formerly were carried out by the households.

Increasing specialization and sectionalization in both the public and the private sectors give rise to problems inasmuch as they lead to a tendency of deferring the co-ordination between the different sectors to that stage of the production and planning process when the finished product or scheme is available. As against this, the principle behind a de-specialization policy should be to attempt to co-ordinate the activities at the stage when the problem is formulated, i.e. as close to the consumer as possible. One example of such de-specialization would be the co-ordination of ordinary buses and school buses already referred to. Other examples are the attempt to solve pollution problems by more integrated production chains; the planning of large supermarkets and discount stores in such a way that business gains from rationalization of the retail trade are not more than offset by the necessary transport investments made by the public and the transport costs paid by the consumer; the co-ordination between medical doctors, social workers, and others—as proposed in the new Danish social reform—so that the consumer of the social services does not need to visit more than one public office to solve his problems; or the experiments with group technology and production cells—as carried out mostly by some mechanical industries, for instance the Volvo automobile factory—in which the assembly lines are replaced by groups of workers who colla-borate on finishing a motor or a whole car at a time, and thereby avoid a number of co-ordination problems that exist along the assembly line.

It is this type of de-specialization which in the educational sector has led to the slogan about problem-oriented education. The goal is not so much to reduce specialization as it is to demolish the traditional sector boundaries and create a more flexible system.

The kind of de-specialization that has the greatest direct impact on the individual household is that which takes place at the interface between the households and the trades. A number of examples show that such a de-specialization is either planned or has already been carried out:

a) As the bus routes in outlying areas can no longer be maintained without very large subsidies, it has been suggested that the car owners in these areas should be paid for conveying those who have no cars;

28

b) As it has generally been impossible to satisfy the demand for kindergartens and day nurseries, and the costs of these facilities also have increased rapidly, local communities are now paying housewives to work in their homes as day nurses for 2-4 children;

c) A growing proportion of all new one-family homes is built partly or in full by the households themselves.

d) With the transition from conventional retail shops to supermarkets, some of the expenses incurred by the shops have been externalized and passed on to the consumer in the form of increased transport costs; and

e) In many public services the service level is reduced when labour costs go up, with the result that part of the work is transferred to the households; that is for instance the case when the mail service requires that mail boxes for all apartments be set up at the entrance to multi-storey buildings, so that the mailman will not have to climb upstairs.

De-specialization of the kind carried out or called for in these examples is promoted by the increase in the general level of education, by the general increase in income, and by more equal income distribution. The increase in educational level reduces the disadvantage of some of the relatively poorly educated, especially in the service sector; the general increase in income makes it possible for many to buy tools and machinery that formerly were available only to the specialist; and a more equal income distribution makes it impossible for the upper class to continue to buy a number of personal services.

The increasing marginal tax rate, which in the Scandinavian countries often is above 50%, will also further the transfer of activities from the specialist to the households, because the specialist must be several times more productive than the non-specialist to be able to compete with the tax-free work of the households themselves.

Already many people today want part-time employment or at least more flexible working hours so that they can devote more time to the activities that are being transferred to the households. In many thinly populated areas with problems of high unemployment and a low level of services one solution would be part-time jobs, so that people worked part-time in industry or agriculture and part-time in some of the services which are in danger of closing or which are already closed. This would, however, require a much more flexible organization and administration than that which today is exercised by the sectorized authorities, organizations and firms.

Legislation that has regional consequences must to a larger degree than is true today take specific regional conditions, regional differences in needs and resources availability, as well as the co-ordination between sectors, into consideration, especially when norms and standards are being established.

The questions which here arise are these: How far can and should a de-specialization policy be taken? Which specialities should be abolished or combined? and, What is the effect on the transport and communications structure and on the regional structure?

5.4. The Extent of De-Specialization

Most of the examples of de-specialization are derived from the service sector, which has also generally been the last to be affected by specialization. If this holds true in general, it is quite in keeping with the observation that has been made in many innovation studies to the effect that those spheres in which an innovation is adopted last are those where it first becomes out-dated. We should therefore be able to regard the specialization process in the same way as any other innovation process, and to regard de-specialization as the rationalization that eventually affects most innovation processes.

That de-specialization occurs first of all in the service sector may also be due to the fact that the advantages of large-scale operations here mainly stem from the multiples of persons rather than capital. In industry, where the advantages of large-scale operation are to a greater extent due to direct savings in resources or to the multiples of capital equipment, de-specialization is no doubt a more difficult proposition.

5.5. De-Specialization and De-Centralization
in the Organizational and Physical Sense

One of the principal aims of a de-specialization policy must be to enhance the standard of living. The Swedish report on low incomes defines the standard of living as "the availability to the individual of resources in the form of money, property, knowledge, mental and physical energy, social relations and security, etc. which enable him to assess and deliberately control his way of living".[12] The pre-conditions for raising the standard of living in a peripheral area are, therefore, that the individual must have greater possibilities for making his own choice, i.e. organizational decentralization, and that he must have more relevant alternatives to choose from, i.e. a physical de-centralization of activities from the towns.

De-specialization will undoubtedly give rise to an organizational decentralization, but will it also result in a physical de-centralization? There are a number of examples where physical de-centralization has taken place at the expense of organizational de-centralization and vice versa. For intance, the development of industry in the peripheral areas has been characterized by the fact that local activities have been superseded by branches or sub-contractors of companies centred in the large cities. In the school system, the growing number of options which have become available to the pupils in recent years were made possible only through increasing physical concentration. The transition from the production line to group work already mentioned may be capable of leading to a physical de-centralization not only of the production of semi-finished products but also of the assembly works. To what extent, however, will this lead to an organizational de-centralization? Will the de-centralized groups not continue to be dependent on input deliveries and marketing organizations to such an extent that their self-government will become illusory?

A de-specialization policy will undoubtedly improve the conditions for those who are already resident in the peripheral areas but will it also result in a greater number of options for the young people who will be growing up in such areas? Kristensen[13] answers this question in the affirmative since he considers that a fair number of the advantages offered by the large cities are of interest only to a limited number of academics and other upper class persons and not to the population in general. The options available in the peripheral areas as compared to those in the cities are therefore seen in a better light here than is usually the case: Kristensen merely sees the former as different from, not as inferior to the latter. But does this argument hold true? And how will an increase in the general level of education and incomes affect the argument?

5.6. The Consequences of De-Specialization with regard to the Demand of Communications

De-specialization has been represented as a solution to the growing problems of transport and communications. But will it solve them? It will undoubtedly solve some problems but it will also create others.

The already discernible trend towards part-time work and more flexible working hours will have the effect of reducing the peak hour traffic. On the other hand, it will, if more people are at work for a shorter period of time, cause an increase in the total volume of travel between the home and the work place. It will also give rise to problems in respect of contacts between people who work at different times of the day.

In the peripheral areas, de-centralization will increase the demand for communications since some of the co-ordination between the sectors which previously took place in the large cities will have been moved out. However, the demand for transport and communications between the large city and the peripheral area will not, for that reason, decrease since the material production will continue to be specialized.

De-specialization will therefore not be able to solve the communications problems by reducing them but rather by involving more people in the communication process.

Notes

1. For a detailed examination of the causes of scale economies, see Gunnar Ribrandt, "Stordriftsfördeler inom industriproduktionen", ("Advantages of Large-Scale Operation within Industrial Production"), *Statens Offentliga Utredninger*, 1970:30, Stockholm.

2. *Garden Cities of Tomorrow*, Swan Sonnenschein, London, 1898.

3. Erik Bylund, "The Central Place Structure and Accessibility to Services in Northern and Western Sweden", *Plan*, International Special Issue, 1972, pp. 31-35.

4. See Alan R. Pred, *Major Job-Providing Organizations and Systems of Cities*, Association of American Geographers, Commission on College Geography, Resource Paper No. 27, Washington, D.C., 1974.

5. See Mats-G. Engstrom, *Regional Arbetsfördeling (Regional Distribution of Work)*, Gleerups, Lund, 1967.

6. J. Friedman and J. Miller, "The Urban Field", *Journal of the American Institute of Planners*, Vol. 31, No. 4, 1965, pp. 321-329.

7. See Poul Ove Pedersen, "Innovation Diffusion within and between National Urban Systems", *Geographical Analysis*, Vol. 2, No. 3, 1969, pp. 203-254; and *Urban-Regional Development in South America: A Process of Diffusion and Integration*, Mouton Publishers, Paris and The Hague, 1975.

8. See Poul Ove Pedersen, "Vaekstcentre og bysystemer" ("Growth centres and urban systems"), *Økonomi og Politik*, No. 2, 1971, pp. 141-167.

9. Erik Wallin, "Yrkesvalprocessen og den regionale strukturen" ("The process of choosing a profession, and the regional structure"), *Urbaniseringsprocessen*, 51, Lund, 1972.

10. Staffan Burenstam Linder, *Den Rastlosa Valfardsmenniskan (The Restive Welfare Man)*, Bonniers, Stockholm, 1969.

11. Erik Wallin, *op. cit.*

12. For a survey of alternative concepts of the standard of living, see Hans Kristensen, "Levevilkar og udkantsomrader" ("Standard of Living, and Peripheral Areas"), *Økonomi of Politik*, October, 1972.

13. *Ibid.*

2

INTENSIVE GROWTH, SCIENTIFIC SYSTEM, AND URBAN DEVELOPMENT: A RESEARCH PROJECT

Bruno Jobert

Each stage of development has its own mode of organizing social space. Present changes in urban space cannot be likened to a simple extension of the urban forces produced during the extensive growth period of traditional industrialization.[1] On the contrary, they seem to be elements of a true mutation, the meaning of which needs to be analyzed.

Some have called present society the "opulent society", and have described the effect that private mass consumption has on urban forms.[2] The mechanical growth of the number of workers in the conventional services sector has led others to study office blocks and the "city" phenomenon.[3] The emergence of a technobureaucratic élite has been recognized in certain urban renewal operations and in the constitution of directional centres. Others have stressed the influence of this or that particular technique (cars, telecommunication methods, etc.) on urban systems. In this same spirit we have elsewhere[4] tried to describe the changes that have taken place in urban planning systems as a result of the introduction of new research and intervention techniques. It seems to us, however, that the most important phenomenon is not one or other of the innovations, but rather the new position of scientific and technical system in the economic system. These new planning methods and the concomitant transformations in urban structure should, therefore, be linked to a major change in economic growth: the introduction of science as a direct productive force. Our purpose, accordingly, is now to explore the interrelations between urban development and scientific and technical system as an essential element of economic growth.

The introduction of science as a productive force is manifested by the progressive eviction of man from his direct executant, handling, and manipulative functions within the manufacturing process. As automation progresses, man finds himself pushed further and further to the fringes of the immediate production process. The sphere of straightforward work diminishes and that of complex preparative, conceptual, and supervisory

33

production work increases. As science comes closer to production, research institutes take on quasi-industrial dimensions, and in them collective work supplants individual research. Conversely, work in leading industries might be likened, in certain aspects, to a gigantic experiment.

At this stage of development, therefore, economic growth does not depend only on the number of workers, the amount of equipment and investments attributed to production, but also on the growth of knowledge and its application to the manufacturing process.[5]

The major contradiction central to this growth is that it necessitates at the same time an ever increasing control and hierarchy, and a social and intellectual dynamism without precedent. Technical innovation saps authority at the same time as this authority becomes more necessary than ever.[6]

The main industries affected by this contradiction are those that are based on scientific and technical research and that mobilize the creative capacities of "intellectual technicians" with a view to maintaining or conquering dominant positions in the system. However, management studies show the importance of an adaptable, non-authoritative atmosphere for technical innovation in a company: the best results, for the company, are obtained when individuals have the widest choice of the technical means to reach a target that management has succeeded in making the personnel feel is a socially superior one.[7] In other words, scientific and technical development is all the more rapid, the better the scientific workers internalize the social target, real or presumed, of the companies employing them. This explains the importance of psychological and economical methods of social control for this category of personnel: participation, human relations, etc.

By centering our analysis on the various interactions between scientific and technical system and the urban system, we think we can bring out some of the most stimulating aspects (and the ones richest in potential contradictions) of urban development, and the strategies which claim to regulate it. Let us make it clear at the outset that by this we do not mean to describe how urban systems "reflect" the characteristic features of the social system: in our opinion these are not simple projections without autonomy, nor specific effects of economic development. The object of our project is, rather, to define certain functions fulfilled by urban systems in this new mode of growth, and some of the tensions and contradictions associated with the emergence of the new mode of organizing social space that has arisen from it.

We intend to base the study of these interactions on three theoretical propositions concerning:
1. Social change;
2. The complex and contradictory character of change in urban systems; and
3. The notion of the polarization system.

1. An approach to social change through contradiction and heterogeneity

Everyone can easily admit that for every stage of development there is a corresponding specific mode of production and use of urban space. Theories differ, however, concerning the nature of the passage from one to another.

In evolutionary theories, social development is seen as manifested by an increasing differentiation and specialization in social activities, and, therefore, in their increasing interdependence. As development progresses diffuse institutions, multifunctional traditional groups (family, primary group) leave room for interacting functional groups. The town is the place of the isolated individual and of large specialized machinery: if a certain demographic density is a condition of specialization, the ever more dense interdependencies provoked by modernization are manifested by an even greater concentration of the population in towns. Like social change, urbanization is seen as a unilinear and continuous phenomenon: in this thesis, the importance of technological innovation in industry appears to be the final aspect of the constant progress of rationality within the collectivity.[8]

This interpretation seems to us too neglectful of the contradictions which are at the root of social change. The dynamism of a functional apparatus, of specialized activities, cannot be understood outside the social relationships which ensure their coherence. For each stage of technico-economic development there is a corresponding specific decision and power system, to which the dominating and dominated classes and strata are compared and defined, "the masters of the means of production, and the servants of these means".[9] The transition from one form of organization to another does not imply a simple unfolding without a break in earlier activities; it is shown by the destruction of the old system of decision, and, therefore, by antagonisms and lasting contradictions between groups and social classes. The transition is not immediate, and recent sociological analyses underline, each in their own way, the heterogeneous character of historical societies.[10]

2. The complex and contradictory character of change in an urban environment

In the same way, urban societies conserve the physical traces of past systems, as the persistence and resurgence of old systems are reinterpreted at times by the dominating mode of production, and reveal elements of new modes of organizing social space. They therefore combine two kinds of contradictions, one resulting from the co-existence of urban systems of differing ages, the other from antagonisms proper to this or that system. Since, moreover, it is not merely a question of these various systems being juxtaposed, there is a risk that analyses of pure types may have little bearing on reality.

Any new structures which might appear thus act on historical material which has its own originality, and can exercise a certain influence on the later course of urbanization. One can presume that the traditional agrarian type organization, and the alliances made between social strata belonging to different periods of development during the process of industrialization, have greatly contributed to modelling the particular image of industrial urbanization in this or that historical society.

The extension of American universities, for example, cannot be analyzed solely in relation to elements of the urban systems which are their contemporaries: the suburban middle classes, the rise of the Central Business District etc., the conflicts and, at times, riots, which mark this episode of the urban re-conquest of the black ghettos are witnesses to the importance of these tensions and contradictions between elements of differing ages.[11]

The problem of transition, which is becoming more and more important in the theory of social change, appears, therefore, to be central to our approach.

This does not mean we will be studying the conditions of production and use of urban space in an abstract model of post industrial society, but rather that we will be analyzing the tensions and contradictions which might arise from the emergence of a new type of economic growth in an already organized social space, by studying one of its essential elements.

There is no doubt that this will permit certain aspects of urban planning to be made more profound,[12] since this is not only a regulating process acting at the heart of a homogeneous urban system, but also a process regulating tensions which may arise from the co-existence and concurrence of several systems in one urban unit. Planning contributes to the institutionalized regulation of the transition from one mode of organizing social space to another within complex urban societies.[13] Consequently, it does not mean merely noting how planning expresses the dominant character of this activity or of those groups, the segregated or dispersed character of one or another, but rather of capturing the way in which it facilitates the substitution of one dominant activity by another one, how it takes into account the expulsion and relegation phenomena of groups touched by the new domination phenomena.

If the processes described by ecologists are used to analyze the urban insertion of scientific and technical system, then the processes of domination and segregation, of centralization and decentralization ought to be understood in relation to the invasion and succession processes to which they might give rise.[14]

3. The notion of the polarization system
   as a means of analyzing urban situations

The principal danger in trying to account for the tensions and contradictions resulting from the coexistence of systems of differing ages within concrete urban units is that of foundering into absolute relativism.

If, for example, the insertion of scientific system in the various urban systems is only demonstrated by problematical liaisons that are incidental to elements belonging to another age, then all systematization of such relations seems impossible. Each urban situation would represent a unique structural combination with no relation to any other. Consequently, scientific analysis should refer to the deepening of homogeneous systems. We have mentioned the dangers of abstraction with this method.

Notions drawn from the economic theory of polarized development ought to permit the definition of an orientation avoiding absolute relativism as well as the formalism of abstract systems. For this, each "urban economic system" must be considered as an element in a system of poles and centres which expresses the division of work within the economic space. Economic growth progresses neither evenly nor haphazardly in this polarization system.

Towns are complex systems combining the remains of old systems and the germs of new, still emerging ones around a dominant system.

Industrial agglomerations feed themselves on the rural world's breakdown that they have provoked: the reception and socialization of rural migrants, the ups and downs in the conquest of new agricultural zones for industry, the alliances, the relationships between urban and rural groups, are all features of industrial centres.

Industrial manufacturing activities are thus chased from the metropolitan centres towards their peripheries or to distant satellite poles, to the benefit of new specialized data processing activities. A large part of the work carried out in these dominant poles is, nevertheless, still simple work relying on the use of only slightly mechanized or automated tools. These inequalities in development are shown by the rush of foreign workers who come to occupy "the transition factories, stop gaps for coming automation".[15] Thus, in France, the transitional population of rapidly undesirable foreign groups install themselves in transitional areas when the French working class abandons them for more comfortable shelters, and these foreign groups stay there until redevelopment chases them to other slums.

It is therefore possible to perceive the functional relationship which might exist between the dominant, motivating town, freeing low skilled labour for the outskirts by accelerating the aging of its activities, and the inequalities in its development.

Contradictory movements can, in the same way, be detected in present urban systems: the effects of domination of the most technically advanced industries seem to combine with those of the slow industrialization of other sectors.

Within the polarization system it seems theoretically possible to determine various types of structural combinations between economic elements of differing ages, depending on the specific situation of urban units and their transformation within this polarization system. Several ways of inserting scientific and technical system into the polarization system can be found: associated with large metropolitan areas (Paris, London, Boston), in certain industrial centres (Grenoble, Birmingham), isolated in segregated poles for the production of knowledge (Cambridge). Our hypothesis is that these different types of insertion form a system, and show differentiated domination effects between urban poles.

It is neither the property market, nor urban planning which found the economic values that constitute an urban pole, but rather its position in a system of poles, the spatial form of the economic division of work. But it may be that the internal contradictions of urban development (for example financial speculation resulting in a housing crisis, or a public transport crisis) provoke a policy at the polarization system level through a backlash: the difficulties linked to the growth of large urban metropoles like London and Paris have contributed to national urban policies. It is, besides, not by chance that a large number of private research establishments are concentrated in certain new towns in the London suburbs (Harlow, Welwyn Garden City, etc.).

It is around this dominating network that urban systems are built and develop.

The necessary understanding of the existing relations between this system of interaction proper to dominant units, with the rest of the urban structure, necessitates a reevaluation of the fundamental concepts allowing us to account for urban phenomena.

The problem seems insoluble as long as one reduces towns to a physico-demographic form which would itself engender a certain style of life, an urban culture.

38

The foundation of urban systems is formed by the spatial interactions between activities and not by the physical and demographic structures, which only serve as a support. From this point of view, theories insisting on the preponderate role of export activities as the foundation of urban dynamism are certainly a step forward. These do, however, reduce urban systems to induced phenomena without any dynamism of their own, and it appears that on the contrary large metropoles base their own development on a network of exchanges and services that permit them to constantly substitute new export activities for declining industries. Thus towns appear to be vast communications networks. It is not spatial proximity but accessibility which is the main property of urban systems. Each individual, each group, participates in multiple spatial interacting networks, in which the "neighbour" relationship plays an ever smaller part.

The idea of territorial collectivities with a global vocation and a homogeneous frontier, reigning over a mathematically fixed series of satellites and rural zones, must give way to that of the urban system as a system of communication, localizing open and multiform exchange systems. There are no relations of equivalency between these networks, these exchange systems. The dominant social and economic units structure the whole of the urban system in accordance with their requirements for relation and exchange.

Working Hypothesis

Under these conditions it seems necessary to distinguish between two series of hypotheses that are themselves linked. The first refers to the productive dimension of interactions between scientific and technical system and the urban systems, and therefore principally concerns the polarization system. It claims to contribute to the definition and analysis of new forms of domination within the urban networks. The second series of hypotheses aims mainly at the "collective consumption" dimension of interactions between scientific and technical system and urban systems. This aims at stating the manner in which various groups are integrated into the urban systems, through scientific and technical system and the impact of different urban strategies on this integration.

1. Research and research-development unit implantation
    and their impact on the polarization system

Here it is a question of grasping one of the most significant aspects of the relation between firms, or leading production units, and urban poles.

Research-development is, indeed, one of the areas where interpenetra-

39

tion of large manufacturing organizations, and of the State and Public Services, is the most advanced. At the product level, however, the large research and development units tend to form a "closed innovation sector"[16], which greatly strengthens the oligopolist character of the capitalist economy. This therefore means studying the contradictory or complementary relations between two integration systems and the diffusion of innovations, one centering on the firm or sector, the other on the urban pole and its environment.

The first hypothesis to be tested concerns the behaviour of firms and production units. It can be supposed that the process of selecting a particular urban system by companies is a cumulative one in which, once above a certain threshold, the actual existence of a complex of research and research-development units is the main reason for implanting new units, and for their proliferation. This cumulative character in implantation may be related to the needs of scientific work, and to the ever greater part played by research and the exchange of information. In this way poles of production and accumulation of knowledge are formed, and the preferential localities might be chosen by companies using the following criteria:

a. proximity of the firm's decision making centre; this would make it possible to ensure, by frequent exchanges of views, that the research conforms to the firm's targets;

b. proximity of political decision making centres, the present main source of research orders; and

c. abundant resources of qualified personnel and especially of the middle rank professional staff and technicians, the availability of which in an urban system is, because of their lack of mobility, an important consideration.

These hypotheses, therefore, take the opposite view to certain suggestions that there is great technical and economical indecision in the implantation of most modern businesses. If the influence of the physical and labour flux tends to decrease, the importance of the information flux becomes preponderant, and with it an urban localization which, because of its polyvalence, permits the multiplication of new combinations characteristic of intensive growth. The greater the concentration, the more the information flux will converge on a small number of decision making centres. Consequently, the domination of the metropoles of knowledge and power on the whole urban pole system tends to be reinforced.

If these hypotheses are correct, one can suppose that companies' reasoning leads to the priority of implanting research poles in the centres of the largest metropoles, the dominating economic poles.

This seems to be largely verified in the case of the Paris region which accounts for 18.6% of the population, 21% of the active population,

23% of scientific degrees, 51% of III Cycle theses, 58% of doctorates, and 61% of research workers.[17]

Consequently processes associated with technological gaps in international relations could possibly help to describe the mechanisms of this reinforcement of dominant centres.[18]

a) Is it possible to discern a brain drain from the peripheral urban systems? A recent enquiry [19] amongst research workers in the public sector in France helps to strengthen this argument.

b) Might not the creation of isolated research units result in the formation of scientific enclaves dominated by external units who transmit the benefits of innovation back towards the centres of power?

The most typical case in this field is probably that of the Centre d'Etudes Fondamentales of the I.B.M. Company at La Gaude near Nice.

Such are the arguments (to be checked) which seem to us to be directly linked to the behaviour of firms and production units. They call for further hypotheses on the role of public action. No doubt we should distinguish, in this regard, between the state and local groups.

As far as the state is concerned, military, political and economical imperatives oblige it to maintain its rank in the international competition in science and technology. These "imperatives" can mean constant mobilization of scientific resources around the dominant pole, whose reinforcement is, over the short term, a better guarantee of the development of science than is the formation of decentralized poles.

In actual fact, these problems concerning the localization of scientific activities seem to have been at the root of an acute conflict over the last dozen years between the Délégation à l'Aménagement du Territoire and the Délégation Générale à la Recherche Scientifique et Technique. The former's social targets for long term rebalancing are in direct conflict with the latter's interest in short term research resulting in the greatest scientific development. Those responsible for scientific expansion are already complaining about the poverty of Parisian laboratories, whilst expensive facilities remain unused in the provinces.

Conversely, however, contradictions in the development of large metropoles, as well as the difficulty that industrially based societies find in integrating their activities, can lead to new urban creations. Thus, the latest paper on research policy of the Conseil Economique et Social evoked the possibility of creating one or more new centres.

The most advanced plans concern the creation of a scientific and technical pole between Nice and Antibes in the South of France, "Sophia Antinopolis", in liaison with the decentralization of a "Grande Ecole", and, above all, the southern part of the Parisian region where there are already a large number of spontaneous developments, both public and private. If this last solution prevails, it would mean an unlocking of the capital, and the consequences on the balance of the territory remain to be evaluated.

Like the Societic Akademiegorosk, there are various scientific towns in the United States which illustrate, in E. Morin's opinion, the need for organizing deviance in hierarchical societies.[20]

On the local level, the problems of implanting research and research development units can signify new forms of competition between local groups: new public relations methods (publicity and personal contacts with investors), and other major considerations such as accessibility of the most direct sources of information, personnel training, and the quality of the environment. A recent study of the strategies of international firms would seem to contradict the importance of this last factor.[21] It seems to us however, that this factor, a minor one for classic industrial implantation, becomes strategic in advanced industries and research. The most influential factor conditioning the location of all research establishments is the need to obtain, keep, and develop a team of research workers and technicians of the required quality.[22] Consequently, the quality of the urban environment for the use of the upper layer scientific professional workers (schools, housing, cultural life) becomes an important element of implantation policy.

2. Urban strategies for the intergration of scientific and technical system

The preceding hypotheses suggest that the position of various groups, amongst which scientific and technical research forms the support in collective urban consumption, is conditioned first of all by the implantation policies we have just spoken of. It is this problem we wish to tackle with a second series of hypotheses.

The strategies of local attraction (such as a firm's policies) can converge towards the concession of a privileged position at the urban collective consumption level. In this case, an element of control and social integration may be formed for this stratum of the population, and the contradictions noted in production relations between the development of creative work and the reinforcement of social controls may be hidden. Inversely, it might be through problems linked to collective consumption that certain groups (in other respects the beneficiaries of mass consumption) can grasp the tensions and contradictions of the whole social system.

Consequently, the way in which social layers are inserted in the urban system can play an important role, either through their transformation into strata or classes, supports of the techno-structure, or in the tightening of their links with all the other categories of workers. It is from this angle that the *new urban strategies* need interpreting in a way that goes beyond the simple technical transformations.

42

Doubtless, two types of strategies could be opposed in a fundamental way, inspiration being taken from the categories defined by Apter:[23] the *strategies of mobilization* (which imply systematic political action in the transformation of social relations) and *strategies of conciliation* (which often refer to a functionalist analysis of social change.)

The strategies of conciliation consider social relations as natural fundamental facts. Urban "problems" to be treated are mainly the product of irrational conduct linked to ignorance and tradition. Beyond these common aims, two main tendencies might be distinguished, depending on whether stress is laid on the individual and the rationalization of his behaviour, or on the primary group and the basic community. We would see the first as functional mechanist, the second as culturalist.

In the functional mechanist approach, it is a question of adapting individuals as well as possible to the plans of the large organizations, regrouped or not in abstract statistical categories. "Participation", like social action, then seems to be a means of marginal correction in relation to these plans. Social action will stress the specific training for each category; it will treat "social problems" as the sum of social cases needing individual social and psychological help. In this context, it is possible that the special advantages enjoyed by the upper scientific and technical strata may permit them to place themselves in prestigious zones, and integrate into the opulent society through the bias of private consumption; it is also possible that the desire to settle this work force may lead to actions designed to create a favourable environment for them. Such actions can come from the production unit (buying housing) or from state programmes, and they can lead to segregation, which might be strengthened by a culturalist conception of amenities.

In the culturalist approach, the stress is laid on the tensions and cultural disparities which result from social change. The privileged point of action is no longer the individual, but the primary group, the basic collectivity unified by a specific sub-culture. The "social" problems result principally from the inability of certain groups to insert themselves into the existing social structure. The solution of these problems would be linked to an evolution in the attitudes and fundamental values of these groups, who ought to find a way of affirming themselves through rational cooperation among their members. Community development is the classical form of this approach, which finds new incentive in the movement for integrated amenities. The new stress placed on the breakdown of hierarchical barriers, on the capacity to work in groups, participation reduced to non-conflictual areas of social life, seem like the echo, in life outside work, of the changes being made in the management methods of large companies (the same as their common "forgetfulness" of institutional relationships which form the framework for psychological relationships).

43

On the contrary, it is the relationship between the different social groups and the urban space production system which would form the main axis of mobilization strategies. The level of privileged action thus becomes that of the various groups and social classes which form a differential relationship to power, to the decision making systems. Social problems are, therefore, considered to be principally the result of social relationships. They are the product of tensions and contradictions between social classes and groups. In this perspective, a mobilization strategy would first consist in counter-balancing the intellectual technicians' tendencies to integrate into the techno-structure and, parallel with this, in removing the resentments of the less qualified workers and the tensions between executants and technicians, through the ever wider diffusion of instruments of creative thought, by constructing a community of life among them.[24]

The ability of a local group to put this or that strategy into action depends, however, largely on the institutional and political conditions under which they operate. The adoption of a local mobilization strategy in a political system based on reproducing social relationships, runs into institutional norms elaborated at another level, and might have only partially integrating results. The final impact of a strategy on urban structure constitutes, therefore, an essential element in appreciating its meaning. It depends largely on extra-urban factors: institutional standards, national socio-political relations, the polarization system. This is why a study taking into account several national cases would, no doubt, better elucidate the most essential characteristics, both on the economic level and on the local and national political level, of the insertion of scientific and technical groups into urban systems.

Do regional planning and sociology not risk being one step behind if they centre themselves exclusively on the problems of classical industralization? Should they not draw on the consequences of the "new international economy"[25] characterized by the domination of the large units controlling both technical innovation and the creation of new products? It is to this type of problem that this research programme[26] would hope to bring the elements of an answer.

Notes

1. For notions of intensive and extensive growth, see R. Richta, *La Civilisation au Carrefour,* Anthropos, Paris, 1970, p. 20ff.
2. See E. Salzano, *Urbanistica e societa opulente,* Bari, Ed. Laterza, 1969.
3. See for example, H. Delayre, C. Dessane, F. Godard, and Ch. O'Callaghan, *La Renovation Urbaine à Paris,* D.G.R.S.T., 1971.

4. Bruno Jobert, "Urban Planning and Political Institutions", in J. Hayward and M. Watson (eds.), *Planning, Politics and Public Policy,* Cambridge University Press, Cambridge, 1975.

5. Cf. I. Kourakov, "La Science et l'Efficacité de la Production Sociale", translated in *Cahiers du C.E.R.M.,* no 58, p. 22-40; and A. Touraine, *La Société Postindustrielle,* Coll. Mediations Dunod, Paris, 1970.

6. F. Bon and M. A. Burnier, *Les Nouveaux Intellectuels,* le Seuil, Paris, 1971; and *Classe Ouvrière et Révolution,* le Seuil, Paris, 1973.

7. E. Jantsch, *La Prévision Technologique,* O.C.D.E., Paris, 1970, p. 295ff.

8. See for example R. Parsons, "Impact de la Technologie sur la Culture", *Revue Internationale de Sciences Sociales,* no 4, vol. XXII, 1970, p. 660-681.

9. François Perroux, *Industrie et Création Collective,* P.U.F., Paris, 1964, p. 72.

10. See for example the contributions of G. Balandier and J. Berque in G. Balandier (ed.) *Sociologie des Mutations,* Anthropos, Paris, 1970.

11. Cf. M. Castells, "La Renovation Urbaine aux Etats Unis", *Espaces et Sociétés,* no 1, November 1970, p. 131ff.

12. Study of this regulation process should not be limited to the institutional practices called "urbanism" in so far as this traditionally covers only the physical dimension of local public action. However, one of the major characteristics of the present evolution in planning is the ever closer connection between physical and social action with a view to controlling the transformation of urban space. As the subjective aspects of production develop, and society makes innovation the driving force of growth, public social action tends to overflow from the traditional frame of circumstantial assistance to become a permanent element in the adaptation of groups and individuals to urban change. The study of urban planning and of urban development strategies must, therefore, beam more than ever on the whole complex formed by physical and social action.

13. Cf. Castells, *op. cit.,* p. 128.

14. Cf. F. S. Chapin, *Urban Land Use Planning,* University of Illinois Press, Urbana, 1965, p. 23f.

15. S. Mallet, *La Nouvelle Classe Ouvrière,* le Seuil, Paris, 1971, p. 11.

16. S. Erbes, *L'intégration Internationale,* P.U.F., Paris, 1966.

17. Cf. M. Brocard, "Recherche Scientifique et Régions Françaises", *Le Progrès Scientifique,* 152, March-April 1972, pp. 4-33.

18. Schiller Thébaud, "Problèmes de Politique Scientifique dans les Pays Sous-Developpés", IREP note, February 1971.

19. "Les Chercheurs du Secteur Public en Sciences Exactes et Naturelles", *Le Progrès Scientifique,* February 1968, pp. 84-85.

20. E. Morin, "Note sur la Communication des Faits Sociaux", in *Sociologie des Mutations, op. cit.*

21. M. Falise and A. Lepas, "Les Motivations de Localisation des Investissements Internationaux dans l'Europe du Nord-Ouest", *Revue Economique* no 1, January 1971, pp. 102-109.

22. R. J. Busswell and E. W. Lewis, "The Geographical Distribution of Industrial Research in the United States", *Regional Studies,* Vol. 4, No. 3, October 1970, pp. 297-306.

23. David Apter, *The Politics of Modernization*, Chicago University Press, Chicago 1963.

25. See Celso Furtado, "Dépendance externe et théorie", *L'homme et la société*, no 22, October-December 1971.

26. This research programme is financed by the Délégation à la Recherche Scientifique, Action Concertée de Recherche Urbaine in France under the 1972 urban economic system programme. The continuation of a comparable enquiry in other countries would doubtless permit these theoretical propositions to be better founded.

3

INFORMATION SYSTEMS FOR REGIONAL POLICY AND NATIONAL PLANNING IN THE FEDERAL REPUBLIC OF GERMANY

Rainer Thoss

1. *Introductory Remarks on the Issue of "Ideological Substance" versus "Technical Perfection" in Regional Policy*

In a recent discussion paper Antoni Kukliński stressed the need to distinguish between the criterion of ideological substance of regional policy, and the criterion of technical perfection of methods and models applied in the process of planning that policy. He pointed out that "the generation of a new stream of innovations in our field is possible only via the integration of ideological and technical approaches to regional policy and planning".[1]

It is one of the purposes of this paper to show possible ways for such a synthesis. It is true that "the ideological approach is much more controversial, full of tacit assumptions which are not well prepared for explicit discussions".[2] The relevance of Kukliński's plea cannot be controversial. We are, however, convinced that any issue of ideology in the regional and environmental context may be expressed explicitly in quantitative terms by suitable social indicators. Thus "tacit assumptions" can become "open value judgements" if the discussants decide to reveal their systems of values, preferences, and priorities.

Instruments applied in the planning of policy measures may take the form either of a verbal or of a formalized abstract of the real world phenomena to be analyzed. A priori there is no reason to prefer one or the other type. Since, however, both society and nature are highly complex systems of interdependent relations—and since it is desirable to avoid ideological evasiveness—there is much to be said in favour of the construction of formalized mathematical models to assist the human brain in understanding all the feedbacks and chains of causation that have to be considered by planners wishing to study, simulate and evaluate the direct and indirect effects of their activities.

Analytical instruments may be classified according to the logical interpretation of the relations included in the system under study. Those relations may be of the following types:

a. Tautologies, i.e. equations which are true by definition and only state one variable in terms of others (definitions, balance equations);

b. Impact functions, i.e. empirical hypotheses about the impact of one variable upon other parts of the system (technical and behavioural equations);

c. Targets, i.e. normative prescriptions to specify those conditions of the system that are considered as "satisfactory" or "optimal". Targets may be stated in the form of equations, inequalities, or functions to be maximized or minimized. They are explicit expressions of the ideology of the decision maker.

Models which contain only the first type of relations are useful as ex-post accounts of ecological and socio-economic situations. Like input-output tables, they may also serve as a statistical basis for impact models. In this paper they are called "accounting models".

"Impact models" consist of hypotheses *and* tautologies. They may be used for the description and prognostication of environmental and socio-economic effects.

The term "decision model" is applied to models which *in addition* to tautologies *and* hypotheses include socio-economic and/or ecological targets.[3] Cost-benefit analyses are a variety of this type.

Note that a decision model always includes an impact model, and an impact model usually includes balance equations. Time is, of course, an important variable in all social, economic, and ecological considerations. Thus any impact model has to include dynamic or recursive relations.

2. Recent Progress in the Development of Tools and Aids for Environmental Socio-Economic Planning in the Federal Republic of Germany

In order to distinguish between "methods already tried out" and "experimental methods" it is convenient to first describe some of the official activities of government agencies and then present some selected research activities.

2.1. Offical activities[4]

2.1.1. *Accounting models*
Accounting models are generally the first step in the construction of impact models. They supply the necessary data for the subsequent steps of testing empirical hypotheses on the relations between pollution and

production.

The report of experts on problems of the environment for 1974 contains an example of such a model for sulphur and sulphur emissions. It states that in 1970 of the total supply of 4.5 million tons about 40% was emitted to the atmosphere and that 90% of emissions resulted from combustion processes.[5] Another example of this type is the city of Cologne survey of emissions (Emissionskataster).[6]

2.1.2. *Impact models*

2.1.2.1. *Environmental planning and information system.* One of the greatest difficulties in environmental planning is that there is no consistent system for the collection of statistical data and information. The environmental program of the Federal Government and our Council of Experts on Problems of the Environment have, for this reason, stressed the necessity of constructing a computerized information system (Umwelt-Planungs-Informations-System, UMPLIS).

UMPLIS is to provide data and methods which will aid in estimating the consequences of considered actions. It will help to answer questions such as:

Who will be affected by an action?

What are the economic benefits and costs of an action?

What are the consequences if development goes on as before without intervention?[7]

It will contain information about products and production processes and about standards and sensitivity ranges for critical environmental variables. The impacts of these variables are to be specified and therefore the system will be an aid in the preparation of impact statements.[8] The construction of this tool is one of the tasks of the Federal Environmental Protection Agency (Umweltbundesamt).

2.1.2.2. *Environmental impact statements.* In 1973 the Federal Government prepared a bill on environmental impact statements (Umweltverträglichkeitsprüfung).[9] The importance of this tool has been strongly emphasized by the Council of Experts on Environmental Problems.[10]

As in the United States[11] this bill demands that all governmental agencies should continuously monitor and evaluate their activities to protect the quality of the environment and to direct them towards the protection of the environment. The agency in charge of a proposed project has to check if the project will have adverse impacts on natural, ecological, cultural or scenic resources, if it will be controversial because of the relocation of housing, if it will divide or disrupt an established community or disrupt orderly planned development, if it is incompatible with other

49

goals adopted by the community, and if it will cause pollution of air and water or excessive noise.[12]

The agency in charge has to discuss the impact statement with other agencies, institutions, departments, etc. in an iterative process. This may lead to revisions of the proposed action.

In essence, an environmental impact statement is a simulation of probable effects. In order to describe indirect effects it must include an (at least rudimentary) impact matrix to take account of possible feedbacks. In particular, it must show the goal conflicts resulting from proposed activities. If the targets are added to this matrix, the impact statement takes the form of a decision model. These models are cost-benefit studies because all activities are evaluated by their opportunity cost in units of the objective function.[13] In this way it is possible simultaneously to simulate *and* evaluate the impacts of alternative environmental strategies, as well as to avoid the iterative process of simulation and judgement by different agencies.

2.1.2.3. *Input-output model of* SO_2 *pollution.* For the "Umweltgutachten 1974" the impact of the economy on the quality of air was simulated by a 14-sector input-output model on the national level. Data was derived from the accounting model of SO_2 production mentioned above.[14]

2.1.3. *Decision models*
2.1.3.1. *Program for Regional Development.* For the preparation of the Federal Government's Program for Regional Development (Bundesraumordnungsprogramm) a decision model was used.[15] In this model the territory of the Federal Republic of Germany was subdivided into 38 regions and the economy was aggregated into 6 sectors. Impacts on the ecology were considered mainly with respect to land use. Besides socio-economic standards, the model also included a number of ecological targets, mainly referring to the protection of areas for regeneration of natural resources and to waste and sewage disposal. The model was designed to show the limits of economic growth as well as to outline the kind of regional distribution of economic activities, population, and infrastructure that would optimally meet the targets.

2.1.3.2. *Target values of social indicators.* During the preparation of this program it became obvious that there was still not enough information in existence about social indicators to measure the actual situation of regions and to specify the targets to be reached. For future editions of the Bundesraumordnungsprogramm the Council on Regional Planning (Beirat für Raumordnung) is therefore at present setting up a list of social indicators and trying to specify their minimum levels. Roughly one third of these

50

indicators refer to the quality of the environment. The others specify regional targets for public utilities, economic activities, and social structure. At some later point in time this set of targets should be combined with an impact model to find the optimal values of the instrument variables. Since conflicts of goals are not for the moment being considered, it may be necessary to revise targets later on, in order to achieve feasibility (consistency), or because of large trade-offs.

2.2. Research activities

2.2.1. *Accounting models*
Descriptions of interdependencies between the ecologic and economic systems are based on the "materials balance approach" developed by Kneese.[16] By way of definition, balance equations describe the final amount of pollutants as a difference between the amount existing at the beginning of the period, the pollutants generated within the period, and the reduction of pollutants by the natural environment and by human protective action plus exports and imports. Examples of this type have been developed in connection with the control of radioactive material.[17]

2.2.2. *Impact models*
For the explanation of the generation of pollutants as by-products of socio-economic activities the well-known input-output analysis has proved to be a powerful tool.[18] In such a model it is assumed that the quantity of inputs as well as of polluting by-products is a function of output. This assumption enables us to estimate the total quantity of pollutants emitted as impacts of alternative values of the final demand vector. The model thus simulates the ecological consequences of satisfying economic demands.[19] Impact models of the Systems Dynamics variety lay particular emphasis on temporal repercussions.[20]

2.2.3. *Decision models*
A model of this type is being constructed for the Frankfurt area as a contribution to the UNESCO research program on "Man and Biosphere".[21] For the purpose of this model the metropolitan area of Frankfurt and its surroundings is subdivided into 20 sub-regions. The aim is to determine the best socio-economic and ecological uses that each of these sub-regions can be put to. The solution has to satisfy the different goals to be pursued in order to improve the quality of life.

2.2.3.1. *Socio-economic relations.* The tools and aids furnished by the theory of quantitative economic policy have proved very useful in planning socio-economic development.[22] This theory provides a framework for linking economy and ecology if a sectoral disaggregation of the economy is introduced, because different sectors of production involve different types of ecological impacts. Explicit consideration of sectors leads to the inclusion of a Leontief-type impact matrix showing direct, as well as indirect, consequences of economic activities.

There can be no doubt that the highest priority in maintaining the quality of life is the protection of nature. Within the limits drawn by this goal, however, there is no reason for ignoring factors of production. The objective of economic-ecologic policy must be to maximize production, subject to the constraints imposed by ecological targets and available factors of production.

Since the absolute levels of activities may be determined in this way, it suffices for structural considerations to apply a (generalized) closed input-output model. This avoids the problem of exogenous forecasts of final demand.

Economic interdependencies for the Frankfurt area are therefore described by an input-output matrix with 56 sectors of production, which is closed by targets for the shares of private and public consumption, private and public investment, and export surplus. A labour balance and sectoral employment constraints serve to describe economic production possibilities and employment targets.

Finally, the objective is to determine the type of regional distribution and the types of processes of production that will maximize output, i.e. to plan economic development so as not to surpass the limits of growth within any given period of the planning horizon. Intertemporal changes of parameters will be considered in a recursive manner.

2.2.3.2. *Land use.* Land use is one of the most important connections between the economic and the ecologic systems. Land is, firstly, the base for all socio-economic activities. Further, it is needed for recreation and for the reproduction of natural resources like water, fresh air, etc. It is also necessary for the disposal of waste materials, which are generated as joint products of the socio-economic activities (cf. 2.2.3.3).

The land use equations of the model can be divided into two parts. The first consists of capacity constraints. These describe the amounts of different types of land available in each sub-region. Quality types are defined by ecological criteria (supply constraints).

The second set of restrictions specifies norms for the demand of land, which may result from the production of goods and services, from waste disposal, and from housing demand. Land use coefficients quantify the technological and behavioural hypotheses which link the demand for economic goods to the demand for land. Apart from the traditional economic land using activities, special attention is given to the need for

52

the protection of landscape, for the reproduction of natural resources, and for land to be used for recreational purposes. The norms state the minimum requirements for each of the competing demands. Growth is limited in a sub-region if one of the landuse targets becomes a binding constraint.

2.2.3.3. *Solid and liquid wastes.* Solid and liquid wastes pose important problems for the ecology of metropolitan areas. For this reason it is necessary to include this aspect in any model for ecological socio-economic development planning.

Material flow equations for each sub-region therefore specify the sources of wastes (production, imports), and the activities which may be considered for their disposal (incineration, composting, deposing, exports). A set of technological hypotheses then describes the impacts of economic activities in terms of the several types of waste and the inputs and outputs of disposal activities. Treatment activities themselves create outputs of reusable goods and final wastes.

Reusable materials then may be delivered to the sectors of production and the final wastes disposed of. The option of recycling means that in each sector there should be possibilities of substitution between alternative processes of production in order to find the best combination of inputs of raw materials and reusable wastes. Limits to growth may exist because of shortages of factors of production or of suitable land for disposing activities.

2.2.3.4. *Waste water.* The sub-regions are inter-linked by exports and imports of goods and other materials. If regions are connected by the same water-course, they also have to be linked together by waterflow equations, because a discharge of pollution at one point of a river affects the entire downstream part of the river.[23] The constraints concerned with the impact of waste water on the ecology may be divided into three groups: production and treatment of residuals (waste water balances and BOD-balance), impact of residuals on water quality, and water standards.

The generation of household sewage is described as a certain amount of sewage per head per day. The generation of waste water in the productive sectors is represented by discharge coefficients, defined as a constant proportion between the output of waste water and gross production in each of the sectors. Whereas personnel industrial waste water as well as house-hold sewage receive obligatory treatment, cooling water as well as pro-cessing water may be discharged without treatment or may be treated in different ways.

For measuring water quality a special form of the population equivalent biochemical oxygen demand is used. This is capable of integrating the effects of organic and toxic wastes into a single number. The impact of the discharged waste affects the amount of dissolved oxygen in the river water. It is one of the ecological targets to keep dissolved oxygen above a certain lower limit. This implies that there are upper limits of waste discharge to be observed, and this in turn means that there is a limit to growth with respect to water pollution also.

From an esthetic and hygienic point of view, however, it is not sufficient to provide merely for a minimum of oxygen in the streams. This could be achieved by artificial aeration, but it leaves the water in a very poor condition for recreation purposes. The model therefore also contains upper limits for the load of BOD, which also may lead to limitations of economic activities in certain subregions.

2.2.3.5. *Air pollution.* As was shown above (2.1.1), the impact of economic activity on air pollution cannot be studied without a detailed description of consumption and conversion of energy.[24] For this purpose the energy sector of the model was further disaggregated by commodities.

The part of the model dealing with air pollution therefore contains energy balances for thirty-four types of energy, which may be produced (as main products or by-products) by fifteen processes. Again, an impact matrix of technical and behavioural coefficients links energy demand to other economic activities. In addition, this part of the model includes constraints for the supply of energy from international sources.

The impact on the environment is accounted by pollutants balances for eight types of air polluting substances. The sources of these unwanted by-products may be either production-activities or consumption of different types of energy. Air quality standards for each of the pollutants then serve to specify upper limits of pollution, which again imposes limits to regional growth.

3. Conclusions

There can be no question but that each of the tools and aids mentioned in this paper is valuable in the preparation of decisions on policy measures to control ecological repercussions of socio-economic development.

Accounting models provide important information on the state of the ecological and economic systems and on the sources of positive and negative impacts. They usually serve as base for the calculation of probable impacts.

Impact models simulate the foreseeable effects of exogenous impulses, like policy measures, changes of economic activities, changes of the state of the environment, etc. Since they contain no explicit normative components they stay in the realm of positive science and therefore seem to be preferred by executive agencies. Probable impacts can—as a separate step of deliberation—be compared with ecological and socio-economic targets and, by a process of trial and error, solutions can be found which satisfy these constraints. The shortcomings are:

    a. that targets are not stated explicitly;

    b. that the alternatives considered may not include the optimal one; and

    c. that these models provide no information about the size of trade-offs of targets.

Decision models avoid these shortcomings. They simulate the instrumental consequences of pursuing certain ecological and socio-economic targets. To have this capability, they have to include an impact model (which, of course, could be used also without targets). Such models are of special value in situations where—in a series of consecutive steps of an iterative process—decisions must be taken and targets must be revised according to social preferences.

For this iterative process the dual solutions of decision models provide information about the opportunity costs of the different targets. Targets are made comparable because they are all measured in terms of the goals of the objective function. In the well-known cost-benefit studies (which maximize the difference between benefits and costs) marginal net benefit per unit of target indicator would be the common denominator; in the case of the model of 2.2.3. above it would be the marginal quantity of output foregone; in a model with the objective to minimize environmental disruption it could be marginal pollution per unit of other targets.

Information about opportunity costs thus provides a more rational basis for the improvement of targets by reviewing and revising the original value judgements. One of the most frequent misunderstandings with regard to decision models results from the fact that in order to reach the level of post-optimality analysis one has to use some preliminary value judgements about targets as a starting point for the iterative process of finding and revising targets. It should be pointed out, however, that all normative components must always be regarded as preliminary in the sense that their specification constitutes only the first step in the iterative process of specifying and revising the ideological goals of regional environmental, social, and economic policy.

Notes

1. A. Kukliński, "Notes on Regional Planning", mimeo, Ottawa, February, 1974, p. 3.

2. *Ibid.*

3. For the structure of this type of model see UNESCO, *Final Report, Expert Panel on Perception of Environmental Quality,* MAB report series Nr. 9, Paris 1973, pp. 28-29, 70-73.

4. For details see *Der Rat von Sachverständigen für Umweltfragen. Umweltgutachten* 1974, Stuttgart (Kohlhammer) 1974 (subsequently referred to as "Umweltgutachten 1974").

5. *Ibid*, p. 212; cf. K. Lenhart, *Die Emission von Schwefelverbindungen,* VDI-Berichte Nr. 186, Dusseldorf 1972.

6. Cf. K. H. Lindackers, H. May, D. Meinhardt and O. J. Zuendori, *Aufbau und Auswertung des Emissionskatasters,* Cologne (Heymann) 1971.

7. Bundesministerium des Innern, *Das Informationssystem zur Umweltplanung* (UMPLIS), Umweltbrief 2, Bonn 1973.

8. *Ibid*, p. 13.

9. Cf. Bundesminister des Innern; *Roh-Entwurf für ein Gesetz über die Prüfung der Umweltverträglichkeit öffentlicher Maßnahmen* (UA I 5-500 310/1), Bonn, 31.8.1973.

10. Umweltgutachten 1974, p. ix.

11. Cf. L. J. Sumek, *Environmental Impact Statements: More Myth than Reality,* National Conference on Managing the Environment, May 14-15, 1973. U.S. Environmental Protection Agency, Office of Research and Monitoring, Environmental Studies Division, Washington D.C., part I, pp. 39-52.

12. Cf. *Ibid,* p. IV-43; and W. Obenhaus, "Überlegungen für eine Konzeption zur Prüfung der Umweltverträglichkeit öffentlicher Maßnahmen", in *Umwelt,* 3 (1973), pp. 58-60.

13. Cf. R. Thoss, "A Dynamic Model for Regional and Sectoral Planning in the Federal Republic of Germany", in *Economics of Planning,* 10 (1970), p. 110.

14. Umweltgutachten 1974, p. 234.

15. Cf. R. Thoss, "Resolving Goal Conflicts in Regional Policy by Recursive Linear Programming", Paper presented at the 13th European Congress of the Regional Science Association, August 28-31, Vienna 1973, p. 20; to be published in *Regional Science Association Papers.*

16. A. V. Kneese, R. U. Ayres, and R. C. D'Arge, *Economics and the Environment: A Materials Balance Approach,* Washington (Johns Hopkins) 1970, p. 9.

17. D. Gupta, and others, "Umweltbilanzen, ein Kernproblem der Umweltschutz-Politik", in *Durchsetzung des Verursacherprinzips im Gewässerschutz,* Ergebnis der 2. internationalen Expertengespräche am 10. und 21. November 1972, Gesellschaft für Kernforschung m.b.H., Karlsruhe 1973, S. 129ff.; see also Die ökologische Bilanz, Protokoll des Kolloquiums am 30.-31.8.1972 in Hamburg, mimeo. paper (BP Benzin und Petroleum AG), p. 2.

18. Cf. W. Leontief, "Environmental Repercussions and the Economic Structure: An Input-Output Approach", in *Review of Economics and Statistics,* 62 (1970), p. 262; and W. Isard, *Ecologic-Economic Analysis for Regional Development,* London 1972.

19. H. Juergensen, K. P. Jaeschke and P. Laemmel, "Allokationseffekte der Social costs im Umweltsschutz", *Umweltbrief* 3, Bonn 1973

20. Cf. E. Zepf and K. Britsch, "Ökologische Kriterien für die Begrenzung regionalen Wachstums", in *Raumforschung und Raumordnung,* 31 (1973), p. 138; and A. Voss, "Ansätze zur Gesamtanalyse des Systems Mensch-Energie-Umwelt", *Berichte der Kernforschungsanlage Juelich,* Nr. 982.

21. See UNESCO, *Final Report, Expert Panel on Ecological Effects of Energy Utilization in Urban and Industrial Systems,* MAB report series Nr. 13, Paris 1973, p. 60; and R. Thoss, "A Generalized Input-Output Model for Residuals Management", paper presented to the 6th International Conference on Input-Output Techniques, Vienna, 22-26 April 1974.

22. Cf. J. Tinbergen, *Centralization and Decentralization in Economic Policy,* Amsterdam (North-Holland) 1954, p. 7; H. Theil, *Economic Forecasts and Policy,* Amsterdam (North-Holland), 1970, p. 385; B. G. Hickmann, "Introduction", in B. G. Hickmann (ed.), *Quantitative Planning of Economic Policy,* Washington (Brookings), p. 2.

23. See R. Thoss and K. Wijk, "An Empirical Linear Model for Water Quality Management", in J. G. Rothenberg and I. G. Heggie. (eds.), *The Management of Water Quality and the Environment,* London (MacMillan), 1974.

24. Cf. R. Thoss and H. P. Doellekes, "Energy and Environmental Planning", in OECD, *Energy and Environment,* Paris 1974, p. 77.

4

SOCIAL ISSUES IN REGIONAL POLICY AND REGIONAL PLANNING IN THE SCANDINAVIAN COUNTRIES

Briitta Koskiaho

The Development of Social Regional Problems

Regional problems in Scandinavia are related to the geographical, geo-physical, and cultural location of the countries. The fact that they are sandwiched between two cultural regions, East and West, and the fact that such large areas of their land lie so far north, have had considerable implications for these countries' development.

Like other European countries situated on the borders between East and West, the Scandinavian countries have their most populated, cultivated, and active areas in the west, and like other northern countries they have a further concentration in the southern areas of their territories. In Finland, for example, two thirds of the population lives in the south and west in a narrowish zone covering only a third of the country's area, while just over a tenth of the population lives in the provinces of Oulu and Lapland which cover almost the entire northern half of the country. This alone is enough to create regional problems, since the predominantly rural east and north is relatively poor. Several other interrelated factors are, however, also involved.

The first of these is urbanisation, a world-wide phenomenon that has been very strongly marked in the last few decades in Scandinavia. In Finland the percentage of the total population living in rural areas dropped from 68% in 1950 to 49% in 1970. The southern parts of the country have grown considerably, particularly in urban areas. Thanks to a high birth rate, the population of rural communes in the more northerly areas was still increasing during the 1950's, but it declined sharply in the 1960's as a result of the fall in the birth rate and of the rapid increase in the number leaving the communes. A similar situation has developed both in Norway and in Sweden.

Urban-rural and regional differences in population growth rates have diminished because of falling birth rates in the rural areas.

The age structure difference between urban and rural populations has, meanwhile, become more marked. The falling birth rate and increased migration to the cities have left the rural populations with a higher average age than the urban populations. Accordingly, unless radical socio-political measures are taken to improve living conditions in the rural communes, their depopulation and the consequent imbalance in age structure between urban and rural areas, will continue. This is particularly the case in Finland and Norway; in Sweden the position is somewhat less critical.

Some of the indicators of relative levels of living reveal parity between different regions and between rural and urban areas. Social security in terms of monetary services, for example, is available to the whole population of Finland, and standards of nutrition, children's health, housing (measured according to the ratio between number of rooms and their occupants), etc. are at least comparable over all areas of the country. Disparities are, however, in evidence in other indicators, particularly with regard to the health of the male working-age population, secondary and higher education, and the availability of cultural services in the more sparsely populated areas.

The most disquieting differences are those revealed by the health indicators, and these have been a subject of study for both social and medical scientists. The following table gives the mortality rates for men in urban and rural regions in Finland per 1000 inhabitants:

Age	Urban			Rural		
	1951-55	1956-60	1961-65	1951-55	1956-60	1961-65
0- 4	7.82	6.16	5.24	9.07	7.08	6.20
10-14	0.67	0.50	0.47	0.74	0.59	0.53
20-24	2.00	1.61	1.25	2.19	1.65	1.79
30-34	2.96	2.90	2.29	3.05	2.66	2.48
40-44	6.73	5.82	5.85	5.14	4.95	5.18
50-54	15.73	14.34	14.66	12.96	12.60	13.01
60-64	37.59	34.40	34.71	31.10	30.51	30.64
70-74	80.17	76.03	76.56	69.61	68.58	67.61
80-84	173.43	158.60	160.19	156.57	151.87	154.00

As stated, these figures apply only to the male population. The female mortality rates, in Finland as elsewhere, are usually considerably lower.

Male mortality rates are much higher in large urban centres (eg. Helsinki, Tampere, Turku) than in smaller towns. The problem is, therefore, double-ended: the highest death rates are found both in the poorer rural areas and in the most highly industrialised urban centres. In the former case heavy manual labour is combined with a shortage of health services, and in the latter an abundance of health services is accompanied by the health hazards of the industrial community.

Economic growth in Scandinavia, and especially in Finland, is threatened by structural unemployment, by regional inequalities, by internal migration and emigration, and by the increasing damage that is being done to the environment.

The situation that has developed in the primary industries is an example of the kind of structural unemployment problems facing these countries. In 1970, 23% of the total population of Finland was engaged in working in the primary industries; the figure for the population of the north and east of the country at that time was 36%. Between 1967 and 1970 unemployment in Finland was worst (almost 6%) in areas in which primary industries predominated, and this exacerbated regional discrepancies that already existed. The importance of the primary industries has, moreover, been decreasing over the past twenty years relative to the secondary and tertiary industries: while 26.4% of the GDP at factor cost was contributed by the primary industries in 1950, by 1960 the figure was 20.6% and in 1970 it was down to only 14.8%.

Within the primary industries the proportion of agricultural production has fallen while that of northern forestry production has risen. Until recently Finland was a typical small farmer country, but by now a sizeable number of small farmers have given up their farms and moved to the towns or to another Nordic country, particularly to Sweden, to work in the manufacturing industries. Forestry production has been mechanised and automated, and new methods of forest cultivation introduced. This has reduced the demand for forestry labour and has driven part-time forestry workers to seek full-time employment elsewhere.

Another force that needs to be taken into consideration is the concealed unemployment in the rural primary industries. This is particularly relevant to aging small farmers who, instead of moving into other occupations when their work on the farm decreases, continue living in the country and become increasingly dependent on social security benefits which, by international standards, are fairly high in all the Nordic countries.

The regional distribution of the population has been strongly influenced by both emigration and by the internal migration to urban areas that has already been mentioned. There has recently been a sizeable emigration from the impoverished rural areas of high unemployment in the north and east of Finland and, to a lesser extent, from Norway to Sweden. This is the Scandinavian "Gastarbeiter" problem. The net emigration from Finland was more than 70,000 in the 1950's, and more than 170,000 in the 1960's. The adverse effects that this loss of active population has had on the population structure of rural communes in Finland have already been

61

noted.

Internal migration in Finland has been mainly towards Helsinki and its surrounding industrial areas. The net migration to the south was 274,263 (4%-5% of the population annually) between 1951 and 1970, while there was a net outflow from the north of 57,413 in the same period. The total population of rural communes dropped by nearly 470,000 in those twenty years, and most of the decrease was in the north and east. In the main, the emigrants and migrants from these areas were in the 20-35 age bracket.

Migration is related to the structure of production and thus to the employment opportunities in the areas concerned. Unless Finland's regional production structure is changed in the near future, the rural areas particularly in the north and east will continue to drive people to seek employment in the towns and in other countries. The same is true of Norway. This is the challenge facing regional policy in these countries.

The problems in Sweden are rather different. Sweden, which has the highest standard of living in Europe, has found a shortage of labour the most important of the negative results of development. The very low Swedish birth rate has led Sweden to employ foreign workers in its secondary industries. At the present time Finnish workers are the largest constituent of this foreign workforce in Sweden.

In Finland the problems facing regional and social policy are the problems that have resulted from the disparity between urban and rural areas, between the south and west on the one hand and the north and east on the other. The towns and wealthier areas generally are luring labour away from the rest of the country. This movement has both positive and negative effects on the rural areas surrounding the major urban centres.

The proximity of such areas to the large centre has the positive effect of making a greater number of jobs, services, and cultural facilities available here than in more remote rural areas. At the same time, however, these hitherto rural areas are transformed into something that is neither town nor country. Since the land utilisation policy here is not as controlled as it is in the towns themselves, while the physical environment is subject to as much damage as in the towns, these areas suffer many of the worst side effects of industrialisation.

In Finland the main environmental problem has been water pollution. The lakes are generally slow-moving and shallow and thus easily badly polluted—as also, to a large extent, is the Baltic Sea itself. The worst offender is industry, mainly the pulp and paper mills, and the effects are by no means limited to the immediate surroundings of urban areas. Large expanses of water in all parts of Finland are now so badly damaged that rural inhabitants can no longer use them for fishing or other economic purposes, for consumption as drinking water, or even, in many cases, for full recreational enjoyment. Laws have been passed to alleviate this situation, and location policies for industry are being implemented.

The exploitation of forests in Scandinavian countries is a particular and very important aspect of these countries' economic utilisation of natural resources. Total re-forestation of large areas in Lapland has been introduced in the hope of improving the quality of the forests. The excessively cold climate, however, and ecological monoculture have produced economically negative results. Such measures frequently spoil the environment for the rural inhabitants as well as seriously damaging the ecological system.

Another aspect of the environmental problem is the increase in tourism in Scandinavia, particularly in the lake regions and in Lapland. While tourism creates employment and business opportunities and is generally good for the economy in an immediate sense, it can and often does have irreversible effects on the fragile ecology of the Nordic countries. Ecological renewal takes an extremely long time in Scandinavia, owing to geographical location and climatic conditions.

The Capacity of Theories to Predict Regional Development

The period of industrialisation has seen the proliferation of concepts dealing with the rapid growth of material wealth, and the relative status of various societies is now generally measured according to their prosperity and their rates of economic growth. The same kind of thinking lies, moreover, at the root of most of the models we have for improving the status of the underdeveloped countries.

Economic growth means that more material commodities are produced each year, and the attainment of a higher economic level depends on the amount of production of new commodities. This concept has been roundly criticised recently in Scandinavia. Kyösti Pulliainen, for example, adds a criterion that has far-reaching implications. The production of new goods, he writes, measures the level of prosperity only if the amount written off is smaller than the production. In analyses of economic growth it has traditionally been assumed that this plus stock is constant, and accordingly no attention has been paid to the quality of the goods: quantity was seen as the single important variable. What this traditional view ignores, however, is that a large proportion of the production over any given period is needed just to offset the number of previously produced commodities that are discarded over the same period. The proportion of production that merely replaces commodities that have become obsolescent can not be seen as new production in any proper sense of the term. What we need, according to Pulliainen, is a new interpretation of the whole concept of economic growth: an interpretation that takes both new production and the amount written off in any period into consideration.

When models of economic development that assume certain factors are constant are applied to an actual situation the constants can often be found to *vary*. This has happened in the case of Scandinavia, where social and environmental factors have been shown to be variables rather than constants, and it is exemplified in the ways in which theories of economic growth attempt to forecast future regional development.

When analysing the industrialisation process one can point to the positive effects of the process—even when these develop certain un-desirable side-effects over a period of time—and to those effects which have been neglected or which are actually negative.

Different cumulation theories relating to this question have been worked out by social scientists. Gunnar Myrdal's version, which related partic-ularly to industrialisation, deals with the structure of a society at the strongly positive stage of industrial growth. The negative "backwash effects" of growth in a society at this stage are seen as providing human resources for the industrialisation process elsewhere.

The American social scientist William Simmons proposes, in his "inventory of the future", the following nine components as indicative of a continuation of growth in companies. These components also very well describe the cumulative positive progress in Myrdal's model:

1. Complete industrialisation: people no longer need to worry about the necessities of life—nutrition, clothing, shelter, security—and they take an interest in other matters, i.e. the proper division of resources, the quality of life in the environment, the meaning of life itself. This indicates a change in the system of values: we learn to work for living and no longer live for work.

2. The increasing use of computers.

3. The increase in leisure time.

4. Improvements in the technology of the communications media.

5. The increasing significance of education and, concomitantly, the in-creasing importance of skilled workers.

6. The increasing of "social consciousness" among enterprises: enter-prises will participate more than before in the implementation of social policy measures.

7. The increase in the number of multinational enterprises.

8. Changes—resembling those that are already taking place in bio-medicine—in the control of behaviour and in the transfer of organs.

9. The increasing use of long-term planning.

The assumptions here in Simmons' list are that the process of industrial-isation will actually continue in the future, and that this process will have positive results for human beings. As I understand it, the general technocratic view among, for example, American futurologists, is that of a society in which computers solve social as well as technical problems. This view does, however, give rise to certain questions. The process of industrial development in the West certainly has negative as well as positive features. In Scandinavia many social scientists are now very interested in the whole process, in its positive and in its negative effects, and also in the ideological issues which are raised by theories of society like Simmons'. They see the negative counterparts of some of the effects judged positive by Simmons. Among these we may mention that the benefits of complete industrialisation may be offset by dissatisfaction and by a less appealing kind of life-style; that the increasing use of computers may result in undesirable mechanisation; that the greater amount of leisure time available may lead to artificial amusements or boredom and idleness; and that the benefits of improved education may be annulled by the machine-like work that will still have to be done.

In his theory of cumulative development Myrdal refers to what he calls the enigma of over-developed regions. He considers that certain retarding factors come into play in over-developed, densely populated areas. One such factor might be expenses rising beyond the tolerance limit. This is connected with the economic concept of marginal costs, as in the case of restricting the growth of enterprises beyond a certain limit. Once the limit is exceeded, external negative effects begin to outweigh profits. Myrdal has not developed a model that takes external negative effects into consideration, and he does not deal with the problem posed by factors that, although held to be positive in their effects, turn out to have negative repercussions. This omission is important. When the possibility of such repercussions is not attended to then there is no possibility of controlling them, and they may well cause serious damage both on their own and by influencing other variables negatively. This kind of development has left its mark on the regional reality of all the Scandinavian countries.

Olavi Riihinen writes that the positive external effects of towns and industrial communes have expansion effects particularly on their immediate surroundings, that new centres emerge in the vicinity as satellites of the original centres. Many Scandinavian writers are critical of this kind of development, since they again see the negative external effects relating to the creation of satellites. Yngve Larsson, for example, counters Simmons' notion of complete industrialisation with a view of the effect this may have in exacerbating loneliness, housing problems, differences between income classes, segregation, and the conditions in sleeping suburban towns with poor service facilities. He sees an increase in leisure as being of little benefit, since the strenuousness of the work-days will necessitate a longer recovery period, and since the greater distances that will have to be travelled between the home and the place of work will eat into the "leisure time". The more widespread use of computers he sees as resulting in greater demands on the worker and in a life run by the watch. He considers that education in Simmons' future society would have the effect of increasing stress both for those whose work is routine and monotonous and for those whose work is creative and demanding. The benefits of greater social consciousness he thinks would be countered by feelings of insecurity in the workers, caused by an increased regional mobility of labour markets and by temporary unemployment resulting from structural rationalisation and closing enterprises. And, finally, Larsson thinks the negative effects of closing down smaller enterprises and of increased automation and rationalisation would offset whatever positive effects an increase in the number of multinational enterprises might have.

As is the case with the positive effects considered by Riihinen negative effects of the kind mentioned by Larsson, which have their roots in over-developed areas, have repercussions far outside such areas both in terms of the social system and in terms of the physical environment.

Theories of the economic and the social growth process are thus very poorly equipped to explain what is taking place in over-developed regions. Since, moreover, these regions affect development in rural areas, our theories must further be judged according to their capacity to cope with rural problems. Our existing social and environmental problems further reflect the deficiencies of our theories.

It is, of course, relatively easy to detect deficiencies in existing theories. To decide what our society, and regional development in our society, should instead take as their objectives is rather more difficult.

Problems of Policy

It is clear that the problems of regional imbalances between urban and rural areas call for comprehensive policies. Population policy, economic and social policy, and environment policy are all essential in formulating a regional policy. There is quite general agreement on this point all over the world. The difficulties arise when it comes down to deciding how such a comprehensive policy should be operationalised. How is it possible to take into consideration simultaneously the special requirements both of rural "backwash" areas and of crowded urban centres? In practice no general optimum solution to this problem has been found. In Scandinavia at the present time the view is often propounded that the solution is to direct society along the right path by combining planning and rational decision making with ideological change. What, however, it may well be asked, is the "right" path? Is it perhaps right for the people? In this case the question *which* people are meant is not irrelevant. Very often the operationalisation of goals for decision making reveals conflicts, and one is hard put indeed to decide which group, which region, which nation should have the right to decide on the best solution. In regional policy there is a further conflict between some social objectives and the requirements of the natural environment. To what extent, in other words, will the "right" path be right not only for society but also for the ecological system? Our answer to this question will determine whether or not it will still be possible for future generations to live on this earth.

In the Scandinavian countries, as elsewhere in the West, the problems of goals for decision making are receiving considerable attention. The people and, more gradually, the decision-makers themselves are becoming increasingly critical of uncontrolled economic growth and of the way in which economic values dominate policy on regional (and, indeed, on all social) issues at the present time.

This critical attitude has had several results. It is now felt that everything possible should be done to preserve the traditional forms and values of rural culture for future generations of Scandinavians. There is, moreover, a back-to-the-country trend: people are moving out of the megalopolis to live in the country or in smaller towns whenever this can be arranged from the standpoint of work. This trend is currently most marked in Sweden, but it is gathering momentum elsewhere. The government of Finland, for example, is planning a large-scale regional decentralisation of the administration and the economy. Up to now, the principle has been to bring the labour to the capital; from now on the capital will, as much as possible, be brought to the labour. It is felt that this procedure will improve the quality of life of the rural population and of the inhabitants of underdeveloped areas generally.

Regional and social policies are increasingly attempting to combat the defects that have resulted from the depopulation of the countryside. Assistance from state funds has encouraged private industry to move into underdeveloped areas with high unemployment, and state-owned enterprises have also been established in such areas.

Training and educational policies designed to assist the inhabitants of the underdeveloped areas have been stepped up: Finland, for example, has just introduced a comprehensive school system like that which was set up some years ago in Sweden, and short vocational training courses for adults are being offered.

The social and commercial service facilities, which have always been a problem in the sparsely populated areas, are being boosted in all of the Nordic countries. Sweden, which again has taken the greatest strides up to now, has been experimenting with ways to improve the standards of services in such areas, and has worked out circulation systems of different social, commercial, and cultural services.

While it is very difficult to say what kind of regional policy would be best for Scandinavia at the moment, it is certain that the policies that are being implemented are becoming more "human", more social, than ever before.

Bibliography

Kaasinen, Matti, *Retraining projects as a means of improving possibilities of labour resettlement* (English summary), Acta Universitatis Tamperensis, Ser. A., Vol. 55, Tampere, Finland 1974.

Koskiaho, Briitta, *Differences in the level of living of four Western European countries,* University of Tampere, Institute of Social Policy. Research report #3, 1969.

—, *Environment and Decision making,* University of Tampere, Institute of Social Policy, Research report #32, 1973.

Larsson, Yngve, *Samhallsplanering och teknik: Samhallsbyggandets framtida tekniska problem* (Planning of Society and Techniques: Technical Problems in the Development of a Future Society), Academy of Technical Science, IVA Report 39, Stockholm, 1971.

Meurman, O.-I., "Asemakaavaopin Taydennyslehtia" (Appendices to City Planning Textbook), The Technical University, Mimeo. paper 115, 1957.

Myrdal, Gunnar, *Economic Theory and Under-Developed Regions,* G. Duckworth, London, 1957.

Pedersen, Poul Ove, "De-specialisation—a regional development policy for the periphery?" *Regional Development and Planning,* Mens en Ruimte, Regional and Urban Studies no. 1, 1973.

Population and Development in Finland, Reply of Finland to the UN Secondary Inquiry on Population and Development. The Population Research Institute Series A: 14, Helsinki 1973.

Pulliainen, Kyösti, "Taloudellisen kasvun vaihtoehtoja" ("Different Possibilities of Economic Growth"), *Aika,* No. 4-5, 1972.

Riihinen, Olavi, "Urbanisation and external economies" (English summary) in *The values, objectives and practice of social policy in the 1970's,* English summaries, Acta Universitatis Tamperensis, Ser. A. Vol. 49, 1973.

Simmons, William, *Inventorying the Future,* Management decision No. 3, 1971.

Statistical Yearbook of Finland 1971, Helsinki 1972.

Sweden's Case Study for the United Nations Conference on the Human Environment, "Air Pollution across National Boundaries: The Impact on the Environment of Sulphur in Air and Precipitation", Royal Ministry for Foreign Affairs, Royal Ministry of Agriculture, Stockholm, 1971.

Sweden's National Report to the United Nations on the Human Environment, Royal Ministry for Foreign Affairs, Royal Ministry of Agriculture, Stockholm, 1971.

Vik, Rolf (ed.), *Proceedings of the Nordic Symposium on Biological Parameters for Measuring Global Pollution,* IBP i Norden, No. 9, 1972, Oslo 1972.

5

REGIONAL DEVELOPMENT IN SPAIN: TRENDS, POLICIES, AND PLANNING*

Harry W. Richardson and *Fernando Fernández Rodriguez*

Despite an impressive national growth rate performance since 1960-1,[1] Spain has severe regional problems and remains underdeveloped in terms of physical and social infrastructure. There has been some convergence in interregional per capita income differentials in the 1960s—the evidence is unclear because the available provincial income data are weak—but this probably occurred despite rather than because of policy.[2] In spite of economic liberalisation, Spanish economic policies have remained autarchic and excessively cautious. Moreover, the administration's strategy has been to minimise public expenditure, since the political support of the professional and middle classes has been bought with low tax rates.[3] One obvious consequence has been a strong preference for directly productive investment which makes less demands on public expenditure than infrastructure investment. This has heavily favoured the big cities which already had a substantial stock of infrastructure.

Population Distribution

The population of Spain is about 34 million and is distributed, though not equally, over a surface area of 504, 750 km² (i.e. an average density of 67 persons per km²). The rate of population growth (1.05 per cent per annum) is far from negligible and the rate of urban growth (3.4 per cent per annum) is rapid. The present urban population (i.e. living in towns

---

* The issues discussed in this paper are elaborated in greater length in H. W. Richardson, *La Política Española y el Desarrollo Regional*, Atlanza, Madrid, 1975 (to be published in English as *Regional Policy and Planning in Spain*); and in F. Fernández Rodriguez, "La Política Regional en los Planes Españoles de Desarrollo" ("Regional Policy and Plans for Development in Spain", *Boletín de Estudios Económicos,* No. 86, 1972.

larger than 20,000) is 56 per cent of the total, and is forecast to reach 78 per cent by the year 2000. The spatial distribution is very unbalanced with most of the large urban agglomerations apart from Madrid located on the coast. By 1980 47 per cent of the population is expected to be living in eight provinces covering 13 per cent of the surface area.[4]

The rapid urbanisation rate has had marked differential effects on individual areas and regions because urban expansion has been paralleled by rural depopulation. Each year more than 100,000 persons leave agriculture, and in the 1960s 23 out of 50 provinces suffered a net population loss. Most of the three million people who changed homes in the 1960s moved to the big cities, and hence, apart from the pull to Madrid, tended to move from the centre to the periphery. The effects of population growth at the periphery have been accentuated by the foreign tourist boom, reinforced by an increase in domestic demand for holidays and second homes. The results have included pressure on urban services, invasion of the countryside and environmental degradation.

The unequal spatial distribution of population can be explained geographically and historically by differentials in the natural resource base and by the pace of industrialisation which has had cumulative effects on this initial disequilibrium. Although the imbalances in population distribution and in economic activity have been associated with unequal distribution of incomes spatially (the per capita income ratio between the richest and poorest provinces is probably about 2.5 : 1), interregional income and welfare standards have tended to converge for reasons directly connected with the dynamics of population and migration change.[5] Thus, although rural-urban migration has accentuated the spatial imbalances in the distribution of population it has tended simultaneously to reduce the spatial imbalances in the distribution of income. As Alcaide Inchausti has pointed out,[6] economic activity has become more spatially concentrated in the 1960s but polarisation has been less strong than in the case of population. Out-migration from the land has been associated with higher living standards because of increasing agricultural efficiency and reduced underemployment. In-migration to the cities has been associated with increased competition in metropolitan labour markets, frictional unemployment, housing shortages and pressure on urban services. There has been a dampening of per capita income growth in the bigger cities reinforced by relative deterioration in non-monetary indicators of household welfare. Although expansion of the major urban-industrial concentrations has had beneficial effects on national economic growth and economic efficiency, there have been unfavourable side-effects that have eroded some of these benefits from the point of view of big city residents. These include speculative increases in land prices, deficits in infrastructure endowment, pollution and traffic congestion.

70

The overall patterns of interprovincial migration have been fairly consistent.[7] Although contiguous provinces tend to be closely interconnected with each other via migration flows, the dominant characteristic of interprovincial migration is polarisation in favour of the two dominating metropolitan provinces, Barcelona (the major industrial centre) and Madrid (the national capital and service centre). Particularly strong are the migration linkages between Andalucía and Barcelona, reflecting the critical significance of rural-urban flows and the historical legacy of this traditional migration pattern. Migration into the Basque region has been of regional rather than national significance since most of the migrants have come from adjacent or north-western provinces. Bilbao has not been a major destination for migrants from the country as a whole. These migration trends support the hypothesis that migration is largely determined by economic forces. If the stated national policy objective of minimising interregional migration is to be achieved, it suggests the need for strong measures to promote economic development in the traditional regions of out-migration.

The Heterogeneity of Provinces

The provinces of Spain differ widely in terms of size, population, economic structure, degree of urbanisation and other economic and social variables. For instance, the population levels of over 4 million for Barcelona and Madrid contrast with Soria, Guadalajara, Segovia, Teruel, and Palencia—all of which have populations less than 200,000. In several provinces (Guipúzcoa, Madrid, Vizcaya, Barcelona, Las Palmas, Tenerife, Álava, Oviedo, Zaragoza, Valencia, Valladolid and Sevilla) between 95 and 60 per cent of the population live in cities larger than 100,000, whereas in an even larger number of provinces there is not even a single town of this size.[8] Industry is heavily concentrated in a limited number of provinces; more than 40 per cent of total industrial employment is in two provinces (Barcelona and Madrid) and 65 per cent in eight provinces.[9] Conversely, there are eight provinces with more than 30 per cent of their net output in the primary sector.[10] There is a comparable spread of performance in growth rates, per capita income differentials, and migration rates. This striking heterogeneity between provinces combines with the traditional weaknesses of the provincial administration in Spain to restrict the effectiveness of regional planning severely, especially in view of the fact that the province remains the largest subnational administrative and planning unit.

71

Changes in Provincial Income Banks

Interregional per capita income differentials in Spain are wider than in most developed countries. The ratio between the highest and lowest income provinces (Guipúzcoa and Almería) is at present almost 3 : 1, and this represents a narrowing compared with the 1950s and 1960s. Nevertheless, one-third of the provinces still have a per capita income less than 50 per cent of that of the richest province. Despite indications of convergence in the last two decades, Spain remains a country with a large number of underdeveloped and poor regions.

In view of the inaccuracies of the provincial income data, it is preferable to adopt a simple form of analysis (changes in ranks) rather than a more statistical treatment. Comparing 1955 and 1970, there is a high degree of stability in ranks for many provinces. Almost three-fifths of the total number retained a similar rank (defined as a change of less than five places) over that period, and many of these either retained the same rank or changed by only one place. Moreover, stability was much greater at the top and the bottom of the rank order. No province moved into or left either the top five or the bottom five. However, 22 provinces changed rank by five places or more, 12 in an upwards direction (see Table 1). With one exception (Soria) all the upward moves in rank were of less than 10 places, whereas four provinces suffered a drop in rank greater than this margin.

Table 1. Biggest Jumps in Ranks, Income per Head by Province, 1955-70

Soria	+18	Córdoba	− 5
Gerona	+ 9	Málaga	− 5
Lérida	+ 9	Segovia	− 6
Teruel	+ 9	Las Palmas	− 9
Balearics	+ 8	Oviedo	− 9
Guadalajara	+ 8	Palencia	− 9
Toledo	+ 8	Valencia	−11
Huesca	+ 7	Cádiz	−13
Murcia	+ 7	Huelva	−15
Lugo	+ 6	Sevilla	−15
Salamanca	+ 5		
Tarragona	+ 5		

There were discernible spatial patterns in those provinces that jumped ranks. Five of the ten declining provinces were a spatially contiguous set in Western Andalucía, which testifies to the failure of regional policies in the 1960s to do much for Southern Spain. Three other slumping provinces (Oviedo, Palencia and Segovia) were situated on a central—north west axis. As for the rapidly improving provinces, it is significant that many of these were located around the core provinces of Barcelona and Madrid.

This suggests that there has been some diffusion of development spatially out of the cores. This, however, is not a universal phenomenon, as is shown by the differential experience of the adjacent provinces of Segovia and Guadalajara. It is possible that Palencia and Segovia have suffered negatively because of their proximity to the poles of Valladolid and Burgos. The finding that spatial spread effects predominate around the cores of Madrid and Barcelona, while backwash effects predominate around these poles is not contradictory, in view of the different sizes of the centres, their varying levels of development and the existence of fiscal and other incentives to attract industry to the poles.

Delimitation of Regions

There are no official planning regions in Spain. The geographical scope of most regional plans (e.g. Plan Badajoz, Plan Jaén, Campo de Gibraltar Plan, the poles) has been determined on an *ad hoc* basis. To the extent that there has been a regular mechanism for administering and implementing subnational plans this has been developed at the provincial level, specifically via the CPSTs (Provincial Commissions for Technical Services) established in 1945 and entrusted from 1957 with the execution of provincial plans and the co-ordination of the field projects at the different ministries. However, experience shows that in practice the local agents of the ministries have given little attention to CPST planning.

In November 1973, following the conversion of the Comisaría del Plan (Planning Commisariat) into the new MPD (Ministry of Planning and Development), a decree was introduced dividing the 50 provinces into 14 planning regions in each of which there were to be planning agencies (Territorial Delegations) and parallel representative bodies (Territorial Planning Commissions). This delimitation is merely the latest of a large number suggested by regional analysts in Spain over the last twenty years. The decree was, however, not implemented. This is partly the result of the fact that some of the proposals (e.g. grouping Navarra with the Basque region, keeping Las Palmas and Tenerife together etc.) aroused considerable local opposition, and partly the result of the ministerial changes that took place at the end of 1973. The most recent proposal is to abandon regionalisation with institutional arrangements and to settle instead for a set of seven macro-regions to be used solely for technical planning purposes inside the Ministry. For this approach to be effective it will be necessary to decentralise more planning decisions to the provincial level and to pave the way gradually for interprovincial co-ordination. There are few precedents in Spain for progress on this front.

The Creation of the MPD (Ministry of Planning and Development)

In June 1973 the Planning Commisariat that had been created in the Presidencia del Gobierno in 1962, was disbanded and replaced by a new Ministry, the MPD. Whereas the Commisariat had predominantly a sectoral structure, the MPD is organised functionally, with Economic, Social and Regional Planning Divisions (as well as administrative, technical and statistical departments). This reflects, inter alia, the increasing attention that is being devoted to equity and other social goals. The functions of the Regional Planning Division are to deal with all aspects of regional policy and planning and to prepare and implement the regional component of the national development plan. The Division is divided into three separate departments: the first is the general regional planning department, further sub-divided into groups dealing separately with the developed areas and the underdeveloped areas; the second is responsible for the study and planning of resources; and the third, responsible for programmes and regional action, is in charge both of spatial strategic planning and of drawing up and implementing specific plans and programmes. Also, among the functions of the Social Planning Division is that it should be responsible for environmental planning and act as the secretariat for the Interministerial Commission for the Environment.

The creation of the MPD was accompanied by a stated intention to reform the preparation of the national plan. The first three plans were presented to the Cortes (the national parliament) only after the drafting stage. However, in the fourth plan the MPD will submit the procedure of drafting the plan, the definition of its objectives, and its contents for consideration by the Cortes. This change strengthens political participation in the planning process, and could have far-reaching consequences especially in such fields as regional planning where local interests may make their influence felt through the political process.

Provincial and Municipal Administration

Neither the provincial nor the municipal administrations are well equipped to undertake substantive regional planning. The provincial administrative system was established in the nineteenth century on the French Napoleonic pattern. The fifty provinces refer to areas widely different in size, economic and financial resources and socio-economic characteristics. The provinces of Navarra and Álava retain financial arrangements and organisational structures unknown elsewhere. The Provincial Governor was intended to be a professional administrator on the model of the French Prefect, but has consistently been a political figure recruited from the Movimiento, the

74

Sindicatos, or the military. The provincial administration is frequently by-passed by the Ministries in Madrid which operate directly through their local agents. Municipal authorities are organs of the State and are under close control of the Administration. Local officials, when acting as re-presentatives of the State, are subject to orders from the centre. Even when acting as autonomous agencies the local authorities are kept under regular supervision ("tutelage powers"). The representative bodies of the provinces and municipalities, the Diputaciones and the Ayuntamientos, are indirectly elected, and the distance between the people and local administration is great.[11] Also, the increasing tendency for the State to transfer the administration of its services from local control to the Ad-ministración Periférica has further weakened local involvement. There is a shortage of professional staff at the provincial and municipal levels, where both salaries and the quality of personnel are lower than in the central administration.

Tutelage powers have led to conflicting interests since political control (over local councillors and their decisions) is exercised by the Governor (i.e. by the Ministry of the Interior) while financial control is in the hands of the Provincial Delegates of the Finance Ministry. While the Ministry of the Interior attempts to create viable local administrative units, the Finance Ministry frequently curbs local initiatives because of its desire to reduce public expenditure and to retain potential revenue sources for the central government.

The crucial reasons why provincial and local authorities have operated ineffectually in Spain are financial. Funds have been short, the Finance Ministry has been parsimonious, and taxlevying powers are limited. Taxes absorb a lower share of national income in Spain than in many other countries. Despite a slight increase in the ratio of taxes to national income, 0.183 in 1970 compared with 0.165 in 1930, the share of local and provincial taxes in total taxes has fallen from 28.6 to 18.3 per cent. Efforts to redistribute funds from rich to poor authorities have failed. In view of the deficiencies in local revenue, many projects have had to be financed via central government loans and grants, and thus most of the major financial decisions have been taken in Madrid. Almost 93 per cent of local taxation is determined by the central government in Madrid, which also retains some form of control over about one-half of the resources of local authorities and two-thirds of the resources of the provinces.

These factors explain why neither the provincial nor the municipal authorities are in a strong position to tackle the problems of regional and urban development. Although administrative reforms, including more devolution of powers and more local revenue sources, might remedy the situation, it is difficult for local administrative reforms to run ahead of changes in Spanish society and political structures as a whole.

Before the I Plan

Prior to the 1960s, regional planning in Spain had very few antecedents. In 1918 the establishment of a national parks system represented an elementary spatial strategy confined to one type of facility, while in 1926 regional water supply authorities were created. In the early 1950s *ad hoc* spatial plans were introduced for Badajoz and Jaén which were a crude attempt at comprehensive regional planning. In 1957 the provincial planning functions of the Provincial Commissions for Technical Services were expanded, while in 1959 the beginnings of a decongestion strategy from Madrid was introduced. However, none of these programmes or policies amounted to much, and regional planning in Spain effectively dates from the I Development Plan, 1964-7.

Regional Policy in the I Plan, 1964-7

The policies for regional development introduced in the I Plan reflected the influence of the Report of the Mission of the World Bank (IBRD) which has visited Spain in 1961. The Mission had urged measures to promote the aggregate rate of growth, reinforced by policies to promote the free mobility of labour and capital. This left little room for major regional development efforts. However, the Mission did suggest that a few regions with growth potential should be selected, and that measures should be taken to stimulate development there without interfering with the growth of the economy as a whole.

The I Plan broadly adopted this position, but also paid some attention —or at least lip-service—to regional equity. The plan's most important innovation—the establishment of two industrial promotion poles (Burgos and Huelva) and five industrial development poles (La Coruña, Sevilla, Valladolid, Vigo and Zaragoza)—was not recommended by the IBRD Mission, but instead reflected the influence of French regional development theory on the Spanish technocrats. The I Plan proposed a number of integrated specific regional plans for certain areas (Campo de Gibraltar, Tierra de Campos, and the Canary Isles), and these required new institutions in regional development administration. Finally, the poles instruments stressed capital subsidies (investment grants and official credit) whereas the World Bank had come out in favour of labour subsidies.

76

The II Plan, 1968-71

The II Plan did not contain any major new initiatives in regional planning. The main changes were in philosophical outlook and attitudes rather than in planning instruments and, because stated intentions were never fulfilled, regional policies continued much as before.

The major philosophical changes were: a broadening of the narrow "economic efficiency" approach that characterised the I Plan; a stress on selectivity rather than on macro-economic prescriptions; some shift in emphasis from the problems of growth to those of distribution; a greater role for agriculture, education and social policies; and an increased role for the public administrator and a commensurately reduced role for the private entrepreneur, the dominant actor in the I Plan. In regional planning, the II Plan attacked the overcentralisation of decision making and made a commitment to involve provincial and municipal governments much more in the execution of the plan. However, despite more involvement in some programmes, e.g. tourist infrastructure projects, the degree of local participation in plan implementation has remained limited.

Apart from an elaboration of theoretical statements giving more stress to interregional equity, to the reconciliation of regional with national and sectoral planning, and to feasible spatial strategies, the *content* of the II Plan went little beyond that of the I Plan. The poles policy was continued in more or less its original form, except that some old poles lapsed and new ones were designated. The II Plan also made some advances in tourist planning by the designation of zones of special tourist interest, and this was followed in 1970 by the development of widely dispersed tourist infrastructure programmes.

The III Plan and Regional Development, 1972-5

The III Plan aimed at the integration of regional policy within the framework of national and sectoral planning via a strategy of efficient spatial organisation *(vertebración del territorio)*. This involved the promotion of a hierarchical network of cities and towns (large metropolitan areas, equilibrium metropolises, medium size cities,[12] other urban centres and district capitals) consistent with a rational spatial distribution of population. This had certain implications: more attention to the dimension of space in public infrastructure decisions; more cohesion between the varied scattered regional programmes; a longer-term perspective and more flexibility in policy objectives; and a need for more co-ordination between government departments and different hierarchical levels of the administration.

The national urban system in Spain is spatially skewed with dynamic centres in Madrid, Barcelona and Bilbao-San Sebastián and a few other metropolitan areas located on the coast but with the smaller centres crucial to the diffusion of growth insufficiently developed.[13] One possible strategy (though its phasing could take many forms since there are a great many choices) is clear-cut: promotion of interdependence between hierarchical units and the stimulation of new sub-centres to bring some of the depressed areas into the national urban hierarchy, thereby reducing their isolation and fostering a less polarised spatial growth process. However, such a strategy requires much more discrimination in the spatial allocation of social infrastructure and investment decisions in respect to the interregional transportation network that pay more attention to social criteria and less to current traffic demand patterns. Up to now, the administration has been reluctant to face up to these hard decisions, and the "vertebración del territorio" strategy remains an expression of hopes rather than a practical achievement.

A settlement concentration strategy was also developed for the rural areas. There are about 70,000 separate nuclei, and it is clearly too costly to maintain them all if the aim of urban centres was to make a satisfactory level of urban services *accessible* to all the population. Accordingly, priority was to be given to 286 district capitals and to a second level of selected centres, making 427 in all. The objective was to provide these centres with the industry, infrastructure and services needed to stabilise the rural population and to revitalise the rural regions.

The III Plan also included a shift in emphasis in location of industry policy, away from steering industries to specific locations towards the idea of a national distribution of industry policy based on the location of industries in areas offering locational advantages but at the same time promoting regional development. As a consequence, there was a shift away from the growth point approach. No new development poles were established in the III Plan. Instead, a new concept was developed—that of the "gran area de expansión industrial"—which refers to a much larger area than that of a development pole and contains several nuclei. The objective was to develop a more comprehensive regional planning approach embracing industrial sector planning, urbanisation and a transport and general infrastructure strategy. In the III Plan only one such "gran area" was created—in Galicia. At the same time a regional development society—SODIGA (Sociedad para el Desarrollo Industrial de Galicia)— was created with the support of INI (Instituto Nacional de Industria) to co-ordinate information about investment opportunities in the region, to promote the rationalisation of existing and the creation of new industries, to participate financially in local industry, and to mobilise the flow of investment funds into the region.

Finally, new selective regional programmes were initiated in the III Plan dealing with the Canary Isles, Galicia and the South-East. However, apart from Galicia, which received special treatment as described above, the programmes for these regions amounted to little more than a pooling together of the varied infrastructure projects that would have taken place in any event.

Towards the IV Plan, 1976-9

At the time of writing, the detailed contents of the IV Plan have not been revealed, or even proposed. However, for several reasons it is unlikely that the IV Plan will contain many major new regional planning initiations. The MPD is a new ministry and is still weak relative to longer-established government departments. Also, the bad experience with the ill-fated planning regions of the November 1973 decree will deter the ministry from strong actions. Moreover, the change in the international economic environment has had unfavourable impacts on Spain. The fast growth rate of the 1960s has been interrupted, inflation is serious, and the twin blows of the energy crisis and the recession in international tourism have disturbed the balance of payments equilibrium. In these circumstances, the attention of the policymakers is inevitably turning to problems of the aggregate economy rather than to those of spatial allocation. Finally, the government changes of 1973-4 were associated with a mass exodus of technocrats from planning posts in the ministries, and there is a serious shortage of qualified and experienced regional planners.

Nevertheless, even if little can be expected in terms of new programmes and new instruments, the theoretical debate goes on and the evolution in planning attitudes continues. An ambitious plan for the "ordenación nacional del territorio" is currently being discussed, modelled to some extent on the French "aménagement du territoire" strategies, though also reflecting the comprehensive if idealistic National Plan of Urbanism suggested in the Land and Urban Planning Act of 1956. Although the new plan at first sight appears comprehensive in scope, touching upon all major spatial aspects and variables, it seems upon closer inspection to be little more than a national land use plan, dividing the national space economy into two categories of area, *areas intensivas* and *areas libres*.[14] The trouble with this approach is that land use allocations, especially at the national level, are too rigid and inflexible to form a satisfactory basis for spatial planning. Also, the relationship between economic and social development in a spatial context and land use is one of simultaneous interdependence rather than the former being a function of the latter.

Conclusions

Regional planning in Spain, from the evidence given in the documents of the first three development plans, has evolved quite dramatically. The I Plan's stress on aggregate efficiency, and on intervening at specific locations where opportunity costs were low, gave way in the II Plan to more emphasis on interregional equity objectives, to a closer integration of spatial with the dominant sectoral planning, and to the intention to promote decentralisation. In the III Plan further progress was made, first, by developing the case for national spatial strategies stressing the national urban hierarchy and, second, by softening the growth pole idea borrowed from abroad by substituting the "gran area" concept which may be more suited to Spanish conditions. However, the progress has been much less real than the Plans imply because the evolution in attitudes and statements has not been matched by a parallel improvement in practical planning. Effective instruments and programmes have still not been developed, and any progress in regional performance (e.g. the possible narrowing of interregional per capita income differentials) has been the result much more of spontaneous and natural development forces in the economy rather than of the effects of policy and planning.

The Development Poles Policy

As in so many countries in the 1960s, the keystone of regional policy and planning in Spain was a development pole strategy. Between 1964 and 1972 twelve growth poles were created, some of which have now lapsed.[15] However, the poles strategy in Spain has responded far more to efficiency and national integration goals than to regional equity objectives. In effect, the strategy has been one of national rather than of regional poles. This view is supported by two facts. First, the poles were selected prior to the regions in which they are located and selection criteria stressed growth potential.[16] Leira has argued [17] that the Spanish growth poles policy is an efficiency-oriented policy, and that the selections were made in order to guarantee success. In countries pursuing a *regional* poles strategy it is more usual to choose the regions first (frequently using the "worst first" criterion) and then to designate the most potentially dynamic centres in those regions as poles. Second, the poles have been treated as a spatial instrument for promoting industrialisation in Spain with some stress on large-scale industrial complexes. Thus, the poles were regarded much more as an extension of a national development and sectoral planning strategy, as in French planning practice, than as an instrument for developing the lagging regions of the country.

A weakness in the early poles policy was the wildly optimistic five-year designation period. Although subsequently relaxed, it remains doubtful whether the present ten-year duration should not be replaced by an indefinite period until the selected centre no longer needs subsidies. The incentives offered to pole firms (compulsory acquisition of land for industrial estates on which industrial infrastructure is developed, a 10 per cent capital investment grant, preference in obtaining official credit, and a plethora of tax reductions and exemptions) are rather complicated, and because the benefits are discretionary rather than automatic many firms receive much less than the maximum. This is one reason why the number of projects that materialise is only about one-half of those approved. Also, applications for aid are restricted to specific times, called *concursos,* that occur at intervals of approximately one year. This inflexibility discourages applicants. Furthermore, although the statistics suggest some preference in favour of labour-intensive projects within the policymakers' discretionary powers, all the incentives have a strong capital-intensive bias which is inappropriate for an economy suffering from capital shortage but with labour reserves, at least in the lagging regions.[18] The most important incentive in terms of fiscal resources has been the provision of official credit, particularly because of the low level of self-financing and liquidity constraints in Spanish industry. However, two major drawbacks have been the relative neglect of small firms in terms of access to official credit and the fact that the flow of official credit has been spasmodic because the banks supplying the credit are not insulated from monetary movements in the economy as a whole or from cyclical fluctuations. The minimum size criterion for aid has held back the development of small-scale auxiliary supply plants, and has discriminated against labour-intensive industry and against Spanish indigenous firms which are usually much smaller in scale than the partly foreign-owned companies.

Given the emphasis on large-scale industrial complexes and the capital-intensive bias of the subsidies, it is not surprising that the chemicals and metal industries have dominated investment at the poles. Most of the poles have been highly specialised, with only La Coruña and, to a lesser extent, Sevilla having diversified industrial structures. The typical pattern is for each pole to have a dominant sector: chemicals at Huelva, metal products at Vigo and Burgos, metal products and chemicals at Valladolid, and food industries at Córdoba. This suggests that the theory of functional poles has had a major influence on the character of Spanish pole policies.

The geographical sales and purchases flows of the poles reveal some interesting patterns. Interregional exports account for a high proportion of sales at all the poles, suggesting that the pole has been an effective instrument for expanding the export base. On the other hand, their foreign export performance has been poor even in the case of the coastal poles; only

Vigo has had a favourable impact on the international balance of payments. The links between nearby poles have been weak. Intra-pole sales and purchases have been low, apart from in Huelva (chemicals) and Valladolid (transport implements). Dependence on foreign imports has been very high in La Coruña and moderately high in Huelva, reflecting a reliance on foreign natural resources (petroleum, aluminium, fluorite, etc.). As for integration with their hinterlands, there is a wide difference in experience among the poles. The linkages of Burgos and Vallodolid are primarily interregional with negligible local spread effects. In Sevilla and Zaragoza, on the other hand, hinterland effects are fairly strong particularly on the input side. One reason could be that the intensity of hinterland effects depends on the size of the central pole itself.

The earliest evaluations of the impact of the poles, attempting to measure the relative importance of autonomous, transferred and generated investments, were inaccurate since they were based on a fairly unscientific survey of the pole firms themselves. The II Plan used an elementary form of cost-benefit analysis in which costs were equated with public expenditures while benefits were interpreted as the number of new jobs directly created. This approach is too narrow. Attempts were also made to measure direct, indirect and induced effects as a proportion of provincial income, but these data are difficult to interpret because it is impossible to quantify how much industrial expansion would have taken place in the absence of pole status.

Leira[19] suggests two other kinds of evaluations: first, a cross-sectional test comparing growth at the poles with growth elsewhere in Spain; and, second, an intemporal test comparing "before" and "after" performance at the poles. On both these counts, in general terms, the poles performed fairly well. As Table 2 shows, in the first years of the poles policy (1964-67), the increase in per capita income was much more rapid in the poles than in Spain as a whole, the poorest provinces or the major metropolitan provinces. After 1967 the per capita income performance at the poles deteriorated even though the national rate of change remained constant. Nevertheless, the poles still fared better than the metropolitan provinces. In terms of gross industrial product, the poles showed up impressively. The rate of change in gross industrial product at the poles was almost three times as great as in per capita income, almost twice as fast as the increase in gross industrial product in the metropolitan provinces, more than twice as fast as the country as a whole, and almost four times as fast as in the poorest provinces. Even though industrial output would have increased faster at the poles in any event because of the fact that they were selected on account of their development potential, the growth differentials are so wide that from an industrial promotion point of view the initial seven poles have been a success.

82

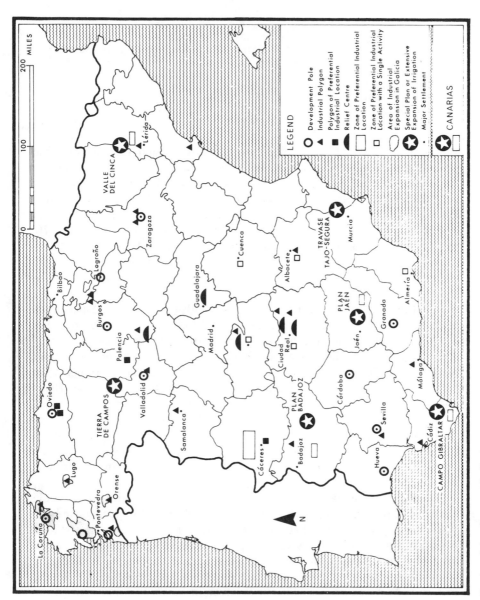

LEGEND

○ Development Pole
▲ Industrial Polygon
● Polygon of Preferential Industrial Location
◗ Relief Centre
▢ Zone of Preferential Industrial Location
▫ Zone of Preferential Industrial Location with a Single Activity
⬭ Area of Industrial Expansion in Galicia
✪ Special Plan or Extensive Expansion of Irrigation
• Major Settlement

CANARIAS

✪▢

Regional development in Spain

Table 2.   Growth in The Original Poles Relative to the Rest of Spain

	1964-7	1967-71	
	Income per capita (% increase)	Income per capita (% increase)	Gross Industrial product (% increase)
Seven Poles	77.4	49.7	137.9
Major Metropolitan Provinces	34.4	36.9	71.3
Five Worst Provinces	55.6	44.8	36.7
Rest of country	37.3	50.2	46.2
National average	44.0	46.6	64.6

Population growth at the poles before and after designation suggests that pole status boosted these cities. With the sole exception of La Coruña, population in each pole grew faster in the 1960s than in the 1950s. The acceleration was particularly striking in the cases of Zaragoza, Valladolid, Burgos and Vigo. The share of the initial seven poles in Spain's total population increased from 4.91 per cent in 1960 to 5.88 per cent in 1970, much faster than in the 1950s (the 1950 share was 4.48 per cent). However, evidence that the *regional* demographic impacts of the poles were either limited or unfavourable is provided by the fact that the pole provinces' share in total population fell from 15.47 per cent in 1960 to 14.81 per cent in 1970, a little faster than in the 1950s (1950 = 15.95 per cent). Even in cases where the pole and the province *appeared* to thrive together (e.g. Zaragoza, Valladolid), the pole grew at the expense of the province.[20] This suggests that hitherto the poles have had a "backwash" effect on their respective regions, promoting intra-provincial polarisation rather than fostering provincial-wide or regional development. In several cases (Burgos, La Coruña, Huelva, Sevilla) the provincial populations failed to expand, and hence these poles must be regarded as failures from the regional development point of view since, despite their own growth and attainment of industrialisation targets, they did not succeed in stemming provincial outmigration. On the contrary, provincial outmigration in the 1960s was much faster than in the 1950s.

Spanish regional policymakers appear to have lost faith in the pole instrument, perhaps because their regional development impacts have been much less impressive than their industrial performance.[21] Since the gestation period of successful poles is very long, it is possible that the strategy has been abandoned too soon. Nevertheless, they could never be treated as a complete solution to Spain's regional development problems. Up to the end of 1971 new jobs created were equivalent to about 3 per cent of the population of the pole cities or less than 0.5 per cent of the national labour force. Moreover, the rate of job creation at the poles (about 7,000 new jobs per annum) was only a small fraction of the annual rundown in agricultural employment (110,000 per annum). Furthermore, the poles strategy neglects the development of Southern Spain (Andalucía). Sevilla has been disestablished, Huelva expires at the end of 1974, little is expected from Granada now that the basic transportation improvements for tourism have been carried out, and Córdoba has failed to take off. North-South dualism—not at present an accurate description of the Spanish situation—might become a reality because of the poles policy.

Major drawbacks to the original poles strategy include: inflexibility in spatial delimitation, recently improved by the larger region delimited at Oviedo and by the "gran area" approach; over-optimistism about the short- and medium-term regional impacts of polarisation; a neglect of regional urban hierarchy considerations and of environmental planning that followed from a tendency to think of the pole in terms of industrial estates rather than as the focus of broad urban and regional development; too little attention to social services and human capital investments; and insufficient balance in the size and variety of firms attracted to the poles. However, these deficiencies suggest a need for gradual improvement, learning through experience and more flexibility, not for total abandonment of the pole strategy.

A more serious indictment of the poles strategy is that it was a sham and was never intended to alter substantially the spatial distribution of resources.[22] This argument is composed of several strands. First, the strategy was an efficiency instrument, and equity arguments were merely used as a cloak to legitimise the poles as a regional policy. Second, it was a conservative, risk-averting strategy. "Natural" poles were selected, i.e. cities that were bound to grow in any event. Thus, it became impossible to separate out the "autonomous" component of growth from the "induced" pole effect. The "success" of the policy was therefore guaranteed in advance. Third, the poles policy was politically acceptable, whereas some of the alternatives, particularly agrarian reform, would have alienated too many of the régime's leading supporters. Fourth, the policy was cheap in terms of public investment resources and fiscal costs. Fifth, a poles policy was compatible with the ideology of the planners. The national plans were indicative plans, and were intended not as a technical solution to the problem of how to allocate resources optimally but rather as a vehicle for encouraging private enterprise. The poles policy avoided difficult structural problems and provided an appropriate setting in which private entrepreneurs might act. Finally, a poles strategy was "trendy", conveying the impression that Spain's technocrats were up to date and using the latest tools of regional planning.

Although these arguments are substantially true, they refer to the reasons why and to the time when the policy was adopted. Policies can be adapted and transformed over time, and the critical question is the degree

85

to which the poles policy was modified to serve equity objectives and to make it more effective. There were some changes such as the creation of poles in more backward provinces (Granada and Córdoba), lengthening of the designation period, and other reforms. Nevertheless, the poles strategy failed to develop as an instrument for achieving regional policy objectives, and has been abandoned before it could have been expected to generate substantive results.

Zones of Preferential Industrial Location

In 1963, the Law of Industries of Preferential Interest set up areas of preferential industrial location as an instrument of regional development in the hands of the Ministry of Industry. Areas were delimited within which firms would obtain the fiscal and other benefits that were offered to industrial establishments at the poles (tax exemptions, subsidies, official credit, compulsory expropriation, etc.). Simultaneously with the development of the poles, the Ministry of Industry delimited several such areas in Tierra de Campos, Campo de Gibraltar, Valle del Cinca, Cáceres and Canarias.

In the I and II Plans, the different instruments of policy remained un-co-ordinated. However, with the III Plan the Government aimed at integrating the different aspects of policy into a broader consolidated strategy. Consistent with this goal, the Ministry of Industry in 1973 de-clared certain industrial estates originally developed within the context of other instruments to be zones of preferential industrial location. For example, industrial estates within the territory of poles which had been rescheduled (e.g. La Coruña, Sevilla, Valladolid, Vigo, Zaragoza), where land remained for industrial development, were included in order to maximise the social return from public infrastructure investments already made. The industrial overspill estates around Madrid which had failed to achieve the hoped-for results (Aranda de Duero, Manzanares, Alcazar de San Juan and Toledo) were also brought within the scope of the scheme. Guadalajara was excluded, because its relative proximity to Madrid had helped it to be more successful. Nine other estates [23] were included where industrial development strategies on development axis or zones of in-fluence lines were in operation in order to compete with more attractive dynamic areas and regions. The general idea behind this consolidation was to combine the zones of preferential industrial location, the existing poles, the "gran area" and other selective regional programmes into one consistent and coordinated policy framework.

Conclusions

Any assessment of regional development policy and planning in Spain is faced with the paradox of dramatic improvement in the policymakers' perception of their problems and clarification of their ideas on the one hand, and deterioration in the real world situation on the other. There are undoubtedly major theoretical advances in the Spanish approach to regional planning as one progresses from one Plan to the next. Today the conception of regional planning in Spain is much broader than it was ten years ago in many respects: recognition of the need to take a long-run perspective, appreciation of the necessity of comprehensive, cohesive and co-ordinated programmes; more attention to interregional and intra-regional equity; more flexibility in the design of instruments and selection of areas; and paying lip-service at least to social and environmental considerations. The practical achievements are, however, far from satisfactory. There is some evidence of interregional per capita income convergence, but its causes have nothing to do with policy. Both population and economic activities have become more spatially concentrated in a few areas, namely Madrid and the major metropolitan coastal provinces. The experience at the poles has been very mixed, but even the "successes" have been of a limited kind, with high rates of industrial growth but negligible, and in some cases negative, regional impacts. The heavily centralised administration has functional rigidly and unresponsively, and there have been no meaningful attempts to decentralise decision making or to reflect regional preferences. Key sectors such as education, agriculture, tourism, pollution control and land use still lack a policy cutting edge to make them viable instruments of regional development. The problems of spatial polarisation, increasing metropolitan congestion, rural depopulation, and imperfectly developed national and regional urban hierarchies are even further away from being solved in spite of more than a decade of efforts in regional planning.

Notes

1. Spain was the fastest growing economy in Western Europe with a growth rate in real GNP in the 1960s averaging 7 percent.
2. Interregional migration has narrowed interregional incomes per capita, if only arithmetically (more people in the rich regions, fewer in the poor), while spontaneous growth forces have resulted in some spatial diffusion of development. Within regions, on the other hand, with a few exceptions such as Cataluña, urban-rural income differentials have widened.
3. Cf. J. R. Lasuén, "Spain's Regional Growth", Mimeo. paper, Universidad Autónoma de Madrid, 1973.

4. These provinces are Alicante, Barcelona, La Coruña, Madrid, Oviedo, Sevilla, Valencia and Vizcaya.

5. This conclusion is tentative because of the imperfections of the income data. The most important work in this area is *Distribución Provincial de la Renta Nacional,* published biennially since 1955 by the Banco de Bilbao in Madrid.

6. J. Alcaide Inchausti, "La Distribución de la Riqueza y de la Renta en la Sociedad Española: Balance de Tres Planes de Desarrollo", mimeo. paper, Madrid, 1974.

7. For analysis of interregional migration in Spain in the 1960s see: Instituto Nacional de Estadística, *Migración y Estructura Regional,* Madrid, 1968 and *Las Migraciones Internas en España—Decenio 1961-70,* Madrid, 1974; A. B. Barbancho, "La Migraciones Interiores Españolas en 1961-70", *Revista Española de Economía,* Jan.-Apr. 1974, pp. 113-158; and J. Angelet, "Interregional Migration Movements in Spain: A Quantitative Analysis of Economic, Urban and Spatial Characteristics", mimeo. paper, 1974.

8. The list includes Albacete, Ávila, Cáceres, Ciudad Real, Cuenca, Gerona, Huesca, Jaén, Lérida, Logroño, Lugo, Orense, Palencia, Segovia, Teruel, Toledo and Zamora.

9. The other six are Valencia, Vizcaya, Oviedo, Guipúzcoa, Alicante and Sevilla.

10. These are Lugo, Cuenca, Zamora, Badajoz, Ávila, Soria, Cáceres and Orense.

11. A new Local Regime Bill presented to the Cortes in May 1974, providing for the direct election of Mayors and the Presidents of the Diputaciones, goes some way towards remedying this problem.

12. For instance, 6 metropolitan areas, 17 equilibrium metropolises and 20 intermediate size towns were designated.

13. Racionero argues that the *national* urban hierarchy is reasonably efficient for interregional diffusion but that there are incomplete urban hierarchies *within regions* to promote intraregional diffusion; L. Racionero, "Desarrollo Regional y Sistemas de Ciudades", Banco Urquijo, Reuniones Internacionales de Economía Regional, Barcelona, 1973.

14. Each of these categories has four further sub-divisions.

15. The original seven poles and their designation periods were: Burgos, 1964-74; Huelva, 1964-74; La Coruña, 1964-71; Sevilla, 1964-71; Valladolid, 1964-70; Vigo, 1964-71; and Zaragoza, 1964-7. The more recent poles are: Granada, 1970-79; Córdoba, 1971-80; Oviedo, 1971-80; Logroño, 1972-81; and Villagarcía de Arosa, 1972-81.

16. Another economic criterion has been to choose suitable centres for expansion along major (present or intended) transport and development axes. Local lobbying and pressures, whether for a pole as in Almería or against a pole as in Zaragoza, had no influence on the decisions of the centralised administration.

17. J. Leira, "Growth Poles in Spain: A Legitimising Instrument for an Efficiency-Oriented Policy", mimeo. paper, University of California at Los Angeles, Berkeley, 1973.

18. In addition, there is underemployment in the cities and a large number of Spaniards working abroad.

19. J. Leira, *op. cit.*

20. Only in the case of Vigo was the absolute increase in population of the province (Pontevedra) greater than that of the pole.

21. This is particularly striking in the case of Huelva, a marked success in industrial terms but an enclave economically isolated from its surrounding region.

22. Cf. J. Leira, *op. cit.*

23. These were at Lugo, Orense, Salamanca, Lérida, Tarragona, Badajoz, Albacete, Cádiz and Málaga.

6

POPULATION GROWTH AND DISTRIBUTION IN CANADA: PROBLEMS, PROCESS AND POLICIES *

D. Michael Ray and *Paul Y. Villeneuve*

1. *The Issue of Growth*

The challenge of growth and change is a fundamental theme underlying much of what has taken place in the century since Confederation in Canada, and pervading much of what is written about future national prospects and problems. Canada has grown very rapidly in land area, population and productivity per capita during the last century. In 1867, Canada comprised four small provinces centered on the Great Lakes— St. Lawrence water system. By the time Newfoundland joined the Confederation in 1949, the country comprised ten provinces and two northern territories. It is now exceeded in land area only by the USSR. Since Confederation, Canada has also sustained one of the world's fastest growth rates of population and of both GNP and GNP per capita. Population increased from a little over three million at Confederation to 22 million by early 1973,[1] while the GNP per capita (constant 1961 dollars) increased approximately from $1080. in 1926 to $3127. in 1971.[2]

These aggregated growth figures hide a complex reality. For instance, immigration has contributed surprisingly little to population increase because of heavy emigration. Between 1851 and 1961, the number of emigrants from Canada has been about three quarters the number of immigrants. But immigration has produced a cultural heterogeneity that increases progressively from east to west across the country and that has, together with urbanization (Table 1), significant consequences in terms of

*   This text is a revised version of a paper presented at the Conference on the Management of Land for Urban Development held in Toronto on April 5 and 6, 1974, and sponsered by the Canadian Council on Urban and Regional Research. The authors are grateful to CCURR for the permission to reproduce the paper and to the Ministry of State for Urban Affairs for research contracts allowing the undertaking of this work. The ideas expressed are those of the authors and not necessarily those of MSUA.

occupational and class structures. In 1867, half the labour force was employed in agriculture, lumbering and fishing and by 1971 this figure was down to less than 10% (Table 2). Porter argues that "If large-scale population movements have inhibited the development of a Canadian consensus they may also have inhibited the emergence of class cultures and class polarization with strong class identifications".[3] Income statistics suggest that the distribution of wages and salaries among wage-earning families became somewhat more equal between 1931 and 1951 (Table 3). They also indicate however that regional disparities at the interprovincial scale are very substantial and have been extremely persistent (Table 4). The per capita employment incomes of the highest-income provinces, Ontario and British Columbia, have generally been twice as high as those of the Atlantic provinces: Newfoundland, Prince Edward Island, Nova Scotia and New Brunswick. There has been little change in interprovincial disparities from 1926, the first year for which regular national accounts data are available. This is in sharp contrast to the United States' experience of a steady and significant convergence in the interregional spread of incomes since the early 1930's.[4]

Table 1. Percent of Population Urban in Canada and in Major Regions: 1851-1971

Census Year	Canada	British Columbia	Prairies	Ontario	Quebec	Atlantic *
1851	13.1	—	—	14.4	14.9	9.0
1891	29.8	42.6	23.3 **	35.0	28.6	18.8
1931	52.5	62.3	31.3	63.1	59.5	39.7
1971	76.1	75.7	66.9	82.3	80.6	55.6

Notes:
* Excluding Newfoundland for all years except 1971
** Manitoba Only

The 1851 and 1891 percent urban population figures refer to incorporated cities, towns and villages of 1,000 and over. The 1931 and 1971 figures are based on the 1961 census definition of urban and include incorporated places of 1,000 and over and unincorporated suburbs regardless of population size that were adjacent to cities, towns and villages which had both a population of 5,000 and over and a density of at least 1,000 persons per square mile.

Source: Leroy O. Stone, Urban Development in Canada, Statistics Canada, Information Canada, Ottawa, 1967, p. 29; and Statistics Canada, Canada 1973, Queen's Printer, Ottawa, 1972, p. 114.

92

Table 2. Occupation Structure of the Labour Force: 1881-1971

	1881	1921	1951	1971
Primary	51.3	36.6	19.8	8.3
Manufacturing	24.3	20.8	25.1	22.2
Construction	4.5	5.8	6.2	6.0
Transportation	2.9	7.8	9.5	8.8
Trade	5.3	9.4	10.1	16.9
Services	11.6	19.2	28.2	37.6
TOTAL	100.0	100.0	100.0	100.0

Note: The labour force is composed of civilian non-institutional population 10 years of age and over in 1881, and 14 years of age and over thereafter, who were employed or unemployed. The figures may not add up to exactly 100% because of rounding error.

Table 3. Percentage Distribution of Wages and Salaries of Wage and Salary Earning Families, by Quintiles, 1930-31 and 1951

Quintile	Percentage share of wages and salaries	
	1930-31	1951
First quintile	5.3	8.0
Second quintile	11.3	13.9
Third quintile	17.3	17.9
Fourth quintile	23.5	22.6
Fifth quintile	42.6	37.5

Note: The figures may not add up to exactly 100% because of rounding error.

Source: J. Podoluk, *Incomes of Canadians,* Statistics Canada, Ottawa 1968, p. 268.

Table 4. Personal Income per Capita by Province (as a Percentage of the National Average)

Province	1926	1941	1951	1961	1971
Newfoundland	—	—	48	58	65
Prince Edward Island	56	47	54	59	64
Nova Scotia	61	78	69	78	77
New Brunswick	65	64	67	68	73
Quebec	85	87	84	90	89
Ontario	114	129	118	118	117
Manitoba	108	93	101	94	94
Saskatchewan	102	59	107	71	82
Alberta	114	80	111	100	100
British Columbia	122	121	119	115	109

Source: David Stager, *Economic Analysis and Canadian Policy,* Butterworth and Co. Ltd., Toronto, 1973, p. 465.

Why have such disparities been so persistent in Canada, what have been the structural dynamics shaping Canada's impressive long term growth, and what have been (and are) the institutional responses to the problems of growth and disparities? These are the questions guiding us throughout this paper. We begin by discussing the fact that the problem of congestion in the fast growing regions has now been added to the pervasive concern with regional disparities and the problems of the lagging regions. We then go on to suggest that problems of growth are fundamentally problems of distribution, and that distributional forces, economic, social and political in nature, operate in a time-space envelope in which a series of hierarchical levels can be identified. This leads us into the eleboration of a model of the structural dynamics of growth in Canada. The model exposes some of the basic determinants of disparities and congestion, and also allows an interpretation of the evolving institutional responses to the problems of growth regulation and spatial allocation.

(a) Absolute Growth and Relative Growth

Many problems of pressing concern to Canadians, such as urban congestion and environmental decay, are directly associated with rapid urban growth and the increasing concentration of population in a few metropolitan areas. Urban growth in Canada has been concentrated in three cities: Montreal, Toronto and Vancouver. If past trends continue, these three metropolises will double their population between 1971 and 2000, at which time Montreal and Toronto alone will account for more than a third of the national total. Such concentration of urban growth in three provinces, Quebec, Ontario and British Columbia (Table 1), is not independent, as will be shown below, of interprovincial differences in earned income per capita (Table 3). It furthermore aggravates problems of urban poverty, housing costs, transportation congestion, environmental decay (visual, noise and water pollution, solid waste disposal), social unrest and fiscal squeeze.[5]

One of the most important lessons of the problems of regional disparities and urban congestion is, indeed, that they include the consequences of both *absolute* growth and *relative* growth. We are faced first with what Kingsley Davis[6] calls the double multiplier: a growing population whose resource demands and environmental impact are augmented by rising standards of living. We are faced too with the regional and social inequalities created by differences in the relative growth rates of different regions and social groups. We need to recognize, in fact, that the issue of growth and the issue of regional disparities are a single issue expressed from the perspectives of different geographic scales. Similarly, policies to influence the size and growth of individual urban centres are, at least implicitly, policies to influence the national distribution of population: "A hierarchy of levels is involved, so that what is viewed as an issue of growth at a lower level is an issue of redistribution at the next higher level".[7]

(b)   A Hierarchy of Growth Forces

There is not only a hierarchy of geographic growth scales, but also a hierarchy of historically ordered growth forces. These forces, each one of which prevails during a given time period, tend to concentrate growth at some single nucleus which, according to the geographic scale, may be the world's industrial heartland, a national manufacturing belt, or a metropolitan area. At each scale, a centre-periphery pattern of trade and communication, of settlement and economic interdependencies is established.[8] It is increasingly recognized that such patterns of spatial dominance may well be attributable to processes of circular and cumulative causation[9] and to positive feedbacks, these being much more salient than negative feedbacks in human and societal systems.[10]

In Canada, this hierarchy of centre-periphery growth forces serves, at the international scale, to articulate the country into the world economy. At the national scale, it links the western, Atlantic and northern hinterlands to a central Canadian manufacturing belt stretching from Windsor to Quebec City. And, at successive sub-national scales, it ties urban hinterlands to their urban centres in systems of central places that focus ultimately on Montreal, Toronto and Vancouver. Additional growth forces are involved that are not centre-periphery in pattern, such as English-French contrasts in occupation structure and population growth rates, and foreign investment which has accelerated economic development and urban growth in Toronto and southwestern Ontario particularly.

These are the themes then presented in this paper: that the issue of growth and size and the issue of distribution of population and economic activity are a single issue seen from different perspectives and involving considerations of both absolute growth and relative growth. Understanding this issue and the processes that give rise to the problems of growth and disparities that challenge Canadian society and policy makers involves the recognition of a hierarchy of scales and sets of centre-periphery and other growth forces that together constitute the total geography of the country. The components of growth are the dimensions of regionalism. They are also historically ordered in the sense that some of them dominate certain periods of Canadian evolution. Past regional development policies have been inadequate responses to these components of growth. Policies to shape the future of Canada must be acceptable at all scales of the geographic hierarchy and must comprise the total mix of social, cultural and economic ingredients if they are to have a hope of success.

2. A Model of the Regional Dimensions of Growth

The framework for examining the underlying growth processes and the policy responses needed to deal with problems of population growth and distribution may be presented in the form of a model. The model involves three steps: the measurement of the relative growth of each part of Canada; the identification of the growth forces; and the scaling of each force according to its contribution to growth. Indeed, it is possible to show that the relative growth performance in each part of Canada is the sum total of the growth contributed by each individual dimension of regionalism.

(a) Relative Population Growth Rates in Canada

Relative population growth rates are computed for each county or census division for the period 1911 to 1971. This is the longest period for which population totals could be adjusted for boundary changes. The growth rate of each county during this period is $a = b/d$, where b and d are respectively the regression coefficients in the following simple exponential functions adjusted to the population growth of each county and to that of Canada:

$$P_{ij} = ae^{bt_j} \; ; P_j = ce^{dt_j}$$

P_j is the population of Canada at t_j, $j = 1911, 1921, \ldots, 1971$; P_{ij} is the population of county i ($i = 1, 2, \ldots, 229$), at t_j.

The value of alpha usually ranges around one. A value of 1.0 is the special case of proportional growth: the county population is growing at the same rate as the national total. Counties growing twice as fast have a value of 2.0 and counties growing half as fast have a value of 0.5. Those in which the population is actually declining have a negative growth rate. This way of expressing relative growth allows for system-wide effects and is thus appropriate for studying intrasystemic redistribution. It is widely used in biology and may be used in social science when there are reasonable grounds for suspecting that proportionate effects are at play.[11]

Three distinct categories of counties emerge in Canada: those growing at a faster rate than the national total; those growing at a slower rate; and those actually declining (Figure 1). Most settled areas have, surprisingly, experienced relative or absolute population decline. Only 56 counties, out of 229, exceeded the national average population growth rate. These 56 include the counties with the 21 Census Metropolitan Areas (Table 5).

96

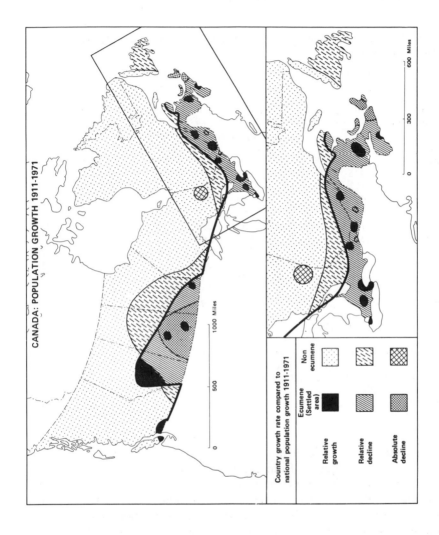

Figure 1. Relative Growth Rates of Population: Canada 1911-1971

Only eight grew more than twice as fast: three countries which experienced population overflow from Toronto and Montreal, and five census divisions located on the northern resource frontier. Apart from these islands of relatively fast growth, the only area of above-average relative growth is the northern resource frontier generally.

Table 5. Population for the Principal Regions of Metropolitan Development in Canada: 1901 to 1971

Principal regions of metropolitan development	1901	1911	1921	1931	1941	1951	1961a	1961b	1971
	Population (in thousands)								
Halifax	51	58	75	79	99	134	184	193	223
Montreal	415	616	796	1,086	1,216	1,504	2,156	2,216	2,743
Quebec	117	133	158	207	241	297	383	379	481
Hamilton	79	112	154	190	207	266	359	401	499
London	52	61	74	87	97	129	181	227	286
Ottawa	103	133	168	197	236	296	436	457	529
Toronto	303	478	686	901	1,002	1,264	1,942	1,919	2,628
Windsor	22	32	66	117	129	163	192	217	259
Winnipeg	48	157	229	295	302	357	476	477	540
Calgary	8	56	78	103	112	156	290	279	403
Edmonton	15	48	87	116	136	211	374	360	496
Vancouver	—	—	224	338	394	562	790	827	1,082
Canada	5,324	7,192	8,776	10,363	11,490	13,623	17,743	17,743	21,568

Note: Population figures for 1901 to 1951 and 1961a were calculated using an expanded definition of metropolitan area (see Stone, p. 132). Population figures for 1961b and 1971 are CMA populations using 1971 definition of metropolitan area.

Source: Leroy O. Stone, op. cit., p. 278; Statistics Canada, 1971 Census of Canada, Ottawa, 1972.

The relative growth profile along the 5,000 mile Trans-Canada Highway which crosses the country from St. John's, Newfoundland to Victoria, British Columbia, illustrates these same points while emphasizing the considerable inter-county variation in growth rates (Figure 2). The peaks are the metropolitan counties or counties with population spillover from adjacent metropolitan counties. They include the census divisions containing St. John's, Newfoundland, Halifax, Montreal, Toronto, Winnipeg, Regina, Calgary, and Vancouver. Note that the profile used digresses from the Trans-Canada Highway between Montreal and Sudbury to follow Ontario Highways 400 and 401 in order to pass through Toronto.

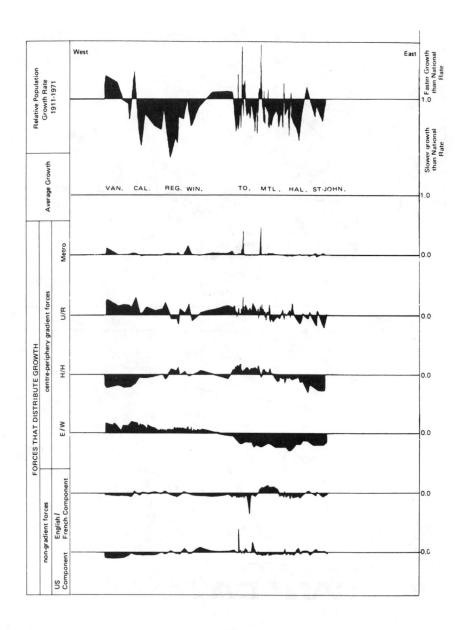

Figure 2. Components of Growth as Measured Along the Trans-Canada Highway

99

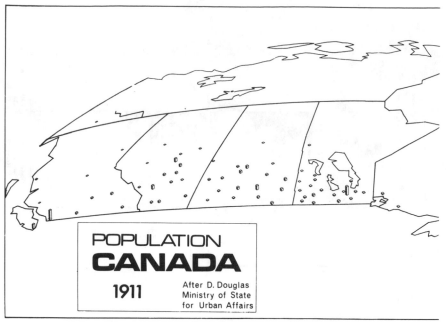

Figure 3.   Population Canada: 1911

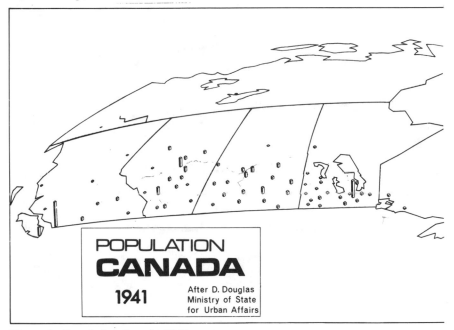

Figure 4.   Population Canada: 1941

100

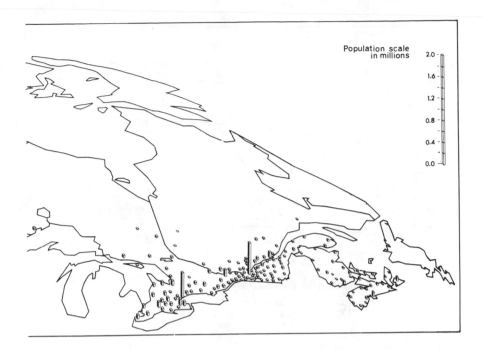

Population scale
in millions   2.0

1.6

1.2

0.8

0.4

0.0

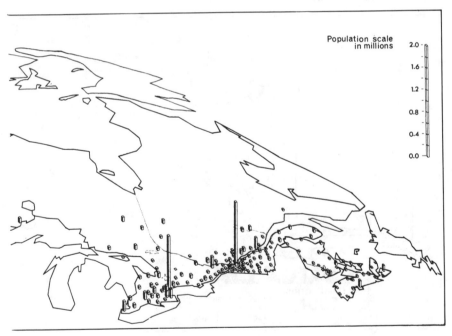

Population scale
in millions   2.0

1.6

1.2

0.8

0.4

0.0

101

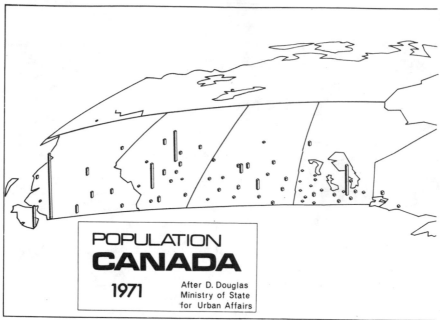

Figure 5.   Population Canada: 1971

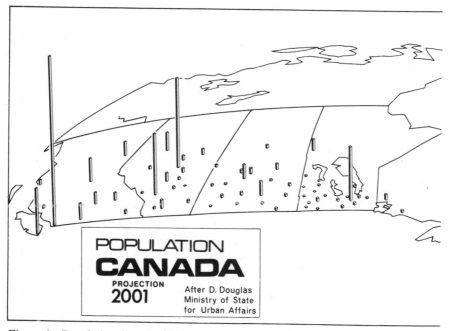

Figure 6.   Population Canada: 2001

102

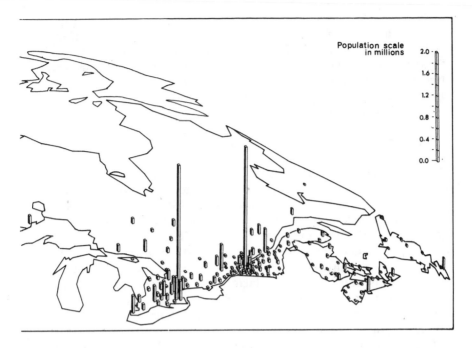

Population scale
in millions

2.0
1.6
1.2
0.8
0.4
0.0

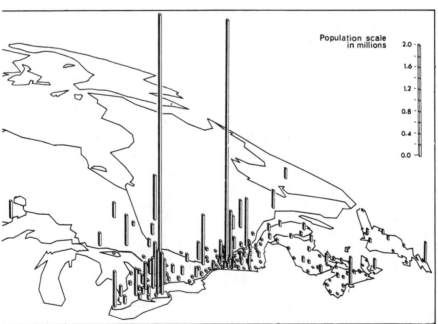

Population scale
in millions

2.0
1.6
1.2
0.8
0.4
0.0

103

The current trend toward population concentration in metropolitan areas is dramatized if the procedure applied to obtain the growth rates is used to project the population distribution in Canada to the year 2001 (Figures 3, 4, 5 and 6). Such strong metropolitanization tendencies can be effectively dealt with only if it is realized first that they are the outcome of a secular developmental pattern gradually constituted by the cumulative superposition through time of a series of growth forces.

(b) The Identification of the Growth Forces

The second step in the growth model is to identify the growth forces. The top profile shown on Figure 2 is a composite of the individual growth forces that together comprise the geography of Canada. The importance of each of these components is illustrated by successively graphing their individual contributions to the growth profile. The component profiles are much more regular than the aggregate growth profile, and the growth gradients for the centre-periphery components emerge quite distinctly. The six dimensions were obtained by factor analyzing a matrix of seventy-six economic, cultural and spatial variables taken mainly from the 1961 census on the basis of the 229 counties or census divisions mentioned above. The factor analysis is discussed in detail elsewhere.[12] Here it will suffice to mention the variables showing the highest loadings on each dimension (Table 6), and to interpret these in terms of the planning responses they have elicited.

(i) *The East-West Dimension of Regionalism.* A first systematic set of demographic, cultural and economic contrasts reflects the vestigial impact of the early production of staple exports for European markets and the tendency for the development of the country to proceed westwards from the Atlantic seaboard. Immigration, particularly immigrants landed before 1931, cultural heterogeneity, and also the percentage of the labour force in farming increase systematically east to west across the country.

The east-west progression in Canada can be understood largely in terms of an economic development process in which hinterland Canada supplied heartland Europe with staple exports in accordance with Europe's needs and Canada's resource endowment and market accessibility. Staples are typically distinguished by ease of production due to abundance and low labour requirements, ease of transportation, reflecting imperishability and high value to bulk ratios, and noncompetitiveness with heartland products.[13] Canada's staples can be ordered from east to west as well as in terms of time of market entry. The two orderings are almost the same: salt cod fish, furs, lumber, potash, pork, beef, wheat, pulp and paper, minerals and fuels.

Table 6. Multivariate Analysis of the Components of Growth

Components	Associated Characteristics (high loadings in factor analysis)	Leverage (regression coefficient)	Statistical Confidence (t test)
Centre-Periphery Gradients			
	higher incomes, house values, education levels and more post World War II immigration in urban areas	.400	16.81
metropolitan	financial and manufacturing activity, Jewish and Italian ethnicity	.072	3.04
heartland-hinterland	unemployment, income disparity, logging, fishing, and other primary activities in hinterland	.206	8.74
east-west	ethnic heterogeneity, with substantial East European representation established by pre-1931 immigration and farming tending to increase east to west	—.050	—2.12
Non-Gradient Components			
English-French	contrasts in age-structure and family size, immigration rates and education and occupation structure	—.186	—7.83
U.S. Control of Manufacturing	mainly secondary manufacturing activity	.180	7.62

Note: The leverages exerted by each component are determined by multiple regression analysis in which the dependent variable is the relative growth rate for each of the 229 census counties.

The independent variables are the components which are measured using standardized factor scores. The components are described in detail elsewhere (by D. M. Ray, *Dimensions of Canadian Regionalism,* Information Canada, Ottawa, 1971). The multiple correlation coefficient for the six components is 0.83 and with an F ratio of 80.27. The overall model and individual regression coefficients are all statistically significant at the .01 level. The regression intercept is the unweighted mean of the relative growth rates: 0.655.

105

The east-west process of regional development operating at the inter-continental scale had, by Confederation, already created important differences that remain as a basic dimension of Canadian regionalism. The low incomes and the lagging population and economic growth of the Atlantic region compared with the Prairies and British Columbia can in part be understood in terms of the Atlantic region's difficulty in coping with declining staples in contrast to the resource boom in western Canada. The sheer size of the country coupled with the concomitant contrasts in regional resources, as well as with timing of settlement and form of economy help in explaining the persistence of severe regional poverty.

At the time of the east-west progression, regional economic development and population growth largely depended upon the exploitation of Canada's physical resource base in a laissez-faire, free-enterprise political climate. Indeed, one must wait until the Great Depression for an emerging concern with regional development policy: "Before that time the development of the country was under the spell of the attitudes reflected in Macdonald's "National Policy". The instruments of that policy, tariffs, land settlement, immigration, railways, freight rates, etc., had a decided regional incidence; the characteristic "centre-periphery" pattern of Canadian development was being forged." [14]

(ii) *French-English Contrasts.* This second basic dimension of Canadian regionalism had an early influence through contrasts in age-structure and family size, immigration rates, religion, and education-occupation structure.

In Canada, the very homogeneous French cultural area has introduced since the beginning a discontinuity in the east-west gradient. The French and English groups show strong spatial segregation. The two cultures have opposite locations rather than independent distributions. This geographic separation can be traced to three causes: (1) the locational differences in initial colonization; (2) the tendency of English settlers to migrate from any area that is becoming predominantly French-Canadian; and (3) the strong tendency for other ethnic groups to learn the English language. [15]

In a very real sense, the federal form of government instituted in 1867 can be considered a response to the French-English dimension of Canadian regionalism, for the 1841 Union of Upper Canada (Ontario) and Lower Canada (Quebec) had not succeeded in assimilating French Canadians. The persistence and growth of an autonomous French cultural group, based largely on high birth rates, has been considered the primary reason for adopting a federal system of government. [16] The federal structure with its division of jurisdiction between Ottawa and the Provinces produces "a lack of clear purpose on the part of the Canadian government" and leads "to extreme caution in implementing national policies designed to redistribute population or industry".[17] Now that differences in birth rates between the French and other ethnic groups have narrowed and even been reversed,[18] and that Quebec has almost reached zero population growth, the legacy of French-English contrasts takes on new forms in terms of regional development and planning. These will be discussed below.

(iii) *The Heartland-Hinterland Dimension.* The east-west progression, complicated by French-English contrasts, was largely a function of international (mainly European) demand for natural resources. However, staple exports have gradually stimulated the domestic economy through economic spread effects to promote the growth of secondary and tertiary activity. The export-base and the sector theories of regional development [19] merge to explain how the heartland-hinterland dimension of Canadian regionalism has built upon the east-west gradient. Economic spread effects promote growth through three types of linkages: (1) backward linkages to increase production in the export sector; (2) forward linkages involving domestic processing of staple exports; and (3) final demand linkages, with consumer goods produced domestically for consumption by workers in staple export industries. Final demand linkages particularly favoured the development of Ontario and Quebec with the establishment there of a bipolar manufacturing heartland. The superposition of a national heartland-hinterland gradient upon the east-west gradient became clear only at the turn of the century when the gradient of population potential from Halifax was reversed from negative to positive, but the east-west gradient was already weaker at the time of Confederation (Table 7). Furthermore, the heartland embodies French-English contrasts reflected through metropolitan bipolarity (Montreal and Toronto) and structural divergence in manufacturing between Ontario and Quebec. Gilmour and Murricane [20] have recently explained the differences in manufacturing between Ontario and Quebec by Ontario's greater market potential at the beginning of the twentieth century. In particular, commercial agriculture was more developed at that time in Ontario and this created a greater demand in metal-working industries. Thus, the heartland-hinterland factor builds upon both the east-west dimension and the French-English contrasts.

Essentially, this national centre-periphery gradient emphasizes the lumbering, fishing and mining economy in hinterland regions. Associated with this are a high male-to-female labour force ratio and lower incomes, and a lower accessibility to national markets and greater economic disparity within the hinterland. Heartland-hinterland differences in age structure also occur because of the flow of net migration in response to econo-

Table 7. Population Potential Gradients from Halifax and Montreal: 1871 to 1971

Year	Gradient of population potential from Halifax (b_1)	Montreal (b_2)	Coefficient of multiple determination (R^2)
1971	0.132	—0.393	0.56
1961	0.114	—0.383	0.59
1951	0.093	—0.363	0.60
1941	0.095	—0.360	0.63
1931	0.108	—0.353	0.62
1921	0.082	—0.327	0.63
1911	0.098	—0.278	0.67
1901	0.065	—0.283	0.57
1891	—0.004	—0.319	0.53
1881	—0.091	—0.367	0.54
1871	—0.129	—0.388	0.55

Note: 1. The population potential gradients are given by the multiple regression coefficients in the equation:

$$\log Y = a - b_1 \log X_1 - b_2 \log X_2,$$

where Y = population potential for each census division for given census year,
  X_1 = distance of each census division from Halifax,
  X_2 = distance of each census division from Montreal.
The equation is computed for each census year separately.

2. Distance from Halifax is surrogate measure of heartland-hinterland forces at an international scale. Distance from Montreal, the point of highest potential 1871 to 1961 is a measure of these forces at the national scale. By Confederation (1867), the east-west gradient was already weaker than the national heartland-hinterland gradient and was reversed from negative to positive.

mic opportunity. Hinterland regions have a relatively high proportion of population under thirty and a relatively low proportion between the ages of thirty and sixty-five years.

Of all the heartland-hinterland contrasts, none has caused more pervasive concern to Canadians than regional disparities in income. Corrective policies were however delayed before being finally triggered by the great economic depression of the thirties:

"The unequal regional incidence of the economic collapse led (1) to extraordinary efforts to shore up the regions that were hardest hit; and (2) to a reappraisal of relationships, particularly fiscal, between the Federal Government and the Provinces. The Prairie Farm Rehabilitation Act (1935) was the most typical expression of the first; and the Royal Commission on Dominion-Provincial Relations, and the system of equalization grants it inaugurated, was the vehicle for the second." [21]

108

The next crucial moment in the evolution of regional development policy in Canada took place more than twenty-five years later and was still characteristically rural in outlook. The Agricultural and Rural Development Act (ARDA) was passed in 1961. It attacked problems of living standards, economic development and resource use in designated rural areas but "solutions of rural poverty often pointed towards the cities." [22] The Area Development Agency (ADA) was at the time empowered to promote programs in urban areas but it operated in isolation from ARDA and did not apply a growth poles and growth centres strategy. Such a strategy was badly needed considering that "Canada may have had the fastest rate of urban growth among the countries of the Western world in the post-war period as a whole".[23]

(iv) *The Urban-Rural and Metropolitan Dimensions.* Two of the most important and recent forces, which together account for much of the variation across Canada in demographic, cultural and economic characteristics, are the urban-rural and metropolitan dimensions of regionalism. In particular, there are substantial contrasts associated with size of settlement —in the education level, occupation structure, and income level of the labour force. Sharp urban disparities in population growth are not new: they have existed in Canada since before Confederation, and every decade has witnessed an increase in the proportion of the population that is urban. What is new is the post World War II metropolitanization of the country. Variables such as financial and manufacturing activity, as well as Jewish and Italian ethnicity load highly on the metropolitan demension (Table 6). Furthermore, King [24] has shown, in his analysis of Canadian urban dimensions, that metropolitanization shows up more clearly in 1961 than in 1951. No doubt the consolidation of metropolitan dominance has continued since 1961. Metropolitan centres such as Montreal, Toronto and Vancouver, are developing "complex organizational forms, detailed patterns of inter-dependence, sophisticated communication media, high levels of tertiary employment, and considerable socio-economic stratification".[25] Strategies of regional development cannot ignore these basic facts.

The difficulty, however, with a strictly metropolitan strategy of urban development in Canada is that the Prairies and especially the Maritimes do not include large scale urban centres. This shows the legacy of the three previous dimensions upon the urban-rural and metropolitan dimensions. Urbanization itself reveals heartland-hinterland and east-west gradients. Half the Canadian cities with over 10,000 inhabitants are located within four hundred miles of Toronto. Only 14% of the population in the Atlantic Provinces live in cities over 100,000, compared with 52% in Quebec, 55% in Ontario and 43% in the Prairie Provinces. French-English contrasts also affect urbanization. In Quebec, mainly because of strong cultural homogeneity coupled with the traditional lack of immigration, the recent drop in birth rate, and a time-lag in urbanization, the urban system shows unique characteristics.

The urban population in Quebec originates from the surrounding rural areas in a greater proportion than elsewhere in Canada. Toronto attracted almost twice as many immigrants as Montreal in 1968.[26] This may produce stronger urban-rural bonds in Quebec, where growth poles and growth centres ideas have been, following the example of France, more popular than in the rest of Canada.[27] A continuation of this trend can be expected considering that Quebec is reaching zero population growth and that economic growth in Montreal has slowed down in recent years. The lack of intermediate-size urban centres has long been a concern in Quebec. It is hoped that a well coordinated policy of growth centres will contribute to the filling up of the urban hierarchy which, at present, still exhibits strong primate tendencies.

In Canada, where the economy has traditionally been based on staple exports, it has only recently been realized that the cities have become the engines of economic development, and this realization is only beginning to have an impact on policy formulation. The relationship between levels of urbanization and regional disparities is, however, clear. Inter-regional differences in average family income for cities in the same size class are much smaller than differences within regions between cities in different size classes (Table 8). The number of manufacturing functions found in cities also has an impact on regional disparities. When the geographic distribution of manufacturing employment in cities of over 10,000 inhabitants is mapped for 1911 and 1961 (Figures 7 and 8), it is found that the Montreal and Toronto manufacturing districts have increased their share of the national work force in manufacturing from 21.8% to 34.9%.[28] Both the heartland-hinterland and the east-west spatial growth gradients discriminate against growth in the Maritimes, where slower relative employment growth in manufacturing industry was associated with a slower increase in the number of manufacturing types. If total city manufacturing employment is plotted against the number of manufacturing types occurring in the 110 cities above 10,000 a semi-logarithmically linear plot is obtained for both 1911 and 1961 (Figure 9). The exceptions in 1961 are either the largest metropolitan centres or the smaller non-manufacturing centres. Furthermore, the plot clearly reveals that any given number of manufacturing types generates less employment in 1961 than in 1911. An aggregate measure of capital-labour substitution over a half-century period is thus provided.[29]

Table 8. Average Income by Region and City Size-class: 1971

Size Class	Atlantic	Quebec	Ontario	Western	National average	Actual national average
1- 24,999	91.6	108.1	98.8	99.7	100	$ 6971.4
25,000- 49,999	98.1	92.5	102.9	103.3	100	7048.4
50,000- 99,999	87.6	92.5	105.7	88.4	100	7409.4
100,000-199,999	89.2	89.8	109.6	92.7	100	7536.0
200,000-999,999	94.5	95.1	104.2	96.2	100	7619.2
1,000,000+	*	96.4	102.5	100.7	100	7676.7
Average income for region	87.3	96.2	105.2	97.8	100	$ 7237.1

* Not applicable

Note: 96 Selected cities as given in *Taxation Statistics 1973*. Average income is the quotient of total income tax revenue and the number of income tax returns for each city.

Source: Calculated from Government of Canada Department of National Revenue Taxation, *Taxation Statistics 1973,* Ottawa, Information Canada, 1972, p. 10, 11, 17; and Government of Canada, Statistics Canada, *1971 Census of Canada,* Special Bulletin (cat. no. 98-701), Ottawa, Information Canada, June 1973.

Policies formulated in response to the urban-rural and metropolitan dimensions of regionalism are still in the formative stage. The creation of the Department of Regional Economic Expansion in the late 1960's allows for a comprehensive approach but the impact of federal economic policies on the various regions is still inconsistent. While industrial incentives in outlying areas of the heartland have met with some measure of success,[30] many industries assisted in locating in the hinterland have failed to generate the local multiplier effects that were expected.[31] Another newly created federal institution, the Ministry of State for Urban Affairs, on the other hand, has been concentrating on the problems of the large metropolises.

Considering the regional diversity of Canada, it can be expected that a national urban policy will be most difficult to implement. This should not preclude researchers, however, from investigating interorganizational and interregional linkages throughout the total urban system. Trickling down and spatial spread effects from growth centres are much more limited than previously thought and the multiplier effects often take place in larger centres than the ones designated.[32] Policy instruments to combine the objective of reducing exaggerated growth in large metropolises with the goal of stimulating development in lagging regions must consider the whole

111

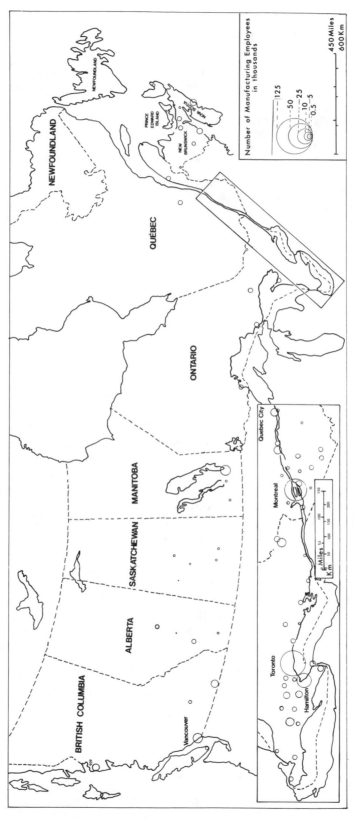

Figure 7. Distribution of Manufacturing Employment: 1911

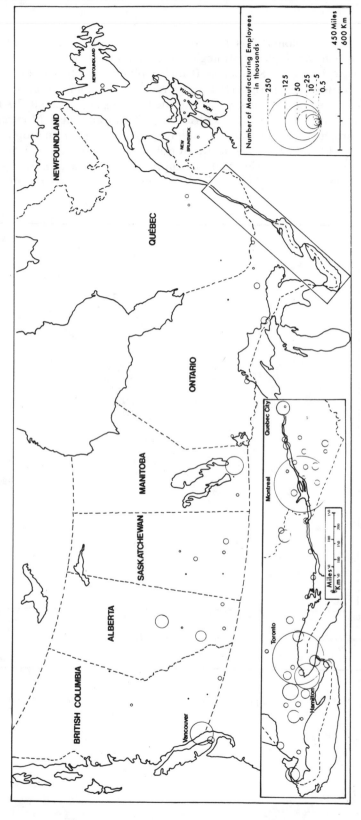

Figure 8. Distribution of Manufacturing Employment: 1961

urban hierarchy. Stöhr[33] has recently identified five basic elements of national urban development strategies: (1) new towns in peripheral undeveloped regions (e.g. Kitimat in British Columbia); (2) new or intermediate-size towns in peripheral lagging regions (e.g. Saint John in New Brunswick); (3) satellite towns at intermediate distance (about 20-100 miles) from large metropolitan centres (e.g. Sherbrooke near Montreal); (4) new urban centres at the immediate fringe of major metropolitan centres (e.g. Flemingdon Park in Metropolitan Toronto); and (5) downtown urban renewal (e.g. Montreal) or "intown" new towns (e.g. Toronto). These strategies have different effects on interregional patterns of de-

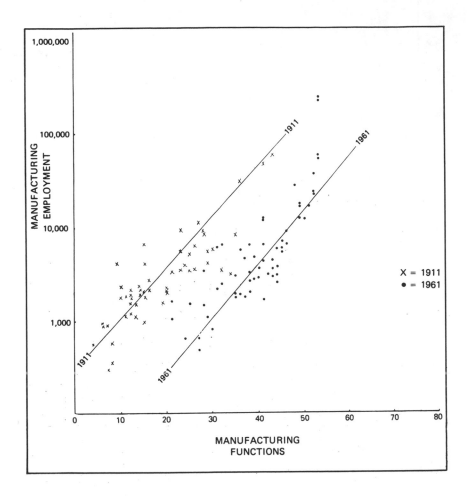

Figure 9. Manufacturing Employment and Manufacturing Functions: 1911 and 1961

114

velopment. The second and the fifth strategies can contribute most to reducing spatial disparities in living standards since they are aimed at depressed areas outside urban fields or within metropolises.[34] It must be noted however that downtown urban renewal, as it is practised in North America, is seldom beneficial to the local population,[35] especially when redevelopers are large multinational corporations.[36]

(v) *United States Investment and the Regional Growth Impact.* A last important dimension of Canadian regionalism is the spatial distribution of foreign investment. Manufacturing [37] is the dominant economic function of most Canadian cities, particularly of those in the heartland provinces of Ontario and Quebec, and the location of manufacturing activity can be expected to have an important impact on urban and regional growth. But more of Canada's manufacturing industry is owned by residents of foreign countries than is owned by Canadians, and there is evidence that the location of manufacturing plants by foreign companies is not independent of the location of their head offices. In particular, almost half of Canada's manufacturing industry is owned and controlled in the United States, and the spatial concentration of United States subsidiaries in south-western Ontario appears to exacerbate regional disparities in urban growth and in average income. United States-controlled establishments and employment make a much greater contribution to those districts of the Canadian manufacturing belt that are contiguous to the United States, such as the Windsor district and the Golden Horseshoe extending from Niagara to Toronto, than to other parts of the manufacturing belt or to other regions of Canada. Manufacturing employment in United States-controlled establishments shows a corresponding concentration in the two contiguous manufacturing districts. In 1961, 83 percent of the American-controlled employment was located within 400 miles of Toronto, compared with 70 percent of the Canadian (Figure 10). United States investment in hinterland Canada has been mainly in primary manufacturing activity such as the pulp and paper industry.

The United States spatial pattern of manufacturing investment in Canada builds upon the other components of growth: it is heavier in the heartland than it is in the hinterland, in the west than in the east, in Ontario than in Quebec, and in urban areas than in rural areas. Despite a number of studies on the topic,[38] Canada has been slow to examine the problems of foreign ownership and hesitant to take any action. There is little doubt that any moves to restrict foreign investment would, unless coupled with strong compensatory action, drastically increase unemployment. But some policies have been put into effect, including the creation of a Canada Development Corporation and a federal government screening agency to evaluate foreign take-over bids, in an attempt to improve the general

115

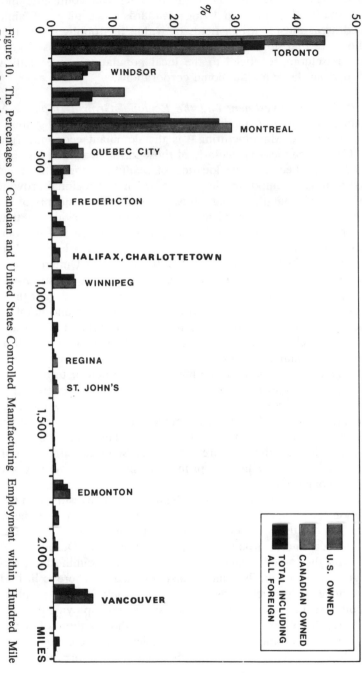

Figure 10. The Percentages of Canadian and United States Controlled Manufacturing Employment within Hundred Mile Distance Bands from Toronto

efficiency of the Canadian economy within the framework of a national economic strategy. This analysis emphasizes the need for a *regional* foreign investment policy as part of a comprehensive programme to achieve more balanced urban and regional growth.

(c)   The Growth Leverage of the Dimensions

The five dimensions of regionalism identified above are the forces that distribute population growth across Canada. The third step in the model is to scale the dimensions according to their contribution to growth. This is accomplished by regressing the relative growth rates computed at step (a) on the five dimensions discussed at step (b). The regression coefficient attached to each dimension is a measure of the growth leverage of that dimension (Table 6). The impact which the components exert on growth is greatest for the urban-rural and weakest for the metropolitan and east-west components. But the metropolitan impact, as can be seen in Figure 2, is much more concentrated than the urban-rural or other components, producing particularly sharp growth rate peaks in the areas affected. The remaining three dimensions—heartland-hinterland, English-French, and United States control of manufacturing—each exert about an equal leverage on population growth. Notice that the regression formulation, in which the independent variables are standardized factor scores, measures each force as though it made no net contribution to the national growth rate. This mathematical convenience enables us to identify directly the leverage which each component exerts on the *distribution* of growth, an important point in assessing the possible intra- and inter-regional impacts of policy interventions. The model, then, makes no attempt to explain national growth rates. Instead, it uses national growth as the yardstick to compute the relative growth rates of the individual regions and to partition these rates among the particular growth forces responsible. In Figure 2, the relative growth profile at the top is the sum of the individual profiles below. The extent to which the relative growth rate exceeds, or falls short of, proportional growth, 1.0, is equal to the net sum of the individual distributive forces.

3.   *Conclusion: Regionalism and the Regulation of Growth*

The final result of the growth analysis is surprisingly simple even though the steps involved are rather lengthy. The likely changes in the projected population growth of each city or county that can be expected from a given policy can be estimated. The estimation procedure involves adjusting the present growth rates for each county by the growth leverage associated with the policy and by the actual values of the socio-economic character-istics in each city or county addressed by the policy. For example, a regional foreign ownership policy to distribute future employment growth in foreign controlled manufacturing establishments on the basis of the present population distribution would eliminate this component of dif-ferential growth. The effect of such a policy, if successful, would be to slow the growth of Toronto and southwestern Ontario but to accelerate population growth elsewhere in Canada. The model presented in this paper presents a mathematical procedure to measure the resulting changes in county growth rates of such a policy and, hence, to compute adjusted population projections.

The model involves the notion that the components of growth are the dimensions of regionalism—a rather new idea in the social sciences though it follows homologically from D'Arcy Wentworth Thompson's seminal work on biological form and growth.[39] The model also involves a rather new concept of regionalism that has some important policy implications. Regions are *not* viewed as unique entities following independent pathways of growth and development. Instead, they are presented as distinctive blendings of common ingredients, progressing along interdependent path-ways of growth. The ingredients form the space-time envelope of Canada. Colonization and ethnic differentiation, two early processes dominating the nineteenth century, correspond to the east-west gradient and the French-English contrasts. Following these, processes of industrialization and urbanization gave rise, in the first part of the twentieth century, to the heartland-hinterland and the urban-rural gradients. Finally, more recent processes of metropolitanization and internationalization are related to a metropolitan and a foreign investment dimension.

These processes and dimensions combine in various ways all across Canada, and it follows that policies to deal with regional problems should not be restricted to designated areas. Instead, they should be applied nation-wide, graduated regionally, according to the net strength of the growth forces that are to be stimulated or dampened.

The question of how much of a country should be designated under various growth and development programmes is a contentious issue. The natural tendency is for all regions that feel they can benefit from pro-gramme participation to attempt to qualify for designation. The larger the national area that is designated for equal treatment, the less effective any such programmes can be. For unless the level of incentives or restraints is graduated to take account of the varying strength of the growth forces across the area designated, growth will be concentrated in those parts with the greatest potential for growth, doing little to help less-favoured areas.

118

Notes

1. B. J. L. Berry, E. C. Conkling and D. Michael Ray, *The Geography of Economic Systems,* Ch. 15, "Canada: The Challenge of Growth and Change", Prentice-Hall Inc., Eaglewood Cliffs, N.J., 1975.

2. Statistics Canada, *Canadian Statistical Review,* Catalogue 11-105, occasional, 1974, p. 16.

3. J. Porter, *The Vertical Mosaic,* University of Toronto Press, Toronto 1965, p. 36.

4. Economic Council of Canada, *Second Annual Review: Towards Sustained and Balanced Economic Growth,* Queen's Printer, Ottawa, 1965, p. 102.

5. Cf. N. H. Lithwick, *Urban Canada: Problems and Prospects,* Central Mortgage and Housing Corporation, Ottawa, 1970.

6. Kingsley Davis, "Zero Population Growth: The Goal and the Means", *Daedalus,* Vol. 102, No. 4, Fall 1973, p. 27.

7. W. Alonso, "Urban Zero Population Growth", *Daedalus,* Vol. 102, No. 4, Fall 1973, p. 205.

8. John Friedmann, *Urbanization, Planning, and National Development,* Sage Co. Ltd., Beverly Hills, California, 1973.

9. A. R. Pred, "The Growth and Development of Systems of Cities in Advanced Economies, *Lund Studies in Geography,* Series B, 1973.

10. R. J. Chorley, "Geography as Human Ecology", in R. J. Chorley (ed.) *Directions in Geography,* Methuen, London, 1973, p. 160.

11. M. Woldenberg, "Allometric Growth in Social Systems", *Harvard Papers in Theoretical Geography,* Paper No. 6, Department of Geography, Harvard University, Cambridge, Mass., 1971.

12. D. M. Ray, *Dimensions of Canadian Regionalism,* Information Canada, Ottawa, 1971.

13. B. J. L. Berry *et al., op. cit.,* Ch. 15.

14. L. O. Gertler, "The Concept of Regional Development", in *Collected Papers: Colloquium on Regional Economic Development,* Department of Geography, Memorial University, St. John's, Newfoundland, 1969, p. 4.

15. D. M. Ray, *op. cit.,* p. 7.

16. J. T. Copp and M. Hamelin, *Confédération: 1867,* The Copp-Clark Publishing Co., Toronto 1966, p. 48.

17. T. Brewis, *Regional Economic Policies in Canada,* The MacMillan Co. of Canada Ltd., Toronto, 1969, p. 81.

18. L. Beauregard, "Le Québec et ses problèmes de population", *Le Géographe Canadien,* Vol. 18, No. 1, 1974, pp. 3-15.

19. W. B. Stöhr, *Interurban Systems and Regional Economic Development,* Association of American Geographers, Commission on College Geography, Resource Paper No. 26, Washington, D.C., 1974, p. 11.

20. J. M. Gilmour and K. Murricane, "Structural Divergence in Canada's Manufacturing Belt", *The Canadian Geographer,* Vol. 17, No. 1, 1973, pp. 1-18.

21. L. O. Gertler, *op. cit.,* p. 5.

22. *Ibid,* p. 6.

23. T. Brewis, *op. cit.,* p. 13.

24. L. J. King, "Cross-Sectional Analysis of Canadian Urban Dimensions: 1951 and 1961", *The Canadian Geographer,* Vol. 10, No. 4, 1966, pp. 205-224.

25. *Ibid,* p. 207.

26. N. H. Lithwick, *op. cit.,* p. 88.

27. L. Bourne, "Urban Canada", unpublished manuscript, Centre for Urban and Community Studies, Toronto, 1974, p. 22.

28. E. F. Koenig, J. S. Lewis, and D. M. Ray, *Allometry and Manufacturing Hierarchy: A General Systems Approach to Manufacturing Employment and Industrial Incentives,* in L. Collins and D. Walker (Eds.), *The Dynamics of Manufacturing Activity,* John Wiley and Sons, London, 1975.

29. *Ibid.*

30. M. H. Yeates and P. E. Lloyd, *Impact of Industrial Incentives: Southern Georgian Bay Region, Ontario,* Geographical Paper No. 44, Department of Energy, Mines, and Resources, Policy and Planning Branch, Ottawa, 1970.

31. L. Bourne, *op. cit.,* p. 20.

32. Cf. A. R. Pred, *op. cit.*

33. W. B. Stöhr, *op. cit.*

34. *Ibid,* p. 23.

35. Cf. M. Castells, *La question urbaine,* François Maspero, Paris, 1972.

36. Cf. EZOP-Québec, *Une ville à vendre,* Conseil des oeuvres et du bien-être, 4 vols., 1972.

37. Cf. J. W. Maxwell, "The Functional Structure of Canadian Cities: A Classification of Cities", *Geographical Bulletin,* Vol. 7, 1965, pp. 79-104.

38. See particularly M. H. Watkins, *et. al., Foreign Ownership and the Structure of Canadian Industry: Report of the Task Force on the Structure of Canadian Industry,* Statistics Canada, Privy Council Office, Ottawa, 1968; and K. Levitt, *Silent Surrender: The Multinational Corporation in Canada,* the MacMillan Co. of Canada Ltd., Toronto, 1970.

39. D'Arcy Wentworth Thompson, *On Growth and Form,* Cambridge University Press, Cambridge, England, 1919.

120

7

REGIONAL DEVELOPMENT IN CANADA IN HISTORICAL PERSPECTIVE

Thomas N. Brewis

It is difficult to form an appraisal of the present without some understanding of the past and the factors and policies which have contributed to
current situations and attitudes. To neglect the past is to lose perspective.
Historical developments can be especially important in the making of
international comparisons reflecting, as they do, the evolution of ideas and
political currents. They merit attention along with a consideration of geographical factors.

As to be expected in a country second in size only to that of the
USSR, there are marked dissimilarities between the different regions of
Canada. Although the population has grown six-fold over the past century,
it still totals little over 21 millions, and areas of concentrated economic
activity are interspersed with others of great size where such activity is
virtually non-existent. In striking contrast to the heavy concentration of
manufacturing activity extending in a fairly narrow belt in central Canada
close to the United States border, several hundred miles separate the main
manufacturing centres of the western provinces.

One of the conventional ways of viewing the country is to see it in
terms of five main regions comprising: 1. the Atlantic region, consisting of
the four most easterly provinces—Newfoundland, Prince Edward Island,
Nova Scotia and New Brunswick; 2. Quebec with its predominantly French
speaking population and culture; 3. Ontario, the largest province in terms
of population and industrial output; 4. the three prairie provinces—Manitoba, Saskatchewan and Alberta; and 5. the most westerly province, British
Columbia, 3,000 miles by air from Newfoundland and separated from the
rest of Canada by the immense barrier of the mountains. These regions
are separated not only by geographic distance but also by dissimilarities
which become more marked as one proceeds north, crossing the 60th
parallel to the very sparsely populated areas of the Yukon and North
West Territories.

Since the turn of the century the regional distribution of population and industry across the country has altered greatly with a strong secular shift to the west and a relative decline of the Atlantic Provinces that shows little sign of slowing down. Within the western provinces themselves, moreover, the shift in recent years has been westward: Alberta and British Columbia have been gaining population rapidly in contrast to the situation in Saskatchewan and Manitoba.

The strengthening and maintaining of a national unity of these disparate regions has been a dominant objective of federal governments since the time of Confederation in 1867. For much of the period following Confederation the emphasis has been on the creation of transport networks, especially through the construction of railways, in an effort to strengthen the east-west links in the face of strong pressures making for closer regional ties with the United States. The imposition of tariffs on imports was designed with a similar purpose in mind. But both the imposition of tariffs and the creation of transport links affected individual regions differently. Thus the tariff protected the predominantly industrial regions of central Canada to the detriment of the Atlantic and western Provinces which depended heavily on the sale of staples in world markets. The improvements in transportation in eastern Canada appear moreover to have been more successful in opening the Maritime market to central Canada than in opening the Ontario and Quebec markets to the Maritime Provinces.

Of particular note is the fact that large parts of Canada which are especially well endowed for the production of one thing, such as grain in the Prairies, pulp and paper in much of British Columbia, or certain minerals in northern areas, offer virtually no alternative economic opportunity. As a result, the fortunes of such areas display a marked instability. Given the spatial distribution of particular industries, measures to assist these industries directly affect the fortunes of particular areas of the country. An illustration of this is the fact that the long history of support to the fishing industry and of naval defence expenditures have particularly benefited the coastal provinces. Whether or not such expenditures were conceived with regional implications in mind, their effect has been regional.

The depression of the 1930's underlined the regional differences within the country. Distress was especially severe in the Prairies which were heavily dependent on export markets. The plight of certain provinces contributed to the establishment in 1937 of a Royal Commission on Dominion-Provincial Relations (the Rowell-Sirois Commission) to examine, among other things, the declining revenue sources available to the provincial governments. The cost of unemployment relief and of other social services, together with the servicing of outstanding debt, had become so burdensome to a number of provincial governments that some form of federal adjustment and subvention was necessary. More generally,

122

it was considered expedient to re-examine the economic and financial basis of Confederation and the distribution of legislative powers in the light of the economic and social developments of the previous seventy years. With the ending of World War II, and with the recommendations of the Rowell-Sirois Commission in mind, fiscal transfers were made by the federal government to enable the poorer provinces to maintain a standard of public services closer to the national average. With many adjustments in scope and magnitude the transfers have continued over the past quarter of a century and are now running at one and a half billion dollars a year. The argument for them has been that where circumstances, whether natural or man-made, have channelled a larger than average share of the nation's wealth into certain sections of the country, there should be a redistribution of that wealth so that all provinces can, without resorting to unduly burdensome levels of taxation, provide their citizens with a reasonably comparable level of basic services.

The fact that these fiscal transfers constitute between 20% and 30% of government revenues of the individual Atlantic Provinces is an indication of their importance. The basis of the equalization formula has been expanded over the years and now embraces some twenty revenue sources.

In addition to such transfers the federal government has made conditional grants to provinces for various purposes, including hospital insurance, assistance to the aged and disabled, road construction, vocational school training, airport development and various resource projects. Conditional grants and shared cost programs of one sort or another have, however, had a mixed reception. While they have undoubtedly tended to standardize certain services across the country, they have at the same time presented problems of administrative control and they have influenced the direction of provincial expenditures in ways which did not always express the priorities of individual provincial governments. Aside from this, there has been a growing belief in the desirability of policies of regional development which would reduce the need for large and continuous transfers.

The fact that there are ten provincial governments in Canada in addition to the federal government complicates the task of policy formulation and implementation. Depending on how it is interpreted, the Constitution can seriously inhibit federal action. Decisions have to be made as to which level of government has the power to do what, and as to the form that cooperation between different levels of government should take. Provincial governments have substantial powers under the Constitution. They are closer to the people geographically as well as in sentiment than is the national parliament in Ottawa, and in some parts of the country regional, rather than national loyalties, remain the dominant ones. Recognition of this is important to an understanding of the Canadian scene.

As the late Lester B. Pearson once remarked, because of regional divergences, Canadian governments find it worthwhile to make great efforts and to exercise great restraint in order to devise policies which will if possible obtain popular support in all the main regions affected. If this is not possible then it is virtually essential to obtain from all sections an acquiescence that is at least willing and understanding rather than grudging or forced.

Attempts to measure the magnitude of income and employment disparities between the different regions rest on the availability of statistical data and for the most part such data are deficient for the period before the 1920's. "Statistics Canada", the national statistical office, was not established until 1918. National accounts data were undeveloped prior to Keynes and were secret during the war itself. Historical estimates extending back to 1926 have, however, since been made. Data on unemployment rates and labour force participation rates similarly go back a relatively short time (unemployment insurance was not introduced until 1941) so that judging the magnitude of disparities in these respects prior to the 1920's is largely a matter of guess-work. Indeed, in the earlier years the lack of data may well have been an important factor in itself in reducing the extent of public discussion and awareness of significant differences between the regions.

What has, nonetheless, become apparent is that substantial income disparities have existed as far back as the data goes, namely to 1926. Moreover, while the degree of income disparity in relative terms has varied with changing levels of economic activity, the longer-run tendency over a period of half a century is one of little change and the ranking among the regions shows considerable stability. The high income regions of fifty years ago remain the high income regions and the low income regions remain the low ones.

A Royal Commission—the Gordon Commission, named after its chairman—concerned with Canada's Economic Prospects was appointed in the 1950's and "Some Regional Aspects of Canada's Economic Development" constituted one of the studies undertaken for it. This, among other studies, served to focus public attention on the problems confronting specific regions.[1] Mention should also be made of a study by a special Committee of the Senate on Land Use.[2] Among the issues to which the Senate addressed itself was that of rural poverty. Investigation revealed that a large proportion of farmers, especially in Eastern Canada, existed on incomes little above subsistence level and that there was an urgent need to improve their lot. More generally the need was felt for a national land use policy which would decide which areas should remain in agriculture, which should be withdrawn from agriculture, which developed and

124

in what ways. One of the recommendations of the Committee was that a joint Federal Provincial Rural Program be instituted to deal with areas of greatest need, and that appropriate action programs be planned and developed. The recommendations fell on sympathetic ears and led to the introduction in 1961 of federal legislation concerned with the "Rehabilitation of Agricultural Lands and the Development of Rural Areas in Canada", commonly known as ARDA. This was, as described below, followed by two other pieces of legislation relating to the creation of an Atlantic Development Board and to an Area Development Agency. These three legislative enactments heralded the more specific concern with regional economic problems that has continued and grown since.

Considerable debate surrounded the ARDA legislation. A basic objective was to improve the standard of living of farmers on small farms who were working marginal land. It was emphasized that a reduction in the number of farmers was not intended but it was—or soon became—obvious that there was little or no alternative to such a reduction and that other types of employment would have to be found for those displaced. With the realization that increasing output on marginal land was not an answer, the emphasis began to shift. In the final stages of the debate, an attempt to get at "the fundamental difficulty involved in the risk of overproduction of food in the world" was claimed as the core of the legislation. Technology had outpaced the demand for food so that the income of farmers was being forced down. Rapid technological change was increasing production on non-marginal farms and the question was whether we could move fast enough under alternative land use programs to provide a greater return to the farmer. It was also realized that while the proposed action focussed mainly on farm people it could not be exclusively agricultural: rural and urban economies had to be related and the program would need to be one of area development.

With the passing of the legislation, agreements for assistance were drawn up on a cost-sharing basis with the individual provinces. For the most part they were administered by departments of agriculture whose concern with the marginal farmer, however, was often limited and there was a mixed response which varied from province to province. Some provinces were hard pressed to put up their share of funds and others were unenthusiastic about doing so. With the expiry of the first agreements which had concentrated for the most part on land improvement and alternative land use, new agreements were introduced shifting the emphasis from the physical aspects of land improvement to the rural people themselves, and increased provision was made for their training and adjustment.

In a 1966 amendment to the legislation, the application of the Act was extended to all rural areas where projects of the nature provided for under the Act could be undertaken with advantage, whether or not the area was mainly agricultural. A third set of agreements introduced in 1973 increased the degree of flexibility to give provincial governments more scope to tailor programs to their individual circumstances and needs.

Of particular interest was the introduction, also in 1966, of the so-called FRED legislation (Fund for Rural Economic Development) which grew out of the ARDA agreements. This provided that a severely disadvantaged rural area, selected jointly by the provincial and federal governments, would be eligible for special assistance if the two governments could agree on a satisfactory regional comprehensive rural development program. Five such areas were selected and the federal and provincial governments together committed over $1 billion to their improvement. Action under the program began with tremendous verve but within three years the legislation creating the Fund was rescinded and, although commitments thereunder will continue to be met (subject to such revisions as are agreed upon), the program has been terminated. For the most part it was felt that the areas were too small and too isolated to permit of effective development, and there were differences of opinion as to what should be done and how. Although the individual plans have features in common—education, training and mobility figure prominently in all of them—the plans are not identical since the needs of the individual areas vary. In the case of eastern Quebec a recommended outmigration of some 20,000 people was withdrawn in the face of political opposition.

Although the labour force in agriculture, forestry and fishing has already dropped substantially—it is now only 9% of total employment compared to three times that figure at the end of World War II—further declines are to be expected. In particular, it has been estimated that nearly half the number of farmers in eastern Canada are surplus to requirements and that this surplus will increase as agricultural production becomes increasingly more efficient and mechanized. The problem is thus to find alternative employment of a more rewarding nature. In the current Canadian environment, employment in low productivity and low paying occupations is unacceptable, and the reluctance to accept low paying employment contributes still further to the trend towards labour saving devices and machinery.

In the administration of the program a number of difficulties have occurred, among them the fact that the problem of rural poverty cuts across many departments—agriculture, lands and forests, fisheries, roads, recreation, water authorities, labour, health and welfare are some of the departments involved—and the task of interpretation has been rendered more complex through frequent changes of government. At the federal level alone there were three Ministers and two governments in the first four years of operation and there have been many changes since.

As an illustration of the way in which policies designed to achieve one

126

objective can unintentionally accomplish something quite different, mention might be made of the case in British Columbia where improvements in water supply designed to facilitate agricultural production have resulted in land becoming attractive for housing development and being taken out of agriculture entirely. Of more general moment, however, has been the inability and indisposition of most agricultural representatives to function effectively with numerous marginal farmers who lack, as they typically do, education, ability and capital. The professional interests of agricultural officials lie closer to those of the larger and more successful farmer.

With regard to the Atlantic Provinces specifically, legislation was passed in 1962 establishing an Atlantic Development Board to inquire into, and to report to the Minister on, measures and projects for fostering the economic growth and development of the Atlantic region of Canada. At the outset the Board was given advisory powers only. It was to assess on a systematic and comprehensive basis factors relevant to growth and the methods by which such growth might be achieved, including the feasibility of specific measures and projects. Almost immediately thereafter, with a change in Government, the legislation was amended and the Board was provided with funds to finance programs and projects considered likely to contribute to growth and for which satisfactory financing arrangements were not otherwise available. With a view to providing a sense of direction, the Board was also empowered to prepare, in consultation with the Economic Council of Canada, an overall co-ordinated plan for the promotion of the economic growth of the region.

In the event the provision of funds determined the main thrust of the Board's operation. Attention was directed to the examination and financing of specific projects, and the advisory and planning function became subsidiary. The consequence was that by the time the Board's life was terminated in 1969 with the establishment of a new department of government, the Department of Regional Economic Expansion (known as DREE), no plan had yet emerged. Several background studies were undertaken and published on various aspects of the Atlantic economy but the attempt to incorporate these into a plan proved abortive. In part, this could be attributed to the absence of experience with planning processes in Canada on which to draw, and to differences of opinion which emerged as to what should be attempted and how. Rivalries within the Atlantic Provinces added to the complexity of the task.

Pressure to take specific action on particular projects dominated the Board's activities and there was reluctance to delay expenditures until a plan for the region was developed. Some things clearly needed to be done and the Board proceeded accordingly. Expenditures were made on social overhead capital, power, water supply, roads, industrial parks, research facilities, and technical and economic surveys. For the most part the

127

desirability of the projects undertaken was not questioned but the feeling grew that a clear strategy of development was not emerging, and the outlining of such a strategy became one of the first tasks of the Atlantic Development Council which replaced the Atlantic Development Board. In the opinion of the Council, the prime objective should be the reduction of unemployment and this called for significant structural changes, chief among which was a substantial increase in the numbers employed in the manufacturing sector.

As noted above, the main expenditures of the Atlantic Development Board were on infrastructure. Direct incentives to industry were considered no less important, but these were the responsibility of the Area Development Agency (ADA) within the Department of Industry.

Legislation establishing ADA was passed in 1963 in order to increase economic development in designated geographic areas characterized by heavy and chronic unemployment. As with the earlier measures, there have been frequent and significant changes of direction and emphasis since. Unlike ARDA, which began with limited objectives and moved at least for a time into the larger realm of regional economic development, the Area Development Agency carved for itself a more restricted role, and those responsible for its administration showed no inclination to become involved in the complex problems of regional development. Originally, it was conceived as a coordinating rather than an executive body but in fact it became the latter. It administered a program of incentives to encourage the establishment of secondary manufacturing industry in areas of the country where unemployment was especially heavy. Aid was provided automatically on a formula basis, originally in the form of tax concessions and later through capital grants. With the establishment of DREE the Agency as such was superseded and a number of significant policy changes were made. Aid became discretionary, and hitherto excluded areas that showed more promise of growth could now qualify for assistance. Designated areas at present cover approximately one third of the labour force of the country. Specifically, a number of "Special Areas" have been designated covering a wide spectrum of economic conditions from medium size urban centres with apparent potential for growth to isolated rural communities especially in need of help.

The establishment of DREE in 1969 was a major step in the evolution of Canadian policies of regional development and the institutions connected therewith. Underlying its establishment was the need to bring a variety of program policies and institutions under the direction of one Ministry rather than several, the hope being to thereby permit a more coordinated approach to regional problems. DREE is a large department with a budget of over half a billion dollars a year and it covers a wide variety of functions such as Industrial Incentives, Plan Formulation,

128

Economic as well as Social and Human Analysis, Policy Development and Evaluation, and a number of others. It has recently completed a survey of the situation in the various provinces.

Among the major changes which are now being undertaken is that of the decentralization of power. Officials are being posted to the various regions to permit a greater degree of flexibility in operation and awareness of the specific problems confronting such regions. General Development Agreements are being drawn up with each individual province.

Evaluation

The net effect of various forms of federal action on the fortunes of individual provinces has long been a source of concern. In 1964 the Department of Finance undertook an elaborate enquiry in an attempt to discover whether individual provincial governments were net recipients of or contributors to federal disbursements. This enquiry took into account all the sums received by Ottawa and all the payments made out of the federal treasury involving fiscal transfers, public works, crown corporations and other federal bodies. For a number of reasons, conceptual and other, it proved impossible to reach any clear answer. Meaningful figures were elusive. A payment made, for instance, to the Head Office of the Canadian National Railway, or to that of Air Canada, could be for expenditures in another province. An attempt was nonetheless made to allocate specific items: in the case of the Department of Citizenship and Immigration, for example, costs of operation were allocated on the basis of destination by province of immigrants, and the costs of the Penitentiaries Branch of the Department of Justice were distributed on the basis of the province of sentence of penitentiary inmates.

In the matter of national defence and national debt charges it was suggested that these expenditures should be allocated according to where the dollars were actually spent. This method of allocation was considered but was not used because it was felt that it would be inconsistent with the concepts upon which the study was based. The vital principle underlying the allocation of expenditure was that of benefit. Accordingly, each expenditure item of the government was scrutinized with a view to understanding its purpose and the nature of the final service provided to the public. The allocation of the expenditure was then estimated upon the basis of some quantitative measure of the benefits received by the residents of each province from the final service resulting from that expenditure.

The only practical alternative to the benefit approach used would have been to employ a purely accounting method based upon data concerning the flow of government cheques. There were several reasons for rejecting

129

this alternative basis. The main reason was that the notion could not be accepted that money spent in one province may not benefit other provinces. To take an obvious example, if money is spent on forestry research in one province, it may well benefit the entire forestry industry of Canada by making it possible for the industry to lower production costs and improve its competitive position. Would it not be unduly narrow to argue that the expenditure was of benefit only to the one province where the research work was actually done?

Another objection to the accounting method to allocation was that this method is defensible only if taken to its logical conclusion. It is not enough to ascertain that federal cheques were mailed to government suppliers in certain provinces; part of the "re-expenditure" may well be for the purchase of goods and services from other provinces. Thus the federal government could pay a contractor in Nova Scotia a million dollars for his services in fulfilling a contract but the great bulk of the money received by the contractor might be paid out by him to producers of equipment in central Canada, and these in turn might have made large expenditures for raw materials from still other provinces. Clearly the allocation of this million dollars to Nova Scotia would be unrealistic.

Inevitably the enquiry involved a great many subjective judgments. Reflecting those judgments, different estimates were made and the conclusion reached was that the exercise was of limited value and unlikely to result in any consensus of opinion. In the absence of detailed input-output tables, uncertainty was bound to prevail. This has not, however, prevented expressions of opinion on the matter: a very common belief is that the two central provinces are the main beneficiaries of import protection measures for secondary manufacturing. This has been a constant theme of the eastern as well as of the western provinces.

Input-output tables may help to clarify the picture. They are being prepared by the federal government and by some provinces. The federal government is supporting the provincial effort and is anxious to maintain close channels of communication among those involved in their preparation so that provincial tables will be compatible with each other. The long-run objective is a system which will permit all the provincial tables to be operated jointly for inter-regional impact analysis.

Turning to the specific programs designed to influence the location of industry, the provision of capital incentives to industry constitutes one of the major policy tools which DREE has adopted for the purpose of job creation. For some time these have been one of the more controversial aspects of federal policy. As has been noted, incentives were given automatically under the old ADA policy to certain types of industry, mainly to manufacturing firms that established themselves or expanded in designated areas. Since aid was given automatically it was inevitable that

130

those firms which would have established themselves anyway in the designated areas received windfall gains. It is for this reason that grants under DREE have been made discretionary. Only if, and to the extent that, a grant is deemed necessary to encourage a firm to locate or expand in a designated area is a grant offered. *In principle* this appears to be eminently sensible.

Clearly there is no point in subsidising firms to establish in designated areas if that is where they are going to go in any case. In like manner, there is little or no advantage in aiding firms to locate there whose prospects of long-run profitability are highly questionable. DREE is seeking applicants who expect to be successful but who will not go to the depressed areas without some subvention. The trick is to decide who they are. How does one read the mind of the applicant? As has been recognized, the difficulty in finding a foolproof system of avoiding payments for what would have happened in any event lies in the problem of establishing motive. If a firm is to set up a branch in an area where it knows the government is ready to offer incentives, and if it knows that these incentives are available only to firms who would not otherwise have gone there, the firm is unlikely to present itself as other than a reluctant mover. In spite of certain obvious merits it may be that discretionary aid is too difficult to handle administratively.

The criteria for incentives assessment were outlined by the Minister in testimony to the Standing Committee on Regional Development. These criteria include judgments relating to the market, manpower requirements, sources of supplies, expected rates of return, costs, public and private, likely effects on other industries and the incentives needed.

The question remains as to how far the incentives do in fact influence the decisions of firms to locate in the designated regions. This question is a crucial one, for such influence constitutes a prime objective of the incentive program. The answer has its roots in the determinants of industrial location in general. One aspect of the latter as it affects the Canadian scene is that related to American investment. A dominant share of much Canadian industry is owned or controlled in the United States and the location of Canadian subsidiaries introduces special factors.

Doubts have been cast on the extent of the influence of certain federal incentives on locational decisions. The reasons for the seemingly modest impact of these incentives have been factors which influence business behaviour. The feeling is prevalent in business circles that the choice of location should be determined by "sound business judgment" rather than by "government intervention". "Sound business judgment" depends on such considerations as expected long-run viability, ready accessibility to markets, adequacy of the labour force and the minimization of risk. There is a strong preference for the traditional zones of economic concentration since, apart from their other advantages, it is in these zones that risks appear to be least. It is not enough just to receive grants which will offset the estimated added costs of a poor location for the present: the matter is one which concerns not only the present but also an uncertain future, and it is even more difficult to put a figure on the latter than on the former.

Companies are reluctant to take the greater risks involved in establishing in the more depressed areas partly because of the consequences for the decision maker if the results prove unsatisfactory. There is a degree of risk beyond which management is not willing to go.

Given the uncertainty of estimation of costs and revenues, it is difficult to see how grants can be tailored with precision. If the projected costs submitted by the applicant appear too high, the application may be considered nonviable and thus be rejected; if too low, the sum received will be less than it might have been. It is not surprising therefore that firms present their case in a way which will maximize the potential grant. This is not imputing dishonesty to business—it is a natural response to the system. Accepting the argument that firms determine their location with only a limited regard for the incentives offered, and combining this with the fact that much of the country is designated for grants, it is difficult to doubt the contention that for many recipients the grants constitute windfall gains. When funds are available, firms will naturally collect them if they can.

To the extent that grants are awarded on the basis of the demonstrated need of applicants, it is the weaker firms that will receive the most. In exercizing discretion in the awarding of grants, seemingly no attempt is made to formally modify the industrial structure of a region: there is no strategy or plan relating to structure. The prevalent view, however, that industrialization is linked strongly to urbanization, has resulted in efforts to strengthen urban centres in areas of the country requiring assistance.

The evaluation of the "special area" expenditures is in some ways even more complicated than that of the Industrial Incentives Program. Not only, as noted above, are the "special areas" heterogeneous, but the programs themselves cover a wider range, involving grants and loans of many kinds. Certain general observations can be made, but ideally it would be desirable to look at each individual case in turn.

The implicit, if not express, assumption underlying much of the expenditures is that improvement in infrastructure will attract industry. But as is widely recognized, such an assumption may or may not be valid. Admittedly, whether or not industry is attracted by infrastructure expenditures, there may be a clear case on social grounds for improving roads, housing, water supplies and so on—industrial development is, after all, but a means to an end, not an end in itself—but the question then arises

132

as to how we are to judge such expenditures. We are faced with the fact that if we interpret regional development broadly enough almost any expenditures can be considered appropriate. There is virtually no limit to the range of activities on which money might be spent. How then are they to be assessed?

In a DREE publication, Regional Development and Regional Policy (1972), reference is made, in connection with the "special area" concept, to ". . . an effort to reinforce market forces through a set of coordinated special programs, applied selectively, where the objective is to assist the so-called "little economies" to participate effectively in the mainstream of the general process of economic growth and social change in Canada." Unless market forces will be reinforced (or it is believed that they will be) expenditures presumably will not be regarded as appropriate by the Department. It would seem, however, from some of the expenditures which have been undertaken that the restraint is not especially circumscribing.

Formally, in both the choice of the "special areas" and the expenditures incurred thereunder, there is a federal-provincial cooperation and joint planning. In practice, planning has often amounted to little more than bargaining over specific projects and allocating the respective financial responsibilities for them. The priorities desired by the provincial governments do not always coincide with those of the federal government and agreements once made are subject to substantial revisions.

An examination of data extending back over almost half a century does not reveal any significant acceleration in the 1960's in the improvement of incomes in the Atlantic Provinces relative to those in Canada as a whole. With the exception of Newfoundland, such improvement as there has been over this entire period in the region has been extremely modest, averaging about half of one percent a year. Nor have comparative unemployment levels shown any significant improvement in recent years, although changes in definition obscure the picture. The inclusion in the 1960's of many seasonal workers among the unemployed has introduced a bias into the data. Newfoundland, which became the tenth province of Canada in 1949, although it is still among the poorest of the provinces, has shown a distinct improvement over the past quarter century.

From a welfare standpoint, unemployment data can be very misleading. The labour force comprises a highly heterogeneous group of people which includes married women and young adolescents with widely varying dependence on employment as a source of income. Composite figures need to be interpreted with caution. Life styles also vary across the country and the high figures of unemployment in the Atlantic Provinces or British Columbia may be less a ground for concern than they would be in central Canada. Similarly, an income level which might appear adequate in one part of the country may appear inadequate in another. There is growing

133

doubt as to what precisely is being measured, and to what extent regional differences are being adequately portrayed.

The foregoing considerations aside, if we are to measure the efficacy of the Department of Regional Economic Expansion in terms of reducing unemployment, we are immediately faced with a multiplicity of variables bearing on unemployment levels and it becomes a matter of considerable difficulty to isolate the specific impact of the Department itself. The need to look at a medium- or a long-run time horizon rather than a short one in assessing the impact of the Department on employment levels is a matter not merely of the inevitable delays involved in the completion of structural changes, but also of the complications in the short run of random year to year changes as well as those associated with fluctuations in the business cycle.

The fortunes of particular areas will often arise independently of anything the Department does or does not do. The discovery and depletion of natural resources, changes in consumer demand or international trading patterns, actions of provincial governments or technological developments influencing the location of industry may result in improvements or deterioration in the fortunes of particular areas. One of the major issues at the time of writing involves the uneven distribution of natural resources and the question as to how far the provincial governments within whose boundaries oil and gas, in particular, exist and whose fortunes have been greatly enhanced as a result, shall be free to determine the price of disposal at the expense of the "have not" provinces.

The actions of provincial governments in the matter of regional development call for special mention. There are several features which are worth noting at the outset, namely:

1) the wide diversity of economic and social conditions prevailing in different parts of the country;

2) the differences in political orientation and in attitudes towards regional objectives;

3) the variations in professional sophistication and administrative style;

4) the multitude of policies, programs and institutions involved specifically with regional development or which, while not falling specifically under a regional development rubric, have nonetheless an important bearing thereon;

5) the fluidity of policies, programs and administrative arrangements, often, though not necessarily, related to changes of government at the provincial or federal level.

It will be apparent from the foregoing that any attempt to obtain a comprehensive view of the prominent features of regional policies as pursued by provincial governments constitutes a major undertaking, quite apart

134

from the added dimension of appraisal. Even within the limited context of such institutions as Development Corporations or Industrial Parks the task of investigation can be one of considerable magnitude if more is to be attempted than the pointing out of certain issues and experiences.

All the provinces, without exception, attach importance to the attraction of industry. The main thrust, indeed, of the regional development effort of most of the provinces is specifically directed at attracting industry. This is reflected in the magnitude of their subventions of various kinds to industry and in infrastructure expenditures designed to induce or facilitate industrial expansion. Among their activities can be cited the preparation of market studies, the provision of various advisory services and technical help, of financial aid of one kind and another, tax concessions, loans, grants and equity participating, the building of factories and the leasing of facilities. Aid has also been extended to resource industries by, for instance, the provision of roads to resources and reduced royalty demands.

In a regional development context expenditures on social welfare and individual adjustment typically play a minor role. The solutions to regional disparities are seen in terms of industrial growth. Where such growth appears impractical the emphasis frequently shifts to migration of the labour force, although official declarations on that subject tend to be muted.

In general, it is in the poorer provinces that provincial governments have been most active in attempting to attract new industry. Many of the ventures which they have helped to finance have proved extremely costly to the governments in question.

The provision of loan funds by Development Corporations is one of the more common forms of provincial aid to industry, and in some cases—as in Ontario, Alberta, and Saskatchewan, for example—loans are forgiveable. In effect these loans assume the form of grants. Quebec and Manitoba have made direct grants available to industry and Quebec, under recent legislation, offers tax concessions to firms which make use of advanced technology or which produce new types of products. New Brunswick has embarked on the establishment of an industrial complex. Almost all of the provinces have established industrial parks, and several offer favourable power rates. It would seem that municipalities in Ontario and Manitoba receive significant help from the provincial governments in attracting industry and both governments have aided in the formation of regional development councils. In addition, it needs to be recognized that almost every city and municipality in Canada is engaged in the quest for new industry—as also are railway companies, public utilities and land developers, each of which offers its own package of inducements and incentives. There is a great deal of competition among municipalities struggling to find new sources of tax dollars. One can only speculate on the

135

net effect of all this activity on the industrial structure and the location of industry across the country. It seems likely, however, that incentives are to some extent self-cancelling—the incentives offered in one province being offset by those offered in another.

In the framing of policies all governments pay at least lip service to the view that public participation in the formulation of plans and programs for individual regions is essential to their success. Thus the recommended strategy for the development of the rural regions in Manitoba includes a requirement for maximum participation and control over the development process by the people actually living in the rural regions. The differences occur not in the expression of the need for public participation but in the manner of its interpretation. Participation is a many faceted concept, and public officials anxious to hasten the pace of change often regard it is an impediment to effective action or as a will-o-the-wisp. Administrative secrecy and lack of publicity is one of the more common obstacles to effective public participation, and the larger the bureaucracy the more difficult the problem of communication becomes.

With regard to the distribution of population, almost all provincial governments recognize the inevitable demise of many small communities but while some provinces, such as Newfoundland, have hastened the process, others, such as British Columbia, are more disposed to let events take their own course. No province, however, denies the impracticability of providing adequate services to small isolated groups of people.

Provincial boundaries have only a limited economic relevance and regional planning by provinces in isolation is inadequate and in some cases it makes little sense. Closer collaboration between the provinces in the formulation of regional objectives and plans, to the extent that it is feasible, is clearly to be desired. Indeed, it should be stressed that regional development ought to be tied in to national developments and to the secular changes occuring in specific industries. We are still a long way from this and what has happened in a number of cases is that firms have been aided to establish in areas of heavy unemployment notwithstanding misgivings about over-production in the industry as a whole

As will be apparent from the trend of discussion up to this point, the main preoccupation of governments involved in regional issues has been with unemployment and low incomes. While this is entirely understandable, regional planning does, however, call for more than this. The distribution of economic activity and social capital affects the employed as well as the unemployed, the wealthy as well as the poor. The preservation and improvement of the environment, the provision of recreational space, the curbing of the disadvantages associated with excessive concentrations of people and industry, are matters which also merit attention. Regional planning confined to areas of distress falls short of what is needed, and

136

from a purely political point of view it is less likely to command widespread support. These are some of the issues which underlie the new direction that policy is expected to take in future.

Notes

1. Howland, R. D., *Some Regional Aspects of Canada's Economic Prospects,* Ottawa: Queen's Printer, 1957.
2. Senate of Canada, *Report of the Special Committee on Land Use in Canada,* Ottawa: Queen's Printer, 1964.

Bibliography

Brewis, T. N., *Regional Economic Policies in Canada,* Macmillan Co. of Canada, Toronto, 1969.

Brewis, T. N., *et al., Growth and the Canadian Economy,* McClelland and Stewart, Toronto, 1968.

Camu, P., E. P. Weeks, and Z. W. Sametz, *Economic Geography of Canada,* Macmillan Co. of Canada, Toronto, 1964.

Caves, Richard E., and Richard H. Holton, *The Canadian Economy: Prospect and Retrospect,* Harvard University Press, Cambridge, Mass., 1959.

Crabbe, Philippe and Irene M. Spry, *Natural Resource Development in Canada,* University of Ottawa Press, Ottawa, 1973.

Creighton, D. G., *The Commercial Empire of the St. Lawrence 1760-1850,* Ryerson Press, Toronto, 1937.

Currie, A. W., *Canadian Economic Development,* (Fourth edition) Thomas Nelson and Sons, Toronto, 1963.

Easterbrook, W. T. and H. G. J. Aitken, *Canadian Economic History,* Macmillan Co. of Canada, Toronto, 1963.

Easterbrook, W. T. and M. H. Watkins, *Approaches to Canadian Economic History,* McClelland and Stewart, Toronto, 1967.

Economic Council of Canada, Second Annual Review, *Towards Sustained and Balanced Economic Growth,* Queen's Printer, Ottawa, 1965.

Harp, John and J. R. Hofley (eds.), *Poverty in Canada,* Prentice Hall of Canada, Scarborough, Ont., 1971.

Howland, R. D., *Some Regional Aspects of Canada's Economic Development,* Royal Commission on Canada's Economic Prospects, Queen's Printer, Ottawa, 1957.

Innis, H. A., *The Fur Trade in Canada,* revised edition, University of Toronto Press, Toronto, 1956.

Innis, H. A., *Problems of Staple Production in Canada,* Ryerson Press, Toronto, 1933.

Innis, H. A., (ed. Mary Q. Innis), *Essays in Canadian Economic History,* University of Toronto Press, Toronto, 1956.

137

Innis, H. A. and A. F. W. Plumptre (eds.), *The Canadian Economy and its Problems,* Canadian Institute of International Affairs, Toronto, 1934.

Innis, Mary Quale, *An Economic History of Canada,* Ryerson Press, Toronto, 1935.

Krueger, Ralph R., *et al.* (eds.), *Regional and Resource Planning in Canada,* Holt, Rinehart and Winston of Canada, Toronto, 1963.

Mackintosh, W. A., *The Economic Background of Dominion-Provincial Relations,* McClelland and Stewart, Toronto, 1964.

McInnis, Marvin, "The Trend of Regional Income Differentials in Canada", *The Canadian Journal of Economics,* May 1968, pp. 440-473.

Royal Commission on Dominion-Provincial Relations, Book 1, *Canada: 1867-1939,* Queen's Printer, Ottawa, 1940.

Safarian, A. E., *The Canadian Economy in the Great Depression,* McClelland and Stewart, Toronto, 1970.

Tremblay, Marc Adelard, and Walton J. Anderson (eds.), *Rural Canada in Transition,* Agricultural Research Council of Canada, Ottawa, 1966.

Wonders, William C. (ed.), *Canada's Changing North,* McClelland and Stewart, Toronto, 1971.

138

8

REGIONAL POLICIES IN THE UNITED STATES: EXPERIENCE AND PROSPECTS

Niles M. Hansen

Regional policy in the United States is based primarily on legislation passed in 1965, during the heyday of President Johnson's "Great Society" programs. There had, of course, been a number of prior experiments in regional development legislation. For example, during the 1930's such New Deal programs as the Tennessee Valley Authority, rural electrification, and the Civilian Conservation Corps were based on public works and resource development and conservation. Following the Second World War a large number of local industrial development groups attempted to attract economic activity, but there were many more of these groups than there were new plants; moreover, many communities denied themselves badly needed public services in order to subsidize marginal firms. In the early part of the 1960's there was a renewal of interest at the federal level in helping "depressed areas". The Area Redevelopment Act of 1961 and the Accelerated Public Works Act of 1962 provided for public facilities in declining and stagnating communities. However, funds were not sufficient to overcome basic problems, planning was carried out on too small a scale, and little attention was given to human resource development.

Although a public works bias was carried over in the 1965 legislation, the two regional development acts passed in that year—the Appalachian Regional Development Act (ARDA) and the Public Works and Economic Development Act (PWEDA)—represented an unprecedented effort to deal comprehensively with regional problems of high unemployment and low income.

The Appalachian Program

The ARDA established the Appalachian Regional Commission (ARC) for the purpose of coordinating a six-year (since extended) joint federal-state development effort—the largest such program yet undertaken in the United States. The ARC maintains[1] that its social goal is to provide the people of Appalachia with the health and skills they require to compete for opportunity wherever they choose to live. The economic goal is to develop in Appalachia a self-sustaining economy capable of supporting rising incomes, improving standards of living, and increasing employment opportunities.

The Appalachian program involves thirteen states—stretching from northeastern Mississippi to southern New York—but the only whole state included is West Virginia. Given this vast expanse of territory it is not surprising that the ARC itself distinguishes "four Appalachias", each with its own needs and potentials. The ARDA gave the ARC a broad range of functions and a narrower set of programs to administer, as well as general guidelines for these purposes. The ARC was given specific program and funding authority in nine functional areas: health, housing, vocational education, soil conservation, timber development, mine restoration, water survey, water and sewer facilities, and highways. The Commission also was given supplemental grant authority and provided with program funding linkages to local development districts.

Strictly speaking, the ARC is not a federal agency, but rather a cooperative venture in which the federal government and the states that are involved participate as equals. The Commission is composed of the governors (or their representatives) of the thirteen states and a federal co-chairman appointed by the President. The regional, state, and local multi-county development district levels each have their own responsibilities. At the regional level the ARC attempts to assess Appalachia's future role in the national economy and is concerned with developing regional programs, planning for public facilities, cooperating in interstate programs, and undertaking social and economic analysis. The role of state planning is to determine areas with significant potential for future growth, formulate long-run programs and annual project plans geared to each Appalachian sub-area in the state, and establish local development districts within which federal, state and local planning efforts are to be coordinated. The multi-county development districts are responsible for communicating local needs and aspirations to the states, identifying local development projects, and coordinating their local execution.

In contrast to the wide scattering of public investments that had characterized earlier efforts to aid depressed areas, the ARDA specified that those "made in the region under this Act shall be concentrated in areas where there is the greatest potential for future growth, and where the expected return on public dollars will be the greatest".[2]

What degree of project concentration has actually been achieved by the ARC? Probably the best indication of success in this regard is provided by the data in Table 1. The four-level categorization shown there was developed by the ARC and applied to each state plan. Level 1 was defined as the highest level of growth potential in each state. Level 4 areas were not designated as growth areas, while the other levels represent different degrees of intermediate situations. The data presented in Table 1 do not include projects that were made before growth areas were defined, and they do not include certain outlays that could not be localized. For all of Appalachia, 62 per cent of investment funds went to the dominant growth areas of each state during the first five years of the ARC's operations. Only 14 percent went to areas that were felt to have no growth potential. Kentucky's low proportion of Level 1 investments reflects the

Table 1. Concentration of Appalachian Program Investments in Growth Areas, by State, 1965-1970

State	Growth Area Levels			
	1 (Percent)	2 (Percent)	3 (Percent)	4 (Percent)
Alabama	84.3	1.4	—	14.3
Georgia	33.2	27.1	—	39.7
Kentucky	2.2	45.8	42.0	9.9
Maryland	86.0	14.0	—	—
Mississippi	87.2	6.9	—	5.9
North Carolina	17.3	36.5	43.4	2.8
New York	80.5	9.9	—	9.6
Ohio	87.2	9.7	—	3.1
Pennsylvania	86.1	4.8	2.9	6.2
South Carolina	69.6	9.1	—	21.3
Tennessee	38.7	26.5	24.3	10.5
Virginia	61.5	—	—	38.5
West Virginia	67.3	3.0	9.5	20.2
Region	62.1	13.9	10.3	13.7

Note: Figures may not add up to 100% because of rounding error.

Source: M. Newman, The Political Economy of Appalachia (Lexington, Massachusetts: D. C. Heath and Company, 1972), p. 156.

fact that there is only one metropolitan county in the Appalachian portion of the state. The relatively low Level 1 outlays in Georgia, North Carolina and Tennessee reflect state decisions to promote growth away from the largest metropolitan areas. Moreover, those states with the highest proportions of Level 4 investments for the most part concentrated their funds on human resource projects, rather than on projects more directly associated with economic development.

The issue of investment in human resources has been a key one in the history of the Appalachian program. The original ARDA made highway development a substantial part of the program on the ground that lack of accessibility was holding back the progress of the region. Of the initial $1.1 billion authorization, $840 million was allocated to highway construction over a five-year period, while another $252 million was allocated to a number of other social and economic programs for a two-year period. Bringing the two types of outlays down to a two-year basis and adding matching state funds meant that about $480 million was authorized for highways and approximately $281 million for eleven other major categories.

The ARDA's initial emphasis on highway construction was severely criticized in some quarters.[3] On the other hand, there has been a strong support for the highway program within the ARC, primarily because it has been regarded as the matrix within which human resource investments will prove their effectiveness. Thus, Ralph Widner, the very able executive director of the ARC during its first six years, could maintain in reviewing the Appalachian experience that:

> The critics argued that it makes far better sense to invest in people than in the concrete of highways. Most of us would agree.
>
> But how carefully thought through is that criticism? If children cannot get to a school for lack of decent transportation, if a pregnant mother cannot get to a hospital for lack of a decent road, if a breadwinner cannot get to a job because the job 30 miles away cannot be reached in a reasonable time, then is such an investment an investment in people or an investment in concrete?[4]

Moreover, in practice there has been a complete reorientation of non-highway funds during the life of the ARC. From an original preference for physical resource investments in the ARDA, the ARC has moved to a three-to-one preference for human resource projects in terms of actual project expenditures. And this comparison understates the case because it leaves out the human resource emphasis of supplemental fund allocations. (Under one of the more innovative sections of the ARDA, the ARC is given funds to supplement local funds in the financing of federal grant-in-aid programs so that the local contribution can be reduced to as low as 20 per cent of the project's cost. By August 1971, $215 million had been appropriated for supplemental funds; almost 82 per cent of this total was spent on human resource development.)

The reasoning behind the shift in emphasis toward human resource investments has been stated by Newman in the following terms:

> By investing heavily in the most mobile form of resources—people—the commision was able to minimize the chance that its investments

142

would be wasted. Though no one could be sure that any particular set of public facility investments could contribute to the development of a self-supporting economy in the more lagging portions of the region, it was clear that better health and education for the people of those areas was a necessary precondition for such development if it was to occur, and, if it did not, individuals could carry them wherever opportunities were available.[5]

This approach would seem to be a milestone on the road from place-oriented policies toward approaches recognizing that the welfare of people is, or should be, the principal objective of economic policy.

The Title V Commissions

Title V of the PWEDA authorized the Secretary of Commerce to designate, with the cooperation of the states involved, multistate regions with common problems of economic distress or lag that cannot be solved by measures taken in any one state. Once a region has been designated, the relevant states are invited to participate in a regional commission patterned in structure on that for Appalachia. In 1966 and 1967, regional commissions were established for the Ozarks (comprising 134 counties in Arkansas, Oklahoma, Missouri and Kansas), the Four Corners (consisting of 92 counties in New Mexico, Utah, Arizona and Colorado), New England (covering all six states in the region), the Coastal Plains (made up of 159 tidewater counties in Georgia and the Carolinas), and the Upper Great Lakes (comprising 119 counties in northern Minnesota, Wisconsin and Michigan). Other commissions have recently been authorized but they have yet to begin effective operation.

The Title V commissions have not received the magnitude of funds made available to the Appalachian program. During their first six years federal expenditures for all of the Title V commissions amounted to a little over $100 million, while those for Appalachia came to $1.3 billion. The ARC was established as an independent agency whereas the other commissions operate under the Secretary of Commerce. In contrast to the ARC, the Title V commissions had little or no advance planning (New England is an exception) and they have had greater political problems. The Title V commissions only have funding powers for planning and demonstration project efforts along with a supplemental grant program. They lack their own cluster of specific programs, and few systematic attempts have been made to build needed linkages between regional and state developmental planning efforts. Moreover, although a few "growth centres" have been designated or approved, the Title V commissions fol-

143

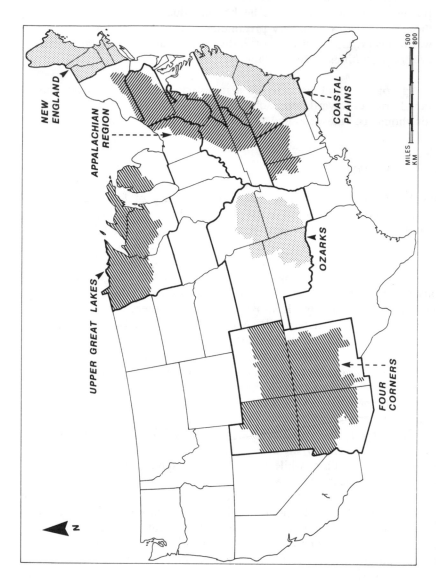

Economic Development Regions in the United States

lowing this strategy have had difficulty in implementing it in view of their limited program and funding authority, as well as the political risks involved. Finally, there has been little or no coordination between the activities of the Title V commissions and the Economic Development Administration even though both are lodged in the Department of Commerce.[6]

The Economic Development Administration

The EDA was created by the PWEDA to assist the regional commissions (a role it has never effectively assumed) and to provide assistance in its own right to areas characterized by chronic economic distress. Eligibility for EDA assistance is based on one or more of the following general economic conditions: (1) a substantial or persistent unemployment problem for an extended period of time, (2) a median family income at a level of less than 40 per cent of the national level, and (3) an actual (or prospective) abrupt rise in unemployment resulting from the closing of a major employer.

To implement its development goals the EDA has at its disposal a wide range of program tools, including grants and loans for public works and development facilities, industrial and commercial loans, and an extensive program of technical, planning and research assistance. As of June 30, 1972, the EDA reported that it had approved 2,508 public works projects amounting to nearly $1.23 billion.

In addition to the multi-state regions discussed earlier, the PWEDA called for three other categories of institutions for dealing with regional development problems. "Redevelopment areas" include counties, labour areas, and certain cities where unemployment and low incomes pose particularly urgent assistance problems. "Economic development districts" are multi-county organizations within which counties and communities work cooperatively on mutual needs and opportunities. "Economic development centres" are communities or localized areas with fewer than 250,000 persons where resources are to be used rapidly and effectively to create more jobs and higher incomes for the population of the surrounding area. Although these growth centres need not be within depressed areas, they are intended to promote economic development in redevelopment areas within the districts of which the centres and redevelopment areas are a part.

Early in its existence the EDA experimented with a "worst first" strategy whereby areas with the most severe difficulties in each category of aid eligibility were to receive top priority for funds from the agency. This strategy, in so far as it was implemented, was inconsistent with the notion of clustering investments in the growth centres of EDA districts. On the other hand, the EDA's experience with the growth centre approach has left much to be desired. A major internal evaluation of EDA's growth centre strategy concluded that:

> On the basis of the twelve in-depth case studies conducted during the growth evaluation, it is not yet clear that the growth centres strategy outlined in the agency's legislation and expanded in EDA policy statements is workable. Residents of surrounding depressed counties designated as redevelopment areas received almost no employment or public service benefits from the EDA growth centre projects surveyed by the evaluation team. Moreover, at the time of evaluation these projects had not resulted in more total job impact than similar projects place in distressed areas, as had been suggested in the past.[7]

The same study also found that:

> ... the twenty-eight completed EDA projects in the growth centres analyzed showed no evidence of stemming out-migration from redevelopment areas or economic development districts. Less than 1 percent of the 850 employees surveyed at EDA-associated firms stated that they would have migrated from the area if their present job had not been available. The percentage of workers who indicated they would have moved to one of the nation's major metropolitan areas in the absence of the EDA-created job was even smaller.[8]

General dissatisfaction with EDA also is reflected in President Nixon's recent proposal to Congress for an Economic Adjustment Act to restructure federal programs for area and regional economic adjustment. The initial report in this regard, prepared by the U.S. Department of Commerce and the Bureau of the Budget, reaffirms the notion that "priority should be given to those areas with the greatest potential of providing higher productivity jobs for the underemployed, rather than attempting to create more productive jobs in all areas of high underemployment".[9] The report also is sharply critical of EDA's past performance:

> The policy of dispersing assistance rather than focusing on those places with the greatest potential for self-sustaining growth has resulted in much of EDA's funds going to very small communities. Over a third of its public works funds have gone to towns with less than 2,500 people, and over a half to towns with less than 5,000 population. There are relatively few kinds of economic activities which can operate efficiently in such small communities, so the

potential for economic development in the communities is relatively small.[10]

The report is equally critical of the Title V regional commissions, but deals more kindly with the Appalachian program, primarily because it has been much broader in scope than the programs limited to alleviation of high unemployment or low income.

Future Directions

Although the Appalachian Regional Commission is likely to continue its operations, the Administration wants to abolish the EDA and the Title V commissions. In their place the federal government would allocate funds to the states (who may choose to form multi-state regional commissions but would be under no obligation to do so) upon federal approval of state plans which outline how the funds would be used to assist distressed areas and present the creation of new distressed areas. While the states are given considerable planning latitude, there is no doubt that the federal government favours concentrating assistance in relatively few areas to permit enough resources in one area to stimulate sustained growth. In other words, although past efforts using a growth centre strategy based on small towns and rural areas have proven not only economically inefficient, but too frequently ineffective, this does not necessarily mean that the strategy would be inappropriate if applied to centres with genuine growth potential.

In another attempt to influence spatial resource allocation in the United States, the Congress, in 1971, called for the establishment of a national urban growth policy, and for a Report on Urban Growth from the President in every even-numbered year. The report is to include data on the state of urban development as well as recommendations for programs and policies to carry out a national urban policy. However, President Nixon showed little interest in developing such a policy.

The issue of population growth has received wide national attention in recent years, but primarily in terms of aggregate growth. The government Commission on Population Growth and the American Future[11] reflected the sentiments of many groups when it recently recommended eventual stabilization of the national population as a means of "buying time" to cope with a host of economic, social and environmental problems. However, a substantial decline in the birth rate has undermined some of the *raison d'être* of policies aimed at zero population growth. Increased attention thus may be focused on the Commission's finding that eventual aggregate population stability would still leave a distribution

147

problem of nearly comparable magnitude.

These demographic issues are closely related to a remarkable increase in public concern about the quality of the environment. Cumberland has argued that:

> Regions today are forced to compete for growth, whether they wish to or not, especially by placing major responsibility to finance public sector services upon local government. The result has been pressures for excessive growth in some areas, as evidenced by exhaustion of local water supplies and massive water transfers, overloading of waste removal facilities, urban congestion, breakdown of transportation facilities, and the intensive settlement of areas unsuitable for development because of periodic drought, brush fires, flooding, seismic activity, earth slides, and other natural phenomena.[12]

Those who share this view maintain that the larger public interest of the nation requires that restrictions be placed on uncontrolled regional growth so that there can be more effective management of water resources, wilderness areas, recreational sites and the quality of the environment. An Environmental Protection Agency has been established to deal with these issues and its powers of enforcement have thus far clearly been more than nominal. Legislation is also pending in Congress to establish a national system of land use planning. Measures for dealing with the inter-relationships between regional development and environmental quality thus appear to be more than a passing fad, and are likely to play an increasingly important part in influencing spatial resource distribution.

Within the larger industrial centres it would appear that while employment opportunities are potentially available to minority groups in the central city ghettos, these groups have been denied these opportunities as much because of housing discrimination as because of employment discrimination.[13] There is clear evidence that blacks (and other minorities) are concentrated in central cities not so much because they are poor, as because they cannot obtain housing in the suburbs where new jobs are increasingly being created.[14] Residents of urban ghettos, like those of lagging rural areas, are badly in need of better education, job training, and generally expanded investment in human resources, but they also need better access to suburban employment sites. Among the means that can be employed toward this end are improved transportation between the ghetto and suburban jobs, expansion of low-income housing outside of the ghetto, vigorous enforcement of open-housing statutes, and rent subsidies. Policies which are based on refurbishing the ghetto, and which therefore assume its permanence, will not resolve the employment problems of big cities. What is called for is, rather, a change in their structure. Of

148

course, if minority groups prefer to live in their own communities, what may be called for is a policy of concentrated decentralization within metropolitan areas.

A major study of the impact of federal activities on regional development concludes that:

> The fundamental requirements of the American economic system —natural resources, labour, capital, and markets—are influenced to some extent by more than forty federal programs which provide assistance to public agencies, private institutions and individuals. But the geographic impacts of these programs, in the aggregate, are modest: they are largely confined to accelerating pre-existing trends toward economic concentration in metropolitan areas or to curbing slightly prevailing trends of economic decline.
>
> At best, even with substantially modified priorities, funding, and administrative processes, the capacity of these programs to alter—and particularly to reverse—geographic patterns of economic development is extremely limited. Isolated shifts in the outcome are possible. These, however, would probably demand greater political consensus and professional expertise than is currently at hand.[15]

Thus, as Wingo observes, at present "putative national urban policy is simply the working out of laws, programmes, administrative decisions and regulations, and judicial rulings which have accumulated over the past two generations".[16]

If individual federal programs cannot be counted upon to alter current spatial distribution trends, it does not necessarily follow that the federal government has no possibility of playing a significant role in this regard. Indeed, the Appalachian Regional Commission experience has demonstrated that a multi-program approach directed toward an entire region can produce positive results.

In conclusion, it may be useful to note briefly some recommendations (with which this author is in basic agreement) made by the Commission on Population Growth and the American Future concerning the future development of urban and regional policy in the United States.

At the national level, it is recommended that the federal government develop a set of national population distribution guidelines to serve as a framework for regional, state and local plans and development. Action should be taken to increase freedom of choice of residential location through the elimination of current patterns of racial and economic segregation and their attendant injustices. To anticipate and guide future urban growth there should be comprehensive land use and public facility planning on an overall metropolitan and regional scale. Vigorous and concerted efforts should be undertaken to promote free choice of housing within metropolitan areas; federal and state governments should ensure provision of more suburban housing for low- and moderate-income families, and more extensive human capital programs should be developed to equip black and other deprived minorities for fuller participation in economic opportunities. Future programs for declining and chronically depressed rural areas should emphasize human resource development, and worker relocation counselling and assistance should be provided to enable individuals to relocate with a minimum of risk and disruption. Finally, it is recommended that a growth centre strategy be developed to expand job opportunities in urban places that have a demonstrated potential for future growth and that are located in proximity to declining areas. The types of growth centres envisioned by the Commission's final report are:

> expanding cities in the 25,000 to 350,000 population range whose anticipated growth may bring them to 50,000 to 500,000. Somewhat lower and higher limits should be considered for the sake of flexibility. Not every rapidly-growing city within this range should be eligible. Only those cities that could be expected to benefit a significant number of persons from declining regions, as well as the unemployed within the centre, should be eligible. Thus, growth centres should be selected on the basis of commuting and migration data, as well as data on unemployment and job opportunities, and physical and environmental potential for absorbing more growth.[17]

The population sizes of the growth centres proposed here may be overly conservative, but this should not preclude at least some demonstration projects linking investments in growth centres to human resource investments in lagging areas and comprehensive relocation assistance programs. It is also important that policy efforts give greater attention to market forces than has been the case in the past. Efforts to reverse market forces are likely to be not only inefficient but also ineffective, though the very notion of regional policies implies some modification of laissez-faire spatial resource allocation. Of course, when we speak of making spatial resource allocation more rational we are implying that we know more than we actually do at present about the locational preferences of the people whose welfare we are trying—in some sense—to further. It is to be hoped that this neglected area of research will receive more attention in the near future.

Notes

1. Appalachian Regional Commission, *Annual Report,* Washington, D.C., 1970.

2. Section 2 of the Appalachian Regional Development Act, 1965.

3. See J. M. Munro, "Planning the Appalachian Development Highway System: Some Critical Questions", *Land Economics,* Vol. 45, No. 2, 1969, pp. 149-156.

4. R. R. Widner, "Appalachia After Six Years", *Appalachia,* Vol. 5, No. 6. 1971, p. 19.

5. M. Newman, *The Political Economy of Appalachia,* D. C. Heath, Lexington, Massachusetts, 1972, p. 150.

6. Cf. D. Walker, "Interstate Regional Instrumentalities: A New Piece in an Old Puzzle", *Journal of the American Institute of Planners,* Vol. 38, No. 6, 1972, p. 359-68.

7. R. H. Milkman *et. al., Alleviating Economic Distress,* D. C. Heath, Lexington, Mass., 1972, p. 204.

8. *Ibid,* p. 206.

9. U.S. Department of Commerce and office of Management and Budget, "Report to the Congress on the Proposal for an Economic Adjustment Program", Washington, D.C., 1974, p. 10.

10. *Ibid,* p. 25.

11. *Population and the American Future,* U.S. Government Printing Office, Washington, D.C., 1972.

12. J. H. Cumberland, *Regional Development: Experiences and Prospects in the United States of America,* Mouton, Paris and The Hague, 1971, p. 138.

13. Cf. J. F. Kain, "Housing Segregation, Negro Employment, and Metropolitan Decentralization", *Quarterly Journal of Economics,* Vol. 82, No. 2, 1968, pp. 175-97.

14. Cf. J. F. Kain and J. J. Persky, "Alternatives to the Gilded Ghetto", Harvard University Program on Regional and Urban Economics Discussion Paper, No. 21, 1968.

15. Economic Development Administration, *Federal Activities Affecting Location of Economic Development,* Vol. 1, Washington, D.C., 1970, p. 11.

16. L. Wingo, "Issues in a National Urban Development Strategy for the United States", *Urban Studies,* Vol. 9, No. 1, 1972, p. 11.

17. *Population and the American Future, op. cit.,* pp. 125-126.

9

DEVELOPMENT AND PLANNING IN ALASKA WITH SPECIAL REFERENCE TO LAND USE AND MINERAL LEASING

John H. Cumberland and *Anthony C. Fisher*

"The future economic development of Alaska will provide a critical testing ground for U.S. regional development theory and practice. It is here that the demands of the future for fuel and economic expansion will confront all of the traditional issues in regional development. But in addition, more recent conflicts in contemporary U.S. values are emerging in Alaska on a very large scale".[1]

1. *Special Opportunities for Alaska*

In the face of sharply increasing national and international demand for its vast untapped oil reserves, and with approval granted for construction of the Trans-Alaska Pipeline (TAP), the State of Alaska now enjoys unique opportunities to use oil revenues to design its future development. With large anticipated revenues (to some degree already realized, in the billion dollars in lease bonuses for North Slope oil), and large unsettled open spaces, the State of Alaska is in a powerful position to observe historical experience in regional development elsewhere and, by avoiding the mistakes that have been made, to develop in ways responsive to the demands of the future. The low density of population and lack of heavy industry have thus far made it possible for Alaska to avoid committing some typical errors of the "lower 48" states in the pursuit of regional development. In particular, serious large scale damage to the environment has been avoided. The State has unprecedented opportunities to observe the experience of other regions and to break new ground in designing development policies to improve the standard of living or the quality of life (where this is defined in broader terms, for example including environmental amenities, than the traditional per capita (money) income measures) for the people of the region and which might in turn serve as a new pattern for reorienting development in other areas. Thus Alaskans, learning from the experience of other regions in the past, may provide lessons for development of still other regions in the future. Both the opportunities and the problems in Alaska are formidable.

2. *Special Development Problems of Alaska*

Major problems for development in Alaska are the harsh climate and great distances involved, which make transportation and communication particularly difficult and expensive. The distances and the low density of human population prevent economies of scale and keep the costs of transporting people, goods, and services very high. This in turn suggests, at least to some residents, the desirability of public sector investment to provide transport facilities for resource development. Because of the climate and distance problems, and the need for economies of scale and transport facilities, Alaskans tend to perceive their development problem as one of subduing a hostile environment. One of the great dangers in this perception is the fact that the Alaskan environment, with its perma-frost and tundra, is actually rather fragile, easily damaged in ways which require extremely long periods of recuperation, or are even irreversible.[2]

Another danger in Alaskan development, suggested by the experiences of Appalachia in particular, is the confusion of resource exploitation with regional development, which we understand as improvement in the overall quality of life in the region. In Appalachia, large scale investment in resource exploitation, mainly coal and timber, has produced benefits primarily accruing to investors and consumers outside the region. Much of the cost—the massive and well documented environmental damage, for example—has, however, fallen on the less affluent local residents.[3]

There is at least some danger that this could be repeated in Alaska, where the development of oil and gas resources by major corporations could primarily benefit absentee stockholders and residents of the continental U.S., with only minimal benefits to the native population. Considering the possibilities of extensive and irreversible disruption of the environment associated with the raising and transporting of oil under such difficult circumstances, the native communities could even wind up as net losers from the development. One very important aspect of coal resource development in Appalachia has been the freedom of the coal companies from liability for damages to surface property occasioned by mining activity. Typically, a lease carries the right to remove the mineral by "whatever means necessary", with no mention of compensation for surface losses. We shall want to consider this question of assignment of liability for damages and its effect on resource allocation in our discussion of planning policies in the next section.

154

The major policy issue for Alaskan regional development is then how to channel the forces of development generally, and demand for Alaskan resources specifically, into pursuits which will improve the quality of life for Alaskans, as well as yielding money returns to outsiders.

3. Gearing Economic Development to Improvements in Quality of Life

In meeting the challenge of channeling the returns which overflow from development of Alaskan oil and gas into true regional development, among the most important considerations are advance planning and protection of the local environment. Major problems of development in the continental United States and elsewhere have resulted from lack of planning and from planning which came too late.[4] That mistake need not be repeated in Alaska. Given the vast revenues which will flow from its oil, the investment of only a small percentage of the total could provide Alaska with regional planning facilities second to those of no other state, and could unquestionably yield benefits far in excess of costs involved in planning. A good start has been made in the establishment of the Joint Federal-State Land Use Planning Commission, discussed further in section 4 below. Though this Commission has advisory powers only, its charge is extensive, and if supported by good research it could play a crucial role.

Advance planning for regional development in Alaska is particularly critical in the environmental area. It is in this area that Alaskans can learn most from the errors of other regions. The application of a number of basic principles can go far to prevent the Alaskan counterpart of the damage from Appalachia strip mining, and the air and water pollution that characterize many areas of the U.S. In particular, the principles which can prevent this type of damage include full liability of the polluter, life cycle planning, region-wide planning, a multi-disciplinary approach, and democratic participation in the planning process.

A fundamental principle is full liability of the polluter-developer for any environmental damage. This may be justified on ethical or political grounds, but is also suggested by economic theory. Advance knowledge by the polluter that he must pay the full costs of his damage provides strong economic incentives to use the best possible technology, and to use his ingenuity and ability to best advantage to reduce pollution. At the same time, the pollution charges and abatement expenditures which they induce raise the prices of products whose production requires intensive use of the environment, in turn choking off demand for these products. In general, the introduction of prices for the scarce assimilative resources of the environment can be expected to move the economy toward greater efficiency in allocation.[5]

Another principle closely related to polluter liability is life cycle planning. It should be obvious that any type of development project goes through a number of phases, including planning, exploration, development, operation, and then finally, termination and restoration. Each of these phases is important and must be given due recognition, particularly in the huge scale developments which are anticipated for Alaska, such as the Trans-Alaska Pipeline and the potentially huge water resource development plans. Such activities involve potential pollution and other environmental damage during the exploration stage as well as during the construction, development, and operation stages. In the frigid Alaskan environment, wastes are not easily assimilated and the scarring of the land surface cannot easily be healed. For these reasons developers could be required to plan adequately for the recycling or removal of wastes and restoration of the environment where possible. An effective way of achieving this is to require that bonds be posted to assure compliance.[6] Where restoration is not possible, an additional charge might be levied on the developer to compensate for the loss of options in perpetuity, as discussed further in section 5 below.

We know from the emerging science of environmental economics that all phases of production and consumption involve waste. The concept of materials and energy balance can be utilized to assist in showing what inputs go into every phase of a regional development project, and what residuals, outputs, and environmental damage result from each phase.[7] We also know from the materials balance concept that pollution treatment processes themselves generate pollutants, and pollutants from waste treatment processes are becoming part of the problem. Developers might therefore be required to show how they plan to recycle, reuse, or otherwise dispose of wastes from each phase of a project, including waste treatment processes. The use of complete materials balance planning plus life cycle planning and posting of bonds to cover any unforeseen consequences can be used to assure the developers will be responsible not only for all of the costs of their projects, but also for restoring, at the end of the useful life of the project, any land, air and water which is damaged. In the case of the Trans-Alaska Pipeline, this would require the formation and disclosure of plans for the eventual dismantling of the Pipeline, the restoration of the surface, and the disposal of any materials involved.

A major shortcoming of regional planning in the continental United States has been domination of the planning process by segments of politically and economically powerful groups in both the private and public sector, usually to the exclusion from the planning of those who are damaged by it. The task of converting regional economic development into socially beneficial regional development oriented towards the public interest, as well as the private interests, of the various social and economic

156

groups in Alaska will be particularly difficult because of the need to include the native populations of Indians and Eskimos as well as the recent settlers. Under both ARA legislation and EDA legislation in the U.S., token efforts were made to assure democratic planning of regional development projects, but all too often these efforts have failed because of the power of established groups.

Another reason for the failure of planning for regional development has been the non-availability of regional planning models and concepts adequate to indicate to local planners the full range of options and the probable impacts and distributional consequences of these alternative development strategies. Using local planning powers of zoning, land use, and similar instruments, regional governments can exercise some discretion over the types of economic activities and development strategies to be emphasized in the region, such as heavy vs. light industry, public vs. private sector investments, or capital- vs. labour-intensive processes. Each of these choices implies alternative sets of impacts and trade-offs for job creation, revenue generation, public expenditure, and environmental management. Regional development models are now available which can help to estimate the impacts of these alternative development programs and aid in the design of development strategies which are optimal, given the particular objectives and priorities of the region.[8]

The task of achieving a meaningful democratic planning process will be made particularly difficult by cultural differences between the growth-oriented settlers on the one hand, and, on the other, the Indians and Eskimos, who had established a viable ecological relationship with the fragile environment of Alaska. This fragile environment is now threatened by the extraordinary pressures that the rest of the world is bringing to bear upon Alaska in order to extract its oil, gas, and other natural resources. Clearly the task of achieving regional development in the true sense, with improved quality of life for all Alaskans including Indians and Eskimos, cannot be achieved through economic initiatives alone. Development of Alaska under current pressures will require new mixtures of insights not only from economists, but also from anthropologists, ecologists, and many others. Perhaps for the first time in Alaska regional development will be perceived as a problem in total social development. Certainly efforts are being made, for example through the Land Use Planning Commission with its native Alaskan representation, to avoid the worst excesses of expropriation (of Indians) and exploitation (of blacks) that characterized some phases of continental U.S. Development.

157

4. The Joint Federal-State Land Use Planning Commission

The Land Use Planning Commission, which has been referred to a couple of times in passing, seems potentially an important enough departure in regional planning to warrant separate discussion. To begin with, it is very much a partnership between state and federal governments, having been created by the Alaska Native Claims Settlement Act (1971) of the U.S. Congress, and an Act (1972) of the Alaska legislature. Co-chairmen are the Governor of Alaska and an individual appointed by the President of the United States. Four additional members are appointed by the Governor, and four by the Secretary of the Interior. At least one member of the Commission must be an Alaska native, and there is, in addition, an advisory committee representing a broad cross-section of Alaskan interests—commercial users, recreationists, environmentalists, natives, and others.

Until very recently nearly all the land in Alaska, some 375 million acres, was under federal ownership. Under the terms of the Alaska Native Claims Settlement Act, 40 million acres will pass to Native Regional Corporations, and another 103 million to the State of Alaska and private owners. Moreover, the Secretary of the Interior is directed to withdraw up to 80 million acres to be studied for possible inclusion in the various federal management systems—parks, forests, wildlife refuges, wild and scenic rivers, and so on. The task of the Commission is to assist in this process of transition and study.

In the first instance, it is to undertake a planning study as a basis for recommendations concerning areas to be retained as part of the federal management system. At the same time, recommendations are to be made concerning the disposition of lands to the state and the native regional corporations, and ways of avoiding conflict in the selection process.

Secondly, the Commission is to advise and assist in the formulation of land use plans for the state' and the native corporations. With respect to both federal and state agency lands, recommendations are to be made on programs, budgets, and changes in law and policy. And interestingly, in view of our earlier discussion, all of these recommendations are to ensure that development improves the economic and social well-being of the native peoples and other citizens of Alaska, and is compatible with national and local environmental policies.

It is clear that in pursuing these objectives, a major focus of the Commission's efforts will be extractive resources—oil, timber, and potentially also the metallic minerals. In what areas, and at what times, are these commercial resources of Alaska to be developed in order to yield maximum net returns, taking into account environmental costs? Since the most important resource in value terms, oil, is extracted via leasing arrangements, as may soon be the case with the metallic minerals, this question can be formulated in terms of leasing policy. As a matter of fact, the Commission recently (December 1973) held a conference on minerals leasing, designed to explore whether and how the oil leasing system could be used to obtain better value from the land bearing other minerals. Among the questions considered were, what should be the objective of a minerals leasing policy, and how can it best be realized? As suggested above, a plausible objective is maximization of net social returns from the mineral in question, taking into account environmental costs of extraction and transportation. How, then, is it to be realized? What areas should be leased, at what royalty rate, and so on? We conclude with some suggestions on these matters from the economist's point of view, drawing also on some of the principles of regional development discussed earlier.

5. *Minerals Leasing Policy and Alaskan Regional Development*

The first question we should address is, whether or not there should be a policy of charging miners for the use of federal, state, or native lands? We said earlier that the related policy of charging for pollution would promote efficiency, but according to a well-known theorem, the same allocation of resources would result if the polluter had the rights to use of the environment, and was paid by others not to pollute.[9]

Changing liability, or property rights, would affect only the distribution of income. Similarly, it might be expected that charging miners a royalty or rent would not affect use of the land. It would still be employed in the use which maximized value, and only a certain amount of redistribution of income, perhaps better accomplished via an explicit policy for this purpose, would result.

Although the Coase theorem is well known, less well known is that it is applicable only under certain rather restrictive conditions, namely when transaction costs and income effects are negligible. In effect, assigning property rights to miners (as under the 1872 Mining Law) can lead to inefficient use of the public lands when—as is increasingly common— mining is not the highest valued use, but the costs of gathering together all of the thousands of affected parties to buy out a mining claim are very high—or more than they can afford to pay.[10] The situation is the same with respect to pollution (with the exception discussed also by Coase of producer-to-producer spill-overs, for which transaction costs and consumer income effects are not relevant). There seems to be a case, then, for a policy of charging for environmental modification and extraction of mineral resources, along with careful benefit-cost analyses of alternative uses of land. Also, though this is not subject to proof, it seems desirable that the

159

rents for scarce mineral resources on their lands should go to the native population or Alaskans generally. As noted above, present leasing arrangements for oil and gas do work this way, and access to the metallic minerals, though still typically free under the 1872 Mining Law, seems to be moving in this direction.

Although there are many varieties of leasing arrangements employed, in the U.S. at least the essence of the system is bidding by mining firms for a lease to a tract of land which confers exclusive rights to the mineral, say oil, there, subject to the payment of a royalty on production. The royalty is a fraction, often around 1/8 to 1/6, of the gross revenues from sale of the mineral, and the amount bid is called the lease bonus. In principle, the objective of the public agency or native regional corporation is, or should be, maximization of the combined sum of bonus and royalty payments (net of environmental costs, which we ignore for the moment). The policy instrument for this purpose can be the setting of the royalty rate. But since the royalty payments are received over a long period of time and are uncertain, it may not be obvious how the rate should be set to maximize rent. In what follows, we offer some guidelines.[11]

Suppose the public agency is less concerned than the typical private mining firm with a quick return from exploitation of the site. This seems a realistic proposition since the government (or native regional corporation) is in the position of a steward of resources for future generations, as the private firm is not. Then a given *future* return from the mine would be worth more to the government. Put another way, the return is discounted at a lower rate (of interest). The government discount rate might be low relative to the private firm's for another reason as well. The private firm would likely be more risk-averse, requiring a higher premium for risk-bearing in the form of a higher discount rate.[12] Now, to the extent that future returns are less heavily discounted by the government for the reasons given above, a higher royalty rate would be desirable. This gives the government a larger stake in the long-lived investment, without unduly reducing the lease bonus it receives, since the firm's bonus bid will be relatively unaffected by loss on an increment of future income. In the limit, the government might set the royalty rate at 100 per cent, in effect assuming the role of entrepreneur, hiring factors of production to exploit the mineral deposit on its property. Against the gains from this policy would have to be balanced the possibly undesirable aspects of government as opposed to private enterprise (bureaucratic inefficiency, and so on).

Apart from its differential effect on discount rates, uncertainty about returns from the mining operation should influence the choice of royalty rate for another reason. If the government is more optimistic than mining firms about the probability of discovery at a side, the size or richness of the strike or the price it will bring, a relatively high royalty rate is indicated.

160

Again, this gives an expected future return greater than the cost in fore-gone bonus. Where private firms seem more bullish, on the other hand—or, for that matter, more inclined to gamble—the rent-maximizing royalty rate is correspondingly reduced.

How much land, or how many tracts, should be leased at a given time? One consideration here is the owner's monopoly power, if any. Where the state of Alaska, for example, represents a substantial share in the supply of a resource to a market, it may realize greater returns by not opening up to development too much of the resource at any one time, i.e., by not "spoiling the market". Monopoly restriction of output, of which this is an example, is generally considered socially inefficient, but may not be in this case. Spreading out extraction over time is, after all, practicing resource conservation. To the extent that this is considered desirable, some element of monopoly return to the state may not be contrary to national policy.

Another influence on the rate and pattern of leasing is the effect of experience with earlier leases on expectations, and hence bids, for new leases. Exploration by the leaseholder develops information about prospects for other tracts. A favourable outcome in one is likely to result in higher bids for others close by or in a similar geological configuration. Certainly this has occurred in the leasing of North Slope oil tracts in Alaska. One counter consideration here is that exploration may be less vigorous if a firm expects that much of the benefit will accrue to others. Large lease blocks may be desirable for this reason.[13]

How do environmental effects fit into the rent-maximizing framework? Our earlier discussion of the desirability of polluter liability is applicable here, and should lead to more stringent control of pipeline breaks, oil spills, acid mine drainage, and so on, as well as compensation to the victims of these effects. In cases where potential environmental damages are very great, or returns from the mining operation marginal, firms may not find it profitable to bid for development rights to a site, and it would remain unmodified.

It is not only the incidental effects of commercial resource development that should be taken account of. Suppose a mineral deposit, a stand of timber, or a site for hydroelectric power production, is also valuable in its natural state, i.e., if not modified for any of these purposes. Minerals and timber often occur in scenic mountain areas, and a hydroelectric site may be a free flowing stream suitable for inclusion in the national Wild and Scenic Rivers System. Loss of the recreation and other values associated with unspoiled natural environments is, or should be, just as much a consideration as potential pollution damages in the decision whether to develop a site. In principle, efficient use of the environment would require that development take place only if the expected gains (*net* of pollution damages) are at least as great as the opportunity losses—the values that

161

are sacrificed by conversion of the environment to developmental purposes. We should acknowledge that both the theory and the practice of measuring these values are currently rather primitive. Hopefully this is due only to neglect, nearly total to date, and will be remedied by future research.[14]

We stated just above that an area should be opened up to development via minerals leasing only if the expected returns, the rents to the mineral, are at least as great as the environmental costs. Although this has to be true, given that the land manager's objective is to maximize net social returns, it conceals a point that is not obvious and should be made explicit. Earlier we spoke of long lasting or irreversible environmental damage. Where the magnitude of the damage, along with the returns from commercial development of a site, is uncertain, development may entail a cost —the loss of "option value"—in addition to the measured losses from the damage (and, of course, the direct resource costs). Option value, as the name suggests, is the value to an individual of an option to consume a good or service sometime in the future. One interpretation is that it is the amount he would pay to avoid the risk of not being able to consume, to assure the availability of the good should he demand it.[15]

Another interpretation, which does not depend on risk aversion, and instead makes use of a Bayesian approach, is the following. Suppose a public agency has under review an (otherwise profitable) activity which will result in the irreversible loss of a natural environment. Suppose, further, that the passage of time results in new information about the benefits of alternative uses—development or preservation—of the environment. Since this information can be taken into account only if the irreversible decision has been deferred, there is a value to refraining from development. Conversely, development entails a cost—the loss of this option value.[16] One important implication for leasing policy is that development of different sources of energy (or for that matter other materials) should be sequenced in a way that permits planners to take account of new information about the full social costs of each.

6. Conclusion

The main point of this paper is that Alaska presents an unusual challenge to the U.S. and to the world to use its non-renewable fossil fuels and other natural resources in ways, and at rates of use, which reflect maturity and responsibility with respect to the rights not only of current generations, but of future generations, not only of those who will use the resource, and gain from its exploitation, but also of those on whose land it has been found. Perhaps then Alaska offers the first and last great opportunity, at

162

least for us in the U.S., to perceive regional development not only as a process of exploiting the earth, but of achieving a new balance between the claims of economic development and those of social and environmental responsibility.

Notes

1. John H. Cumberland, *Regional Development Experiences and Prospects in the United States of America,* Mouton, Paris, 1971, Chapter 11, "The Special Case of Alaska".

2. For a discussion of the special problems for planning posed by environmental losses of extremely long duration, with particular reference to the Alaskan environment, see John Krutilla and Anthony Fisher, *The Economics of National Environments: Studies in the Valuation of Commodity and Amenity Resources,* Johns Hopkins University Press, Baltimore, 1975, Chapter 3, "Irreversibility and the Optimal Use of Natural Environments", and Chapter 10, "The Trans-Alaska Pipeline: Environmental Consequences and Alternatives".

3. The situation is described in moving detail by Harry Caudill, *Night Comes to the Cumberlands,* Little, Brown and Co., Boston, 1963.

4. *The Wall Street Journal* of June 10, 1974 carries a story which indicates that Ataturk, the founder of modern Turkey, was advised back in 1923 not to locate his capital in Ankara, then a city of 30,000 because the enclosed (by mountains) site would give rise to serious air pollution if the city grew much. The advice was ignored and Ankara is one of the world's most polluted cities, even without the effects of substantial auto traffic or heavy industry.

5. The efficiency properties of pollution charges, or effluent fees, are now well-known to economists. Although many have contributed to the literature here, the work of Allen Kneese might be singled out. See, for example, Allen V. Kneese and Blair T. Bower, *Managing Water Quality: Economics, Technology, Institutions,* Johns Hopkins University Press, Baltimore, 1968.

6. This approach is put forward and discussed in John H. Cumberland, *op. cit.*

7. The materials balance approach, which stresses the pervasiveness of residuals in the economy, was developed in a seminal article by Robert U. Ayres and Allen V. Kneese, "Production, Consumption, and Externalities", *American Economic Review,* June 1969, pp. 282-297.

8. See John H. Cumberland and Robert J. Korbach, "A Regional Inter-Industry Environmental Model," *Regional Science Association Papers,* 1973, Volume XXX, pp. 61-75.

9. See Ronald Coase, "The Problem of Social Cost", *Journal of Law and Economics,* October, 1960, pp. 1-44.

10. This assumes that the non-mining values are not easily capitalized.

11. This discussion is based in part on an unpublished NSF grant proposal by Hayne E. Leland and Scott R. Pearson, "The Economic Consequences of Alternative Leasing Policies for Alaska's Natural Resources", Stanford Uni-

163

versity, 1974, and on conversations with Professor Leland.

12. For a review of the discount rate literature, including a discussion of the reasons why government would be less risk-averse than private firms, see Krutilla and Fisher, *op. cit.*, Chapter 4.

13. The "information spillover" in petroleum exploration and its implications for policy are discussed by Frederick M. Peterson, "Two Externalities in Petroleum Production", Study for the Ford Foundation Energy Policy Project, published in Gerard M. Brannon (ed.), *Studies in Energy Taxation,* Ballinger Publishing Co., Cambridge, Mass., 1975.

14. The only organized research effort we are aware of which addresses itself to the issue of valuing the amenity resources of natural environments, and integrating these values into a theoretical resource allocation framework, is the Natural Environments Program at Resources for the Future, Inc. For a statement of results in theory and method obtained in this program, along with some examples of empirical studies, see Krutilla and Fisher, *op. cit.*

15. Option value was first discussed by Burton Weisbrod, "Collective Consumption Services of Individual Consumption Goods", *Quarterly Journal of Economics,* August, 1964, pp. 471-77. It is further discussed and the relation to conventional consumer surplus clarified by Charles Cicchetti and A. Myrick Freeman, "Option Demand and Consumer Surplus: Further Comments", *Quarterly Journal of Economics,* August, 1971, pp. 528-39.

16. See Kenneth Arrow and Anthony Fisher, "Environmental Preservation, Uncertainty, and Irreversibility", *Quarterly Journal of Economics,* May, 1974, pp. 312-319.

II

THE EASTERN COUNTRIES

THE EASTERN COUNTRIES: INTRODUCTION

In the history of planning as an instrument of promoting economic, social and political progress, the role of the socialist countries is of special importance both from the theoretical and from the practical point of view. The planning system in the Soviet Union and Eastern Europe is a dynamic phenomenon in which the experience of the past is integrated with new approaches towards the future. In this context regional planning is not autonomous or isolated, but is rather an integral part of the general system of socio-economic planning. This macro-economic, macro-social and macro-political approach to regional planning is the fundamental leitmotiv in the eight papers presented in the second part of this volume, and it is particularly evident in the papers by Secomski, Granberg, Bandman, Gruchman, and Pavlov, which view the regional dimension of the planning system in theoretical, empirical and technical perspectives.

An important shift in the approach to the spatial element in the process of policy and planning is noted by Secomski, who writes:

There has been a fundamental change in views on the role of the factor of space. The traditional approach, which consisted in locating facts, events, processes and decisions in space which in itself was passive and a mere resultant of other factors, is no longer considered to be sound ... Nowadays the element of space plays a very active part in determining the dynamics of economic growth and social development, particularly as far as quantitative and structural transformations are concerned.

This generalization of Secomski's directs our attention to the second important feature of regional planning in the Eastern countries. This is the comprehensive character of this activity, involving the integrated consideration of economic, social, political and institutional factors. Special attention to the social and institutional factors is seen in the papers by Khodhzaev, Pokshishevski, and Rybicki, which analyze the problems of urbanization and spatial organization in these countries. The theoretical and practical experiences of the socialist countries in this field lead Rybicki to formulate the following generalization:

167

The traditional term "territorial division" should be replaced by the term "territorial structure of the country" under the conditions prevailing now. That is so because the units of the territorial division have become today not only the basis of the operation of the agencies of public administration but also a basis of the operation of local authorities, units of civil and political organization as well as economic and technical institutions.

This generalization of Rybicki is indirectly indicating that the spatial organization of socialist and capitalist countries has different features following the differences in the fundamental assumption of these two systems.

The international aspect of the problem is discussed in the paper of Pavlov where we find the following statement:

"The study of territorial problems arising in the socialist economic integration of the SEV member states is now in the initial stage. With the adoption of the complex program envisaging the further confirmation and improvement of cooperation and development of the socialist economic integration of the SEV member states, the influence of foreign economic relations in the distribution of the productive forces of the USSR and other socialist countries is intensified. Consequently, an important task of economics is the study of the regional problems of socialist economic integration, and of the regularities governing the creation, development and distribution of the productive forces of the combined international economy of the SEV member countries."

These papers do not, of course, constitute a full presentation of the strengths and weaknesses of the experiences of the socialist countries in the field of regional planning. However, they are a good introduction to the field. A more comprehensive discussion of these problems and issues can be found in the following recently published studies:

1. N. N. Nekrasov, *The Territorial Organization of the Soviet Economy,* Progress Publishers, Moscow, 1974.
2. Kazimierz Secomski, ed., *Spatial Planning and Policy: Theoretical Foundations,* Polish Scientific Publishers, Warsaw, 1974.
3. Antoni R. Kukliński, ed., *Regional Disaggregation of National Policies and Plans,* UNRISD-Mouton Regional Planning Series, Vol. 8, Paris and The Hague, 1975.

Antoni R. Kukliński

1

THE MODERN THEORY OF SPACE ECONOMY: PROBLEMS AND TRENDS IN THE SOCIALIST COUNTRIES

Kazimierz Secomski

The most striking features of the present social and economic situation are the dynamic way in which development is taking place and the profoundness and all-inclusiveness of the related structural changes.

The emergence of the theory of socio-economic growth and the subsequent and continuing improvement of its definitions have been helping to reveal more accurately the regularities that occur in the process of growth, to explain its trends and meaning, to formulate findings concerning the rate of growth, and to define the structure of the process of growth in terms of both quantity and quality. This involves the necessity of anticipating the future, occasionally the very distant future, for only thus is it possible to assess the current developmental processes adequately in their totality, as viewed against a close and against a distant time-horizon.

Such analyses, assessments, and findings are, of course, extremely complex, because they have to include a very broad range of phenomena, facts and processes that occur in all domains of social and economic life as well as their mutual relationships and interdependencies. It is obvious, though, that no approach to the social and economic structure of today can be adequate unless it simultaneously introduces prospective elements that make possible a critical comparison between the present and the anticipated future state.

Both spatial planning and the development of concepts for the spatial structure of the national economy have a long tradition and many noticeable achievements. The emergence and subsequent refinement of methods for the presentation of spatial patterns to appear in the distant future has contributed substantially to an increase in the quality and precision of the studies prepared on local as well as on regional and national scales.

By their very nature transformations of the spatial structure of the national economy occur at a relatively slow rate and thus both the policies and the planning of spatial changes involve the perspective and even the supra-perspective period. Only a very long time-horizon permits bringing about basic transformations of the existing spatial problems. For the needs of the current socio-economic policies it is indispensable to have such a model of the desired future spatial structure in order to be able to actively influence the developmental processes in the close and intermediate time-horizons in accordance with the envisaged profound and comprehensive structural transformations to be effected in the long time-horizon.

Thus it is evident that the spatial structure of the national economy, and especially its modelling, is inextricably bound up with the planning of growth and of its changes in the distant future. This feature, so characteristic of spatial planning, involves an inherent difficulty and a danger. Not only an excessively one-sided but also just a functional approach to the form and the substance of the planned very long-term spatial systems may blind us to the realities of the national economy, or to the desired trends and speed of social development.

For these reasons, the most crucial problem of the theory of space economy is how it can be blended together with the theory of socio-economic growth and how the combined theories can then be used in the search for new ideas, by adopting a comprehensive approach to the total body of the economic and social phenomena and processes of development. In fact, the regularities of the present growth cannot be adequately exposed unless the manifold social, economic and spatial aspects that are involved are taken into account. Furthermore, each of these aspects sometimes has a diverse effect on the developmental process, accompanied by the previously described inter-dependencies and feedback relationships. A fundamental principle of the integration of social, economic and spatial planning was thus established, and it has already found wide application in the practice of planning.

The development of spatial planning and studies of perspective and supra-perspective models and spatial systems were in this way given a stimulus as well as a new considerably broadened socio-economic content for further exploration. If it is recalled that the theories of economic growth and social development have made rapid progress in recent decades, it becomes obvious that an extension of the forms, directions and substance of spatial planning is of paramount importance. In some fields of activity, spatial planning has engendered the development of programming and socio-economic planning. At present, however, it is again the planning of economic growth and social development that gives powerful incentives to the development of spatial planning.

This is a consequence of the rapid development of a new field of projections applied to population problems, science and technology, and social and economic life. The visions of the developed socialist society and modern economy created for 1990 and 2000 have been so attractive that

170

they have resulted in a systematic extension of studies and research in the field of projections, in the refinement of methods applied and, finally, in scientifically acceptable projections of various kinds. These projections have become the initial and indispensable link in the whole body of planning socio-economic development.

It has often been emphasized that all phenomena and all growth and developmental processes occur in space. This fact furnished an adequate justification for treating spatial planning and the future spatial structure as a point of departure or as a foundation for general economic planning.

The present tackling of these problems testifies to further progress in developing an integrated approach to projecting and planning. The national economy comprises within its scope an immense number of fields and their specific internal developmental processes, and hence it should be treated as an inherently interrelated economic unity. Similarly, it is necessary to look upon the developing socialist society in a comprehensive integrated manner, notwithstanding the many diverse phenomena and processes which together constitute the successive phases and stages of social development. Furthermore, it is nowadays impossible to separate economic or social projections from planning, and to separate social from economic policies. Now, the fundamental factor of space should be fused into this network of interrelationships, including its essential role in the current economic and social developments. In addition, prognoses concerning various demographic and scientific-technological problems constitute a further element of the integrated approach to the total body of developmental processes. This approach can be eventually said to consist of the following operations in their temporal succession: the forecasting, the programming, and the planning of the total body of phenomena in space.

The most general conclusion to be made about the modern problems and trends in the theory of space economy is therefore that this theory has furnished both a source of, and a model for, new fruitful scientific studies. Many projections as well as researches in the theory of socio-economic development have subsequently laid down new directions for spatial studies, and have given the theory of space economy new problems to be solved, or have brought about the need to review earlier studies thoroughly or to extend them.

It has, in summary, become indispensable to coordinate the efforts of many disciplines of science as this is the only way to arrive at comprehensive proposals contributing to the achievement of goals set for socio-economic development which comprise, in particular, demographic, scientific-technological, economic, social, and spatial aspects.

There has been a fundamental change in views on the role of the factor of space. The traditional approach, which consisted in locating facts, events, processes and decisions in space which in itself was passive and a mere resultant of other factors, is no longer considered to be sound. Certainly, it was necessary in the past to take into account the character and suitability of an area for various uses, but these were supplementary premisses emerging in the course of the process of conscious decision-making. Quite a number of developmental processes and changes were occurring without having had their spatial aspects taken into consideration. The uncontrolled character of this type of events occasionally led even to evident drawbacks and to violations of the tenets of rational space policy.

Nowadays the element of space plays a very active part in determining the dynamics of economic growth and social development, particularly as far as qualitative and structural transformations are concerned. It is unquestionable now that by making use of the factor of space in a rational way, various essential advantages can be achieved which, taken in their totality, stimulate socio-economic development and contribute to its optimalization in a broad sense of this term.

Though this abandonment of a passive in favour of an active approach to the factor of space is at present a common practice, it is still necessary to carry out intensive studies on the improvement of the different methods of making economic use of space, i.e. how to influence the social and economic processes occuring in a given space in accordance with established goals and in an optimal way. Even the already accepted terms and principles of general and detailed location tend to acquire new meanings and require continuing improvement.

This is largely due to the advance of science and technology. In particular, technological achievements account for many fundamental revisions of views on the different uses of space and open up new possibilities of integrating it with developmental processes. The arguments, often related to the perspective visions of socio-economic development, that one occasionally encounters to the effect that space will become irrelevant because travelling speeds will become so high that space will play only an insignificant—if any—role in performing actions or decision-making, often seem to be exaggerated. It is obvious that the importance of new scientific-technical achievements must not be underrated, but definite social and economic processes will stil necessarily take place in space, and hence the most efficient uses of this element wil have to be permanently devised to speed up and improve processes of growth and development.

One of the essential achievements of the post-war period of planning is the supremacy of comprehensive locational decisions. To put it in simple terms, this denotes passing from the location of individual structures or industrial plants to the location of whole groups of structures, industrial complexes, or clusters of enterprises. The application of the latter method results in a change of the total body of problems involved in the optimal extension of the transport system serving the supplementary investments, in planning of service facilities to cater for a group of enterprises, and in comprehensive planning of settlements, centres, whole districts or nodal urban-industrial agglomerations.

There is no doubt that it is in this domain that we are witnessing the outstanding achievements of the post-war development of planning and, at the same time, uncovering great mistakes and numerous shortcomings. This is not to say that there were no achievements or deficiencies in the past. Undoubtedly there were, but it is necessary to remember that the scale and dynamics of the processes of socio-economic growth, and the scope of structural transformations, are much greater today than in the past.

This is the reason why the necessity of applying a fundamentally different approach to locational decisions, of treating them in a much more comprehensive and integrated way, and of putting spatial problems into the proper scale and scope, has become so conspicuous.

The high rate and the complex character of the current developments result in a profound change in views on many aspects of the selection of location. Compared with the present situation, the role of the time element was different under conditions of slow expansion of individual settlements, towns, and even the largest urban-industrial agglomerations. The unprecedented intensification of urbanization processes, especially of the rate of growth of the biggest agglomerations, necessitates an entirely new approach to the element of time. A typical example is the policy of establishing land reserves for future construction in the rapidly developing towns, centres or industrial districts. The time lag between the moment of acquisition of land and the actual expansion of residential districts and whole new settlements is quickly decreasing. There is a major difference in the results of the analysis of the economic and social effectiveness of land reservation when applied to a slow or to a rapid process of the extension of settlement network and its constituting links. The advance of technology and the expectations relating to its further achievements clearly play an important role here.

If no more than the above considerations are taken into account it is evident that the estimate of land value may differ very much, depending on how far the land in question is situated away from a given plant, city district, or city core. The notion of land price in general, and the price of a particular building site in particular, assumes a much broader significance. The meanings of such concepts as the quantity and size of land suitable for various purposes as well as its quality looked upon from different points of view are nowadays different. Whether a site is suitable or not for a specific use cannot be defined by virtue of an individual characteristic alone; additional criteria relating to the settlement, the region, and even to the country as a whole must also be considered. Spatial policies and planning are continuously enriching the set of criteria for socio-economic evaluation and they provide, moreover, a permanent testing of their sequence and hierarchy.

If we now proceed to point out the clearest trends in spatial structure policies, we see that the most striking factor here is undoubtedly the current effort to construct a model of the spatial system of the settlement network. The framework of spatial system in which the big urban-industrial agglomerations constitute the main or leading nodes, linked by a system of technical infrastructure, is now becoming the point of departure for defining the general directions of the development of socio-economic policies and planning. Obviously, in actual practice entirely new facts or circumstances as well as new factors of the socio-economic growth may emerge; in such cases additional nodes or belts have to be created and these modify or transform the original spatial system. Moreover, we should not forget the important problems of finding appropriate ways to stimulate the pace of development and to utilize the space extending between the nodes and the belts so as to fill up the entire territory, i.e. including the areas outside the agglomerations.

The great advance in science and technology has a powerful impact on the pattern and character of the biggest urban-industrial agglomerations. Under such circumstances, it is bold concepts of modernizing and optimizing development of major concentrations of population, industrial establishments, and service centres in spatial terms that become a major problem in the present trends of spatial planning. It is very often pointed out that it is just in the biggest urban-industrial agglomerations that conditions for a particularly rapid development of science and technology arise. The centres of higher education, scientific and research institutes as well as the many laboratories, design offices, and similar units working on behalf of the industries, today lend a specific character to the big urban-industrial agglomerations and decide upon the dynamics and directions of their development. The most advanced branches of industry, such as electronics or automatics, tend to characterize the dynamically developing urban-industrial agglomerations. Thus the most complex problems both of modern spatial planning and of the planning of socio-economic development converge in agglomerations.

Among the fundamental problems of modern spatial planning we should also mention the growing scope of planning of industrial centres and industrial estates. Whereas formerly industrial centres were emerging and developing in an uncontrolled and chaotic way characteristic of the capitalist economy, at present the proper approach to a planned development of urban-industrial centres is generally accepted—even in the capitalist countries—as an indisputable achievement of spatial and socio-economic policies.

However, practical experience has often shown that the actual uses of space in the rapidly developing urban-industrial centres and areas may considerably deviate from the optimizing assumptions included in the plans. Multi-year and long-term (i.e. perspective) development pro-grammes and plans of such districts are worked out. Emphasis is put on simultaneous construction of industrial establishments, social centres, and technical facilities. High priority is granted to the comprehensive and pur-poseful development of large parts of the country designated for indus-rialization. In spite of these efforts, critical appraisals of the development principles included in the plan, and subsequent appraisal of the results obtained in practice, disclose many flaws and even growing disproportions. This suggests both an imperfection and imprecision of spatial plans and indicate that there is no consistent and systematic implementation of these plans.

The protection of the natural environment on a global scale has recently become the most frequently discussed problem. Obviously the importance of this problem differs, depending on whether it occurs in the most ad-vanced, in the relatively well developed, or in the developing countries. For there are considerable differences both as regards the already known harmful consequences of the lack of consistent policies in environmental protection, and as regards the prospects for a constructive approach to the policies of spatial development of a country.

But irrespective of the degree of importance of these problems to each country it is imperative to chart the development and protection of in-dispensable recreation areas, taking into account the growing mass-scale participation in tourism and organized holidays. It is particularly essential to delimit—both in the perspective and in the supra-perspective range—and consistently protect the major national recreation areas to serve the needs of the whole country, its regions, and especially the bigger cities and concentrations of urban population. These recreation areas of different categories which have to satisfy the needs of short and longer rest are a condition for the adequate development of the rapidly industralizing countries. Special protection must also be granted to areas of particular natural beauty and to historical monuments. Finally, it must be added that there is a hierarchy of areas established in accordance with their inter-national, national or local significance.

Our analysis of the current trends in the theory of space economy must not disregard the importance of historical studies. Such studies should not be confined to the limits of the town, region, or country concerned. It is a

175

commonplace to say that each spatial structure now in existence is a result of human activities and developmental processes that took place in the past. This fact must be constantly borne in mind when considering both the spatial pattern of the whole national economy and the picture of the spatial structure of individual settlements, areas, or regions.

A given type of spatial structure is often defined to be more advanced or less advanced judging by the adopted socio-economic and spatial criteria. The analysis of an existing spatial structure reveals its considerable disproportions, both internal and external, as well as structural defects and flaws. Hence the significance of historical studies.

These studies may furnish a thorough explanation of how the studied spatial pattern was developing and extending, what were its constituent elements and when they appeared, why the spatial pattern developed in such and no other directions, and of the reasons for the disproportions revealed now. This type of studies permits us to formulate preliminary conclusions indicating the necessity and scope of the measures to be applied in order to overcome or perhaps only to attenuate the internal deficiencies of the spatial structure in question.

This, however, does not suffice and therefore we tend as a rule to develop comparative studies comprising the historical and international aspects. By comparing different spatial patterns of specific historical periods, or from different countries, we can formulate conclusions and suggestions in a much more comprehensive and diversified form. These fall into two groups:

1) How to improve the existing spatial structure utilizing the experience that results from the historical and international patterns; and

2) How to avoid the earlier inherent deficiencies or disproportions, and even how to combine rationally the elimination of disclosed deficiencies with the optimalization or improvement processes taking place within the new spatial structure.

The above historical and—subsequently—comparative studies, which may also refer to the international level, must now be complemented by prognostic studies. In this kind of studies we attempt to define the optimal spatial structure for the next 20-30 years or even beyond that period, and then draw the pertinent conclusions for the current activities. Accordingly, we obtain new and valuable comparative information which may be of essential significance for the perspective tenets of the spatial policies.

It is not sufficient to analyse and study the past, that is the total of all phenomena and causes that taken together are responsible for the development of the spatial pattern as it is today. Nor is it sufficient to carry out critical re-appraisals or comparisons of the studied spatial structure with their counterparts in other historical periods or in other more advanced countries, although these comparisons often lead to valuable conclusions concerning solutions of specific problems in space economy as applied in other countries. Today it is also necessary to outline the distant long-run perspectives of the model or ideal spatial pattern under the future socio-economic conditions, which will satisfy different and qualitatively higher needs of the advanced socialist society and its modern economy. It is only in this way that the present day and its needs can be adequately associated with the long-run development perspective and the resulting perspective needs.

All the above problems are of crucial importance for the practice of spatial planning. It is understandable that the current policies of space economy as well as the systematic improvement of the spatial structure are to a broad extent based upon cost-benefit analysis.

For these reasons, those policies seem to be especially effective which are intended to purposefully complement the existing spatial structure and to contribute to its modernization. The effectiveness of expenditures on the complementary spatial links, i.e. on the "rounding up" of nodes and belts of technical infrastructure which constitute the given spatial belt, becomes conspicuous. What results in this case is that the areas directly surrounding the given node or belt are made accessible and ready for early development at a low cost.

In another category from the point of view of economic effectiveness are the policies of space that are implemented to effect a partial transformation of the existing spatial structure. That transformation is also often associated with the emergence of new elements of spatial structure, which in consequence necessitates a transformation or selective development of a given part of the spatial pattern, i.e. one of its nodes or belts, in a specific direction. Accordingly, bigger expenditures prove to be indispensable, but they do result in higher effectiveness, though in purely economic terms this is as a rule lower than the particularly high effectiveness obtained when actions aimed only at complementing, slightly extending, or modernizing the given node or belt are undertaken.

The third and final category of transformations of the spatial structure consists of those that result in its major reconstruction; this happens when the objective is to ensure a similarity between the spatial structure to be transformed and the (long- or middle-range) model of the national spatial structure. This falls into the domain of multi-year and perspective spatial policy which is consistently aimed at implementation of the principal tenets of the spatial structure of the national economy.

All the above remarks, together with the division of the policies into complementation and modernization, transformation, and major reconstruction of the spatial structure apply both to the country as a whole and to its individual regions and, subsequently, even to its specific areas, towns and settlements. In any case it is justified and useful to consider thoroughly

177

the economic cost and effects; such an analysis will be of help in defining the sequence of the intended actions to be taken with regard to the space economy and with regard to the rational development of specific areas.

To systematize somewhat the development principles of space economy and the resulting spatial patterns, we can distinguish between those that concern the objectives of economic growth and those that concern the objectives of social development. That is to say, the economic criteria pertaining to the association of economic activities with space are different from the social criteria and premises that associate social and cultural development with spatial units.

Though this distinction between the two categories of criteria is fully justified, it is nevertheless necessary to keep in mind the integrated character of space economy and the comprehensive processes of development that we have already stressed; accordingly, analyses and evaluations of the optimalization of the spatial pattern must be made together both for the needs of economic growth and for those of social development. Obviously, whether the economic or the social aspect will be given predominance will vary from case to case, depending on the specific conditions or on the phase of development. Here, too, the effect of the time factor is conspicuous. This, however, does not mean that the premises of either of the two categories, i.e. the economic or the social, may be ignored. What does become very important is to determine the cost or level of expenditures and the obtained effect. The notion of cost in the economic or in the social sense is not always easy to define as the calculations or evaluations made are often merely estimates. Moreover, it is often difficult to obtain comparable results in calculating the cost as applied to economic and social criteria.

The trends toward minimizing the expenditures or the level of costs defined by virtue of economic and social criteria are generally regarded as significant. In addition, the time factor, i.e. the distribution over time of the volume and kind of the necessary expenditures and their comparison with the dates of obtaining economic and social effects, is also included. The element of time cannot always be introduced into the calculation proper or into accurate comparisons of the magnitude of the necessary expenditures with the expected effects.

It follows that it is occasionally necessary to employ at best approximate results of the analyses made or the comparative evaluations. We should also take into account how the intended action and the magnitude of the intended expenditures involved may affect the given or the closest stage of the resulting changes in the spatial structure, and influence the implementation of its ultimate model.

Among the most difficult analyses are the qualitatively diversified

178

evaluations in which we consider consecutively:

1. The criteria employed by the respective unit, e.g. a factory, when it is making a decision concerning the development of a given area;

2. The criteria and premisses introduced on a broader scale when formulating local development plans;

3. The assumptions, premisses and criteria pertaining to the process of working out the regional plan and constituting the foundation of its development principles; and

4. The general directions, assumptions, premisses and criteria which constitute the point of departure for drawing up the national plan.

Such evaluations indicate that the same decision may be viewed from various angles. An approach restricted to only one set of criteria, however perfect such an approach may be in itself, may lead to actions that are obviously wrong from the standpoint of the intentions as expressed in the local, regional, or national plans. It often happens that even by integrating only the different premisses for the intended decisions from several units, plants or establishments, we arrive at a conclusion that a joint capital investment providing services and facilities to all units involved is purposeful and economically justified.

It is easy to give examples of such evaluations or conclusions. Too often though, we come across the adverse consequences of there being no evaluation or analysis made on any more comprehensive ground. Thus it is necessary to emphasize constantly the indispensability of integrated calculations and integrated treatment of cost at different spatial scales and against the background of combining the economic and social premisses of development.

In conclusion it may be observed that in comparison with different indices of economic growth and social development as well as in comparison with unitary criteria versus those on a local, regional or national scale, the citeria and premisses described above can be divided into the following categories:

1. Identical or very approximate criteria;

2. Convergent criteria which indicate the same direction though occasionally may betray considerable differences as regards the expected expenditures or effects; and

3. Divergent criteria, betraying major differences, which point to entirely different directions or are distinctly contradictory to each other— whether in their contents or in the effects and directions of development.

It is generally accepted that the basic purpose of all spatial planning is to coordinate the total complex of all activities in a given area and to make them optimally purposeful. This can be tested by checking whether what has been obtained is indeed the best result in the form of a planned spatial structure of the national economy and its constituent elements.

Essentially, spatial phenomena can be purposefully influenced by skilful handling of a great number of decisions made by individuals, by particular local and regional organizations, and by the central authorities of the country, according to a spatial development plan which, though comprising some modifiable elements, is still obligatory. Taking as a point of departure the notion that the objective and the task is to influence human activities in space to take place in a planned manner, we have to consider in practice the different degrees of precision and elasticity of specific decisions contained in the plans of different levels. Moreover, irrespective of the adopted decisions of the plan, various circumstances may accompany the implementation of the approved plans or their outlines and this, in turn, may result in certain discrepancies between correct theoretical solutions and their practical materialization, i.e. between spatial planning and the policies employed for its implementation.

This is also due to the general differences between the objective, i.e. the definition of what we want and intend to achieve, and those factors which influence the current implementation process, the latter being often dependent upon the means and measures that are used and on organizational efficiency.

Space economy used to be understood in functional terms. This is especially true of the organization of the process of production and services in space, while studies concerning the organization of the consumption process and the determination of living conditions were undertaken from the spatial point of view.

Such an approach obviously involves a very complex set of problems connected with the optimal utilization of space. In particular, the production and service processes can be linked either with analyses of utilizing space within the given plant only or with analyses that take into account the areas reserved for the plant's further growth. Other premises pertain to the spatial problems of the organization of production and services on a higher level of spatial planning, namely within the given city or urban-industrial centre. Further elements as well as extended criteria for analysis and comparison are associated with the study of the spatial structure as related to the organization of production and service processes in the region. Finally, the highest level of generalization is obtained in studying the spatial problems of the organization of the production processes and services on the national scale, also taking respective international links into consideration.

What is essential here is primarily the introduction of additional premises which in the course of the analysis reveal the inherent contradictions. This happens when the vested interests of a given plant or a given branch are weighed against the interest of the town or the urban-industrial centre concerned, and, subsequently, against those of the whole region or country. Under such conditions it is indispensable to search for optimum solutions from the standpoint of adequate policies of space utilization designed to provide the most appropriate spatial structure, beginning with local plans and proceeding with regional and then national plans.

The planned economy creates favourable conditions for a wide utilization of comprehensive analysis and permits the removal of contradictions as soon as they begin to arise; this is done by employing social criteria and premises, keeping in view the established goals of socio-economic development.

What the theory of space economy is at present confronted with is primarily the problem of how to integrate the questions of economic growth with those of social development in relation to space. It is now imperative to accomplish a close integration of the economic and social factors of development of the national economy and of society. This requires a well-timed, if not simultaneous, solving of the developmental processes constituting the economic and the social aspects. Within a given area both economic and social problems should be solved simultaneously, at least in their conceptual framework. The problems common to the two cases of the developmental processes must not be neglected even in cases of expedient decision making, when social matters may strongly differ from the economic ones.

It is especially worth pointing out that the direct integration of the qualitative and structural transformations in the spatial aspects is inescapable. Today it is impossible to dissociate the successive changes in the nation's economic structure from the directly ensuing transformations of the socio-occupational structure. These two categories of structural change affect each other and they must be consistently interrelated. Accordingly, their spatial reflection should be integrated.

The time factor is here again an additional intervening element. The sequence of economic and social changes implies definite time segments, that is to say the dates marking the onset or advance of the structural changes in the economy or in social life are spanned by only very small intervals. These phenomena, however, should by no means invalidate the principle of observing the unity and integrity of solutions of spatial problems for the needs of the economic and social aspects of development and structural changes. Some differences in treating the two kinds of developments in space may nevertheless result because the tasks involved in the perspective plan may be of such a scale and have such successive stages of structural transformations as would sometimes justify the more significant intervals between the dates of commencing or completing certain structural transformations in the economy and in society.

The dynamics of the present growth of the economy is apparent, among other ways, in the remarkable intensification of urbanization and industrialization processes in Poland. These processes lead to substantially more intensive land utilization and to a rapid take-over of very large areas for development purposes, and often they result in injudicous use of land. Even if concerted counteractions against these adverse phenomena are taken, their persistence is, in a sense, inescapable. Obviously, efforts are made to attenuate the adverse effects of these inadequacies. It is a task of the theory of space economy today not only to improve further many general studies and analyses but also to secure expeditious testing of theoretical ideas and conceptions in practice.

The most frequently raised issue in this respect recently has become that connected with the necessity of intensifying the protection of the environment. Many examples of notorious and often irreversible losses of essential environmental values and of the perceptible deterioration of the natural conditions in the world of today suggest that the efforts intended to secure the practical implementation of many theoretical conclusions should be substantially intensified.

Most valuable, from the practical point of view, have proved to be the studies concerning the prevention of air and water pollution. Some progress has also been achieved as regards the prevention of noise, both in workplaces and in residential buildings. The same can be said of the scientific methods of rational exploitation of the natural resources and of the restoration of the original environmental conditions after resources have been exhausted in a given place.

These unquestionably numerous examples of constructive human activity to combat environmental damage cannot, unfortunately, balance the much more numerous indicators of deterioration of natural conditions in many areas. When we consider that the rapid advance of the scientific and technical revolution results in a further intensification of the processes of economic growth and the accompanying transformation of natural conditions, the imminent danger for man's existence brought about by insufficient environmental protection becomes self-evident.

It is therefore indispensable to give high priority to such theoretical studies and technological innovations as are intended to offset the growing harmfulness of rapid industrialization processes. What is furthermore important is to secure the implementation of those scientific and technological achievements that may at least partly restore what has already been destroyed by technology and by the intensive urbanization and industrialization processes.

These actions are complemented by the various spatial planning activities aimed at a substantial extension of recreation and tourist areas as well as at a considerable extension of afforested areas, especially in the suburban zones which are recreational and regenerative hinterlands for

182

the population of the big urban-industrial agglomerations.

Thus the total body of problems involved in the man-environment relationship opens up new fields of research for the theory of space economy in closest association with a modern spatial organization of the processes of economic growth and social development. This applies in particular to the problems of development and structural transformations under conditions of rapid accretion of the diverse consequences of the scientific-technological revolution.

Within the framework of spatial studies, those devoted to regional policy and planning have enjoyed the most lively interest of researchers in recent years. This growing interest has its roots in the fact that the principles contained in regional plans are being fused with the practical activities of the local authorities. Practice itself imposes many urgent and essential problems both for theoretical studies and for their concrete solution in the course of regional developmental processes.

Among the most significant problems are those resulting from large-scale population migrations. Both in the developing and in the partly advanced countries, migrations from rural to urban areas are the most striking feature of the policy of defining the dynamics of regional growth and of regional structure. These migrations are attended by profound social changes and by complex sociological phenomena. Different field studies, especially dealing with the scale and dynamics of the social transformations in areas of intensive industrialization, have become very numerous. At the same time, the high rate at which the suburban and rural populations are coming to adopt the habits and way of life of urban areas is resulting in many socio-economic changes which also affect space economy.

At present a polycentric spatial pattern is being used on the regional scale as well as on the national scale. The practical consequence of adopting this principle is the development of existing and of new nodes in the form of urban-industrial centres and the reinforcement or extension of the infrastructure, especially of transport facilities, which constitute the belts necessary for the new polycentric pattern.

The policies of intensification of socio-economic growth involve a substantial extension of scientific and research centres and the problem of their spatial distribution. It is a condition of modern development as well as of the rapid advance of the scientific-technological revolution that strong centres, technology, and modern organization should be developing at a very quick rate. These tend to develop mostly in the large urban-industrial agglomerations. Due to natural conditions this applies to a large extent also to centres of higher education. Thus a broad scientific and technological basis constitutes an additional element of the rapid transformation of the economic and social structures as well as of the spatial structure.

183

Studies dealing with the spatial shifts of scientific research centres have become much more intense in recent years. In this connection, it is particularly worth emphasizing the accelerating effect that the high dynamics of the extension of scientific centres have on the modernization of the industrial structure, i.e. on the rate of development of those branches and industrial plants which perform a leading role in the modernization of the industry itself.

We must at the same time emphasize that the studies and researches that have been undertaken so far are insufficient. The same can be said of the conclusions for practice as regards the coordination of the dynamics and structure of development of all regions within the framework established in the national plan. On the one hand the determination of new directions of development for each region and the definition of their developmental pattern is still unsatisfactory, and on the other hand no significant achievements in the establishing of the elements of policies of cooperation of separate regions or their groups have so far been noted. Thus the determination of the assumptions and tenets of interregional planning which leads to highly effective cooperation between the regions has up to now not been satisfactory. On the contrary, too often we have to deal with exceedingly individualistic regional policies and with a similar approach to the determination of the spatial structure of a region, whose links with other regions and potentialities for cooperation are not taken into proper consideration.

Opinions are still being expressed—occasionally in an exaggerated form—on the need to increase the concentration of capital investment in order to accelerate the development of backward regions. As a rule, very limited approaches prevail that are most often connected with the need to make full use of the considerable increments of man-power resources on the spot or within the boundaries of the region concerned.

In this connection it is necessary to recall that concentration of capital investment in a given backward region is not the only way to ensure a rapid development of that backward region. Results of economic calculation show that it is more reasonable to contribute capital investments where they are likely to yield more immediate and substantial results for the entire national economy. The additional increment of investment will then call forth a more rapid development of the national economy as a whole and, whether directly or indirectly, will ultimately stimulate development of the backward regions too. This makes it possible to multiply the investment allotted to levelling out the living conditions of the whole nation in the spatial aspect.

In view of what has been said so far the fundamental importance of perspective regional plans is obvious. These plans, all of which stem from the perspective plan of the socio-economic development of the whole

184

national economy and the perspective plan of the spatial development of the country, provide a many-sided picture of the intentions, tasks and means at hand for comprehensive development and for the attenuation of interregional disproportions. In the case of Poland, whose small size should be borne in mind, we should not overestimate the existing regional disproportions, although it should be a permanent principle of multi-year and perspective planning to employ means aimed at an attenuation of such regional disproportions as exist.

It is also possible to consider the processes of the determination of the spatial structure in more general terms: objects versus space, and man versus space. The former pair of notions, referring mainly to the analysis of historical transformations of the spatial structure, has been widely discussed. The diverse manifestations of man's activities—especially in the form of the immense value of the fixed assets distributed all over the country in its regions and settlements—form historically the successive spatial patterns and add to their incessant improvement, notwithstanding some adverse effects. Simultaneously, to put it generally, the studies referring to objects versus space are very concrete in their character: they deal with the location processes of all kinds of fixed assets, with the resulting transport networks, belts of infrastructure, facilities, and nodes taking the form of settlements, entres, regions, or agglomerations. Here we find a very distinct reflection of the intensifying economic growth, especially in connection with the processes of industrialization and urbanization.

This traditional understanding of spatial transformations must, much more decidedly than has hitherto been the case, be opposed by the approach that concentrates on the relation man versus space. Too often this approach has challenged the traditional view only in the form of supplements, corrections or minor contributions, but what is needed is a more comprehensive analysis of the phenomena of social development. Obviously a major part of these problems have received attention, especially as regards the more striking phenomena such as large-scale shifts of population groups in space, rural-to-urban migrations, changes in life style in the towns, suburban zones, and rural areas, changes in the social structure of the population etc.

At present many more social and cultural phenomena are being emphasized. Man's attitudes, needs and new interests in the developing socialist society are subject to study. We are creating a new vision of our society and its constituent elements in the year 2000. At the same time we should take into account the essential points of the socio-economic changes in the particular regions and urban centres. The modern development processes are marked by the growing role of face-to-face contacts and other human relations. The intensity of these phenomena has grown considerably and has become decisive for economic and social progress. The development of abundant information flows, the direct transmission of the experience of technical and organizational innovations, as well as other forms of direct and efficient contact among people and social and economic organizations, are often mentioned as main factors stimulating modernization of development. Thus in effect what we have here are the accumulating phenomena of the accelerated development of more advanced links of a spatial pattern. These trends are reinforced by the social processes, including the growing rate of development of centres of scientific and technological research. Thus we now encounter a growing impact of human attitudes on changes in the spatial structure. This new approach to spatial transformations requires the initiation or essential development of studies of a different type, namely of studies with a distinctly sociological background. This is especially true of working and living conditions and of the changing needs and habits of people in the big industrial agglomerations, taking into account the problems of recreation of mass-scale automobile tourism. When opening a new or, more strictly, a more comprehensively conceived stage in studies and analyses under the heading man versus space it must not be overlooked that systematic studies of the problems of the objects versus space relationship are equally necessary. The need for integration of relations and processes taking place between people and fixed assets on the one hand, and space on the other hand, remains obvious and decisive.

Thus the modern developmental trend of the theory of space economy gives evidence of new and interesting directions in scientific research. At the same time, the great importance of this research in finding solutions to practical problems is stressed. We draw up plans of socio-economic development for more distant time-horizons; we formulate the purposes of economic growth and social development; and we indicate the concrete directions leading to their achievement. While defining more and more precisely what we intend to achieve, and when, we have also to determine more and more accurately the possibilities and means for the implementation of our plans.

The processes of growth and development are becoming increasingly complex. The criteria of their evaluation and the premises of the socio-economic and spatial policies are changing too. However important the analysis of an individual or a partial point of view may be, our present opinion is that this analysis should be expanded by the introduction of a supreme criterion of the interest of the whole national economy and of the developing socialist society. We study the numerous aspects of the developmental processes: economic, social, demographic, spatial, political and others. It is only on the basis of such a well-founded and many-sided analysis that we arrive at a comprehensive point of view and at an integrated treatment of the problems of development together with its structural transformations of a socio-economic and spatial character.

In conclusion it becomes necessary to secure the optimal cooperation of many scientific disciplines. This is especially true in conditions of the profound changes of the character of modern studies in the theory of space economy and in the practical policies of spatial transformations. It is only through joint and coordinated efforts of many disciplines that we can achieve real progress both in studies and research, as well as in concrete effects of comprehensive and efficient space management.

2

THE CONSTRUCTION OF SPATIAL MODELS
OF THE NATIONAL ECONOMY

A. G. Granberg

Mathematical modelling methods are being applied more and more extensively in regional social-economic investigations. As yet, the most substantial results have been obtained in solving local problems of spatial organization (settlement system models, the distribution of industrial enterprises and service networks, the elaboration of industrial units and territorial-industrial complexes, etc.). The elaboration of problems pertaining to the modelling of national spatial systems was begun in the last two decades, and these investigations are only now beginning to assume practical value.

The first spatial national economic models consisted in a generalization of the "point" model of the interbranch balance (input-output). The best-known balance models in the USSR are those evolved by W. Leontief, W. Isard and L. Moses. All these models incorporate a system of linear algebraic equations having a single (balanced) solution. This is accomplished by recording the major parameters of territorial proportions: either of the structure of the distribution of production, or of the structure of interregional relations. In complicated balance models the single solution is obtained by including specific statistical dependences between the major variables (e.g. of the "gravitational" model of interregional supplies in the model submitted by W. Leontief and A. Straut).

Until recently, interregional interbranch balances were not worked out in the USSR because of great difficulties in systematizing economic information. The possibility of doing so has, however, now been considerably facilitated by the compilation of accounting interbranch balances in all the republics of the USSR and economic regions of the Russian Federation for 1966 and 1972. The first interregional interbranch balances, compiled with the author's participation, covered two economic zones of the USSR (the RSFSR and the rest of the USSR) and three Transcaucasian republics. Analytical estimates by Granberg and Achelashvili were made on the basis of these balances.[1]

Since the major problems of the territorial organization of the national economy are not solved in balance models and are merely reflected in the stage of preparing initial data, these models cannot serve as a principal means of optimizing territorial planning. Interregional interbranch balances should be primarily used in investigating the actual territorial proportions, as well as in the economic-mathematical analysis of solutions obtained on the basis of more general models.[2]

The next step in modelling the national economy as a spatial system consisted in the elaboration of optimizational interbranch interregional models (B. Stevens, L. Moses and W. Isard). Various Soviet authors who have been working on models of this type since 1962 have proposed more than 10 model versions. However, no apparent continuity was observed in the published reports. The models were not approbated in experimental calculations and were not used to obtain even tentative conclusions on the effectiveness of territorial proportions of the national economy.

Experimental estimates of the optimum development and distribution of the productive forces of the USSR on the basis of the interregional model were first made under the author's guidance at the Institute of Economy and the Organization of Industrial Production of the Siberian Department of the USSR Academy of Sciences in 1967. At that time an optimizational problem covering 16 branches of production and 10 economic zones of the USSR[3] was being solved. In 1971 experiments with an interregional model were begun at the USSR State Planning Commission Council for the Study of Productive Forces under the guidance of S. A. Nikolaev. The first estimates covered 18 products and 5 zones.[4] Experimental estimates of an interregional interbranch model were also conducted at the USSR Academy of Sciences Central Economico-Mathematical Institute.

Investigations into interregional interbranch models and their application in pre-planning scientific substantiations have recently been considerably intensified.

1. *Applied optimizational interregional interbranch models*

Our approach to modelling is characterized by the following properties: 1) the interregional interbranch model is constructed as a link in the upper level of the overall system of optimum territorial-production planning models; with its inputs and outputs it is associated with "point" models of the national economy and branch and regional models;[5] 2) the interregional model may "operate" under autonomous conditions as a specialized model of the national economy (the question regarding the relationship between "point" and "spatial" national economic models is examined

190

in the second section of this paper).

The models designed for practical application in pre-planning estimates should be adapted to the existing sources of information, the developed mathematical apparatus, and the available means of computation. All these factors compel us to give up attempts to elaborate a comprehensive spatial model of the national economy, and make it necessary to confine the modelling sphere only to the principal aspects, to consciously simplify the model conditions, and to considerably aggregate the indices.

Let us dwell on the major model version. It incorporates n branches, excluding transportation $(i, j = 1, \ldots, n)$, and m regions $(r, s = 1, \ldots, m)$.

Unknown quantities:

$\overset{\circ}{x}_i{}^r$ – the volume of the production of goods of an i branch obtained during the final year, utilizing productive capacities operating at the beginning of the planned period (the numbers beginning with $k + 1$ refer to the branches producing elements of investments);

$\bar{x}_i{}^r$ – the increment of the production of goods of an i branch in an r region as a result of investments intended for the expansion of capacities;

$x\tau^r$ – the volume of the production of transport in an r region;

$x_i{}^{rs}$ – the volume of the delivery of the goods of an i branch from an r region to an adjacent region s (directly taken into account are the relations only between the adjacent regions);

$u_i{}^{tr}$ – the expenditure of i-type productive investments in an r region in a t year (planned period includes T years);

Z – the overall volume of non-productive expenditures.

Parameters:

$N_i{}^r$ – the volume of goods of an i branch in an r region, which can be obtained in the final year of the planned period when productive capacities operating at the beginning of the planned period are utilized;

$q_i{}^r$ – the fixed portion of the ultimate utilization of the goods of an i branch in an r region;

L^r – the limit of manpower for the productive sphere in an r region;

$\bar{d}_j{}^r$ – the maximum allowable increment of the production of goods of a j branch in an r region;

$\underline{d}_j{}^r$ – the minimum increment of the production of goods of a j branch in an r region;

$\overset{\circ}{a}_{ij}{}^r$ – the consumption of the goods of an i branch for manufacturing a unit of the goods of a j branch in an r region at capacities in operation at the beginning of the planned period ("old" capacities);

191

$a_{ij}{}^r$ – the consumption of the goods of an i branch for manufacturing a unit of the goods of a j branch at capacities put into operation during the planned period ("new" capacities);

$h_{ij}{}^r$ – expenditure of i-type investments for a unit of the goods of a j branch in an r region, obtained at "new" capacities;

$\mathring{t}_j{}^r$ – input of work for the production of a unit of a j branch in an r region, obtained at "old" capacities;

$t_j{}^r$ – the input of work for the production of a unit of the goods of a j branch in an r region, obtained at "new" capacities;

$a_{i\tau}{}^r$ – consumption of the goods of an i branch per unit of work of transportation in an r region;

$t_\tau{}^r$ – the input of work per unit of work of transportation in an r region;

$a_{\tau j}{}^{rr}$ – the expenditures of transportation for intradistrict conveyances of a unit of the goods of a j branch in an r region;

$a_{\tau j}{}^{rs}$ – the expenditures of transportation for the conveyance of a unit of the goods of a j branch from region r to region s;

$\alpha_i{}^r$ – the share of the country's general non-productive consumption fund, used for the consumption of the goods of an i branch in an r region $\Sigma_{i,r}\alpha_i{}^r = 1$.

All the unknown parameters, with the exception of $u_i{}^{tr}$ and $h_{ij}{}^r$, refer to the final year of the planned period. In order to simplify the designation and registry of the models the variables and parameters of the export and import of the goods and the transmission of electrical energy are not indicated.

Conditions:
1) The balances of productive investments for the planned period (10-15 years):

$$\Sigma_j h_{ij}\bar{x}_j \leqq \Sigma_{1 \leqq t \leqq T} u_i{}^{tr} \quad (i = k + 1, \ldots, n; r = 1, \ldots, m) \quad (1)$$

It is assumed that the investments in the development of transport are known.
2) The balances of the manufacture and distribution of the goods of the final year:

$$\mathring{x}_i + \bar{x}_i \geqq \Sigma_j \mathring{a}_{ij}{}^r \mathring{x}_j{}^r + \Sigma_j a_{ij}{}^r \bar{x}_j{}^r + u_i{}^{Tr} + a_{i\tau}{}^r x_\tau{}^r + \alpha_i{}^r Z -$$

$$- \Sigma_{s \neq r} x_i{}^{rs} + \Sigma_{s \neq r} x_i{}^{sr} + q_i{}^r \quad (i = 1, \ldots, n; r = 1, \ldots, m) \quad (2)$$

Condition (2) constitutes a greater part of the total number of the model limitations. When employing the model at the upper level of the USSR's

192

territorial planning, it is necessary to distinguish a minimum of 24 regions (14 republics of the USSR and 10 economic regions of the Russian Federation). If we adopt as a basis the classification of already elaborated regional interbranch balances (approximately 105 branches) the total number of equations of the model for one year alone will greatly exceed 2.5 thousand. Consequently, the problem of dimensionality is of great importance to the applied interregional models. In particular, the operative use of dynamic models on an annual basis does not seem possible for extended-period forecasts.

3) The balances of the work of transportation:

$$x_\tau^r \geqq \sum_j a_{\tau j}^{rr}(\mathring{x}_j^r + \bar{x}_j^r) + \sum_{s \neq r, j}(a_{\tau j}^{rs} - a_{\tau j}^{rr})x_j^{rs} +$$

$$+ \sum_{s \neq r, j} a_{\tau j}^{rr} x_j^{sr} \quad (r = 1, \ldots, m) \tag{3}$$

All types of transportation are unified (expenditures being averaged out). The expenditures for conveyance between adjacent regions are carried by the shipping region. The product is exported and imported through border region stations in the country; only one such station is chosen for each region.

4) The balances of manpower:

$$\sum_j \mathring{t}_j^r \mathring{x}_j^r + \sum_j t_j^r \bar{x}_j^r + t_\tau^r x_\tau^r \leqq L^r \quad (r = 1, \ldots, m) \tag{4}$$

Manpower is registered according to regions; in the model itself the conditions do not provide for the transfer of manpower (however, in fixing manpower limits, possible and expedient population migration flows are taken into account).

5) Limitations for certain variables:

$$\mathring{x}_j^r \leqq N_j^r$$

$$\underline{d}_j^r \leqq \bar{x}_j^r \leqq \bar{d}_j^r \qquad \text{(for some } j, r) \tag{5}$$

$$\mathring{x}_j^r, \bar{x}_j^r, x_\tau^r, x_j^{rs} \geqq 0$$

6) Optimum criteria:

$$Z \to \max \tag{6}$$

The level of consumption by the population of the country at the recorded correlations of the regional levels of consumption and recorded principles of determining the intraregional structures of consumption is

193

maximized. Modifications of the criterional part of the model are connected, in the first place, with the transformation of the notion "regional level of consumption" and, secondly, with the application of various laws determining the intraregional structure of consumption.[6]

The establishment of definite correlations of the consumption levels for different regions reflects the state policy directed towards equalizing the regional levels of living. Optimizational estimates for an extended period may envisage different versions of solving this major task of social-economic development (equalization within the bounds of permissible fluctuations, full equalization, etc.). The model makes it possible to compare the effect the versions of such solutions have on the general level of well-being in the country (value Z). Given specific rules of the elaboration of intraregional structures of consumption, optimization with the aid of the considered criterion provides a version of development and distribution of the productive forces with the following important property of effectiveness: it is not possible to raise the level of consumption in one region without lowering the level of consumption in at least one other region.

In addition to conditions (1)-(6), the model may include limitations to the volumes of investments for the entire planned period (II), which are substantiated in "point" models of the national economy:

$$\sum_{r,j} h_{ij}^r \bar{x}_j^r \leq H_i \tag{7}$$

Proceeding from the specific law of the growth of investments during the planned period, the investments of the final year and their sum for all the years can be represented in the form of functions of the known values of investments of the basic year $\mathring{u}_i^r$ and the unknown parameters of the annual growth of investments ρ_i^r.

At a growth of investments according to an exponential function, i.e. at identical annual rates:

$$u_i^{Tr} = (1 + \rho_i^r)^T \mathring{u}_i^r \tag{c}$$

$$\sum_{t=1} u_i^{tr} = \frac{(1 + \rho_i^r)[(1 + \rho_i^r)^T - 1]}{\rho_i^r} \mathring{u}_i^r \tag{d}$$

The substitution of (c) and (d) and (1) and (2) results in a nonlinear programming problem. However, a piece-linear approximation of (c) and (d) makes it possible to obtain a linear programming problem with additional limitations. A single-stage solution of the linearly-programmed problem provides a solution to the initial problem with any degree of

194

accuracy required.[7]

The first attempt to employ an interregional model for substantiating the versions of the development and distribution of the USSR's productive forces consisted in working out experimental estimates for a 10-year period covering 16 branches of the production of goods and 10 economic zones of the USSR. (Detailed results of the estimates are provided by Granberg).[8] The principal aim of these calculations was to develop methods of an economico-statistical and economico-mathematical analysis of the optimum versions and study the quantitative interrelationships between the factors of the development and distribution of the productive forces.

Since the initial data utilized contained numerous conditionalities, the results of the calculations on the whole could not be recommended for practical use. However, the analysis of the optimum versions made it possible in all cases to obtain a system of conclusions common with the initial data, to predict possible changes in the results when determining the initial information, and to evaluate the economic results of bringing about definite solutions in the field of territorial planning. Many results of the optimizational calculations, which at first seemed unexpected and implausible, were confirmed by other investigations into the development and distribution of the productive forces.

At present estimates are being made for 1976-90. Serving as an information base are the interbranch balances of the republics and economic regions of the USSR.

A simplified version of an interregional model (excluding the investment conditions) is being used to analyze the effectiveness of the actual distribution of industry and resources. The main aim of the analysis is to find "narrow" places (deficit regional resources), the expansion of which results in a rapid economic effect. For the first time, such a investigation has been carried out on the basis of the information of regional interbranch balances for 1966.[9]

The models used in the first versions of the optimizational calculations were consciously simplified in many respects. The transition to improved models is being carried out as specific problems pertaining to modelling methods (as regards transport, interdistrict communication, social-economic problems of labour and consumption, etc.), are being studied and as necessary information accumulates and mathematical security is intensified.

The main criteria of classifying model modifications already elaborated are: 1) the type of combination of production and transportation conditions in the model; and 2) the method of taking account of the dynamics of regional development.

The models are classified in the following manner according to the first criterion:

1) in the regional balances of the goods interregional deliveries are taken into account;

2) in the regional balances of the goods only the balance of interregional exchange is taken into account;

3) the balances of the transportable goods are given for the country as a whole, with regions being singled out as production means.

The first type of model is the main one for the time being; however, it does not make it possible to substantially detail the classification of the branches and regions. The application of the second version becomes a possibility on dividing the single problem into "productive" and "transportation" problems with an iterative agreement on particular solutions. The third version is applied for branches with negligible expenditures for the conveyance of the ready goods; its extension to other branches requires the introduction of specific functions of transportation expenditures.

Three basic types of models can also be singled out according to the second criterion:

1) the main indices (of production, consumption and interregional communications) are calculated in the final year of the planned period, with limitations on the volumes of investments for the planned period as a whole and hypotheses with regard to the utilization of the investment fund in the final planned year;

2) the main indices are also calculated in the final year in conformity with the specified laws of the growth of investments; however, the growth parameters and absolute amounts of the investment funds for the regions are determined in the process of optimization; and

3) for an extended period the main indices of the final years of the time intervals (five-year periods) are determined in conformity with specific laws of the growth of investments for the regions within the time intervals (five-year periods).

In the first two versions the proportions of the final year of the planned period (10-15 years) are accentuated. However, after a solution is obtained for the final year the dynamics of regional development can be "restored" by solving a series of statistical problems for each year. The model of the third type combines the features of "thoroughly dynamic" models (in a large time scale) and of simplified dynamic models with fixed laws of the growth of investments (in a detailed time scale). Moreover, the possibility of restoring the annual dynamics of the main indices is maintained.

The model described above possesses the classification features of 1-2. At present, our task is to "master" the 2-3 model. This will make it possible to substantially detail the model indices (the number of branches and regions) and to increase the possibility of applying it in extended-period forecasts.

The second trend of improving interregional models consists in introducing new conditions and factors. The following problems are of prime importance: 1) the expansion of the unit of interregional exchange and transportation (the inclusion of the statistical dependences of the export and import of the "gravitational models" type, the basic characteristics of the mainline transportation network, etc.); and 2) the compilation of a model including the conditions of population and manpower migration.

2. *The "coexistence" of point and spatial models of the national economy*

Spatial models are a more general type of models of the national economy. The question naturally arises whether in future they might make point models redundant as an *independent* means of economic forecasting and planning. This might be the case if the functioning of spatial models did not require information from point models, and if the summary characteristics of the national economy were obtained by aggregating the results of the spatial models.

Experience accumulated through experimental investigations in systems modelling makes it possible to anticipate the presence of the most immediate tendencies towards the coexistence of point and spatial models. We maintain that the combined use of these two types of models is not a temporary compromise, but that it is expedient in principle.

The system of optimum planning models elaborated at the Institute of Economy and the Organization of Industrial Production of the Siberian Department of the USSR Academy of Sciences includes both types of models of the upper level.[10] The main point model is the dynamic interbranch balance model; spatial models are represented by various modifications of the optimizational interregional interbranch model.

In the first version of the spatial model (1-1) productive investment limits were used as the initial data for the planned period; these limits were calculated after the dynamic interbranch balance model.[11] After finding the optimum version of distributing production, the national coefficients of the consumption of materials, labour and funds were corrected and a new solution to the dynamic interbranch balance model was found.

However, in 1972 the situation changed. The spatial model with optimized parameters of investment growth (1-2) was put into operation. This model can function independently of the dynamic interbranch balance model, while the latter remains fully dependent on the results of spatial modelling. The breach of the bilateral dependence is explained by the dynamic interbranch balance model not including any specified dependences and factors lacking in the modified spatial model.

197

The resulting situation is abnormal. It is explained by the narrow front of investigations based on point interbranch models. As yet, these models are overly "open" and include many exogenous values. For instance, science and education are taken into account only as a tendency of expending resources: their active influence on the development of production is not reflected. Similarly, geological exploration work, and forms of activity in protecting and restoring natural resources, are included in the model. Non-material factors of the population's well-being, the sphere of defence, the influence of external economic and political conditions, etc. are obviously insufficiently reflected in the national economic models.

Many of the possible trends of the development of national economic models can be realized primarily in point models (e.g. the inclusion of scientific and technological progress as an endogenous factor, the spheres of education and the training of specialists, as well as foreign political relations). Furthermore, the knowhow of point modelling of the national economy should gradually be transferred to spatial models. (To do so immediately is both inexpedient and impossible, owing to the drastic complication of methodical information and computation problems.) Apparently, spatial models will continuously lag behind point models in the terms of the degree to which they can reflect general (extraspatial) national economic interrelations and processes.

Simultaneously we shall observe the process of a fuller reflection of specific factors in spatial models (e.g. the interaction between production and the environment). Nevertheless, in the future also, it will be possible to study many aspects of the spatial organization of economy only within the bounds of special regional models.

The question regarding the rational detailing of identical conditions in point and spatial national economic models (e.g. of a list of branch-products and resources) is problematical.

With the existing mathematical and technical security, it is often necessary to artificially limit the scale of optimizational problems. Consequently, spatial problems, in which the typical conditions of point models are duplicated in accordance with the number of regions, and in which, moreover, specific conditions of interregional interaction are present, are affected to the greatest degree. Therefore, in point models the maximally attained detailing of ingredients is considerably higher (by at least one order) than in spatial models. However, it does not follow that the symbiosis of detailed point and aggregated spatial models will become the basic form of coexistence of the two types of national economic models.

Very often greater concretization is required in solving the problem of the territorial organization of economy than in forecasting overall national proportions. In the USSR, for instance, there has always been a tendency towards elaborating detailed versions of the distribution of the productive forces (although frequently this was done even at the expense of general economic substantiations of the system of territorial proportions).

Therefore, we believe that the growing possibilities of computing techniques and mathematical possibilities will be used primarily to accelerate summary national economic calculations rather than to drastically increase the detailing of these calculations. In practice this will mean that calculations for point models can and should be made more frequently and faster than for spatial models.

Thus in our opinion the "division of labour" between point and spatial models of the national economy should be effected along two lines: 1) the intensification of specialization (non-recurrence of models) and the mutual supplementation of new information; and 2) the diverse frequency of utilization by the central planning body.

Notes

1. A. G. Granberg, "Economico-Mathematical Investigations of Inter-republic Interbranch Relations", in *Economy and Mathematical Models,* Vol. 8, No. 6, 1972 (in Russian); and K. V. Achelashvili, "The Elaboration and Analysis of Interregional Interbranch Balances", in *Economico-Mathematical Analysis of the Distribution of the Productive Forces in the USSR,* Novosibirsk, 1972 (in Russian).

2. It is well known that the application of optimizational models is not limited by the calculation of one optimum version; as a rule, a change in an optimum version is analyzed, with certain conditions being recorded. In conducting such an analysis it is convenient to use auxiliary economico-mathematical models. K. V. Achelashvili has proposed modifications of balance inter-regional interbranch models, which are adapted to the economico-mathematical analysis of optimum versions of the development and distribution of the productive forces with a fixed structure of the distribution of production or with a fixed structure of interregional relations, i.e. in accordance with the conditions adopted in the models submitted by W. Leontief, W. Isard and L. Moses (see K. V. Achelashvili, "Balance Interdistrict Models and their Application in an Economico-Mathematical Analysis of the Distribution of the Productive Forces", in *Methods and Models of Territorial Planning,* Issue 1, Novosibirsk 1971 (in Russian), pp. 216-233.

3. *Ibid,* pp. 181-221.

4. Cf. A. Granberg, *The Optimization of Territorial Proportions of the National Economy,* Economy, 1973 (in Russian).

5. The structure of the system of models and a description of its separate links and coordination processes are provided in A. G. Aganbegyan, K. A. Bagrinovskii and A. G. Granberg, *A System of Models of National Economic Planning,* Mysl', 1972 (in Russian).

6. In those models where the population and manpower during the planned

199

period are firmly attached to regions (taking into account the demographic forecast and expected migration) the "regional level of consumption" characterizes the aggregate consumption of the entire population of the region. This same notion in more sophisticated models with a variable population characterizes per capita consumption. The extent of the consumption of concrete material goods, or commodity groups, is defined as a function of the regional level of consumption (see A. G. Granberg, *The Optimization of Territorial Proportions of the National Economy, op. cit.*, Chapter 1. The initially adopted rules of the elaboration of intraregional structures of consumption can be defined more accurately in the process of optimizational calculations.

7.   *Ibid.*

8.   *Ibid.*

9.   A. G. Granberg, "Economico-Mathematical Investigations of Inter-republic Interbranch Relations", *op. cit.*

10. A. G. Aganbegyan *et al, op. cit.*

11. In addition, data on the material goods (branch) structure of the consumption fund were directly used, whereas the regional coefficients of the material, labour and capital expenditures were forecasted on the basis of the average coefficients of the dynamic interbranch balance for the USSR. However, the utilization of all this information was determined not by the requirements of the interregional model itself, but by the difficulties in preparing regional information existing at that time.

3

SCHEME AND COMPOSITION OF OPTIMIZATION MODELS OF FORMING SPATIAL PRODUCTION COMPLEXES *

M. K. Bandman

One of the tasks of regional research at the pre-planning stage is an optimization of the spatial structure of a region or of components of its economy such as spatial production Combinations of different levels: large intra-regional spatial production Complexes, isolated and intra-complex production knots and their agglomerations, zones of conventionally complete exploitation and areas of intensive agricultural development.[1] These various spatial production Combinations are differentiated from one another on the basis of two characteristics—production and territory. Spatial production Combinations are accepted as independent units when the advantages arising from complex economic development, rational distribution, and organization of production can be carried into effect in them. The hierarchical order of a given spatial production Combination is determined by its place in the national economy and spatial production planning, by the nature and intensity of its internal and external economic relations, and by the development level of its productive forces and its production structure. The combinations of every hierarchical order are inherently characterized by specific features of the corresponding form of spatial organization of production, units of economic regionalization, and national economic planning.

Since the basis of the spatial structure of any region consists of large spatial production Complexes we can, in the process of pre-planning research, analyse the following:

1. Specific features of large intra-regional spatial production Complexes as spatial production Combinations of a specific order with certain properties;

---

* In Soviet scientific literature on regional research, the term "Territorial Production Complex" is used more often than "Spatial Production Complex", in order to emphasize that a specified territory (rather than an abstract space) is meant. In this paper "Spatial Production Complex" should be considered as synonymous with "Territorial Production Complex".

2. Factors, determining time, rates and dimensions, and directions of development of a spatial production Complex as a whole and of its individual parts, location of all the elements of economy of the Complex, internal and external relations of the Complex, methods of quantifying these factors and conditions;

3. Specific features of a spatial production Complex as an object of economic-mathematical modelling—properties of Complexes to be taken into consideration in models, means of taking into account with the help of models those factors which influence the forming of Complexes, and conditions of their functioning;

4. Elements of costs which may be reduced as a result of creation and functioning of Complexes in comparison with those necessary for dispersed location of production branches and uncomplex exploitation of an area; methods of their quantification and insertion into corresponding models;

5. Specific features of preparing basic data on Complexes (restrictions, matrix coefficients, functional etc.) needed for solving economic-mathematical problems;

6. Specific features of formulating problems concerning spatial production Complexes and the construction of models of such Complexes; and

7. Place occupied by optimization models of forming spatial production Complexes within a system of models of perspective spatial production planning: logical interrelation of models of such Complexes with each other as well as with models of the national economy and regional industries.

One of the neatest and most complete definitions of spatial production Complexes in general has been given by N. N. Kolosovsky.[2] By large intra-regional spatial production Complex in this paper we understand a planned aggregation of stable interrelated and interstipulated branches of the national economy (industry, agriculture, construction, transport, the nonproductive sphere). This aggregation,

1. Is created for joint solving of one or several major national economy tasks, characterized by large-scale production and clear-out specialization within the framework of the country and their economic regions;

2. Is concentrated within a restricted and compact (not disunited) territory possessing an adequate set of resources needed for them to take part in solving large-scale national economic tasks;

3. Uses local resources efficiently (from the point of view of the national economy); and

4. Has a unified production and social infrastructure.

The spatial organization of production, which is based on maximal use of natural and economical prerequisites of exploitation of separate territories, on joint location of production branches, complex use of resources, and spatial division of labour, ensures a high economic efficiency of spatial production Complexes. Their efficiency (in comparison with that of disunited location or a simple grouping of enterprises) is represented by a saving of natural and labour resources, by investments and current costs reduction, by decreased volume of transportation operations, by accelerating turnover rates of circulating capital, and by a saving of expenditures on construction and the functioning of intrastructure and the non-material production sphere.

Since every such Complex is a link within the national economy as a whole, we may consider as optimal only those complexes in which the state programme relating to output by branches of specialization and to the creation of fair living conditions is fulfilled with minimal social labour expenditure.

The choice of approach and structure of economic-mathematical models of the optimization of forming a Complex is for the most part influenced by specific features of the Complex as a system of a specific order as follows: 1) the structure of the economy is very complex; 2) there are close intra- and inter-Complex relations; 3) the Complex is highly dynamic; and 4) it has a stochastic character.

A spatial production Complex has a complex structure of economy the most important parts of which are resources, industrial and agricultural production, the non-material production sphere and the social infrastructure. These components are closely interconnected. The main transport arteries are of outstanding importance, as is shown in Figure 1. This grouping corresponds to the method of reflecting by means of models differences in the roles and the conditions of functioning of separate elements of a Complex's economy.

Every spatial production Complex is created in order to permit the utilization of one or several kinds of local resources, particularly:

1. *Labour* resources;
2. *Natural* resources: mineral, vegetable, water, land (agricultural areas and territories) suitable for industrial and transport construction or for house building and recreation areas; and
3. *Material* resources: formerly created production and transport objects, elements of infrastructure, and other material goods.

This grouping makes it possible for us to see not only the different purposes of specific resources but also the different conditions of using them and ways in which these can be reflected in models.

The core of any spatial production complex is the production sphere, which consists of a group of specialization branches, a group of completing subindustries, and several infrastructural elements.

The *specialization branches* determine the place of a given Complex within the spatial division of labour of the country and of the economic

203

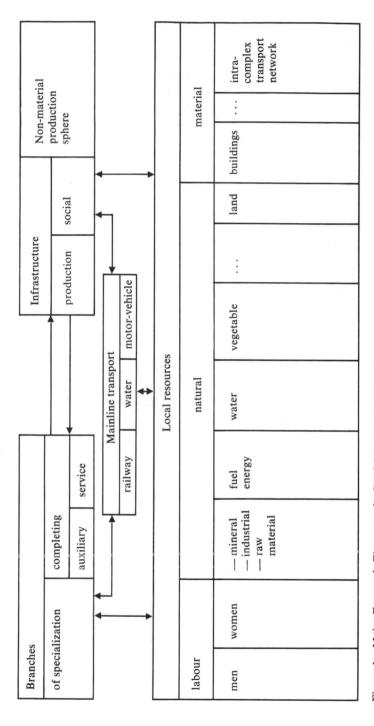

Figure 1. Major Economic Elements of a Spatial Production Complex

region. These branches may be either industrial or agricultural. The kind of specialization branches, and the time and rate of their development, are determined by the resource structure, by the national economic demand, by the geographic conditions of the area, and by production and transportation costs. The specialization branches have as their bases a number of complete or cut off production cycles which have been investigated in the work of N. N. Kolosovsky and many other Soviet scientists.

The second component, the *completing sub-branches,* may be divided into two groups: auxiliary and service branches. Under auxiliary branches we understand those that are required to provide the conditions for the functioning of enterprises of specialization branches entering the Complex. The structure, the time and dimensions of development, the relations and the location of auxiliary branches are all determined by the requirements of the specialization branches, by local resources quantity, and by the efficiency of creating these branches within the framework of a Complex in contradistinction to costs arising when similar products are imported.

Service branches are those which provide the local population with foodstuffs, cultural commodities and household goods. The composition, the dimensions of development, and the location of these branches are, as a rule, determined by intra-Complex demands for production, by the specific features of raw materials, by producing or completed output, and by production costs in comparison with the costs of importing transportable products from other spatial production Complexes.

The problems to be solved for each production sphere component of the Complex are very diverse when the specific conditions of their functioning and the corresponding restrictions are taken into account. For the specialization branches we establish the location of new enterprises and the dimensions of development of existing ones as well as their relations—providing that the producing output task is by all means fulfilled.

As regards the location structure of completing branches, producing output and relations are established when the restrictions relative to each source of local resources have been observed.

Infrastructure and the non-material production sphere are of very great importance for the economy of a spatial production Complex. Productive components of the infrastructure are the construction and energy bases, transport objects, communications, water supply installations and other elements used jointly by the whole Complex and by all the industries. Cultural, instructional, health, and trade institutions, public restaurants, passenger transport and other elements of the service sphere, as well as the housing fund and the administrative and scientific organizations, form the social part of the infrastructure.[3] The infrastructure is formed in accordance with the general level of development of the productive forces in the Complex, and location of its objects is determined by the specific conditions of functioning of the other economic elemens of the Complex and by population as well as by demand.

Completing sub-branches and infrastructure play a very important role in a Complex as they connect separate elements of the Complex's economy. The unity thus formed is one of the defining characteristics of a spatial production Complex, distinguishing it from a simple spatial concentration and from an enterprise grouping.

Inter-Complex, regional, and inter-regional main-line transport has a special function in the economy of a spatial production Complex, which may be explained by the fact that the formation of such transport (unlike other elements of a Complex) is influenced mainly by out-of-Complex conditions. The level of development, the network configuration, the structure and the amount of work performed by main-line transport are determined not so much by the requirements of the Complex as by the national economic need for spatial division of labour in the whole country (international exchange being taken into consideration). There are, however, close two-way relations between main-line transportation and other elements of the economy of a separate Complex. On the one hand, the level of development and the transport network configuration scheme exert an influence on the location of production, infrastructure objects, and population location, and on the other hand development of the productive forces of a Complex requires a corresponding level of development of the separate main-line transportation network elements. Moreover, the transportation network is itself a large-scale consumer of various kinds of multi-purpose resources used jointly by a number of Complexes.

Having such specific features, the transport has to be considered as an independent element of the economy of a Complex and as an object of modelling. As a result of problem solution, a distribution of goods flows may be established among means of transport and directions, as well as a variant of transportation network development under given restrictions relative to carriage capacity in accordance with reconstruction variants of each segment of a unified transportation network.

A compulsory condition of normal functioning of any spatial production Complex as a complex multifunctional formation, and as a component of the national economy, is availability of stable technological, production, economic and organizational external and internal relations. External relations determine the place of a given Complex in the national economy, its specialization in the inter- and intra-regional division of labour. As a rule these relations are bilateral: from the national economy to a Complex (direct), and from a Complex to the national economy (inverse). Direct relations reflect the demand of the country for resources

206

or for the completed output of a Complex (producing task for specialization branches), and the structure and volume of resources (products) which the national economy leaves for a given Complex. The inverse relations contain data on the resources and potentialities of a Complex, on the cost at which the Complex is able to fulfil its production program, as well as on the resources (products) of other Complexes (regions) required for this purpose.

Intra-Complex relations are versatile. They are maintained in accordance with the production process (vertical and horizontal relations), material and technical supply, joint use of resources and infrastructure elements of the complex. Within the framework of each Complex there are close relations between enterprises of specialization and completing branches, within the group of specialization branches and the group of completing enterprises, between the production sphere and the service sphere, within the service sphere, and between the local resources of a Complex and the rest of its economic components. The level of development of intra-Complex relations, their character, their rationality, and their completeness largely determine the degree of economic efficiency of a separate Complex.

The process of forming large-scale Complexes usually takes several decades and is carried out in stages. The most important characteristics of the "maturity" of a Complex are the level of development of vertical, and especially of horizontal, economic relations, a balanced overall use of resources, the degree of economic interrelationship (there is no intention of forming closed economic units), and the degree of engagement of every Complex in the spatial division of labour. Specialization and the production structure are not alone in being dynamic: the dimensions of a territory and the configuration of a Complex's boundaries may vary too.

The considerable extent of time required to form a Complex, the multivariability of eventual development of the Complex's principal objects and relations, and the uncertainty of development perspectives of a separate Complex, greatly complicate the problem of development optimization of the tasks of Complexes. This may be explained not only by the conventional nature of data, but also by a number of external factors. Periodically new national-economic problems arise. Scientific achievements and technological progress contribute to initiating the exploitation of new kinds and sources of various resources and to increasing the efficiency of their use. As a result the potentialities of separate Complexes and their place in the spatial division of labour have to be revised, and this leads to changes in the composition of objects, in the production structure, in internal and external relations, and in the time, rate and plan of the formation of a Complex. Consequently we have to regard a Complex as a probabilistic-uncertain economic system and to admit an uncertainty zone of optimal development. The research on this zone is one of elements of economic-mathematical analysis of optimization problems.

By optimization of the formation of a Complex we understand the determination of the best (from the point of view of the national economy) way of using natural, manpower, and other resources, the determination of the optimal time limits, rates, scales and proportions of development, the structure and spatial organization of all elements of the economy of a Complex, and its internal and external relations—providing that the economy of social labour expenditure necessary for fulfilling producing output tasks of specialization branches will reach a maximum and that the projected living conditions of the population will be secured.[4]

As the point of departure in solving this problem we accept following assumptions:

1. That there exists a centralized management of the economy and that local authorities have a great degree of freedom in decision-making, i.e. the main parameters of the formation of a Complex of any order are established on the higher level, while the determination of ways of forming particular Complexes is left to corresponding territorial authorities.

2. That there exists a system of models and problems at the national-economic level and that all-Union industrial problems have already been solved—or there is an approved general scheme of development of the productive forces of the country, and the place of every region in the all-Union labour division is defined.

3. That the study of the region is carried out in two stages. First of all the region's place in the inter-regional division of labour is specified, the structure and proportions of its economy are optimized, and a variant of the formation of inter- and intra-regional infrastructure elements is fixed. After that the optimization of the spatial structure of the regional economy as a whole and of its separate parts is carried out.

4. That the most progressive forms of spatial organization of the economy of any economic region are spatial production Combinations.

5. That the major spatial production Combinations of a region as objects of modelling are open complex dynamic systems, the formation and functioning of which is influenced by a great number of different factors. In this connection an analysis of the spatial organization of their economy is not possible if the relations to separate Combinations are not considered, i.e. by means of only one model and in the process of only one solution.

Members of the Institute of Economics and Organization of Industrial Production of the Siberian Branch of the USSR Academy of Sciences (IEOPP SO AN SSSR) have, in order to solve this problem, proposed a logical scheme—"approach" and techniques—known as the "Group of models of the optimization of forming spatial production complexes"

208

(Group of SPC models), for the optimization of spatial organization of the economy of intra-regional Complexes.[5] Subsequent studies confirmed the assumption stated formerly that the above approach and models may be used also to optimize the formation of the spatial structure of the economy of an economic region as a whole.[6]

This approach is based on stage-by-stage and element-by-element analysis of the components of the regional economy and successive transition from the solution of general problems to the solution of particular ones, from problems of forming the totality of large-scale Complexes of an economic region to those of the development and location of separate elements of the economy and territorial subunits of each Complex. At every stage, production, infrastructure, resources, and units of spatial organization of production are analyzed. However, the scope and details of this analysis are different (see Figure 2).[7]

As the main criterion of optimization, minimum expenditure in the creation and functioning of a Complex is accepted—and as the correspondence to the national-economic optimum is established thanks to all the parameters of decision-making freedom—the restrictions and conclusions can be taken from the results of problem solution on a higher level of the optimal spatial production planning system.

The principal sources of information for the optimization of spatial organization of the economy of an economic region and its spatial production Combinations are data obtained from the solution of problems of a higher level. In addition, data of drafting bodies of industrial branches, of scientific organizations and local governments are used.[8]

The Group of SPC models is proposed as a research device, the consequent use of which ensures, to our mind, the solution of a complex of problems necessary for the determination of the spatial economic structure of an economic region (see Figure 3).[9] The basis of this Group (models of the first, third, fourth stages) are regional mezzomodels developed especially for this purpose. These belong to the model of spatial—(in contradistinction to point—) economics with simultaneous analysis of all the regional—(in contradistinction to branch—) economic elements, resources, and forms of spatial organization of production within the boundaries of the region being studied. The models of an economic region take, as to their combination of conditions and degree of aggregation, a middle (mezzo) position among regional models: between macro- (models of the national economy) and micro-models (models of arranging objects within the framework of limited territories).

Regional mezzomodels of optimizing the spatial organization of spatial production Combinations are characterized by a block structure (see Figure 4). Each block specifies conditions of the formation and functioning of separate economic elements, or the use of each kind of resource, or the

209

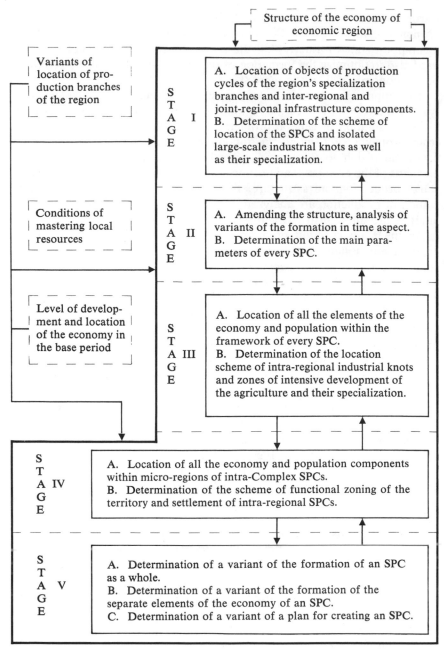

Note: SPC = Spatial Production Complex
      SPCs = Spatial Production Combination

Figure 2. Stages of Optimizing the Spatial Organization of the Economy of an Economic Region

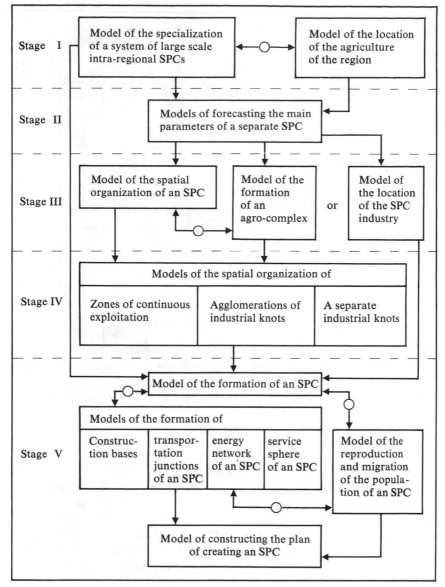

Figure 3. Group of Models for the Optimization of the Formation of Spatial Production Complexes

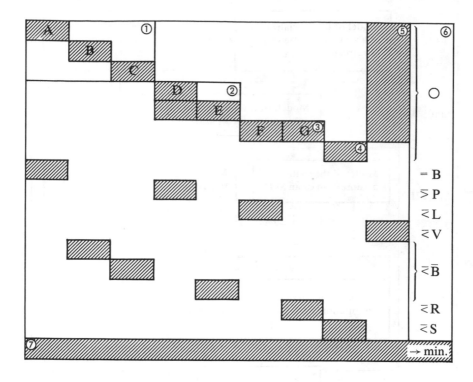

Figure 4. Block-scheme of the Regional Mezzomodel of Optimizing the Spatial Structure of an Economic Region

engagement of a given Combination in the spatial division of labour. The quantity and contents of separate blocks depend on problem setting and the hierarchical order of a Combination, e.g. the models of specializing a system of regional Complexes are based on five blocks: production (1), infrastructure (2), labour resources (3), local resources (4), external relations (5), as well as on vectors of restrictions (6) and the functional (7). Each of the blocks is, in its turn, divided into sub-blocks. So in the production block, sub-blocks of specialization branches (A), auxiliary (B), and service sub-branches (C) are distinguished; in the block infrastructure there are sub-blocks of production and social infrastructure elements, the importance of which does (D) or does not (E) exceed the bounds of a given Combination; the labour resources block consists of sub-blocks "local resources" (F) and "importing resources" (G), etc. The sub-blocks are divided into separate sub-branches, separate infrastructure elements, separate kinds of resources, etc.

Objects of modelling in the regional mezzomodels for each level of a

212

Combination are elements of specialization branches of the given Combination and completing sub-branches, production and social infrastructure and spatial divisions (areals, sites, etc.). The above ways reflect conditions of the formation and functioning of the Combination being studied. The restrictions are represented by input information on the place occupied by a Combination in the spatial division of labour; this information is obtained from the solution of higher level tasks (as well as from data of branch and from statistical organizations) which define the level of economic development in the base period and the possibility of using local resources.

Regional mezzomodels of the optimization of the spatial economic structure of Combinations of any hierarchical order include, as a rule, the following groups of equations and inequations:

1) Conformity of producing output and demand of specialization branches and completing sub-branches output;

2) Conformity of development dimensions and demand for services of production and social infrastructure branches of each Combination, taking into consideration the requirements of Combinations of a higher order;

3) Conformity of availability and use of local resources in major internal units (areals, sites, etc.) of each Combination;

4) Conformity of availability and use of labour resources, taking into consideration possibilities of attracting such resources from other regions of the country;

5) Conformity of availability and use of mobile resources, taking into consideration their eventual import from other regions;

6) Restrictions imposed by top authorities, i.e. the production output programme of specialization branches (B) and development rates of infrastructure elements (P), the importance of which exceeds the bounds of the Combination being considered;

7) Additional restrictions relative to separate variables, reflecting possible limits to the use of local (S) and labour resources (R), capacities of separate enterprises ($\overline{B}$), and deficient resources (V, L) ceilings; and

8) The functional, principal elements of which are indices of expenditures connected with the creation and functioning of production sub-branches and infrastructure elements, with maintaining external relations, exploiting local resources, attracting and settling the population, taking into consideration the projected standard of living.

When choosing an optimal variant the impacts of production and spatial factors are taken into consideration: relations concerning the receipt of raw materials and the exchange of products, the conditions of the provision of labour, land and water resources, the conditions of settling and stabilizing the population, and of the creation and functioning of transport networks, buildings, and agricultural bases (the latter condition is of particular importance in regions of new exploitation).

At all the stages of the research it is proposed to solve three types of problems which are characterized by specific contents and which require specific structures of economic-mathematical models and principles of construction. We may distinguish the following types of problems:

1) The determination of the best variant of the spatial organization of the economy of every Combination;

2) The analysis of the formation process of separate Combinations taken as a whole; and

3) The determination of a variant of forming particular infrastructural elements and the establishment of the plan of creating Combinations.

The problems of the first type may be formulated in general form as follows: determining the variant of using resources, location of sub-branches, and elements of the corresponding Combination infrastructure, provided that it fulfils its role in the spatial division of labour and that calculated expenditures on its creation and functioning are minimized. In order to solve this type of problem a series of models is proposed which correspond to a definite order of Combination: for a region, a model of the specialization of the Complex system and model of agriculture location; for a separate Complex, a model of the spatial organization of a Complex and that of agro-complex or model of industry location; for a part of a Complex, models of spatial organization of the economy of all-round exploitation, of a separate industrial knot or an agglomeration of industrial knots (see Figure 3). All the above models belong to the regional static models type of general form and are developed in conformity with continuous and mixed formulations of problems.

With the help of either formulation we consider simultaneously 1) sub-branches, 2) infrastructure, and 3) resources of the corresponding Combination.

In order to test each of the above models in the IEOPP SO AN SSSR a number of experimental problems of large dimensions have been solved on the basis of Siberian data. We used some results of these solutions when developing the regional lay-out of Prichulymye, province of Irkutsk and territory of Krasnoyarsk and when preparing pre-planning materials for East Siberia as a whole and for the territory of Krasnoyarsk. The formulation of the problems mentioned above, the models actually used and a short description of several solutions have been already published.[10]

The second type of problems may be formulated in general form as follows: testing coordination of succession, terms and rates of the creation of specialization branches objects, of the dimensions, time and rates of completing sub-branches and infrastructure elements development and of using resources, provided that investments in creating the corresponding

214

Combination are minimized. These tests are carried out for several intra-regional Combinations.

To solve this problem a dynamic optimization model with a mixed formulation model of forecasting Complex basic parameters is proposed. With it possible variants of forming specialization branches are proposed and a free formation of variants of completing sub-branches development, of all the infrastructure elements, and of using resources admitted. Joint and interrelated consideration of all the sub-branches and all the infrastructure elements is a great merit of the given model since it allows of a representation of the process of the formation of the particular Combination as a whole. This is also the essential difference between these models and those that are developed for the solution of the third type of problems.

On the basis of the model of forecasting the basic parameters of a Complex, a series of experimental problems have been solved using data on the Sayany Complex.[11] The analysis of the obtained results permits us to maintain that it fulfils all the required functions within the Group of SPC models, but the work on it is not yet completed. Considerable difficulties arise when information necessary for the solution of this problem is collected and processed.

The essence of the third type of problems is specification of the variants of location, relations and structure of each of the infrastructure forms of the corresponding Combination, provided that the calculated expenditures on the creation and functioning not only of the whole economy of the given Combination, but also of the given infrastructure form within the whole region are minimized. This is a separate analysis of the formation of every infrastructure form (transport system, building base, fuel-energy system, etc.) instead of an analysis (as in the second type of problems) of them as a whole. In this case we study the interrelations of every separate infrastructure form and the whole economy, and as a result an opportunity arises not only of obtaining a detailed scheme of the formation of the given infrastructure form, but also of undertaking a correction of cost indices relative to it.[12]

Solutions for every infrastructure form of any Combination are co-ordinated, with the results of the solution designed to construct models of the corresponding infrastructure form of a higher order of Combination or of the region as a whole.

Practical calculations according to these types of problems have been carried out for the time being at the IEOPP only in order to optimize the formation of the building base of separate isolated Combinations—the industrial knots of Bratsk[13] and Bogychansk[14] in Middle Siberia. There are some propositions as to approaches and models for the solution of this question. An analysis of the results of experimental calculations make it possible for us to state that in this case network linear dynamic models

215

may be used.

On the whole the experience in experimental calculations carried out at the IEOPP has shown that the proposed logical scheme and a part of models of optimizing the spatial organization of the economy of an economic region may already now be used in the practice of pre-planning studies that are necessary for working out general schemes of the development of the productive forces of the region, and for working out schemes and projects for drawing up general plans for the regional layout of industrial knots.[15]

A great advantage when using the techniques of economic-mathematical modelling in pre-planning studies of territorial systems is the opportunity of analyzing simultaneously a great variety of types of engagement of all orders of spatial production Combinations of an economic region in the spatial division of labour, the use of all the kinds of resources, structure and spatial economic organization, and of internal relations and settling systems, under different situations of their formation and conditioning. The work already carried out has shown that the variants obtained as a result of the solution of optimization problems yield an economy of about 10 percent of costs in comparison with those variants obtained without using the techniques of economic-mathematical modelling.[16] However, the value of the work should not be viewed solely—or even mainly—in terms of percents of economy (although these amount to considerable sums when the dimensions of modern new territorial exploitation programmes are taken into consideration), but also in terms of the new opportunities that it affords of comprehending the formation process of territorial systems. Modern techniques permit us not only to obtain a final result, that is a scheme, but also to determine the impact of every condition and factor, as well as to reveal quantitative correlations. The latter fact is to our mind of exceptional importance for pre-planning territorial studies in the light of the insufficient certainty of basic information, and the stochastic nature of the process of formulating and functioning of territorial systems elements, which are responsible for the stochastic nature of the results of any forecasting study. The emergence of the opportunity to quantitatively represent (it was formerly possible to do this only verbally) a prediction of the behaviour of a system when some of the indices are changing is making it possible to further extend the field of the application of economic-mathematical models.

216

Notes

1. B. I. Shniper and M. K. Bandman, "Objects and contents of intraregional consolidated planning of different levels", in *Regional Economics and Territorial Planning,* Part I, IEOPP SO AN SSSR, Novosibirsk, 1971, pp. 3-42.

2. N. N. Kolosovsky, "Production-territorial combination (complex) in Soviet economic geography", in *Fundamentals of Economic Regionalization,* The State Publishing House, Moscow, 1958, pp. 133-175.

3. In this paper the whole non-material production sphere of the Complex is considered together with its material base within the framework of the social infrastructure.

4. Living conditions are of particularly great importance for Complexes in newly exploited regions since labour is there one of the most expensive resources. The demand for labour resources in pioneer regions can be reduced through increased use of technical equipment, advanced technology and engineering, and through creating a standard of living in such regions that is higher than that of developed regions. Additional expenditure on realizing a planned increase in the standard of living can be justified from the national-economic point of view as a result of the total economy of working time at the expense of lowering migration intensity, increase in accommodation rate of the population, reduction of arrangement, training specialists costs, and a number of other factors. Thus the standard of living index is closely connected with the requirements for maximal use of local labour resources and with reducing expenditures on attracting working people from other regions of the country. This corresponds to the generally accepted criterion of minimization of total calculated costs in the formation and functioning of spatial production Complexes.

5. First variants of the approach and models were published 1966-1969. In 1971 a collection of articles was published where the results of previous work were generalized and positions of the sector of the formation of Complexes of the IEOPP SO AN SSSR relative to this question expounded. See *Modelling SPC Formation,* IEOPP SO AN SSSR, Novosibirsk, 1971, p. 330; and M. K. Bandman, V. V. Vorobyeva, V. I. Yezersky, V. S. Zverev, V. D. Ionova, N. I. Larina, M. A. Malinovskaya, and I. V. Mymrin, "Optimization of spatial organization of complex utilization of Siberian resources", in "Geographical problems of Siberia", *Nauka,* Novosibirsk, 1972, pp. 22-43.

6. M. K. Bandman and N. I. Larina, "Using SPC models for optimizing sub-branch location in an economic region", in *Spatial production complexes* ("Geography problems", No. 80), M., Mysl' 1970, pp. 59-66.

7. For details see *Modelling SPC Formation, op. cit.,* pp. 32-36.

8. See *ibid,* pp. 37-114.

9. See *ibid,* pp. 130-279.

10. See *ibid,* also M. K. Bandman, V. V. Vorobyova, A. I. Gaft, V. D. Ionova, Ye. I. Pertsik and Ye. S. Shatsilov, "Optimizing principal elements of regional lay-out schemes of the province of Irkutsk", in *Economic-Geographical Problems of Forming Siberian SPCs,* Issue III, Part II, IEOPP SO AN SSSR, Novosibirsk, 1971, pp. 26-64; and V. S. Zverev and V. Yn. Malov, "Problem

217

formulation and experimental calculations by means of a model of industrial knot spatial organization", *Izvestia SO AN SSSR*, No. 6, Series on the Social Sciences, Issue 2, 1972, pp. 109-115.

11. See *Modelling SPC Formation, op. cit.*

12. A. M. Alekseev, V. N. Dolinina and V. N. Kriuchkov, "Using automated calculation for formation of SPC construction programmes", in *Economic-Geographical Problems of Forming Siberian SPCs*, Issue 3, Part II, IEOPP SO AN SSSR, Novosibirsk 1971, pp. 102-117.

13. V. A. Shubert and L. G. Lavrov, "Using network techniques when modelling the process of formation of a separate SPC", in *Economic-Geographical Problems of Forming Siberian SPCs*, Issue I, West-Siberian Publishing House, Novosibirsk, 1969, pp. 117-136.

14. A. M. Alekseev, V. N. Kriuchkov and V. A. Sholkin, "Constructing long-range regional programmes", in *Regional Economics and Territorial Planning*, Part I, IEOPP SO AN SSSR, Novosibirsk, 1971, pp. 88-100.

15. M. K. Bandman, V. S. Zverev, V. D. Ionova, N. I. Larina and M. A. Malinovskaya, "Results of experimental calculations by means of SPC Models", *Izvestia SO AN SSSR*, Series on the Social Sciences, Issue 3, No. 11, 1970, pp. 64-70.

16. M. K. Bandman, and V. D. Ionova, "Experience in defining effect of the solution of optimization territorial problem", in *Economic-Geographic Problems of Forming Siberian SPCs*, Issue IV, IEOPP SO AN SSSR, Novosibirsk, 1972, pp. 175-187.

4

THE CONCEPT OF A UNIFIED SETTLEMENT SYSTEM AND THE PLANNED CONTROL OF THE GROWTH OF TOWNS IN THE USSR*

David G. Khodzhaev and *Boris S. Khorev*

The aim of this study is to present a general concept of the development of settlement[1] in the USSR, and through this to work out the basic policy assumptions for controlling the growth of towns and other settlements. This concept, without which it would be difficult to carry out rational regional and urban planning, must have both a theoretical and an empirical basis.

The Marxist thesis about eroding the differences between town and country during the building of communism is of great importance in connection with the theoretical basis.

The division of settlement types into those that are urban and those that are rural, resulting from the social and territorial division of labour and, in particular, from the separation of industry and agriculture, goes hand in hand with the class differentiation of society. "The division of labour in any society leads above all to the separation of labour in industry and trade from that in agriculture, and similarly to the separation of town and country".[2] In a class society this division between the two kinds of settlements creates an antagonism between town and country. With the liquidation of the class structure, and with the rebuilding of society along communist lines, the existing differences between town and country will gradually be eroded. Certain features of agricultural production and its related form of settlement will, however, remain, distinguishing it from other branches of the national economy and above all from large scale industry and its related forms of settlement.

The important point to be made about long-term changes in the growth of towns is that the erosion of the differences between town and country will lead to a *unified system of settlement*. The planned control of this system may make it possible for an excessive growth of towns to be avoided. Whereas in bourgeois societies the town governs the country,

* This article is reprinted from *Geographia Polonica,* 27, Warsaw 1973, pp. 43-51.

the elimination of the old division of labour in a classless society will, Engels writes, signify "the fusion of town and country".[3] This does not mean the absorption of the country by the town, as some urbanists hold, but rather the fusion of these two forms within a unified system of settlement. In the country man is at present usually subject to nature, and in the town he is unnaturally cut off from it: in the future unified system of settlement man will be in harmony with nature.

Engels' discussion of the liquidation of the differences between, and the subsequent fusion of, town and country is often neglected either because it is interpreted as presenting a goal for the distant future, or because it is considered to be unconnected with his main concerns. Both these views are completely erroneous.

In "The Housing Question", and particularly in "Anti-Dühring" he both propounds and justifies his thesis about eroding the boundaries between town and country. His justification involves economic, sociological and ecological issues, and is at the same time connected with the urgent tasks of social development. From the economic standpoint "liquidating the antagonism between town and country is not only possible, but it becomes a necessity for both industrial and agricultural production".[4] "The prospect of eliminating the old division of labour stands before us", Engels emphasized, "this, and the division between town and country".[5] From the sociological standpoint, the task of eliminating the antagonism between town and country is justified by Engels by the necessity "of plucking the agricultural population from the isolation and dullness in which it has vegetated for thousands of years".[6] And from the ecological standpoint the elimination of the antagonism is, according to Engels, "necessary in the interest of social hygiene. Only by merging town and country can the present poisoning of air, water and soil, be eliminated".[7]

The classic works of Marxism-Leninism not only justify the necessity of eliminating the antagonism between town and country and of their subsequent fusion, but they also outline how this can be achieved:

(1) through the harmonious development of productive forces according to a single overall plan;

(2) through a greater equalization of the distribution of large-scale industry and of the population over the country;

(3) by creating strong internal links between industrial and agricultural production;

(4) through the development of communications; and

(5) by overcoming the excessive concentration of population in large cities (as the capitalist means of production is eliminated). Socialism will lead to "a new settlement pattern of mankind (with the elimination of both rural neglect, isolation from the world, its barbarism, and of the unnatural concentration of huge populations in the large towns)".[8] The need "to

220

strive with every effort . . . for the rational distribution of workers" was expressed in the Party Programme, accepted at the 8th Congress of the RKP(b), and worked out on V. I. Lenin's directives.[9] An important methodological recommendation made by V. I. Lenin is "the unconstrained distribution of population throughout Russia", which is connected with "the rational economic use of the outlying areas of Russia".[10]

In implementing these theoretical legacies, the Party sees to the rational and planned development of the economies and cultures of the peoples of the Soviet Union by locating production and distributing settlements throughout the country. The question of rational settlement is referred to in the Programme of the CPSU, accepted by the 22nd Party Congress:

> "The developed building of Communism requires an even more rational distribution of industry which will ensure an economy in social endeavour. The integrated development of regions and special-ization of their economies will eliminate excessive concentration of population in large towns, will help overcome the existing differences between town and country, and will make the level of economic de-velopment of regions more equal".[11]

These propositions are of prime importance for working out the scientific concept of the distribution of population.

Socialism was the first system to set out with the intention of bringing an end to the antagonism between classes which would open the era of the classless society, and make possible the liquidation of the conflict between town and country. The formation of a single communist ownership; the linking of agricultural with industrial labour; the transformation of the former into a variant of the latter; and the establishment of the social equality of urban and rural workers; these are the socio-economic pre-conditions for eliminating the differences between town and country. In the USSR the general socio-economic process of eroding the boundaries between town and country is manifested in many ways, including: the mechanization and industrialization of agriculture (the change to a greater industrialization of the livestock branch of agriculture in recent years has been particularly important in the current plan); the spread of agro-industrial combines; the growth of "urban" occupations in the village, and as a result of this the increasing homogeneity of urban and rural workers; the growing local movement of population and increasing commuting be-tween village and town; making the flows of information more equal; spreading the network of developed urban centres so as to draw the large rural population into its economic and social orbit; making the small towns more active, and so on.

In this connection we must turn our attention to certain principal changes that have been affecting the development and distribution of the

221

forces of production in the Soviet Union, and that are important for solving the problems of settlement.

(1) It is well known that the number of large towns has been increasing in the USSR. An important aspect of this process, particularly in recent decades, is that the development of a network of large towns proceeds according to the principle of an "expanding geography of productional forces", helping the economic activation of formerly backward regions. The importance of cities in the population structure of the country is gradually decreasing. Thus the proportion of the population of the seven old million-cities—Moscow, Leningrad, Kiev, Tashkent, Baku, Kharkov and Gorki—in the total population of large towns has changed during the Soviet period from 60% in 1926, to 40.7% in 1959, and 23.4% in 1970.

(2) There has, in recent decades, been a significant increase in the levels of urbanization of formerly underdeveloped *oblasts* and republics. This is clearly seen in the data of the 1959 and 1970 population censuses, which show that the higher growth rates of the total urban population are usually found in those *oblasts* with a low proportion of urban population. This testifies to an intensive "pulling-up" process of the urban network to a higher level in previously backward *oblasts*. There are now hardly any weakly-urbanized *oblasts* with a low rate of urbanization. The urban population rose by 36% from 1959 to 1970, and the proportion of urban population reached 56%. Out of 138 *krays, oblasts,* Autonomous Republics, and Union Republics which have no *oblast* divisions, the proportion of urban population exceeded 55% in 49 cases; was between 50% and 55% in 13 cases; and less than 50% in 76 cases. Lower than average rates of growth took up 65.3% of the administrative-territorial units in the first of these groups, 38.5% in the second, and only 18.4% in the third.

The current growth of large towns testifies to a more equal distribution of the forces of production over the country. It does not testify, as some economists who limit themselves to a superficial look at the process of the concentration of population in large towns believe, to a deepening of an inherited "inequality" of development.

(3) In recent years, there have been fundamental changes in the distribution of industry in the Soviet Union. These have come about through the establishment of branches and separate sections of large industrial enterprises in many peripheral towns (of both small and medium size). This happened on a small scale before 1966, but was particularly remarkable during the 1966-1970 five year period. At this time enterprises opened up branches not only in towns and villages near Moscow, Kiev, Riga and other cities but also in remote regions in the European part of the country. In the Mari A.S.S.R., for instance, branches have been opened

up of factories that are based in Yoshkar-Ol, Kazan and even in Leningrad, Kharkov an Kuznetsk (Penzen *Oblast*). Two branches were located in such towns as Volzhsk and Kosmodemyansk, and one in the worker settlements of Krasnogorskiy and Morki. The Moscow ZIL factory also established branches in a series of town in many *oblasts* in the European part of the USSR. This phenomenon represents a serious step forward in solving the so-called "problem of small towns" in which ample labour resources are available, but which do not have the technology required for modern industrial production. These factories which do have the required technology provide the needed opportunities for young people in these areas and simultaneously solve the problem for industry (particularly for the labour-intensive machine-building industry) that had been posed by a labour deficit in the large towns and by the difficulties involved in attracting supplementary labour from elsewhere.

(4) The practice of organizing separate scientific research and project institutes in small towns is becoming more widespread. In the small towns these have different productional objectives from the main branches, which are usually located in the large towns. A related trend, which is of great importance in the current scientific-technological revolution, is that involving towns whose development depends entirely on the scientific-productional complexes that are established in them.

(5) In the USSR, as elsewhere, there has in recent years been a great increase in the mechanization and industrialization of the livestock branch of agriculture (through the construction of large poultry farms and livestock complexes to replace the previously small-scale dairy farms, pig farms, etc.). The collectivization of agriculture in its time led to crop mechanization and helped to solve the grain quality problem. The current changes can be seen as the second very important step forward. Along with an increasing use of chemical and other processes, they testify to an important spread of the technological revolution in our agriculture, that will have considerable impact on the distribution both of basic capital in agriculture and of the rural population.

(6) Since 1950 there have been significant qualitative changes in the local mobility of population through inter-village labour movements and cultural links between different regional settlement systems. These changes result particularly from the great effort put into developing suburban and inter-urban transport, especially bus transport. The number of bus routes increased considerably, as did the distances covered; in 1950, 51.9 million passengers used the inter-urban bus routes, in 1960 551.3 millions, and by 1968 this figure had doubled.[12] Local aeroplane services were also developed. These seemingly trivial indices of the development of transportation networks in fact reveal that great changes have taken place in the general lifestyle of the population, particularly the rural population,

223

because the increasing mobility of the rural population has created links between rural and urban areas and has changed the face of what used to be called the "deep provinces". An increase in the scale of commuting to work between village and town is connected with this. At present this process involves 3 million people throughout the USSR.[13]

(7) The development of channels of information and communication have also helped to bring the lifestyle of people living in outlying regions closer to that of people in the capital cities.

These important changes are already having considerable influence on all aspects of the process of the development and distribution of productional forces in the Soviet Union: they are undoubtedly helping to make this distribution and development more equal, and they are eroding the boundaries between town and country. Their influence will be even more marked in future.

Looking at the historical aspect of the development of the forces of production and social relations, one can distinguish two basic trends that had a significant effect on the process of settlement: an increasing territorial division of labour, and differentiation of the distribution of the products of this labour. These resulted in a concentration of industrial production and urban population, as could be seen in the rapid growth of large towns. Revolutionary changes in management, in the techniques of distribution and exchange, and in inter-settlement links, are, however, now leading to the establishment of a unified settlement system, the basic features of which are: first, a freer distribution of population over wide areas which form communities of interest and are characterized by intensive interrelations rather than intensive forms of urban development; and second, an equal distribution of production and population throughout the country. It is possible to glimpse the outline of the future "unified settlement system" in the regulation and combination of the various types of settlement distribution. In the trend towards an increasing radius of large-scale settlements of workers in places which act as supplementary sources of labour, and in the development of commuting due to improved transportation facilities, one can see the future map of the world.

On this map, settlement will not have to depend on the distance to sources of supplementary labour.

A general conception of the development of settlement is particularly necessary for working out the long-term control of the development of the forces of production and of the process of urbanization. Interest in long-term settlement problems, which has a long tradition in the Soviet Union (N. Milyutin's work in the late 1920's is particularly notable[14]), has grown considerably in recent years. This is partly due to the fact that a general scheme is now being prepared, under the direction of the all-Union Gosplan, for the distribution of productional forces in the USSR

224

up to 1980. This has made it necessary for us to work out scientifically a general scheme of settlement over the USSR, for the Economic Regions and Union Republics, up to 1980.[15] The scientific sub-departments of the all-Union Gosstroi are working out forecasts for the development of Soviet urban growth for even longer periods (a special conference in Moscow in February 1970 was devoted to this problem).[16] Because of the need to work out the long term distribution of population, Soviet geographers and urbanists have done a lot of work, especially in the last ten years, on questions of group and agglomeration settlement distribution and on analysing territorial systems of settlement. (The work of V. G. Davidovich and his followers is particularly important in this regard.) At present we can already speak about a definite concept of the long-term distribution which, however, still needs a theoretical foundation (from the standpoints of urban science, sociology, economics and geography). We will call this the concept of a unified settlement system (jedinnoi sistemy rasseleniya) abbreviated to JSR. In general, this term is taken to mean the functionally differentiated and structurally interlinked network of all the settlements in a given area. The network, which is part of a unified system of regional planning, is established through several subordinate stages and is being evenly developed and controlled through planning for society as a whole.[17] The essence of the concept is that in the long term, through the regional distribution of the forces of production of separate regions, the historically formed settlement pattern (both its concentrated and dispersed forms) will be transformed into integrated regional systems of settlement units that are socially and economically interlinked; their size will depend on local conditions. These units will together form the unified (economic) system of settlement.[18]

The political aim in establishing the JSR is to secure the necessary comparable conditions of work and lifestyle for all the components of the system.[19] This does not mean, however, that the conditions of settlement in an existing small town will become like those in a large town. Within the system the very structure of settlement distribution must change significantly.

There are several types of permanent inter-settlement links which have a great influence on the structure of settlement distribution: (1) productional, (2) cultural, (3) labour, (4) recreational and (5) informational. The development of these various types of links proceeds unevenly in time and space. This is the reason for the differences between settlement systems in the level of development and structure. The intensive development of the different types of inter-settlement links leads to the transformation of existing towns into agglomerations and "settlement regions". These can be taken as new units of territorial and urban planning with their own peculiar internal structures. Z. N. Yargina has demonstrated one of the possible lines this transformation may take.[20] A practical example of designing the internal structure of the JSR is provided by the work done by Lithuanian scientists and planners on a scheme for regional planning in their republic.[21]

Under the concept of the JSR the relative importance of separate urbanizing factors with regard to the development of a given settlement is altered. Educational establishments, internal transport, a zone of recreation and even a complex of institutions maintaining the important inter-urban services, can all act as an urbanizing base for the various types of settlement within the system. A change in the role of the separate factors in the whole system naturally changes the normative importance of their combined influence in calculations on the total population of particular towns. Such calculations must be carried out above all for the system (region) as a whole. Even in the near future the basic "urbanizing" or "town-forming" factors must be examined in the wider regional aspect as "region-forming" factors. We entirely agree with the well-known Polish urbanist K. Dziewonski, when he writes that with an increasing mobility of population, goods, and information, and with the growing area of the towns, potential fields of urbanization arise. As a result, the "opening-up" of a town increases, and the urbanizing base increasingly assumes functions which are not limited to a defined area.[22] This important theoretical observation can be found in Gorynski's concept of a "regional-urban model".[23]

The formation of the JSR represents a new stage in the development of settlement, and also a step forward compared with the universally observed expansion of uncordinated settlement forms of local combinations of settlements, including large-town agglomerations. The emergence of agglomerations and the JSR are both characterized by an intensification of inter-settlement links, but there is an essential difference between them: a well organized and regulated agglomeration can be one of the components of the JSR, but the system as a whole represents a higher stage in the development of inter-settlement links. The JSR presupposes a certain intensity of these links (which have, moreover, to be of a suitable technical standard) and a certain level in the network of services, that will ensure comparable opportunities for all the inhabitants of the regional system to use all the services and places of recreation. In the Soviet Union, especially in the older developed regions, this means that as well as improving transport, one should also create appropriate networks of focal centres of population in which various service institutions would be concentrated. Their distribution should ensure that they will be equally accessible to the whole population. The large urban agglomeration with its centripetal tendencies can be distinguished from the JSR by the way it divides the adjoining areas into those privileged nuclei with services and the remaining

226

outlying areas without services. Under the JSR this division is overcome and the conditions are created for the "more equal distribution" of productional forces recommended by Engels. However, the JSR is often mistaken for the process of deconcentration of these forces, and thereby contrasted with the "law of concentration".

There are two basic types of settlement network formation occurring in the process of concentration of population itself (and in the concentration of the forces of production in general):

1) Concentration in the chief, often excessively developed, centre, or in the chief town and its satellites. An example is the concentration in a country's capital or in the administrative centre of a region (or in a corresponding agglomeration) and the slackening development of "residual" settlement networks;

2) Concentration both in the chief centre and in several additional centres. An example of this would be concentration not only in the capital of a country, or in its two or three chief towns (if it is a large country), but in all its large towns or regional centres; or concentration not only in the central towns of a region but in several additional centres of average size.[24]

We think that this second type can be the policy basis of the formation of the JSR in most older-developed regions of the USSR and that in the European part of the country the development of settlement according to this type can lead, as Z. N. Yargina says,[25] to the formation, in the next 50-100 years, of equal living conditions over the whole territory from the point of view of accessibility to centres of social activity. Only under these conditions can we overcome the excessive and disproportionate growth of individual large centres.

Under the concept of the JSR one cannot speak about a contrast between the lifestyles of, on the one hand, large towns and agglomerations and, on the other, small towns, as erroneously held by some writers (for example V. I. Perevedentsev, A. S. Akhezer and A. V. Kochetkov). This approach, we should stress, appeared in the Soviet Union in recent years in discussions of the problems of limiting the growth of very large towns, and also in discussions of the fate of small towns or, more precisely, towns requiring development. It resulted directly from the social "demands" which appeared in several party and government resolutions made of our scientific and planning departments. There has been a lot of practical work done in the last decade, particularly between 1966 and 1970, in activating those towns requiring development. This was indispensable at this stage in the formation of the JSR for increasing the role of individual areas in the national economy.

The direction of the national economic planning of the forces of production and distribution of settlement over the country undergoes im-

227

portant changes in the various stages of the development of society. In the political background to the formation of the JSR in the post-war years the following stages can be distinguished: 1) the extension of the network of large towns—the local centres of *oblast* rank—through strengthening the industrial development of several "provincial" centres in the *oblasts* and Autonomous Republics (e.g. Ryazan, Kaluga, Cheboksary, Kurgan); 2) increasing economic activation of small and middle-size towns; and 3) the formation of a network of important focal centres within an *oblast;* these are the so-called regional centres where new industrial investment, as well as services to meet the needs of the entire population of the region within the *oblast,* are now being concentrated.

A very important practical political task in establishing the JSR is the control of the distribution of production and population in all the developed parts of the USSR. This task is difficult when dealing with local combinations of settlements. Under the JSR, recreational areas such as national parks, reserves, and areas set aside for tourism and leisure, are as important in planning as industry, agriculture, science and education. This will be very effective in improving the ecological situation. The JSR is a form of spatial organization which must be an organic combination of the natural and artificial environments.

The basic geographical task of the JSR is the economic regionalization of the country. Only through this is it possible to distinguish regional systems of settlements of various ranks, and to carry out a regional-network analysis which above all tries to define the location of the focal centres of population in the whole system. In economic planning the formation of the JSR is one of the tasks behind the politics of the distribution of productional forces. We should point out here that the formation of the JSR requires special criteria.

The general criterion of the rational distribution of the forces of production is an increase in the effectiveness of the whole of production which in its turn helps raise the standard of living of the population. This criterion is normally used in assessing the rational distribution of population and the development of a settlement network. However, we think this criterion is insufficient for the latter problem. One should take as a second criterion an improvement in the standard of living and the creation of opportunities for comparable living conditions for the population in the various regions and settlements of different sizes and types, from the village to the large town, throughout the settlement system.

The universal creation of comparable working and living conditions for the population is the fundamental solution to the problems of rationalizing the distribution of production, regulating the growth of towns, and so decreasing the demographic pressure on large towns. At present, the rational and even distribution of production is unquestionably one of the important conditions for levelling the standard of living and for stimulating urban development. This means that these economic and social problems must be treated together.

Notes

1. The term *rasseleniye naseleniya* in the Russian literature on the subject can refer to both the process of the distribution of population over an area and to the result of this process (the settlement network). Such a wide term has no equivalent, as far as we know, in English.

2. K. Marks and F. Engels, *Sochineniya (Works)*, 2nd. ed., Moscow, Vol. 3, p. 20.

3. F. Engels, "Anti-Dühring", in K. Marks and F. Engels, *op. cit.*, Vol. 20, p. 308.

4. *Ibid*, pp. 307-308.

5. *Ibid*, p. 308.

6. F. Engels, "K. zhilishchnomu voprosu" ("On the Housing Question"), in K. Marks and F. Engels, *op. cit.*, Vol. 18, p. 277.

7. F. Engels, "Anti-Dühring", in K. Marks and F. Engels, *op. cit.*, p. 308.

8. V. I. Lenin, *Poln. sobr. soch.* (Complete works), 5th ed., Moscow, Vol. 26, p. 74.

9. V. I. Lenin, "Programme RKP(b)" in *op. cit.*, Vol. 38, p. 443.

10. *Op. cit.*, Vol. 16, p. 227.

11. *Programma Kommunisticheskoy Partii Soveiskogo Soyuza* (The Programme of the Communist Party of the Soviet Union), Moscow, 1969, p. 72.

12. See "Narodnove Khozyaystvo SSSR v 1969" (The Soviet National Economy in 1969"), *Stat yezhegodnik*, Moscow 1970.

13. B. S. Khorev, T. K. Smolina, A. G. Vishnevskiy, "Mayatnikovaya migratsiya v SSSR i ee izuchenye" ("Commuting in the USSR and its study"), in *Problemy migratsii naseleniya i trudovykh resursov*, Moscow 1970.

14. N. Milyutin, *Sotsgorod*, Moscow, 1930.

15. Cf. D. G. Khodzhaev, "Nekotoriye problemy regulirovaniya rosta gorodov i razvitiya naselennykh mest" ("Some problems of controlling urban growth and the development of urban settlements"), *Problemy gradostroitelstva* 1, Kiev 1970.

16. Cf. "Perspektivy razvitya sovetskogo gradostroitelstva" ("On the development of Soviet town planning"), *Arkhitektura SSSR*, 6, 1970.

17. Cf. B. S. Khorev, "Rasseleniye naseleniya: kriterii i kontseptsii" ("Population distribution: criteria and concepts"), in *Materialy Vsesoyuznoi nauchnoi konferentsii po problemam narodnonaseleniya Zakavkazya*, Erevan 1968; and "Rasseleniye i territorialnosistemnaya organizatsiya proizvoditelnykh sil" ("The distribution and the territorial-system organization of productive forces"). *AN SSSR, ser geogr.*, 2, 1971.

18. Cf. N. Baranov, "Problemy perspektivnogo razvitiya sovetskogo gradostroitelstva" ("Problems of the perspective development of Soviet town plan-

ning"), *Arkhitektura SSSR,* 4, 1970; and articles by N. A. Solofnenko, S. I. Soldatov, V. S. Ryazan, G. A. Kaplan and others, in *Nauchniye prognozy i formirovaniya sovetskikh gorodov na baze sotsialnogo i nauchno-tekniches-kogo progressa (Scientific predictions concerning the development and the forming of Soviet towns on the basis of social and scientific-technical progress),* 3, Moscow 1969.

19. The reason why the necessary living and working conditions are described as *comparable* is that differences in the natural environment make it impossible to achieve complete equality.

20. Z. N. Yargina, *Sotsialniy progress i nekotoriye voprosy perspektivnogo rasseleniya, (Social progress and some questions on the perspective settlement network),* Paper presented to the VIIth International Sociological Congress in Varna 1970, Moscow 1970.

21. The main ideas in this work can be found in the doctoral dissertation of K. Sheshelgis, "A uniform system of settlement in Lithuanian SSR", 1967.

22. K. Dziewonski, "The concept of the urban economic base: overlooked aspects," *Regional Science Association Papers,* 18, 1967; and "Present needs and new developments in urban theory", 21st International Geographical Congress, India 1968, Abstracts of Papers, Calcutta 1968.

23. J. Gorynski, "Problemy gradostroitelstwa v svete sovremennoi urbanizatsii" ("The Nature and character of the urbanization process"), *Trudy Kom. po delam Territ-Ekonom. Razvitiya Strany PAN,* 16, Warszawa 1967 (in English: *Studies, Committee for Space Economy and Regional Planning of the Polish Academy of Sciences,* 19, Warszawa 1968).

24. In the USSR towns of "average size" in a system are those with between 50,000 and 250,000 inhabitants (formerly up to 500,000). These towns are more economical from the point of view of expenditure in the urban economy.

25. *Op. cit.*

230

5

URBANIZATION AND ETHNOGRAPHIC PROCESSES*

Vadim V. Pokshishevski

The processes of urban development are "universal" with regard to the many forms involved, depending on the system of production, and give rise to varied social effects. An important aspect of these effects, and one which has so far been underestimated by geographers engaged in urban geography, is the influence of urbanization on ethnic processes.[1]

Research on the impact of urbanization on ethnic processes is becoming very important in countries with a multi-varied population structure. In this paper the author analyzes this problem mainly in connection with the USSR, a land faced with great urban expansion and populated by more than 100 nations living in a close community. The author is of the opinion that many aspects of this problem have transformed analogies abroad, particularly in the developing countries.

The growth in the level of urbanization is accompanied in the USSR, as (to a generally lesser degree) in other countries, by the penetration of the features of the urban way of life into rural areas. In this regard, it is worth recalling that reducing urbanization solely to the quantitative increase in the ratio of urban population to the total population is possible only if this is considered an approximation (although this is a very important index of urbanization). Another essential feature of urbanization, though only a quantitative one, is the increase in the proportion of the total urban population living in the large and largest cities. The statistical data for the USSR on this point are given in Table 1.

Thus urban development both radically changes the "statistical structure" of the population (proportions of urban and rural populations), and is associated with the transfer of the urban way of life to rural localities. It is because of the mobility of town residents and their access to information that their impact on social (and also ethnic) self-determination may be considerably greater than their proportion of the total population. While

---

* This article is reprinted from *Geographia Polonica* 27, Warsaw, 1973, pp. 79-85.

Table 1. Demographic Conditions for an Increase in the Effect of Urbanization on Ethnic Processes (given in whole Percentage Figures)*

	Census or computed years			
	1926	1939-1940	1959	1970
I. Proportion of the urban population in the total population of:				
(a) the USSR	18	33	48	56
(b) Union Republics (the RSFSR not included)	18	30	42	50
(c) Union Republics (the RSFSR and its Autonomous Republics not included)	16	29	41	49
II. Proportion of city inhabitants who live in:				
(a) cities with more than 100,000 population	41	46	49	55
(b) cities with more than 0.5 million population	16	21	24	27
III. Proportion among the population of the Union Republics (the RSFSR not included) and Autonomous Republics incorporated in the RSFSR of:				
(a) inhabitants of cities with more than 100,000 population	13	19	19	25
(b) inhabitants of cities with more than 0.5 million population	1	5	9	12

* Calculated from the data in *Itogi vsesoyuznoy perepisi naselenya 1959 g. SSSR* (svodnyi tom), Moscow, 1962; *O predvaritelnykh itogakh vsesoyuznoy perepisi nase-lenya 1970 g.*, Soobshchenye CSU SSSR, Moscow, 1970.

this is true of other countries also, it is particularly important in the USSR, as explained later in this paper.

The traditional idea among ethnographers and geographers that the countryside is the "mainstay of ethnographic features" (unlike the towns, which are considered to be "anti-ethnographic" with their material culture and their mixture of ethnographic components) is currently undergoing a revision. Such a notion was justified for the historical period during which towns presented a kind of "demographic exception" because of their low population numbers, and the ethnic sub-stratum was believed to be a phenomenon spread over a whole country, a phenomenon that was not subject at that time to the social conscience. Neither of these premises is relevant any longer, at least not in the USSR, and particularly not for the leading nations forming the Republics of the Union and their incorporated Autonomous Republics. The simultaneous development of commodity

232

and monetary relations has led to an influx of manufactured goods, factory products and the associated material culture into all rural areas, and this influx has considerably weakened the "spontaneous" and insufficiently conscious ethnographic character of these areas.

The joint effect of urbanization and ethnic processes involves many historical, social, demographic, and town planning features. The latter can be seen particularly in developing countries, which often preserve separate ethnic settlements or districts within town boundaries. They can also be seen in highly developed capitalist countries having racial segregation or mass immigration, which leads to preferential residential districts. The resulting "nodes" or "junctions" of interaction between urbanization and ethnic processes are a particularly fertile field for geographic research, because the complex nature of geography essentially aims at detecting ties between these kinds of phenomena.

It is generally known that cities, particularly large ones that attract migrants from an area considerably larger than the original ethnic region with which the city has been developing, frequently become multi-national centres. The multi-national composition of population in the overwhelming majority of cities in the USSR is not only the result of these cities' historical past, which often favoured the migration of various nations over long periods (including particularly the migration of Russians to cities throughout the USSR), but also, and above all, the result of Lenin's national policy during the period of the building of socialism. This policy allowed representatives of all nations "to put down roots in the cities", and at the same time strongly stimulated the national consciousness and ensured a rapid diffusion of culture, socialist in content and national in form, to all nations of the USSR. Lenin's policy is also reflected in the organization of the state, in the system of the multi-stage national and state formations (the Republics of the Union, Autonomous Republics, Autonomous Oblasts, National Okrugs).

The development of various national and state organs was accompanied by an accelerated expansion of the economy into the non-Russian areas (particularly through industrial growth), and led in these areas to rapidly expanding urban centres which have become focal points for the development of national culture and ethnic consciousness. In these centres were established headquarters of scientific institutions, in order to educate a national labour force of skilled workers and professionals, as well as social institutions and organizations which carried out the research on and the development of the national culture. These centres have furthermore become sources of literary and publishing activities and of broadcasting in the national language, etc. Since they need national personnel for management positions and for intensively training the national labour force, they have come to attract the rural intake of the indigenous population. (Some-

233

times they attract representatives of nationalities from beyond the boundaries of their ethnic territory, i.e., from other Republics of the Union, including urban inhabitants from such Republics). Thus one can state at the present time it is probably the cities, more than the rural areas in the USSR, that are becoming "carriers of ethnic features".[2]

A similar process of cities becoming the centre of ethnic features can be seen in many less developed countries in different forms. This applies particularly to those which gained independence during the last decade. Apart from being ethnically "mosaic", the cities in these countries play an extremely important role as the "ethnic uniter" at the initial stage of emergence of a nation.

In the composition of a certain national area in the USSR, the occurrence of major national groups that are normally resident in adjacent Republics, Autonomous Republics, etc., may sometimes be the outcome of historical settlement circumstances (eg. the Tadzhiks in Samarkanda and the Armenians in Tbilisi). At other times it may also reflect a drawing together of the individual nations (eg. the attraction exerted by Kazan upon the nationals of neighbouring republics, e.g., those of the Volgan-Vyatkan and the Ural regions). This is accompanied by neighbouring nations (which for this, if for no other, reason are subject to the economic and cultural gravitation towards cities), having their own ethnic territory within a particular republic, and sometimes also an autonomous status. Thus, the effect of Tbilisi on the Ossetians differs from that exerted on the Azerbaidzhans for example.

The mechanism of the formation of national composition of the urban population in the Union Republics and in the Autonomous Republics is determined by the relationship between two mutually opposed trends. The first trend is the influx of the native population to these towns. This is the result of a planned policy of accelerating the training of home staff for the "urban professions" on the one hand, and on the other of releasing the native population from the rural areas as the mechanization of agriculture gains headway. The second trend is a rapid increase in the demand for labour in towns, due to the growth of the economy, which is particularly concentrated in urban areas; the quality requirements of such labour (skill, training in "urban professions") are particularly important. Should the demand for "urban" staff outstrip the rate at which it is possible to train the newly arrived native population, labour from beyond the boundaries of a particular ethnic territory would be "drawn in" instead. In practice, this very often leads to an increase in the proportion of Russians (as well as White Russians and Ukrainians attracted in the same way) in the population of a particular town.

Both the above trends are most clearly seen in the capitals of the Union Republics which have become at the same time the leading economic

234

Table 2. Changes in the Total Figure, and National Composition of the Population of the Capitals of Four Union Republics of the USSR

City	Year	Population in thousands	National composition of the population in %		
			natives	Russians	others
Baku	1897	111.9	36.0	33.4	30.6
	1926	425.9	26.3	35.3	38.4
	1959	987.2	37.7	34.2	28.1
Kiev	1897	247.4	22.2	54.4	23.4
	1926	513.6	42.2	24.5	33.3
	1959	1104.3	60.0	22.7	17.3
Tashkent	1897	155.4	75.1	9.7	15.2
	1926	323.6	52.6	32.4	15.0
	1959	911.9	33.9	43.8	22.3
Tbilisi	1897	159.6	26.4	28.0	45.6
	1926	294.1	38.2	15.6	46.2
	1959	694.7	48.5	18.2	33.3

centres of their Republics. That these trends are mutually opposed, is illustrated by the examples in Table 2.

The transformation of Tashkent under Soviet authority, not only into a large capital city, but also into a first order industrial centre, has caused such a great demand for trained labour that it has proved impossible to meet this demand solely by training the native population within scheduled time periods. This explains the rapid increase in the proportion of Russians (although the native Uzbek population has also grown rapidly; it increased by 140,000 from 1926-1959). The population of Tashkent has almost tripled during the Soviet era, while that of Baku has increased scarcely more than twice. This growth resulted both from an outside influx and the natural increase. The Azerbaidzhans and Russians in Baku, which was an important industrial centre even during the pre-revolutionary days, have grown in number. The proportion of the third leading national component, the Armenians, has diminished in Baku, while the Persians who migrated to the city during the earlier periods and were employed as unskilled labour in the operation of oil wells, have disappeared altogether. It was the "industrial past" of Baku that stood behind the rapid rate of training of new personnel recruited from the native population; this has resulted in an almost unchanged proportion of Russians in the population of the city.

The great achievements in the training of native labour in Tbilisi during the Soviet era has resulted in the native population approaching 50% of

235

the total number of inhabitants (the number of Armenians in Tbilisi exceeded that of the Georgians up to the Revolution and during the first years of Soviet authority). The influx of Russians and Armenians during the Soviet era has been negligible, and their proportion to the total number of inhabitants in Tbilisi has decreased sharply. There has been a considerable influx of Ossetians (which is due to the incorporation of the South-Ossetian Autonomous Oblast into the Georgian Soviet Socialist Republic), and of certain other nations, represented in Trans-Caucasia by their largest ethnic enclaves (the Kurds, the Greeks). The increase in the number of Georgians in the population of Tbilisi (about 224,000 during the period 1926-1959) was also accompanied by an assimilation of part of the autochtonic population. Thus, almost 12.5% of the Armenians and nearly 20% of the Ossetians in Tbilisi considered the Georgian language their native tongue in 1959.

The proportional increase of the Ukrainians in Kiev was the result of two simultaneous factors that followed the same trend, i.e. (1) the influx into the Ukrainian capital of Ukrainians from all over the Ukrainian SSR (including the nearest neighbourhood); (2) the further consolidation of the Ukrainian nation, due to a growing national consciousness. This resulted from the great achievements of Ukrainian culture. It can be assumed that a part of the Kievans who hesitated over admitting their Ukrainian nationality,[3] later acknowledged this with sufficient conviction. Also children born of mixed marriages have increasingly declared themselves Ukrainians (as noted in a special study).[4] The total Russian population of Kiev has doubled during the period 1926-1959 (i.e. it grew at almost the same rate as the total population of the city), and its proportion has hardly decreased during that time. On the other hand the proportion of the "miscellaneous" nationalities has decreased very rapidly; the Jewish population of Kiev virtually started from nothing after the atrocities of the Nazi occupation; the number of Poles in Kiev has decreased both in relative and absolute figures (due to repatriation and mixed marriages); and the numbers of Germans has also decreased in absolute figures.

The data given above [5] illustrate the most extreme examples; they permit, however, a discussion of some definite types of ethnographic relations between urbanization and migration. Thus, the "Tashkent" type of changes in the ethnic composition of population could also be seen for example in other large cities of Central Asia and Kazakhstan characterized by a rapid economic growth (in 1959, Russians constituted 73.2% of the inhabitants of Alma-Ata, 71.8% of Frunze, 52.5% of Ashkhabad, 74.4% of Karaganda, 56.7% of Dzhezkazgan, etc.).

The population influx from other republics is not so much the outcome of the unsatisfactory "quality" of a local population unable to meet the requirements of a rapidly expanding economy, but rather of an absolute

236

shortage of people to fully develop the industrial potential. Such a situation is faced, for example, by the Baltic republics. The census of 1970 has recorded an increase in the population influx, particularly to the cities of the Estonian Soviet Socialist Republic. The positive balance of migration to the above cities has been calculated for the period 1959-1970 as 131,600, including 92,500 from beyond Estonian SSR. This latter figure is nearly half (45%) the entire natural increase of the urban population of the republic during the intercensus period.

A rule that can be adopted to describe an ethnographic trend clearly seen throughout the USSR would run as follows: the influx of the Russian population in cases with a rapid growth of industrialization "exceeds" the pull exerted by the national and ethnic centres on the native population; in cases with a slower economic development, the proportion of the native nationality in the total population of a city may be considerably higher. An interesting relation between the proportions of the native and immigrant population (the latter being mainly Russian), depending on the size of the city (i.e. total population), occurs in the towns of Union Republics (except the Russian Soviet Federal Socialist Republic) and in the towns of Autonomous Republics incorporated into the Russian Republic. It is not only the capitals, but also the larger cities whose size largely depends on the development of industry, that rapidly attract their population from outside their republic. It is for this reason that the composition of the population of such cities has a mosaic pattern, with the simultaneous increased proportion of Russians. This proportion may be smaller in medium and small towns. In urban types of settlements, however, many of which form newly established industrial centres, the proportion of Russians may also be rather higher.

In an earlier paper, the author looked at the dependence of the ethnic composition on the size of a city for the Lithuanian and the Tadzhik Soviet Socialist Republics.[6] The dependence was fully confirmed. On the other hand the picture thus obtained about a settlement of the urban type has proved more variegated. This proves beyond doubt that they should be considered differently, and those which form newly established industrial centres should be put into a separate group.

The specific social features, essential to ethnography, of ethnic processes in cities include: a very deep division of social activities that cuts across the national divisions of the population; a great variety and activity in contacts (personal ones, as well as those between whole professional or social groups); a high level of mutual exchange of information (including national cultural values); the knowledge of two, and sometimes several languages; an increased participation in non-material activities; availabillty of durable equipment (including household equipment) which tends to equalize the way of life of the various population groups; architectural

237

forms which reduce the possibility of preserving many traditional domestic ethnic features: an absolute prevalence of factory-made commodities for meeting the requirements of the population (these commodities sometimes preserve ethnic features; this, however, almost exclusively concerns items of applied art).

One more important feature can be seen in Soviet cities, particularly in those which have become capitals of the Union and Autonomous Republics, centres of Autonomous Oblasts or of Oblasts within the Union Republics (and it is these cities that form the "officer corps" within the urban network beyond the Russian Federal Soviet Socialist Republic, and in the territories of the Autonomous Republics of the Russian Republic). In these cities one finds special organizations and institutions, whose activities try to develop national forms of socialist culture.

An essential feature of "urban ethnography" in non-socialist countries may be the spatial segregation of racial or ethnic groups, an ethnic discrimination in the labour market, a struggle between languages, and other manifestations of ethnic antagonisms.

Three main ethnic processes characterize our epoch. First, the consolidation of nations, particularly of those involved in the development of the victorious conditions of the Socialist system, and those in the developing countries which are only passing the initial stages in their integration. Second, nations drawing closer to one another and whose life paths are inter-weaving. Third, the assimilation of minor nations by major nations which are more economically, socially, and culturally advanced.

These three processes are more active in urban areas. The effect of the urban environment in levelling off external ethnic features and encouraging assimilation is often accompanied by an opposite trend; ethnic consciousness is sharpened through the daily opportunities of comparing one's "own" culture with others', as represented by other ethnic groups. In the USSR and other Socialist countries this sharpening stimulates creative competition and cooperation between neighbouring national cultures in the cities. It does not oppose a rapprochement of nations since each of them wholly preserves its individuality and can freely manifest its features. In contrast, in capitalist countries such a sharpening of the national consciousness may lead to evergrowing national and ethnic conflicts.

Notes

1. There were strong appeals at the International Congresses of Anthropologic and Ethnographic Sciences VII (1964) and VIII (1968) to make ethnography "the face of the city" and demands for further "demographic trend" within the broad scope of ethnographic research; the problems of urban pop-

238

ulation are moving discernibly ahead in ethnographic and ethnodemographic research.

2.   An interesting example is presented by the Armenian cities, particularly by Yerevan. With a very high proportion of Armenians (93% according to the 1959 census) in this city's population we can consider it uni-national. The influx into Armenian cities of Armenians from beyond the republic (including immigration from outside the USSR, by repatriation), marks a turning point in the historical process of the "Armenan Diaspora", which has dispersed the martyred Armenian nation over numerous countries. We must recall that during the 18th and 19th centuries the Armenians founded many settlements over the present area of the USSR beyond the original boundaries of Armenia. (The territory of the Armenian Soviet Socialist Republic of today was incorporated into the Russian Empire as early as the 1820's.) According to the 1959 census, 55.7% of the Armenians in the USSR lived in Armenia; 15.9% lived in both neighbouring Georgia and Azerbaidzhan. One should stress at this point that the Armenians, including those outside Armenia, are a relatively "urban" people: in 1959, 57% of them lived in urban areas; the average for the USSR as a whole was 48%. Armenians who move to the cities in Armenia have usually already acquired an urban way of life, and an "urban profession".

3.   It should be borne in mind, when comparing the data of the Soviet census records with those of the 1897 census, that the latter did not have any questions about national status; the ethnic structure under that census was determined by the mother tongue only. The policy of Russification under the Tsarist rule led to a neglect of the Ukrainian language and its social prestige was lower compared with that of Russian (also of Polish, within specific groups). It was because of the similarity of the Russian and the Ukrainian languages that the ethno-linguistic boundary was by many standards a relative one (a similar indefinity could hardly have occurred in the non-Slavic peripheries of the Russian Empire where the Russian language distinctly differed from that spoken by the native population).

4.   V. V. Pokshishevski, "Etnicheskiye protsessy v gorodakh SSSR i nickotoric problemy ikh izucheniya" ("Ethnic processes in cities of the USSR and selected problems of research"), *Sovietskaya Etnografiya*, No. 5, 1969.

5.   For particulars see V. V. Pokshishevski, *ibid.*

6.   V. V. Pokshishevski., *ibid.*

FUNCTIONAL AND SPATIAL ORGANIZATION IN RELATION TO ADMINISTRATIVE TERRITORIAL DIVISIONS — THE EXAMPLE OF POLAND

Zygmunt Rybicki

1. *Determinants of the Territorial Division of Poland*

The efficient performance of the managerial functions as well as the execution of socio-educational and economic-technical tasks[1] by the government in Poland is determined by the territorial structure[2] of the country. With the changing functions of government encompassing new spheres of responsibilities it generally becomes necessary to introduce changes in the territorial structure of the country.

Many factors influence the territorial structure of the country, the number of territorial units and the number of tiers.[3] The most important of these factors are the following:

1. The size of the territory of the country, the density of population, and the type of population concentration;

2. The scope of tasks performed by government, and the intensity with which the government fulfils its managerial functions, particularly as far as the social and economic-technical questions are concerned;

3. Historical traditions which, irrespective of the subsequent changes in the socio-economic system, continue to exert an influence on the delimitation of the territorial units;

4. The problems of minorities which, in multinational countries, have a bearing on the question under consideration;

5. Geographic conditions, such as the relief map of the territory, the system of transportation lines, etc; and

6. The developing requirements and needs of the people with regard to cultural life and social services as well as to municipal and technical facilities.

All the factors involved in the process of restructuring the territorial division of the country must be taken into account. The respective weights of the various factors are defined by the executive body on the basis of actual priorities declared by the state.[4]

The most important of these factors are undoubtedly the functional substantive scope of responsibility of the territorial administration, the intensity of influence to be exerted by the state on the processes of social life, and, in particular, the active part played by the state in the economy.

The policies carried out by the state administration are contained—to varying degrees—in four major spheres. These are:

1. Implementation of the administration policy in a given area; this activity consists in defining goals, in ascertaining what resources are necessary to attain each of the set goals, in planning, forecasting, and initiating new actions;

2. Licencing, distributive, and protective activities, which consist in enforcing law and order, issuing permits, and following-up citizens' obligations vis-à-vis the state (collection of taxes, military drafting etc.);[5]

3. Organizing economic activities and public technical services, i.e. organizing state-owned enterprises and ensuring that the facilities indispensable for their efficient performance are available, establishing transportation systems and energy supply systems, executing policies as regards cooperative and private enterprises, establishing municipal facilities, etc; and

4. Implementation of the administration's service roles, i.e. establishing public health institutions, educational, cultural and scientific institutions, and ensuring social welfare and rehabilitation, etc.

Changes in the structure of territorial division are also brought about by the necessity of increasing state involvement in contributing to the satisfaction of growing social needs; this results in an increase of the scope of functions performed by the state and this increase is particularly evident in the third and fourth of the spheres described above. The growing scope of the organizing functions carried out by the state is particularly apparent in the socialist countries. Following the changes in the socio-economic structure the government in the socialist countries became one of the major instruments of promoting economic growth, as well as an important factor implementing social reforms and guiding cultural, educational, technical-economic and other transformations. The growing involvement of a government in the internal social and economic life of the country is, however, also characteristic of countries with different socio-economic systems.[6]

The new scope of responsibilities resulting from the growing organizational functions of modern government necessitates certain transformations in the territorial structure of the country. Hence, the new territorial units being established now have to be framed in a way which provides favourable conditions for the fulfilment of the increased government responsibility for social, cultural, and economic affairs. In defining these new territorial units, the high dynamics characteristic of the phenomena of collective life have to be taken into consideration. The processes of concentration and specialization of manufacturing production (and partially also agricultural production) are striking examples of such dynamic changes in the national economy. If a local government unit is to be capable of collaborating with large economic organizations it must have adequate powers to implement its policies, and thus it must be able to exert its authority over a larger geographic area. It is this that has provided the impulse to the search for new solutions, a field of study that has come to be known as regionalization.

A region can be defined as a large territorial unit the government of which has the powers to perform complex socio-economic functions, and which is able to be a fully competent partner strong enough to interact with large economic organizations. The problems of regionalization occur in varying degrees in practically all countries; the degree depends, inter alia, on the character of tasks declared by a state as priority tasks, and on the willingness of government to undertake action aimed at the implementation of these tasks. It is in those countries which undertake organizational tasks (i.e. those relating to the third and fourth spheres),[7] that the above problems come to the fore. That is why the emergence of regions can be treated as an example of the influence that the tasks (particularly the economic tasks) undertaken by government exert on the territorial structure of a country. Under such circumstances it is not surprising that in most cases the discussions concerning administrative changes or comprehensive government improvement programs tend to include the problem of the territorial division of the country. This is why changes in the structure of the administration have almost always accompanied investigations relating to the transformation of the territorial division of the country.[8]

The subject matter under consideration here is the transformation of an existing territorial division of a country rather than the introduction of a completely new division. This approach results from the fact that the existing units of the territorial division have developed in a historical way and are related to certain traditions of the population residing in those units. Any change thus becomes highly complex and expensive to execute, which is why it is an evolutionary change of the territorial division that is characteristic of most countries. This, however, does not mean that there is no growing need to introduce more basic changes[9], but that because of the complexity and the cost of changing a country's territorial division, any proposals along such lines have to be extremely precise and comprehensive.

2. The Territorial Division in Poland

There are three existing systems of territorial division in the Polish People's Republic. They are: 1. the basic system; 2. the special purpose system; and 3. the supplementary system.

It is the local administration that operates in the basic units of the territorial division of the country. This administration performs general duties and its operation contributes in particular to the satisfaction of the social and welfare as well as the economic needs of the population. In the socialist countries the representative local authorities of the government (people's councils) [10] operate in the basic units.

Not all emerging problems can be solved within the confines of the basic unit of the territorial division. For example sea coast administration, mining administration, health resorts administration etc., require that the territorial units of their operations coincide with the relevant features of the tasks performed by such administration. Consequently, special purpose units come into being. The local authorities operating within the basic units of the territorial division perform also certain coordinative functions as regard other bodies at the same horizontal level; that is why there is a general tendency to limit the number of special purpose territorial units and to keep them as small in size as possible. Special purpose authorities can also operate in the basic units of the territorial division. Under such conditions the direct contacts of the various authorities become easier and the coordinative function within the horizontal framework is greatly facilitated.

The supplementary units of the territorial division are areas of operation of the supplementary authorities. For example, in the collective communes each village has a local representative (soltys) who acts as supplementary authority vis-à-vis the commune authority. In urban areas such supplementary functions are performed by voluntary block committees or settlement councils which perform supplementary functions vis-à-vis the city and (in cases where a city administration is subdivided into districts) district authorities.

We are here mainly concerned with the basic territorial division. It is in the areas of the basic units that the fundamental tasks of government are carried out, particularly as regards economic and spatial planning. In the socialist countries those basic units constitute the areas of operation of the representative local authorities; these authorities are established by popular election, and they define tasks for the local administration and perform the functions of civic control.

The basic units of the territorial division can be subdivided into tiers and types. The main types are the following: cities, rural communes and aggregative units. The larger urban agglomerations constitute a special type.

These agglomerations, because of their growing importance, are frequently accorded a special legal status.[11]

Cities and aggregative units can belong to various tiers. There are two or three tiers of the territorial division in most of the European countries.[12] As a result of long-standing tradition the present system of territorial division in Poland consists of three tiers. These are the following:

1. The lowest tier—rural communes, small towns, and medium-size city districts. Until the end of 1972 there existed also industrial, fishing and health resort settlements, but these have recently been classified as cities or rural communes;

2. The intermediate tier—boroughs (which are aggregative units comprising all the units of the lowest tier with the exception of medium-size city districts), medium-size cities, and large city districts; and

3. The highest tier—provinces (aggregative units comprising boroughs and medium-size cities) and the five largest cities of Poland (subdivided into districts).

The people's councils and, subordinate to them, the local administration operate in all units of the territorial division described above, i.e. communes and cities, city districts, boroughs and provinces. Furthermore, agencies of independent administration which are not directly subordinate to the people's councils can also operate in some units. The activities of the local bodies of political parties, mass civic organizations, trade unions and others are also confined to the territorial units. Consequently, it is this unit that constitutes a focal point of all fundamental phenomena of group activities.

The following is the specification of the territorial units existing in Poland on January 1, 1974:

— *The lowest tier* (communal):
  2048 rural communes
   437 town communes
   318 rural town communes
    11 districts (in cities belonging to the intermediate tier)
— *The intermediate tier* (borough)
   317 boroughs
    74 cities
    28 districts (in cities belongng to the highest tier)
— *The highest tier* (provincial)
    17 provinces
     5 province-cities (Warszawa, Lodz, Krakow, Poznan, and Wroclaw).

245

3. The Territorial and Substantive Scope of Activities of the Government Agencies

The substantive and the territorial scope of the activities, i.e. the responsibilities, of government authorities and administration [13] are interdependent. One of the very important other factors on which they depend is the territory upon which the tasks of a given agency are to be performed. The process of restructuring rural communes in Poland, for example, clearly indicated that agencies operating in small territorial units are not able to discharge wide responsibilities. These agencies had to function with the aid of a major subsidy from the central budget because their own income was too small to allow them to undertake larger projects. [14]

The small size units of territorial divisions were also not conducive to the enhancement of the organized form of political, cultural-educational, economic and similar activities which induce civic and self-government forms of popular involvement. [15]

The functions of licencing, distribution, and protection can be effectively performed in small-size units. However, with the widening scope of the organizing functions of the government administration the problem of territorial expansion of the activities of government authorities increases in importance.

The various responsibilities of government authorities and government administration as a rule appear in different spheres of activity in varying degrees. These responsibilities may be classified as follows: [16]

1. The extent of decision-making powers, i.e. making specific legal decisions and issuing general legal acts. The extent of powers depends on the importance of the problems entrusted to a given agency;

2. The scope of direction, supervision and control exercized on subordinate agencies. The agencies at the lowest tier are devoid of such responsibilities. In all other cases the law must clearly define the scope of responsibilities and quantitatively fix the means at the disposal of the supervising bodies;

3. The scope of obligatory collaboration with other government agencies and organizations, the responsibilities for coordination vis-à-vis independent agencies, as well as the ways of stimulating the various civic organizations, institutions and individuals to undertake collective works of local importance; and

4. The scope of proposals and initiatives to be submitted to the superior agencies, the transmission of individuals' comments and requests as well as the preparation of documents for the decision of the superior agencies. This does not of course apply to the highest or to the central agencies.

The responsibilities concerning direction, supervision and control and

246

of the submission of proposals are particularly wide in a system of centralized government administration, where collaborative and decision-making responsibilities are relatively underdeveloped. As against this, within the decentralized system local authorities are given particularly wide responsibilities for decision-making and collaboration.[17]

As indicated previously the tasks ascribed to certain spheres and the resulting responsibilities are executed primarily by the local authorities of government functioning in the basic units of territorial division. The role of each of the tiers of government as related to the territorial division of the country can be described in the following way:

1. The main task of the agencies at the lowest tier (communal) is to satisfy the basic every-day needs of the population. As far as their licencing, distributive and protective powers are concerned, these agencies carry out the registration of marital status, vital statistics, and movement of population, they organize fire protection, enforce law and order, collect basic taxes, etc. As far as their economic activities and public technical services are concerned they organize the construction and operation of municipal facilities and they initiate civic actions to construct local roads, green open spaces and other social facilities. The agencies of rural communes provide agro-technical advice to the private cultivators and veterinary aid to their livestock and they control and supervise the number of shops in the villages. In accordance with the legal framework now in existence the agencies at the communal level are further responsible for the adequate provision of rural and communal school buildings, health centres, cultural groups and local clubs, and they carry out social welfare actions utilizing budgetary provisions for this purpose. They also devise and initiate civic actions. The agencies at the communal level have a fairly wide scope of decision-making powers and powers of collaboration with other agencies and organizations.

2. Agencies of the intermediate tier (borough) undertake tasks which exceed the capacity of the agencies at the communal level. The borough agencies define the ways in which policies devised by higher authorities should be implemented, ensure such implementation, and see that initiatives and actions taken by various institutions are coordinated in their totality whatever their formal dependence may be. They organize civic control over all government agencies operating in a given area; they also assist the agencies at the communal level in execution of their tasks. In the sphere of licencing, distribution and protection, the agencies at the borough level supervise public meetings, organize military drafting, supervise the activities of the people's militia and other organizations concerned with public order, and give verdicts on appeals made against the decisions of communal agencies. In the sphere of economic activity and public technical services the borough agencies set up local construction

and maintenance enterprises, state pools of agricultural machinery, and plant repair and municipal enterprises etc. The agencies organize local transport, heating and lighting systems, and supervise the operations of local post offices. In their service roles the agencies at this level set up hospitals, secondary and vocational schools, borough cultural institutions, public libraries and social welfare establishments.

3. The agencies of the provincial tier implement tasks the scope of which exceeds the capacity of the lower tier agencies. For example, they assist in running specialized hospitals, support theatres financially, set up and direct specialized local enterprises and consulting offices, and promote local cultural, artistic and scientific activities. However, the main task of these agencies is the coordination of the activities of various institutions operating at the same tier (what is called horizontal coordination) as well as the coordination of the activities of institutions operating at the lowest tier.

The powers of coordination (i.e. obligatory collaboration) derive from the accepted principle of harmonizing the activities of institutions having a large measure of independence, (i.e. a wide scope for their own decision-making). The problem of coordination is of particular importance when the responsibilities of the lower tier agencies are increased. The establishment of trusts comprising local enterprises can serve as an example of coordination relating to the institutions of the same tier within the system of people's councils. These trusts organize by themselves the activities of local enterprises entrusted to them (retail trade, restaurants, small scale manufacturing and so on); at the same time the trusts are subject to overall control and supervision by the administrative agencies of the provincial tier.

The institutions which are not directly subordinate to the people's councils are subject to horizontal coordination. This coordination concerns such institutions as agencies of specialized administration (e.g. mining administration, sea coast administration, energy supply administration, forestry administration and so on), government enterprises which are not subordinate to the people's councils (e.g. larger manufacturing enterprises), and non-governmental organizations (e.g. associations of artisans and cooperative unions). The powers of coordinating the activities of the above mentioned agencies and institutions were given to the people's councils by the People's Councils Act. These powers are expected to create conditions under which activities aimed at satisfying the needs of the population can be carried out in a more consistent manner. The goal of satisfying the needs of the population thus defines the framework of the powers of coordination. Within the framework of these powers the people's councils are authorized to comment on the location proposals submitted by large enterprises and their branches. They undertake housing projects financed from the budgetary provisions and from the resources of specific enterprises, they devise and execute employment policies, etc.

Under the conditions of a fairly wide range of responsibilities entrusted to the borough agencies, coordination becomes a part of the function of direction, supervision and control. Utilizing powers of coordination the provincial agencies ensure an equitable development of various areas, the rational siting of new investments, the desired level of protection of environment and so on. The main objective is that the needs of the population should be adequately and constantly satisfied.

The instruments by which coordination is effected by the agencies of the provincial tier are in the first place the economic plans, the local budgets, spatial development plans, etc. The procedures established for the preparation of projects and plans, their approval and implementation, provide for the participation of agencies of the lower tier and also for the participation of other institutions involved. The principle of devising plans from below makes it possible to combine civic initiatives, activities of various groups, and local want-satisfaction with more general objectives connected with policies of coherent and dynamic development; they also make it easier to combine the economic with the social objectives.[18]

4. *Collaboration as the Main Method of Solving Regional Development Problems*

The question of interaction of the government agencies operating in the units of territorial division is closely connected with the problem of consistency between the existing territorial division and the emerging regional entities. It is necessary to distinguish between the interactions taking place among the people's councils of the same tier and type (e.g. the link between the neighbouring borough people's councils) and the interaction of the people's councils of the same tier but of a different type (e.g. the link between the borough people's council and the city people's council in a borough-city). There is further interaction between people's councils of different tiers and of different types (e.g. the link between the people's councils of province-cities and the people's councils of the suburban communes). The collaboration of various people's councils is the principal method by which emerging regional problems are currently being solved in Poland.[19]

It is the inconsistency existing between the formal territorial structure of the country and the emerging regions that requires close collaboration of the people's councils. The fact that already today one can observe the emergence of the supra provincial and supra borough socio-economic links and interactions appears to indicate that the question of a thorough analysis of the territorial division of the country should be made. For example, from the formal-legal point of view no supra-provincial units of territorial division exist in Poland today. This is not, however, to say that there are no particular solutions employed in practice, based on mutual inter-provincial agreements. To give a few examples:

1. The concept of the "Warsaw agglomeration", comprising the city of Warsaw and a part of Warsaw province, has been developed with the aim of creating conditions to ensure the future rational growth of the Polish capital. This concept involves an agreement between the local authorities of Warsaw and those of the Warsaw province.

2. In order to ensure coherence between the design and implementation of the transportation network, living and cultural facilities, and protection of environment, collaboration is essential among the neighbouring highly industrialized areas of the southern part of Poland in Krakow, Katowice, Opole, and Wroclaw provinces.

3. Development of the sea-oriented industry has brought about a common base for the coordination of all activities connected with the particular sphere in Gdanski, Koszalin and Szczecin provinces.

On the other hand, the existing regions do not constitute fully developed entities at the moment.[20] It is premature to speak today about the regions having taken their final shape, since a planned action (partly resulting from new geological discoveries) aimed at restructuring the spatial distribution of industrialized centres is still in progress in the country.[21] Nevertheless we should emphasize that a certain measure of stability of the territorial division of the country is indispensable.

The above mentioned examples do indicate the important role that the processes of industrialization and urbanization can play in the emergence of new territorial links.[22] Obviously, it is not every new link which will necessitate a change in the territorial division. Aside from the need for some stability, a large number of problems requiring a consistent co-operation in the regional scale can be handled successfully within the existing territorial division, provided that certain conducive conditions are created. It is the political principles which are of major importance in this connection. The reason for this is that the task of government is always to execute its stated political principles; these principles exert a major influence on the operation of government as well as on the methods of their implementation and on the general approach taken to them (in spatial terms also).[23]

From this point of view the unity of the political principles related to problems that have a regional dimension is of prime importance if the consistency of the administration's operation is to be ensured. This is particularly so because of the incoherence between the territorial division of the country and the developing regions now in existence. This unity is achieved in Poland also through a definite spatial delimitation of the spheres of interests of the local boards of political parties. For example only one party unit has been given the responsibility for all the agencies of government administration operating in the area of a large urban agglomeration, irrespective of whether those agencies operate in the cities or in the suburban areas. This approach has greatly contributed to consistent problem solving in the entire area of an urban agglomeration. There are, however, limits to the possibilities of devising solutions to problems which transgress the existing boundaries of the territorial division of the country. If such links and interactions tend to become permanent and if they extend over a number of spheres of activities of government agencies it becomes unavoidable to give due consideration to the problem of restructuring the territorial division of the country.

The continuing collaboration among the local administrative agencies operating over an area delineated by the emerging socio-economic relationships in Poland has led to the conclusion that a common development plan comprising all the agencies involved should be devised. This is exactly what occurred in the supra-provincial collaboration described above. Originally the development of the sea-oriented industry brought about the collaboration of the provincial authorities within the framework of the "Interprovincial Commission for Collaboration with Sea-Oriented Industry" established by them in 1962. This Commission was a civic agency operating on the principle of voluntary collaboration among all institutions and corporations represented in it. Subsequently, a new unified macro-regional plan of the Baltic coastal area has been developed, comprising all the territorial units which previously collaborated on a voluntary footing. The preparation of macro-regional plans[24] has been initiated within the framework of the perspective plan, integral to which is the national spatial development plan. Beginning in 1962, work started on the elaboration of three macro-regional plans: one for the Baltic coastal area; another covering the complex of industrial areas in Upper Silesia-Cracow provinces; and the third including the north-eastern part of the country, where accelerated development is envisaged.[25] These macro-regional plans came into being as result of close cooperation within the interprovincial commissions established especially for the preparation of these plans and with the Polish Government experts board for spatial development.

The importance of the problems described above, far from decreasing, has become more prominent as the responsibilities given to the people's councils have been widened (as a result of the recent 1972-73 reform). The accepted principle stating that the tasks which exceed the scope of responsibilities of a given people's council should be executed by a higher tier council does not always contribute to a satisfactory solution. The

251

reason for this is that no perfect territorial division can be devised. Such a division is by necessity based on some fundamental premises with the result that other tasks of supplementary and secondary importance have to be solved through other arrangements. The borough and provincial boundaries should not cut across the obvious economic, social and cultural links that emerge in a natural way.

It is significant that the progressive collaboration among the people's councils, its form and its procedures, has been primarily brought about by practical needs. The analysis of the developed forms of collaboration among the local agencies will reveal three basic stages of such collaboration as far as the comprehensiveness of these forms is concerned. We should note that the sequence adopted for these three stages here is primarily connected with the ordering principle which illustrates the scope of the collaboration involved. The various forms of collaboration in fact supplement each other and are often applied side by side in practice.

The first stage of collaboration, when the existing organizational structure is taken for granted, consists in harmonizing the tasks performed by the local agencies. During that stage the following forms of collaboration evolved:

a. Joint meetings of the people's councils concerned, joint meetings of their committees, etc.;

b. Nominations of the representatives of collaborating people's councils on their collective bodies, e.g. local economic planning commissions; and

c. Elaboration of one integrated general regional plan [26] for the province-city and the areas of the province surrounding it and preparation of detailed regional plans for parts of the neighbouring provinces where important projects or other economic activities which will exert a profound influence on the economic development of the area will be carried out. (A general regional plan is as a rule confined to the administrative boundaries of the province).

The expanding scope of problems requiring an integrated approach tends to bring about the development of new mechanisms of collaboration. At this stage, the solutions already existing in the law are utilized with the important qualification that they are applied to more than a single people's council. The following are examples of such collaboration:

a. Nominating joint consultative, coordinating and controlling agencies by the people's councils;

b. The establishment of a joint local authority for two people's councils;

c. The establishment of joint local enterprises;

d. The establishment of a joint people's council for a commune and the neighbouring borough-city. There are numerous small towns the development of which is so intimately linked with the development problems of the neighbouring commune and vice versa that it is considered justified to entrust a joint people's council with executing the task of their joint development, although they will retain their administrative identity. There are presently 318 joint people's councils for small towns and neighbouring communes in Poland; and

e. Collaboration between commune people's councils with the neighbouring people's councils in all cases which are considered to be justified on the ground of the character or type of the task being undertaken. The collaborating people's councils may in particular: i) Pass joint resolutions; ii) Enter into agreements concerning the execution of a particular task and its financing as well as establishing, if required, new enterprises to carry out the execution of that particular task; iii) Establish principles of joint utilization of selected premises and plants; iv) Set up joint funds for selected purposes; v) Organize social actions in specific fields; and vi) Initiate joint social, cultural and health actions.

It is to be stressed, however, that at this stage of development the collaborating units carry out tasks of their own. This is to say that here, as in the first stage, collaboration consists in summarizing the efforts of collaborating agencies. The only new features are that these efforts yield results through the activities of joint agencies. In contradistinction to this, the third stage of collaboration is characterized by *joint* management by the local authorities in a region, irrespective of the existing territorial division and substantive links. At this stage the crux of the matter is not to combine efforts in selected fields but rather to entrust the expanded activity to an agency which is more capable of carrying it out successfully. This means that instead of, for example, setting up a transportation system in the suburban zone by establishing a separate enterprise for that purpose or by entering into agreement as far as the activities of the city and suburban zone enterprises are concerned, the collaborating councils may come to a conclusion that the transportation needs of the suburban zone in question can be covered more satisfactorily by the existing city transport enterprise; in exchange for this service the local authority of the suburban zone will undertake to provide commensurate recreational areas for the city inhabitants. The collaboration in this field is facilitated by such legal instruments as, for example, making the suburban communes subordinate to the people's council of the neighbouring (borough) city or by making these subordinate to a district council of a province-city, i.e. to an agency of a higher tier. The application of such resolutions may be particularly useful in all cases in which a suburban commune tends to become a part of an urban agglomeration, or when a small town comes under the direct influence of a larger and more dynamic city.

5. Concluding Remarks

The problems of regionalization are, as we have seen, treated in Poland as part of a much wider question, namely the problem of the delimitation of the territorial division of the country.

The experiences we have had in Poland and also the experiences of other socialist countries lead us to conclude that the problems of territorial division are very complex and that they emerge as a resultant of many factors. Consequently any proposal for a change of an existing territorial division must be approached in a cautious and thorough way.[27] It is also not possible to experiment with a proposed change in a part of the country. However, it is possible to try to solve the problem in a sequential way, and this is exactly what the Polish authorities did when they undertook a comprehensive and thoroughly prepared reform of the territorial division as far as the territorial units of the lowest tier are concerned.

The communes established in 1972 have become strong units of the territorial division. The local authorities at the communal level took over a number of responsibilities previously discharged by the borough agencies. It is definitely to be expected that this process will continue in the future. At the same time, it is to be pointed out that the average number of communes per borough has decreased substantially when compared with the situation that existed before the reform was undertaken. On January 1st 1972 there were an average of 14 communes in a borough; by January 1st 1974 that average had decreased to about 7. The average number of administrative units in a borough at that time was 8 when small towns were counted in: 14 was the smallest number of administrative units of a borough tier in a province; the biggest did not exceed 34.

The administrative solutions described above are, however, not fully satisfactory because the intensity of the development of Poland constantly poses new problems.[28] The existing and emerging urban agglomerations are bound to exert an increasing influence on the tasks to be performed by local administrations.[29] At the same time the process of concentration of production is in progress, as is illustrated by the emergence of huge economic corporations. This is why we are already faced with doubts about whether the provinces as presently delineated will be capable of performing the role of economic regions in an efficient way. It is to be expected that the macro-region will play an increasingly important part as the economic development of the country is intensified. Thus the macro-regions may provide a foundation for a new territorial division of the highest tier in the future.[30]

Although the work on the modernization of the territorial division of Poland is still in progress, it has been possible to organize administrative

254

activities at the regional level. The principal method applied in this respect has been the collaboration between the people's councils and their agencies. This method was selected because the territorial division in Poland constitutes the basis for the activities of the unified system of authorities and government administration: the people's councils directly or at least indirectly govern the total body of problems in the areas of their activity.

Other forms of organizing the activities of government at the regional level are also used to a large extent in Poland. These are the establishment of special development funds, the merger of administrative agencies in neighbouring units of territorial division etc. It is thus justified to state that Poland can be quoted as an example of a country in which numerous forms and methods of regionalization are applied, depending on the recognized needs. The common characteristic of the solutions applied in Poland is their elasticity, which consists in the selection of those organizational forms of regional activities that reflect the specific requirements of the fields under consideration. One of the advantages of the Polish approach as far as regionalization is concerned is the relatively low cost of the applied solutions, and this results from the fact that activities at the regional scale are carried out by the agencies of public administration i.e. no separate agencies are established to carry out such activities. It should also be noted that the experiences of Poland show that the administrative activities on the regional scale can be developed under the conditions of an existing traditional territorial division. That division has to be supplemented to a smaller or greater degree by mechanisms allowing of administrative actions that are commensurate with the scale of dynamically developing regions.

The features and experiences of the Polish method of organizing the administrative activities at the regional scale thus appear to deserve to become a subject of wider international research and presentation.

Notes

1. The function of the socialist state is elaborated in N. W. Czernogołowkin, *Tieorija funkcji socjalisticzeskogo gosudarstwa*, Juridiczeskaja Lit., Moscow, 1970.
2. The traditional term "territorial division" should be replaced by the term "territorial structure of the country" under the conditions prevailing now. That is so because the units of the territorial division have become today not only the basis of the operation of the agencies of public administration but also a basis of the operation of local authorities and units of civic and political organization as well as economic and technical institutions.
3. See also M. Jaroszyński (editor), *Administrative Law,* Vol. 1, PWN,

Warsaw, 1952, p. 67 et passim.

4. As a rule the problems of minorities have to be taken into consideration in the process of introducing changes in the territorial division of the country. However, the way in which they affect the intended changes depends on the policy vis-à-vis minorities exercized by a given state. For example, in the USSR, which adheres to the principle of the equality of rights of all nationalities, special autonomous units (districts and areas) are established in such a way that their boundaries encompass the main population centres of a given nationality. Those countries which take the blending of the nationalities residing in them as a goal define territorial divisions along different lines.

5. Licencing, distributive and protective activity is used here in the subjective sense; see Walter Antoniolli, *Allgemeines Verwaltungsrecht*, Manzche, Vienna, 1954, p. 254 et passim.

6. J. Zawadzki, *Modern Capitalism: Economic Essays*, Warsaw, 1964; and B. Chenot, *Organisation économique de l'état*, Paris, 1965.

7. See also Pierre Viet, *De la planification régionale à la région politique et administrative en Europe*, Bulletin de l'Institut International de Administration Publique, No. 9/1969, p. 31 et passim; and E. Kalk (editor) *Regional Planning and Regional Government in Europe*, IULA, The Hague, 1971, p. 39 et passim.

8. Gerald E. Caiden, *Administrative Reform*, Penguin Books, London 1970.

9. These problems have been investigated by several writers, including Kosta Mihailovic, *Regional Development in Eastern Europe*, United Nations Research Institute for Social Development, Geneva, 1972, p. 46 et passim.

10. M. Jaroszyński, *Aspects of People's Councils: a political and legal study*, PWN, Warsaw, 1961, p. 27 et passim.

11. See also *The History of Urban Growth*, Report of the International Colloquium, Brussels, 2-4 December, 1969, Brussels, 1971.

12. See also Samuel Humes and Eileen Martin, *The Structure of Local Government, A Comparative Survey of 81 Countries*, International Union of Local Authorities, The Hague, 1969.

13. On this subject see also M. Jaroszyński, *op. cit.* p. 64 et passim.

14. Research has shown that shortcomings of this type are usually associated with the functioning of the majority of local agencies operating in small territorial units. For further information on this subject see *Local Government in the Twentieth Century*, 35 national reports on a general report for the International Union of Local Authorities Jubilee Congress, 1963, The Hague, 1963.

15. Although popular participation in decision-making is a concept often stressed nowadays, there seems little in the way of a consensus on which this means or might mean. See also James V. Cunningham, "Citizens' Participation in Public Affairs", *Public Administration Review*, Special issue, V. XXXII, October, 1972, p. 589 et passim; A. K. Bialych, *Uprawlienije i samouprawlienije*, Nauka, Leningrad 1972, p. 89 et passim; and Giuseppe di Palma, *Apathy and Participation, Mass Policies in Western Societies*, Macmillan, London 1970, which includes an analysis of the participation crisis in Great Britain, the Federal Republic of Germany, Italy, and the USA.

16. This subject has been elaborated on in my study *The System of People's Councils of the Polish People's Republic*, PWN, Warsaw, 1971, p. 218 et passim.

256

17. See also my study "La descentralización su importancia para reformar la administración pública", in *Cuadernos de la Sociedad Columbiana de Planificación*, No. 8/1972, p. 5 et passim.

18. This problem was elaborated in my study *Administrative and legal problems of the planned economy*, PWN, Warsaw, 1971, p. 246 et passim. Planning problems have been also described in Jerzy Kruczała, *Local Government as Promotor of Economic and Social Development*, IULA, The Hague, 1971; see also W. Kawalec, "Regional Development and Planning in Poland" in *Regional Government*, IULA, The Hague, 1971, pp. 253-259.

19. The forms and scope of People's Councils collaboration are described in detail by Jerzy Słuzewski in "The Collaboration of People's Councils", in L. Nara (editor), *Studies in the field of Administrative Law*, PWN, Warsaw, 1971, p. 113 et passim; see also *The Activities of Government Agencies in the Area of Urban Agglomerations*, Wyd-Prawnicze, Warsaw, 1965, p. 126 et passim by the same author.

20. See also Tadeusz Mrzygłód, *Spatial Development Plan of Poland*, Warsaw, 1971.

21. These problems are considered to be the subject of forecasting in Poland today. See S. Leszczycki, P. Eberhardt, and S. Hefman, *Prognosis of the Spatial Development of the Country up to the Year 2000;* and B. Malisz and P. Zaremba, "Prognosis of the Settlement Pattern in Poland in the Year 2000", in *The Development of Poland in Prognoses,* prepared by the Polish Academy of Sciences, the Committee for Research and Prognoses "Poland 2000", Ossolineum, Warsaw, 1971.

22. See also J. Goryński and Z. Rybicki, "The Functional Metropolis and System of Government", in *Metropolitan Problems,* Methuen, London, 1970, p. 291 et passim; and "Symposium on Governing Megacentropolis", *Public Administration Review,* No. 5/1970.

23. See S. Leszczycki, "The Concept of Space and its Role as a Factor in Modern Economy", in K. Secomski (editor), *Elements of Spatial Planning Theory*, PWN, Warsaw, 1972, p. 31 et passim.

24. This problem is elaborated in A. Kukliński, "Macro-Regional Planning in Developed Countries" in A. Kukliński, R. Petrella (eds.), *Growth Poles and Regional Policies: A Seminar,* Mouton, The Hague, 1972; The problems of spatial development of one of the macro-regions in Poland are described in A. Pyszkowski, "The Development of a North-Eastern Macro-Region" in *People's Council — Economic — Administration,* No. 15/1973, p. 23 et passim.

25. As given in Regulation No. 10 of the Prime Minister dated January 24, 1972 concerning the preparation of the national spatial plan and regional plans.

26. The problems of regional planning are elaborated by St. M. Zawadzki, *The Bases of Regional Planning,* Warsaw, PWE, 1972.

27. This is also referred to in Wacław Brzeziński's "The Shaping of the Territorial Division of the Country: Problems and Methods", in *State and Law (Państwo i Drawo),* No. 3/1963, p. 401, et passim.

28. K. Secomski, "On the Way Toward Modern Structural Changes in the National Economy" in *Nove Drogi.* No. 10/1970.

29. See also Annmarie Hauck Walsh, *The Urban Challenge to Government, An International Comparison of Thirteen Cities,* Institute of Public Administration, New York, 1969.

30. A. Kukliński, *op. cit.*

7

KEY FEATURES OF REGIONAL DEVELOPMENT AND PLANNING IN EASTERN EUROPE*

Bohdan Gruchman * *

There are a number of similarities between regional development planning in Eastern Europe and in other parts of the world, most of which stem from the common spatial nature of the problems dealt with in both areas. However, there are also profound differences, connected with the basic characteristics of the economic and political systems of the countries concerned, between the practice of regional development planning in Eastern Europe and elsewhere, and these differences tend to be overlooked or minimized. The issues of regional development and the methodology of regional planning in Eastern Europe cannot be fully understood without reference to some of the basic features of the socio-economic and political system.[1]

Of these features, public ownership of the bulk of the means of production is particularly important. This is the base of a decision-making system in which the key development decisions pertaining to all segments of the economy are made at the centre and evaluated from the national point of view. Planning as a particular way of making development decisions is similarly characterized: it is basically normative and not, as in many other countries, indicative. This centralization of planning and its normativeness come especially clearly to the fore when planning decisions are being taken with respect to future capital formation and distribution of income.

* This note addresses itself to some of the major features and issues of regional development planning that are common to all Eastern European countries. However, there are aspects of the problem which are dealt with differently in individual countries and on which the author was not able to dwell in this paper. In particular, the specific features of regional planning in the USSR merit special attention. For particulars, the reader may refer to the literature mentioned in the following pages.

* * The views expressed in this paper are those of the author and do not necessarily reflect those of the United Nations Organization with which the author was connected in the period 1972-1974.

Two other features have a considerable bearing on regional development planning in Eastern Europe. The entire development system is socially oriented: the socialist economies are committed to a full employment policy and to an income distribution that will create equal opportunities for all segments of the population living in each part of the country. The other feature pertaining to development in Eastern European countries is that most of them inherited from the past an under-developed, predominantly agricultural economy with strong spatial disparities.[2] It became imperative that substantial changes be made in the sectoral and spatial structure of each country, and the heavy capital outlays involved in such changes did not remain without influence on the implementation of the previously mentioned social orientation of development.

Overall Characteristics of Regional Development Planning

Against the above background, regional development planning in Eastern Europe developed features which differentiate it from that experienced elsewhere. The difference is already evidenced in the scope of the regional approach to development. Regional planning in Eastern Europe was from the beginning an action-oriented activity geared to tackling economic as well as spatial (physical) and social aspects of regional development more or less comprehensively. It is only relatively recently that such an approach has come to dominate the issue in many other countries.

Regional planning as it is practiced in Eastern European countries involves all the economic sectors (industry, construction, agriculture, etc.) as well as all the so-called social sectors (education, health, social welfare, etc.). This wide coverage enables the planners to formulate economic and social programmes that complement one another. The need for integrating economic planning with social planning, which at present is a widely debated issue in many countries around the world, was hardly an issue at all in the socialist planning system.

The planners in the Eastern European countries further co-ordinate the socio-economic with the physical (spatial) aspects of development. They determine the location of productive investment, of technical infrastructure (highways, communication lines, water supply systems, etc.), of social facilities, and they formulate policies for development of settlement systems. All this results in regional land use maps which usually constitute an integral part of regional development plans. The explicit treatment of physical aspects in these plans considerably reduces the difficulties found elsewhere in co-ordinating economic planning with urban planning.[3]

Regional development planning is an integral part of the national planning process in Eastern Europe. It is recognized as vital in the three-dimensional development planning accounts system which involves central macro-planning, and sectoral as well as regional planning.[4] Each of these kinds of planning deals with development in a specific way, and contributes to a comprehensive vertical and horizontal treatment of the entire development process.

Within this system regional planning has two tasks: to secure the most efficient location of all development activities, and to bring about an income distribution among inhabitants of all parts of the country which would create opportunities for equal sharing in the benefits of development. The first of these tasks does not arise in the regional planning of the western countries, owing to dominant private ownership in most segments of the economy; the second is undertaken, mainly in the practice of those capitalist economies which pursue a national policy of regional development.

Over the many years of implementing regional planning, the countries of Eastern Europe have devised a system that reflects the specific features of regional planning in this part of Europe. This system represents a practical implementation of the concept of "planning stages". First the long-term regional development plans are prepared. These cover a period of ten to twenty or more years and outline the basic objectives and strategies of long-term regional development. Then, each socialist country makes its middle-term regional development plans, usually covering a period of five years. These have the function of translating the long-term goals and strategies into defined targets and action programmes which are assigned to concrete units and institutions for implementation. The final stage in the planning process requires the preparation of executional plans which set out the immediate tasks that are to be performed in one or two years by all those involved in the implementation of the targets and objectives of the previous plans. In conjunction with the annual budgets and financial plans, the executional plans define the resource allocations necessary for plan implementation. As the execution of development plans is divided between central and regional/local authorities according to their spheres of operational competence, two versions of the short-term plans are prepared: the regional executional plan (sometimes called the "territorial plan") for the regionally and locally supervised parts of the economy in each administrative district; and national sectoral plans for each centrally controlled sector. Both of these form part of the annual national economic plan.

The socialist countries of Eastern Europe have developed methodologies and procedures designed to make it possible for these plans to be prepared in a co-ordinated and comprehensive fashion. In these methodologies and procedures, the main emphasis is on the elaboration, transmission and proper application of planning parameters: from long-term development

261

plans through middle-term to operational plans; from national macro-plans through the mezzo-level to plans at the micro-level; in the lowest administrative units and in individual enterprises.

Regional Planning and Optimal Location of Investment

It is well known that, in order to find an investment location that will be optimal from the social point of view, it is necessary to consider not only the direct but also the (sometimes wide-ranging) indirect costs and effects. Among the factors affecting locational calculations, agglomeration economies are nowadays becoming increasingly important. Their impact, and also that of deglomeration factors, can only be assessed on the basis of advance knowledge of the future inputs and outputs of other branches of industry, particularly those located in the same area and related to the industry in question through forward and backward linkages, the planned inputs and outputs of trade, storage and transport enterprises, investment in urban infrastructure and in many other ways. Such knowledge is normally beyond the capabilities of individual enterprises. In a market economy, agglomeration economies can generally be assessed only *ex post*, and even then with considerable difficulty. The look into the future is then an extrapolation of past trends or a conjecture based on more or less intelligent assumptions.

In a socialist economy the above difficulties are already considerably reduced or even eliminated by the comprehensive nature of regional plans, which contain most of the information on future development of all other sectors and enterprises needed to assess a substantial part of possible external economies and diseconomies connected with particular locations. If the locational calculations for all major sectors are made at the same time, during the regional planning process, there is a good chance of arriving at a coherent set of locational decisions representing an optimal solution for the entire subsystem.[5] This is exactly the role that regional plans in the socialist countries of Eastern Europe are assuming with growing competence. Most of these countries initially concentrated particularly on the assessment of factors contributing to agglomeration economies of industry, since this sector was the prime agent of structural change in the spatial pattern of national economy. In the process of regional planning, deglomeration policies for industry were also formulated (Hungary, Poland). While continuing and even strengthening this function, regional planning is currently increasingly competently tackling the perhaps even more complex task of assessing urban economies connected with the restructuring and development of entire settlement systems *(inter alia* in Czechoslovakia, Bulgaria and Poland).[6]

The capability of regional plans in socialist countries to take into consideration all the relevant inputs and outputs contributing to agglomeration economies would not be as significant as in fact it is, were it not for the fact that these plans serve either directly or indirectly as the basis for most locational decisions on development: directly when the locational decision is taken while the plans, which usually account for a major part of development investments, are being worked out; indirectly when the locational decision is taken after the preparation of the plans, particularly with regard to the location of investment outlays of smaller scale, which are not dealt with individually in the regional plans or which occur during the implementation of the plans. Since such decisions are nowadays usually taken autonomously by various enterprises and economic agencies, it is necessary to develop locational incentives for these enterprises to follow the development directions embodied in the regional plans. Prices of such inputs as water, gas, land, and transportation, which are differentiated from city to city on the basis of the regional plan, serve this purpose by pushing autonomous locational decisions in the desired direction. For some years now work has been carried out in most of the socialist countries aimed at finding, with the help of regional plans, the most effective parameters with which to guide decentralized locational decisions and thus to reconcile the interests of individual enterprises with the spatial rationale.[7]

Regional Planning and Income Distribution

Owing to the national ownership of the means of production and to several other structural features, the authorities in a socialist economy may, it is widely acknowledged, directly decide about the distribution and redistribution of a much greater part of income produced than in a capitalist economy. In geographical terms income distribution in the socialist countries may be accomplished with more independence from income generation than is possible elsewhere. Naturally, for the country as a whole the total volume of income distributed cannot exceed the volume of income produced, but income distribution may be more easily redirected to different social groups and, what is of particular interest to us here, to different regions, out of exact proportion to their share in income production. Among the instruments that are most effectively used for this purpose are the investment fund, covering both production and social sectors, and the public consumption fund, i.e. goods or services supplied free of charge or at reduced prices.

Income distribution of the scope and nature of that which is being effected in the socialist countries requires not only the establishment of individual operational programmes in numerous fields but also the ap-

263

plication of more general measures to help co-ordinate these programmes and guide them in the desired overall direction. These measures, which should be based on a thorough knowledge of the various needs and priorities of social groups living in different parts of the country, should facilitate the implementation not only of short-term policies of income distribution but also of the long-term policies of a structural nature.

The regional planning process as practiced in Eastern Europe seems well suited for the application of such measures. The process commences at the local and regional levels. The authorities at these levels, under general guidelines from the centre, are required to prepare draft local and regional plans expressing the needs of the region's population and outlining development proposals for meeting these needs. Through arrangements which vary from country to country, such plans are accepted by representatives of the population and are then transmitted to the centre to be included in the over-all national development plan which is prepared by central planning authorities. When this national development plan has been approved, binding parameters are transmitted back to the regions in order to guide them in the preparation of the final regional and local development plans. These plans may differ, sometimes substantially, from the initial drafts because what is optimal from the purely local and regional point of view may not be optimal when national interests are taken into account, and also because priorities of a higher order may supersede some of the local and regional priorities. Since, however, the central planning authorities make a considerable effort to meet local needs and priorities, it is unusual for there to be a wide disparity between the draft and the final regional plans.

The broad scope of regional development plans offers a good platform for co-ordinating various programmes of income distribution, particularly —as in the case of low income housing and the location of health and educational facilities—when the programmes are complementary. The role of these plans may be considered even more crucial in the regional co-ordination of programmes relating to income production with those relating to income distribution. While the socialist system is able to go quite far in dealing separately with these two kinds of programmes there are limits which, under certain circumstances, should not be exceeded. If too high a portion of income produced is transferred from one region to another, the growth process of the former may slow down, its labour productivity may decrease and other negative consequences may result. On the other hand, overfavouring a region with income coming from outside may have an adverse effect on its efforts to increase its own production, its own productivity and, ultimately, its own income.

There is no general rule which can help establish a correct balance between regional income production and distribution. The interdependencies[8] between productive and social programmes are usually intricate and often indirect in nature; moreover they differ at different times. To trace and adjust them requires a thorough knowledge of existing local conditions, of future plans for numerous regional sectors, and of the background of national needs and priorities. Such knowledge can be acquired through a regional planning process that has the scope and nature of that which exists in the socialist countries. Regional plans and all their co-ordinating instruments (regional income and expenditure accounts, manpower balance sheets, etc.) make it possible for an optimal (in relation to given constraints) balance between regional income generation and distribution to be found.

Substantial changes in regional income distribution can be brought about only through structural changes in the spatial pattern of the economy. Programmes of income redistribution of a short-term character cannot have a lasting effect since structural changes of the regional economy require longer time periods to bear fruit. The correct framework for effecting lasting change in this regard is that of the long-term—i.e. covering 10-20 years—regional plans in the Eastern European countries. A distant time horizon in regional planning is also advantageous in assessing the profitability of social overhead investment directed to an underdeveloped region and its impact on the development of productive activities. Finally, as regional planning in Eastern Europe, besides being long-term, is also operational (mid- and short-term), it allows long-term policies of structural change to be harmonized with short-term social policies, in particular with those of income distribution.

Some Key Regional Development and Planning Problems of the Future

The regional approach will continue to play a major role in the national development efforts of the Eastern European countries,[9] and it is at least arguable that its role will be greater in future than it has been up to now. The socialist countries are determined to maintain or even to increase their high rates of growth. This implies the need for further profound structural changes in their economies and for optimal utilization of their development resources. Proper location of activities which would satisfy these needs could considerably increase the efficiency of the economy and thus contribute to the overall rate of further growth. At the same time, regional development planning will become much more responsible for environmental protection than ever before. With further growth, environment problems—both local, or regional, and national—will increase in scope and in importance. These will require a national environmental policy which will have to be implemented mainly in a regional framework.

The majority of the countries in Eastern Europe, until fairly recently

265

predominantly agricultural in character, are in the process of transition to urban societies. One can predict that this process will be intensified in the future. The process in itself is characteristic of countries all over the world. What makes it different in Eastern European countries is the intensity of the process and, even more, the controlled way in which it is being implemented. Development of a national urban structure which would secure the optimal living conditions for the bulk of the population and simultaneously be conducive to further national growth is a challenging task for regional development in the future. Particularly crucial will be the regional framework for the rational development of the biggest urban agglomerations.

The countries of Eastern Europe will continue to alleviate the remaining spatial imbalances of their economies which cause differences in the living standards of the population in different regions. Considerable progress in speeding up the growth of less-developed regions has been achieved in the past, despite the limited possibilities of capital accumulation and the pressing needs of growth.[10] However, the interregional differences inherited from the past were so deep that it has not yet been possible to eliminate them totally. Differences in regional production and income which reflect shifting patterns of technological innovations and development strategy will of course never be totally overcome: such temporary differences in a changing regional pattern are an inevitable corollary of growth. What must be eliminated are the chronic differences of a structural nature which result in some regions invariably being considerably below the national average of per capita income (or any other meaningful measure) and others invariably being well above that average.

Against the above background of regional development problems, the methodology of regional planning as it is currently exercised in practice will have to be changed in a number of ways. The common aim of these changes will be to increase the impact of regional planning on all major economic decisions. This is necessary not only because of the growing spatial interdependence of development and the increasing scarcity of space, but also because of a tendency towards greater decentralization in the decision-making system, particularly with respect to industrial enterprises.

Thus, it will most probably be necessary to further broaden and strengthen the system of planning parameters which guide regional developments in the economy.[11] Besides improvements in the operations and in the quality of direct, normative parameters, indirect ones derived from regional planning projections will have to be widely used if a proper framework for decentralized decisions with spatial implications is to be established. These regionally conditioned parameters would reflect spatial conditions of long-term demand and supply of land, labour, water, infrastructure, etc.

266

Such parameters with different spatial scope and content are needed particularly in two situations: when the macro-development plan is being disaggregated into regional components; and when individual projects in different locations are being analyzed and evaluated. In the first situation the regional parameters are necessary in order to shape sectoral plans according to a national policy of regional development. In the second they have the task of reflecting the full opportunity costs in each location. The planning parameters ("prices", "costs", etc.) will have to be generated in a chain of programming operations, many of which will have to be of a non-linear type (in order to deal with, *inter alia,* urban agglomerations). This will require a remodelling of the present planning procedures and statistical reporting.

With the further expansion of modern information techniques and the implementation of new planning models which meet the above requirements, it will probably be possible to simplify the regional planning procedures by reducing the number of planning levels which co-operate in a hierarchical system of development plan formulation. Although in theoretical considerations usually two-level models are discussed, in reality there are far more planning levels.[12] Merging some of them would shorten the planning process and facilitate statistical and planning explorations. Such an operation would most probably require the establishment of some new regional planning levels which would stand somewhere between the eliminated ones.[13] Since planning for such new regional levels would also have definite implications for plan implementation, this could lead to changes in the territorial division of the country. For reasons which stem from the characteristics of the existing system as explained earlier, it is of paramount importance for the countries of Eastern Europe that territorial administrative units coincide with development and planning regions. A periodic review of the situation and, where necessary, an adjustment of administrative borders would, therefore, be required.

Notes

1.   These issues and their background as they relate to the Soviet Union, Czechoslovakia, Yugoslavia and Poland, have been dealt with extensively in articles by V. V. Kosov, A. J. Probst, P. Turcan, K. Mihailovic, B. Winiarski, B. Gruchman and B. Prandecka in *Economies et sociétés: Economie régional et pays socialistes,* Cahiers de l'I.S.E.A., Tome III - No. 1, Librairie Drozd, Geneva, January 1969.

2.   This is well described in Chapter I of Kosta Mihailovic, *Regional development: Experiences and prospects in Eastern Europe.* United Nations Research Institute for Social Development, Geneva, Regional Planning Series, Antoni Kukliński (ed.), Vol. 4, Mouton Publishers, Paris-The Hague, 1972.

3.   The United Nations Secretariat, New York, found it necessary to organize

from 10 to 14 September 1973, a special meeting of experts to discuss problems of integration of economic and physical planning and to suggest lines of action to solve the problem. See the official documents of the expert meeting registered under ESA/HPB/AC.10 (English).

4. The scope and functions of each part are defined in K. Porwit, *Theoretical and methodological questions in the construction of comprehensive models for regional planning*, RSA Papers, XXII, 1968.

5. These calculations, in order to be as approximate to real-world conditions as possible, have to be based on rather extensive mathematical models with non-linear functions. But even simple alternative calculations performed manually in an iterative process can be very useful and better than extrapolation and guesswork.

6. One can consider urban economies as a particular group of agglomeration economies or, to use W. Isard's term, economies of juxtaposition. See W. Isard, *Methods of Regional Analysis: An Introduction to Regional Science*, Cambridge, Mass.: MIT Press, 1960.

7. Extensive experiments in this direction have been organized in the Soviet Union. See N. N. Nekrasov, "Economic Policy of the KPSU and the Distribution of Productive Forces", *Komunist*, No. 3, 1972, pp. 70-71. (In Russian.)

8. An overview of these interdependencies as they operate in socialist countries is given in M. Kabaj, "Selected aspects of long-term social planning and forecasting—central planning", in Economic Commission for Europe, *Approaches and methods used in long-term social planning and policy making*, United Nations, New York, 1973 (Sales No.: E.73.II.E.7), pp. 37-56.

9. The present and future role of the regional approach in Eastern Europe is analyzed in A. Lukazewicz, *"Problems of regional development planning in the Eastern European planned economies"*, paper presented at the Sixth Interregional Seminar on Development Planning: regional (sub-national) planning, held in Quito, Ecuador, from 20 September to 1 October 1971, United Nations document (ESA/DPPP/Meeting/PL.VI/8.).

10. These changes are extensively documented in K. Mihailovic, *op. cit.*, Chapter II.

11. The role of such parameters within the entire framework of planning is described in K. Porwit, "Techniques of interregional plan formulation in Poland", in David M. Dunham and J. G. M. Hilhorst (eds.), *Issues in Regional Planning*, Publications of the Institute of Social Studies, Paperback Series IV, Mouton Publishers, The Hague-Paris, 1971.

12. On the question of existing planning and decision-levels in most of the socialist countries of Eastern Europe see *Planification et élaboration des décisions à plusieurs niveaux*, Documents présentés à la sixième réunion des conseillers économiques des gouvernements des pays de la CEE, United Nations, New York, 1970.

13. At the national level this would most probably require a change in the division of the country into macro-regions. The role of that level in regional planning is analyzed in A. Kukliński, "Macro-regional planning in the developed countries; problems and issues", in *Growth poles and regional policies*, A. Kukliński and R. Petrella (eds.), Mouton Publishers, The Hague-Paris, 1972.

8

REGIONAL PROBLEMS OF SOCIALIST ECONOMIC INTEGRATION

Jurij M. Pavlov

The 25th session of the Council for Mutual Economic Aid, held in July 1971, adopted a program for further expanding and improving cooperation and for developing socialist economic integration among the member states. The CMEA envisages gradual convergence and profound accommodation of the national economic structures, based on the principles of socialist internationalism, respect for national sovereignty, national independence and national interests, full equality, mutual advantage and mutual assistance. The CMEA member states' decision to enter into a new phase of large-scale economic integration is a logical result of long-term cooperation among the socialist countries in all spheres of social activity.

Increasing internationalization of social and economic activities and the further development of the international division of labour constitute an objective process determined by the state of the productive forces and by the latest developments in the scientific and technical revolution. Internationalization of the reproduction process has created conditions leading to a new stage in international social and economic relations—a stage of economic integration of separate states and of the establishment of large regional interstate communities. This, in turn, makes it possible to considerably extend the sphere of economic activity as a result of the ever-increasing possibilities of intensifying the concentration of production on an international scale and of organizing production on a cooperative and combined basis. Karl Marx pointed out that with the formation of a socialist economy the working class would advance towards "a harmonious national and international coordination of social forms of production".[1]

At the present time there are two types of economic integration: socialist and capitalist, and these differ radically in their principles, goals and methods.

Economic integration of the CMEA countries is based on public ownership of the means of production, on centralized planning, and on the

269

principles of socialist internationalism. It is conducted on a voluntary basis, involves no supra-national bodies, and does not touch upon questions pertaining to domestic planning and the economic activity of states. Socialist economic integration within the system of the CMEA countries ensures a harmonious interaction of international and national interests, and promotes a rapid alignment of the levels of economic development of the countries belonging to the socialist commonwealth.

Capitalist economic integration is based on state-monopolistic ownership, on the internationalization of large capital. In the exercise of this type of economic integration the contradictions characteristic of the capitalist social-economic formation are manifested in full measure. Here, integration is characterized by competitive struggles among state-monopolistic groupings. At the same time gigantic supermonopolies of international capital appear, and these encroach on the national interests of countries, particularly of those which are economically underdeveloped. "The international interpenetration and intermingling of capital and the various forms of cooperation of industrial activity among them constitute the industrial-economic basis of the integrational process".[2] Capitalist integration radically differs from socialist integration not only in its state-monopolistic character but also in the continued presence and intensification of the irregularity of the economic development of the integrated countries and their regions, an irregularity that is aggravated by inflational tendencies and competition for markets.

Economic integration, the essence of which lies in a coming together of countries, and, eventually, in a mutual accommodation of national economic structures, as well as in the formation of a single international economic body, is an intricate and contradictory process, in which two tendencies are intertwined. The first is a rapid internationalization of the reproductive process, and the second is the further development and perfection of the national states, with all the peculiarities of their centuries-old economic and spiritual activity on a well defined territory.

In analyzing the capitalist mode of production, V. I. Lenin noted that "the economic, political and spiritual life of mankind as a whole becomes increasingly internationalized already under capitalism. Socialism internationalizes it to the full".[3] Discerning, moreover, two historical tendencies—1) towards the formation and consolidation of national and state segregation of certain countries, and 2) towards the development and consolidation of international relations between them[4]—V. I. Lenin foresaw the possibility of "creating a single, world economy controlled according to a general plan by the proletariat of all nations . . ."[5]

Economic integration has a markedly regional character. Of considerable scientific interest is the study of the localization of international integrational communities, which, of course, first appeared in Western

Europe. In the last 15 to 25 years two large integrational communities have appeared in the world: the community of West European capitalist states known as the Common Market (EEC), and the community of East European countries belonging to the Council for Mutual Economic Aid (CMEA). As we have seen, the essence, goals and tasks of economic integration, as well as the character of the integrational measures of these two communities radically differ.

Interstate integration originated in Western Europe as a result of the existence in that area of a great number of relatively small, but economically developed, countries. The contradiction between the demands arising out of the development of the productive forces of capitalism and the narrow bounds of domestic markets achieved maximum acuteness. Other factors also involved were the specific political conditions under which monopolistic capital developed in this region, the formation and consolidation in Europe of the socialist system of states, the maturity and solidarity of the communist and workers' movement, as well as the heavy loss which the West European bourgeoisie suffered as a result of the disintegration of the imperialist colonial system. However, the fact that, as a result of the strengthening of the position of the U.S.A., the monopolistic capital of the West European countries lost the leadership of the world economy, played a special role in the development of integrational tendencies in West European countries. The founding of economic organizations (the European Coal and Steel Community in 1951, the Common market in 1958, etc.) made it possible for West European capital to establish an extensive industrial-financial basis for competition with American capital.

Integrational cooperation of the East European socialist countries began in the midst of their political and economic isolation during the Cold War period. This necessitated a unification of their forces to restore the national economies ruined by the war and to launch large-scale construction of the material and technical basis of socialism and communism.

"The CMEA member states consider that the high level of development of productive forces which they have achieved, the great changes in the production and consumption spheres, the urgency of the tasks involved in conducting the scientific and technological revolution, the all-round acceleration of technical progress and the raising of production efficiency and living standards, as well as the nature of socialist relations of production and the requirements of the class struggle against imperialism, make it vitally important to constantly expand and improve the economic and scientific-technical cooperation among the CMEA member states and to develop socialist economic integration . . ." [6]

271

The limited manpower and material resources of small and average-sized countries is also an important consideration as regards integration. Such countries are unable on their own to develop all branches of science and technology and to implement the resulting achievements in production. Consequently, they strive to develop their industry, science and technology jointly with a group of countries.[7] This is particularly true of Western Europe.

The CMEA countries have at their disposal the greatest industrial-territorial potential in the world. They account for approximately 18 per cent of the territory, 10 per cent of the population (over 360 million), over 25 per cent of the national income, 33 per cent of the industrial and over 20 per cent of the agricultural production, and approximately 10 per cent of the world foreign trade turnover.[8] Concentrated in these countries is 4/5 of the world reserves of manganese ores and apatites, 2/3 of the reserves of nickel, tungsten and asbestos, approximately 1/2 of the reserves of iron ore, zinc and copper, approximately 2/5 of the reserves of natural gas, approximately 1/3 of the world reserves of coal, etc.

The development of the economic integration of the socialist countries, the process of convergence, and, in the long run, the merging of their economies, are facilitated by the similarity of their social-economic structures—all based on socialist relations of production and public ownership of the means of production—by the rapid development of the productive forces, and by the principal economic changes which have occurred in the last two or three decades. The extensive implementation of scientific and technical achievements is of particular importance in this connection.

In carrying out the complex program of economic integration that the CMEA countries have adopted, economists are faced with the necessity of solving a number of concrete problems and of conducting scientific feasibility studies of the development of the productive forces. In studying the economic essence of socialist integration great importance is attached to a comprehensive analysis of the policies and accumulated experience in its territorial aspect. This is due to the fact that the international socialist division of labour is becoming an important factor in the development and distribution of industry in the socialist countries.

In our opinion, the study of regional problems of economic integration should be conducted along three basic lines:

a) The first is the study and scientific generalization of the territorial features of economic integration in a macrosphere, the process of forming a combined, interstate, integrated economy, the regularities of establishing such an economy, and the development and distribution of the productive forces. In this study the projection of macro-economic tasks to the territory and the investigation of and a search for a solution to problems connected with an optimum distribution of industry geared to a newly-forming spatial unit become increasingly important. Needless to say, in this study the basic principles of socialist economic integration must be fully observed.

b) Next, and very importantly, is the study of economic interrelations between separate states in the system of integrational unification and of a gradual rationalization and optimization of these interrelations. V. I. Lenin sharply criticized the assumption that a democratic state where socialism had triumphed would be without borders. National distinctions mediated in many phenomena of the social-economic sphere would continue existing for a long time even after socialism was victorious on a worldwide scale. A purposeful activation of the participation of certain countries in the international socialist division of labour improves their national economic structure, and consolidates the economic potential of the combined economy.

c) It is necessary to investigate the territorial properties of economic integration in a microsphere. This study relates to the influence integration has on the development of separate regions within the country, the solution of concrete problems of cooperation between contiguous border territories, and the coordination of the development of "contact economic zones", etc.

Naturally, these conventionally evolved trends of scientific research reflect the single process of a systematic formation of an economic territorial structure of an integrated economy.

Joint integrational practices are becoming increasingly evident in the CMEA member states. Thus different interstate economic and international economic organizations are founded, industrial centres are constructed jointly with the participation of the interested states, and certain technologically—or scientifically— inclined industries are developed jointly. Such international integrational measures conducted by the CMEA will undoubtedly have a significant and ever-increasing influence on the distribution of productive forces in all the individual member states. Their economies will conform more and more to the functions performed in the system of international socialist division of labour. The systematic regulation of the international socialist division of labour directed at optimizing foreign economic relations results in the establishment of a combined economy and in the strengthening of relations. This process, however, is due not to a mere levelling, but to a strengthening and development of the individual national economies, their complex development and the effective specialization of industry to the extent allowed by the integrational community. In future, it will be necessary to find ways of rationalizing the earlier distribution of productive forces throughout the economic system of the CMEA countries.

The period following the adoption of the complex program has been characterized by a further expansion of cooperation and by all-round development of socialist economic integration. Thus the production of the national economies, and of the commonwealth's economy as a whole, have been made more effective. At the present time practical solutions are being found to major economic problems which involve both the national and the international interests of the fraternal countries. Moreover, the economic development of the CMEA countries is being determined to a great extent by the extension of all-round cooperation.

The 26th session of the CMEA (July 1972) passed a decision on the coordination of national economic plans for the next five-year period (1976-80) and, by mutual agreement, for a longer period up to 1990.

The national economic plan of the USSR and of other CMEA countries for 1976-80 are being coordinated in two stages. In the first stage a study was made of the basic trends of cooperation with the other socialist countries, and mutual consultations were held on coordinating these trends. In the second and current stage (1974-75), specific conditions of cooperation are being worked out, e.g. in the field of the mutual supply of goods. The central planning organization of the CMEA member states and the leading bodies of the Council for Mutual Economic Aid, have been very active in preparing economic cooperation projects for the coming five-year period, and this will make it possible to sign final protocols on the coordination of plans and long-term trade agreements among the integrating countries in accordance with the decision of the 26th CMEA session. Simultaneously, integrational measures for economic and scientific-technical cooperation between the USSR and other CMEA countries are being more completely coordinated with the principal tasks of the USSR's national economic development during the coming five-year period.

All this will make it possible to draw up, on an extensive planned basis, a coordinated five-year plan of multilateral integrational measures to be taken by the CMEA member states. This plan "will embrace all necessary activity in the combined effort of the countries involved to build projects and productive capacities, develop the specialization and co-operation of production on a multilateral basis and to conduct joint measures in solving major scientific and technical problems, etc."[9]

Of special interest from an economic standpoint are the socialist countries' mutually coordinated decisions regarding the localization of major fuel-energy and mineral-raw material supplies, the international specialization of production, and the extensive development of cooperative relations among the collaborating countries. These decisions are coordinated by a special committee for cooperation in the field of planning. This committee has worked out joint production plans for certain types of industrial products, particularly in those fields which determine scientific and technological progress.

In recent years important argeements have been concluded on the construction of large industrial projects on the territory of the USSR, with the participation of interested countries. Among these is the agree-

274

ment on the construction of the Rayon Pulp Mill in Ust'-Ilinsk, the Asbestos Concentration Plant in Kiembaev, a large isoprene rubber factory, and a 750-kilovolt power transmission line from Vinnitsya to Albertirsh (in the Hungarian People's Republic). At the 67th session of the CMEA Executive Committee (1974), general multilateral agreements were signed on the development of the production of iron ores and certain types of ferroalloys on the territory of the USSR. According to these agreements, the export of iron ores and concentrates from the USSR to the other CMEA countries in 1980 will have increased (on conversion to metal) by 25 per cent compared to the 1975 level. This will result in intensified extraction and concentration of iron ore in the Krivoi Rog Basin as well as at the new ore concentration plants of the Kursk Magnetic Anomaly. An agreement has been signed on cooperation in the joint construction of a large gas pipeline from Orenburg to the western frontier of the USSR. All these agreements, as well as many others either in effect or being worked out, greatly influence the character of the territorial organization of production and result in the improvement of the industrial structure of the national, regional, and local economic complexes. It is significant that a great number of large-scale agreements on cooperative construction or specific crediting concern projects developed in the eastern regions of the USSR. That country's participation in the process of economic integration thereby objectively contributes to the economic development of poorly developed areas, and accelerates the rate of building large fuel-energy and mineral-raw material bases in the east of the USSR. International economic organizations (such as the "Mir" power system) are continuing to develop, facilitating the acceleration of the economic integration of the socialist countries. Decisions pertaining to the perfection of the forms and methods of foreign trade, currency and financial relations, etc. have been taken. Measures have also been taken to accelerate the development of the economy of the Mongolian People's Republic. The Republic of Cuba has been accepted as a member of the CMEA.

The next ten to fifteen years should see the launching of a colossal program of development of the commonwealth of socialist nations. During this period the economic potential of these countries will almost double, and science and technology will develop at a rapid rate. According to preliminary estimates, in 1985 the CMEA countries will account for approximately one-half of the world production of industrial goods.

Industry in the capitalist countries is distributed spontaneously. The application of state-monopolistic methods of regulation only partially restricts this spontaneity. The attempt at a transition from national forms of solving territorial problems and regulating the processes of distributing the productive forces in the Common Market countries to a higher, interstate, form of influencing the territorial structure of the economy is still ineffective. Until recently the established supra-national body—the European Economic Community Commission—had virtually no real possibility of conducting an independent regional policy. The regional measures in the European Economic Community are financed from the national budgets. Interstate credits are provided by the European Investment Bank, the Orientation and Guarantee Fund, etc. Moreover, the capital is used, as a rule, for the construction of private projects, which exert a very limited influence on the "general background" of the distribution of the productive forces.

A gradual, conscious, and scientifically-grounded specialization of the member states is taking place within the CMEA integrational system—which, however, does not display a unilateral character. The economy of each socialist country develops in a complex manner, relying on its own industrial base and proceeding from the available social-economic and natural prerequisites, and simultaneously specializing in the combined economy of the CMEA member states. The assumption that socialist economic integration reinforces the formerly existing division of labour among the member countries, so that some countries remain industrial while others preserve their agrarian character, can thus be seen to be erroneous.

Branch and territorial economic proportions in the combined economy of the CMEA countries are regulated by coordinating the national economic plans. Thanks to this measure the domestic national economic proportions change and the international socialist division of labour develops purposefully. At the same time, the necessary economic proportions in the entire socialist commonwealth are combined with the necessary interstate proportions of the development of the national economy. These can, naturally, change as a result of scientific and technical progress, improved cooperation, etc.

A most important condition for authentically effective integration is the gradual levelling of economic development and the raising of formerly economically underdeveloped to the level of the highly-developed countries. In this respect special importance is attached to the question of accelerating the economic development of the Mongolian People's Republic. The complex program of economic integration envisages steps to stimulate this Republic's economy through, for instance, the joint construction and operation of industrial and other projects by the interested countries, the issuance of credits, etc. A case in point is the agreement between the USSR and the Mongolian People's Republic on the construction of a large mining complex at the Ergenetiin-Obo copper-molybdenum deposit.

The development of economic integration in Western Europe, though only in its early stages and progressing unevenly, is also promoting a drawing together and mutual adaptation of various economic formations, of a number of economic branches and—to a much lesser extent—the national economies of the member countries. This process is coming about extremely slowly and is beset with difficulties.

Although a certain levelling of the overall economic structures of the Common Market countries can be observed, considerable gaps exist not only in terms of the overall economic and scientific-technical potential of these countries, but also in terms of the overall industrial output per capita. This tendency will, moreover, according to development forecasts, be aggravated in future.[10]

The internal regional policy of the CMEA member states is based on their national programs. During the years of socialist construction all these countries have witnessed an upsurge in those regions which were once economically backward (e.g. the economic development of Slovakia and the Czechoslovak Socialist Republic, the northern regions of the German Democratic Republic, the southern regions of the People's Republic of Bulgaria, etc.).

An important result of the development of the foreign economic relations of the CMEA countries has been the change in economic structure of the territories bordering on the USSR. Large industrial centres have been growing up in the CMEA countries (other than the Soviet Union) on the main lines along which fuel and raw materials are transported from the USSR (e.g. the petrochemical industry, ferrous metallurgy enterprises, etc.). Thus, while the national regional programs are being realized, international measures, particularly in the sphere of production and scientific-technical cooperation, exert an ever greater influence on the development of certain territories inside the countries.

Economic integration is a system of overall economic interrelations, under which the solution of a particular regional problem may have bearings on common problems. In the process of economic integration of the socialist countries an interrelated circle of territorial problems, both in the macro- and micro-spheres, is systematically and consistently solved. The combined economy of the CMEA countries is established in planned sequence, international and national interests being harmoniously combined.

Socialist economic integration creates a new type of international economic relations that are stable and systematic and ensure the development of specialization and cooperation, and the creation of cooperative industrial, transport and other projects, by redistributing investments among the integrated countries. The possibility of such a redistribution increased considerably with the organization of the International Investment Bank. This provides long- and medium-term crediting of measures connected with the development and confirmation of international socialist division of labour and the development of the economy of the collaborating countries. It is necessary to bear in mind, however, that during the effective period of the CMEA's complex program (fifteen-twenty years) its realization will be based on preserving national and government property and the economic sovereignty of the integrated states.

At the present time the EEC countries are making a transition to a new stage of regional policy, increasing the authority of the supra-national body, and intensifying interstate forms of influence on territorial structure. A special body, the Permanent Commission for Regional Development, has been formed. This has the right (on the basis of the regional plans of the member countries) to coordinate activities in developing backward agricultural areas, regions affected by constant unemployment, frontier territories, etc. To facilitate the implementation of regional plans, this Commission can finance regional measures in separate countries, extend aid in the form of advantageous credits, etc. In its work it has, however, encountered serious difficulties in determining which of the underdeveloped regions need economic aid most urgently.

The regional policy of the EEC is subject to several contradictory influences. The factors that stimulate the formation of a common economic area are that economic relations are internationalized and that certain scientific and technical problems are shared by all the countries. These factors act as the centripetal forces of integration. Centrifugal forces are the contradictions among the bloc executive partners, the contradiction between the communitarian aims of regional policy and the national means of effecting it, and, finally, the tendency towards an expansion of the general economic area as countries with greatly varying economic levels and considerable regional disproportions join the commonwealth. This circumstance, along with the extraordinarily heterogeneous character of regional problems existing in the member countries, creates new obstacles in the way of implementing the regional policy of the EEC.

The study of territorial problems arising in the socialist economic integration of the CMEA member states is now being undertaken. With the adoption of the complex program envisaging further cooperation and development of socialist economic integration, the influence of international economic relations on the distribution of the productive forces of the USSR and other socialist countries is intensified. Consequently, an important task of economics is the study of the regional problems of socialist economic integration, and of the regularities governing the creation, development and distribution of the productive forces of the combined international economy of the CMEA member countries.

In this respect, a complex evaluation of the natural resources of the CMEA member countries both as a group, according to world standards, and separately, as compared to the economic system of the CMEA countries, is of prime importance. Without a scientifically grounded natural

278

principle of the international socialist division of labour it would be difficult to create an effective model of interstate economic relations for the next fifteen to twenty years within the framework of the CMEA.

Bilateral and multilateral construction of combined industrial centres and complexes (with shares of capital investments being contributed by different countries), and international cooperative organizations are, as we have seen, becoming more and more widespread in the CMEA countries. The creation and localization of these centres, complexes and organizations are playing an increasingly important role in the distribution of the productive forces of the CMEA countries taken separately. Taking into account the integrational measures conducted by CMEA, changes can be made to the existing specialization and distribution of industry in the regions of the European socialist countries, and in the republics and expansive economic regions of the USSR. Great importance is attached to the coordinated distribution of fuel-energy and mineral-raw material bases, and of power- and material-consuming branches, as well as to the joint planning of the development of certain industries that are crucial to scientific and technological progress.

In future, cooperative specialization and the cooperation of production will expand sharply, particularly in a number of branches of machine-building, in small-tonnage chemistry, in the production of certain types of ferrous and non-ferrous rolled stock, etc. Investigation of the territorial aspect of this problem and scientific elaboration of effective models of collaboration in this field, are still in their infancy.

In the USSR the study of the present distribution of the Soviet Union's export-import industries, and scientifically grounded extended-period forecasting in this field are assuming great practical significance in promoting the rationalization of the distribution of the Soviet Union's productive forces and greater efficiency of the international socialist division of labour.

The considerable expansion of economic relations between the USSR and other CMEA countries in the last ten or fifteen years has resulted in a considerable increase in the volume of freight traffic. In 1970, over 120 million tons of bulk cargo were exported from the USSR to other CMEA countries alone, and this figure is still increasing. The development of transportation-economic relations among the CMEA countries is stimulating them to develop a single transportation system. In connection with this, the USSR is confronted with great problems in further reinforcing land transport in western regions and in the development of sea transportation facilities.

The territories situated in the European part of the USSR have from the beginning been engaged in the international socialist division of labour. In future, numerous types of mass cargoes will be exported from the country's more remote eastern regions. In this connection special importance is attached to the scientifically grounded and coordinated solution to the problem of developing and distributing fuel-energy and mineral-raw material bases to satisfy the needs both of the USSR and of the other CMEA member states. Another important scientific problem consists in determining a rational regional and interstate specialization of the processing industry. It should be noted that specialization and cooperation affect such leading branches of machine-building as the electric-power, motor vehicle, and agricultural industries, the production of machine tools, atomic tools, electronic computers, etc. Due to the increasing number of enterprises participating in this process it is necessary to work out scientific recommendations for determining the optimal zones of their localization, taking into account the economic, labour and natural resources of different regions of the USSR.

All these factors predetermine the founding, within the bounds of regional economy, of a new and significant branch of science dealing with the study of regional principles of economic socialist integration. Economists and regionalists of the socialist countries are confronted with the important task of together working out scientific and methodical principles of the influence the international socialist division of labour has on the distribution of productive forces within the economic system of the CMEA countries.

Notes

1. K. Marx and F. Engels, *Collected Works,* Vol. 17, Moscow, p. 553.
2. L. I. Glukharev, ed., *Problems of integration of industry under capitalism,* Mysl', Moscow.
3. V. I. Lenin, *Complete Collected Works,* Vol. 23, Moscow, p. 318.
4. Cf. *Economic Problems of the Development of the World Socialist System,* by K. F. Solov'eva, Moscow, 1971, p. 74.
5. V. I. Lenin, *op. cit.,* vol. 41, p. 164.
6. "Multilateral Economic Cooperation of the Socialist States", *Yuridicheskaya literatura,* Collected Documents of COMECON, Moscow, 1972, p. 30.
7. Cf. P. Bozhik, "Problems of Economic Integration", in the Polish Journal *Nove Drogi,* No. 2, 1971.
8. For the sake of comparison we should note that the territorial-economic potential of the Common Market countries constitutes: 1.4 per cent of the world territory, 7.2 per cent of the world population, 18.4 and 10.9 per cent of the world industrial and agricultural output, respectively, and 37.0 per cent of the world foreign trade turnover.
9. O. Rybakov, "Socialist Economic Integration: The Main Sphere of National Economic Planning", *Planned Economy,* No. 4, 1974, p. 13.
10. Cf. M. Maksimova, *Basic Problems of Imperialist Integration,* Moscow, 1971, p. 293.

III

THE DEVELOPING COUNTRIES

THE DEVELOPING COUNTRIES: INTRODUCTION

Both the theory and the practice of regional development are under-developed. The approaches we have are largely a product of the so called "first" and "second" worlds and it is, therefore, perhaps not surprising that attempts to apply them to the "third" world have not as yet been marked by notable success. The papers in this section of the book are contributions by authors resident in all three worlds and are an excellent reflection of the continuing search for adequate theory and meaningful practice.

The contributions are marked both by similarities and differences. All of the authors, to a greater or lesser degree, are obviously dissatisfied with existing approaches and with the limitations these have both in analysis of existing situations and in prescriptions for change. Coraggio is the most explicit and vociferous in his dissatisfactions. His attack on the theories of Pedrao, Boisier, and Lasuén is powerful and direct and, although his case tends to be argued from a particular ideological viewpoint, his paper gives considerable food for thought. He reveals weaknesses in existing theories but gives only an indication of how these should be revised. Higgins, on the other hand, is perhaps least critical, and has clearly made up his mind that urbanization is the key to development. He simply offers Malaysian decision makers a choice of various strategies with which to achieve that aim.

Between these two extremes the other authors raise a number of inter-related concerns. Ganguli makes a strong plea for social considerations to loom larger in policy and theory, and this call is echoed by Wood, Lefeber and several of the other authors. Grosman draws particular attention to the need for strategies which include employment creation, and Taylor and Pióro both argue the need for restructuring what they consider to be dysfunctional colonial spatial structures.

Another common theme running through all nine papers is the need for local involvement in the planning process. This is considered in different ways and to different degrees. Both Wood and Taylor discuss attempts which have been made to measure what the people want from the de-velopment process as a possible input to planning. From studies in all parts of the developing world this need emerges but there is little agree-

ment on how local involvement can be effectively achieved.

The United Nations has adopted the phrase "a unified approach" which Higgins uses in the title of his paper. Other authors pick up this theme, although the terminology used often differs, and the need for an "integrated" or "systems" approach appears in various forms. Arguments are made for strategies which include equity, income creation, economic growth, employment creation and an improvement in both the quality of life and human dignity. No author views "development" simply, or even primarily, as economic growth. Both Pióro and Taylor use the term "growth centre" but it is clear that the term does not adequately describe the type of changes the authors envisage. Perhaps "development centre" would have been more appropriate, although one hesitates to add more jargon to this already overjargonized field.

Differences, perhaps not surprisingly, are even easier to find than similarities. This is particularly evident in the discussions by the authors of the type of strategies required to achieve change. Some authors argue for functional change, others for structural change, and several for both functional and structural change in different sectors and to varying degrees. There are also marked ideological and methodological differences. Arguments related to the full range of theoretical disagreements in the social sciences involved in the study of the developing nations can be discerned even when these are not made explicit by the authors. Nor are these arguments confined only, or even mainly, to the theoretical issues: different policy approaches are argued with vigour.

The papers provide some answers but they also leave many questions unanswered. Several authors raise new questions to which they provide only partial answers, or in some cases no answer at all. Yet the questions have been defined with clarity and throughout the papers one can sense the urgency and impatience of problems which will not wait for the "perfect" answer. The difficult task of developing a more appropriate and effective approach to regional development in the third world is incomplete, but these contributions from researchers from various disciplines, countries, and ideological backgrounds, using empirical data from different areas, represent a significant step in the right direction. Further steps, however, must be taken and taken very soon.

D. R. F. Taylor

1

NATIONAL PLANNING AND REGIONAL DECENTRALIZATION

Louis Lefeber

Introduction

The function of regional planning is to provide a design or blueprint for the regional allocation of resources. However, if central planning is practised, the harmonization of regional plans and the coordination of regional resource allocation decisions with the central plan represent a complex problem which cannot be resolved without reference to the meaning or concept of nationhood. Each discipline in the social sciences may have a different interpretation of this concept, but for purposes of economic analysis the natural definition seems to be in terms of the welfare function (or functions) to be maximized through planned economic development policies. National unity is represented by a unique and well defined welfare function or set of weighted objectives which is accepted as guide for resource allocation in all component regions. In contrast, a loose federation of autonomous states implies that each state has individual and distinct welfare objectives which are independently pursued subject only to certain well defined constraints.

If there is no unified concept of welfare, implying that the nation is composed of a federation of autonomous states, the role of central planning is restricted to those areas where the common interests of the component regions are predominant, such as national defence or inter-state commerce. As a consequence the problem of regional decentralization in plan preparation and implementation is minimal; planning is undertaken individually by each state. On the other hand, if there is a strong concept of nationhood represented by a dominant, nationally agreed-upon set of welfare objectives, and even if there is a detailed national plan, there is

* This paper is revised from the author's notes on "Coordination of National and Regional Plans and Regional Decentralization" contributed, at the request of Professor A. Mabogunje, to the Conference on Regional Planning and National Development in Africa, University of Ibadan, Nigeria, 1972.

285

the problem of how to induce regional decision makers to act in harmony with national welfare priorities. In particular, if the component regions themselves are political units with elected governments, so that plan implementation cannot be through central control or fiat, it may not be possible to find regionally decentralized means for the pursuit of national welfare interests.

Decentralization can work only if all individual private and institutional decision-makers can be induced to behave voluntarily in a way that is consistent with social welfare criteria. In other words, conditions must be created to make it desirable for participants to act in the social interest. In the fictional purely competitive market organization this is attained by making use of profit and loss incentives based on the price mechanism, and by suitably selected means for income redistribution. Unfortunately, such an approach cannot be directly adopted for the purpose of regional decentralization. This is because regional governments are not profit maximizers in the economic sense of the term. Furthermore, the decisions of regional governments with respect to resource use may directly and significantly affect large segments of the total economy, so that the economic behaviour of one regional government can and often will affect the welfare of other regions. Hence, conflicting interests and various externalities may also arise.

Regional Decentralization in India [1]

The problems of regional decentralization can be well illustrated in the case of India. The real difficulties in planning and plan implementation did not become evident for nearly twenty years after independence and the introduction of central planning. The dominance of a single political party from 1947 to 1967 both in the Indian Union and in its component states gave the *appearance* of smoothly functioning central planning and control over implementation. Conflicts among the states, and the problem of inducing state and local decision-makers to behave according to the national interest existed all along; but conflict resolution and cooperation was obtained through highly personalized political rather than institutional channels, primarily through the individual abilities of Prime Minister Nehru in persuading the participants to cooperate. The system failed to produce an institutional mechanism for conflict resolution. Its absence became evident after the general election in 1967, when the ruling Congress Party lost its dominant position. Since the change in the political structure happened to coincide with the termination of the Third Five Year Plan, no political agreement could be obtained on national plan formulation and on the concomitant problem of dividing the scarce resources among the states of the union.

The period of what would have been the Fourth Plan was bridged over by a sequence of annual plans. In the meantime, however, an Administrative Reforms Commission made a series of recommendations for the improvement of the planning mechanism through decentralization and broader based political participation in plan formulation.[2]

The Commission's report suggested that there was a need to bring into the process of plan formulation those decision-makers who ultimately have to comply with and implement the plan. Accordingly, it was recommended that the National Development Council, composed of the Chief Ministers of the states and union territories as well as of the union Cabinet Ministers, should be the highest forum in plan formulation not only in name but also in practice. It was hoped that if agreement on plan purposes and inter-state resource distribution could be reached by the representatives of the states, compliance with the national plan and resource use according to nationally instead of regionally established welfare criteria could also be assured.

The National Development Council soon discovered, however, that the conflict over the inter-state distribution of resources, i.e. the division of central assistance, could be resolved only with the help of well specified criteria.[3] The impasse was resolved when the Council reached agreement on a set of relatively weighted objective criteria consisting of state population, income tax effort and development expenditure with respective weights of .6, .1 and .2. By placing the largest weight on population relative to income and performance, it was recognized that interstate income redistribution must be determined primarily by interstate income inequalities.

This formula for the distribution of central assistance among the states reflects a national concern with social justice. It is, therefore, interesting to note that resource transfers from high to low per capita income states do not necessarily result in improvements in personal income distribution. In some instances the opposite may even result. For example, the State of Maharashtra contributes to union finances more than it receives in the form of central assistance, and Uttar Pradesh is a net recipient of inter-state income transfers. The central assistance received by Uttar Pradesh is employed for the continued development of its already prosperous western areas rather than for the advancement of the eastern regions where severe unemployment, underemployment and poverty continue unabated. Since resources are utilized more equitably in Maharashtra than in Uttar Pradesh, the inter-state transfer of resources may well result in a deterioration of interpersonal social justice, even though it is motivated by concern for inter-state equity.

This example illustrates a general problem which centrally planned economies must solve if decision making and implementation are to be regionally decentralized. The conflicts inherent in the regional distribution of national resources may be resolved by the use of relatively weighted criteria. However, a formula is not sufficient to guarantee that regional decentralization will lead to the implementation of national welfare objectives. The heart of the problem is that cohesion can only be given to a group of semi-autonomous regions through plan harmonization which, in turn, necessarily implies some degree of regional economic integration. Without it, regional plans representing the aggregation of specific projects in each region cannot be related to each other, and particular projects cannot be selected so as to conform to both national and integrated regional interests.

These are not merely academic considerations. Evidence in India and elsewhere overwhelmingly indicates that there is no general correspondence between aggregate national and regional plans on the one hand and project planning on the other. Hence, it is only rarely possible to show how projects selected by regional planners fit either into an overall regional or into a national framework.

Regional integration or the integration of states into a union requires not only that the barriers to the movement of productive inputs and outputs should be diminished, but also that the criteria for investment decisions should be made compatible over all regions. For this it is necessary that certain basic information should be made available to regional planners on prices, wages and discount rates which, in turn, can only be extracted from the national plan. Implicit in the selection of a specific national plan is a corresponding social time preference or social rate of discount which in an integrated group of regions should indicate the rate at which current sacrifice is to be balanced against future benefits. Plan coordination requires that this same social rate of discount should be used in the evaluation or selection of all regional projects from which regional plans are aggregated.[4] In addition, other relevant information on, for example, the welfare valuation of foreign exchange and other rates and prices, can also be extracted only from the national development plan. Herein lies the significance of obtaining agreement among regional political leaders, such as state Ministers and other regional economic decision makers, on national plan formulation: in addition to regional income redistribution, as discussed above, consensus on a particular path of development establishes quantifiable and uniform criteria for regional project selection and plan formulation.

It must be recognized, however, that even if the necessary information for plan coordination existed in India, the compliance of regional decision makers, i.e. project selectors and local planners, could still not be taken for granted. Current state planning practices vary according to the particular interests and politics of the different states. State planning is dominated not only by local political considerations, but also by the tactics of presenting regional projects to national planners in a way which state officials believe will increase their own state's share of the national investable resources.

A training program for state planners held in 1970 at the Institute of Economic Growth (Delhi University) revealed that there is—at least in the current practice—a nearly irresolvable conflict between particular state interests and national political economic rationality. The approach to state planning considered to be strategic by state officials consists of overstating the benefits and understating the costs of regional projects so as to maximize the likelihood of approval by the union government. In other words, state planners have a built-in motivation to mislead national planners with respect to the merits of their plans in the hope that by so doing they will increase the flow of resources to their respective states. Needless to say, such tactics might work if only one state resorted to them while others followed nationally agreed-upon criteria; however, when all participants play the same game, some or all have to be losers and the planning process is bound to lead to waste.

Regional Balance and Resource Use: Evidence of Performance

In any politically integrated set of regions, such as the Indian Union, the question of regional balance is continuously at issue. If perfect mobility of resources existed and if labour were also perfectly mobile, there might not be any need for regional income transfers: an appropriate market mechanism combined with measures for increasing employment and other means of improving inter-personal equity would be adequate to bring about socially desirable patterns of resource use. Resources and labour are, however, not always mobile and large pockets of unemployment and poverty may persist in less developed regions. Hence, the problem of how to induce development in retarded areas must be resolved. Since the primary means for improving inter-personal equity consists of increasing the rate of employment, this problem comes down to the question of how the demand for labour can be increased in regions of unemployment.[5]

The Indian effort to industrialize during the 1950's was based on separate criteria for the localization of heavy industries and consumer good industries. In keeping with the strategy for development attributed to Professor Mahalanobis, heavy industries and large industrial complexes

289

of national significance were to be located according to strict and narrowly conceived economic efficiency criteria. Smaller consumer good industries, on the other hand, were supposed to be distributed regionally in such a way as to promote regional balance and absorption of unemployment.[6] Apart from such nonspecific directives, there was no unified set of criteria for the determination of social desirability in program design or project selection.

In order to accommodate the heavy industrial complexes, the government undertook the formation of entirely new urban concentrations and the development of existing towns at those geographic points which, in terms of transport and communication facilities, raw material supplies and other economic determinants, were judged suitable industrial locations. In this process of centrally controlled development of large industrial centres, small scale consumer goods industries and ancillary engineering and other enterprises were also attracted. Opportunities for smaller private entrepreneurs and the viability of small industries around the newly established government enterprises were assured by the growth of local markets in a setting where the necessary social overhead capital (transport, power, communications) as well as repair facilities and technical expertise became available for their use also.

The industrial cities which grew up around the new government enterprises represent interesting examples of induced regionally decentralized industrialization. The point is that the giant public enterprises have the capacity to survive even in remote areas and can generate urban complexes around them. The resources available to the public sector firms are generally beyond the reach of the private sector, and their size is such that the urban and industrial overhead capital which would be external to most private sector industries can be internal to them. Herein lies the explanation of why towns planned around public sector enterprises can be expected to attract private industries also. As stated elsewhere, "those factors and supplies, i.e. the diverse input and output markets, repair shops, social overhead services and transport and communication links to other production centers, the absence of which discourages private investors in non-industrial town centers, are available in the urban areas around the public sector enterprises".[7]

The effort to disperse small scale consumer goods industries for regional balance had no success. The government, aware of the importance of social overhead capital and the externalities without which small enterprises cannot maintain themselves, undertook a wide-ranging industrial estate program which, however, proved to be a waste of capital and other resources. It is interesting to note that those industrial estates which happened to be located in close proximity to, or which were linked with, already existing industrial areas readily survived and, in fact, prospered.

290

The majority of the industrial estates were, however, located in regions removed from industrially established or agriculturally prosperous areas. These have been unsuccessful and underutilized in spite of the considerable subsidies that have been offered to potential investors.[8]

The experience confirms that the provision of industrial infrastructure and social overhead capital is not sufficient to motivate potential investors: investors must also be assured of ready access to either national or local markets as well as to supplies and other inputs. The problem is that industrial estates established in retarded regions cannot rely on local markets, because either these do not exist or they are too thin to absorb the output of local producers. On the other hand, small producers in remote locations cannot realistically hope to produce for national markets either. Hence, insufficiency of demand makes location in remote industrial estates unprofitable. The deficiency or unreliability of the transport and communication system may further increase the uncertainty inherent in such an investment decision.

Another instructive example of deficient regional development planning is provided by the effort to develop a retarded region in Central India.[9] This Dandakaranya Project was originally undertaken after Partition in order to settle East Bengali refugees in partially virgin territories newly opened up for colonization. However, the development authority failed to provide the settlers with adequate agricultural infrastructure or with the means for creating it on their own. As a consequence agriculture could not develop and a large proportion of the colonists still remain either unemployed or underemployed. In order to relieve the depressed conditions, the development authority then considered establishing small-industrial centres. But the problem with this is the same as with the industrial estates: the local markets are insufficient to sustain even small scale consumer goods production, and the national markets are unattainable for technical and other reasons, including the insufficiency of transport routes.

These examples demonstrate that industrial dispersal programs which are not justified by sufficient local demand or linked to already established industrial regions result in waste of capital and organizational resources. In the case of retarded regions and pockets of unemployment distant from industrial centres, the first planned effort must concentrate on the upgrading of agriculture. This, in turn, requires the building up of agricultural infrastructure, i.e. water control, irrigation and local transportation. If agriculture can be made to prosper, the source of a growing local demand for ancillary services and consumer goods is also established. Under such conditions, it becomes reasonable to expect that potential investors in small scale service and consumer goods industries will find the motivation to locate in dispersed and remote areas.

291

It is evident that rural prosperity is a basic requirement for inducing dispersed or regionally decentralized industrialization. But what then are those regional policies that are likely to bring about rural prosperity consistent with regional and personal equity objectives? Here again the Indian experience is instructive.

Because of the scarcity of organizational and material resources, the initial Community Development Programme failed to generate a widely dispersed agricultural development. Once it was realized that the available effort was necessarily too thin for effective application over all states and regions, the government adopted a new and entirely different strategy. The Intensive Agricultural District Program (IADP) was initiated in 1960 in order to concentrate effort and resources in a few potentially promising agricultural areas. The hope was that if the regionally concentrated effort were to succeed, agricultural advancement would also spread to other non-program areas. In this, however, the IADP was not successful. Though in certain program districts (notably in Ludhiana of Punjab and West Godavari of Andhra) agriculture advanced rapidly, in most other original program districts progress was not noticeably faster than in neighbouring non-program districts.[10] But whatever productivity changes the program can be credited with, the income distributional effects of the selective approach implicit in the IADP concept were detrimental to the attainment of either personal or regional equity objectives. The IADP seemed to increase income inequality not only in relative terms but in many regions also in absolute terms. Even in the successful program districts unemployment was not eliminated, while the ranks of the landless increased because of land consolidation and termination of tenancy. Furthermore, because of certain adverse factors acting on the demand for labour, such as increasing capital intensity of production, employment has not been increasing pari passu with productivity increases.[11]

Whatever the case, the consequences were twofold. First, to the extent that regional agricultural policy is supposed to harmonize with national plans and national objectives, the IADP may have been a failure, since it ran counter to the personal and regional equity objectives of the union. This in turn, may have the additional and, perhaps, paradoxical welfare consequence of interrupting the momentum of agricultural development because of inadequate growth of low income demand for food and staples.[12] Secondly, to the extent that widespread rural prosperity is a prerequisite for decentralized industrial development, the IADP approach, which increases rather than diminishes regional income disparities, cannot contribute to dispersed industrialization. An alternative regional policy, consistent with national objectives, may have to focus on raising the productivity of the average farmers instead of that of the farmers who are already capable and efficient.

292

The greater the degree of regional disaggregation, the more specific the plan must be. In the limit, disaggregation consists of detailed project design and the execution of planned projects. Accordingly, as disaggregation increases, the need for detailed knowledge of the local geographic, climatic, economic and social conditions also increases. At the same time, the disaggregate regional or local plans must also fit into the state or national planning framework so as to assure overall consistency and observation of social welfare priorities.

Local administrators and planners do not always have adequate information about the intentions of the state or national government concerning new plan projects. As a consequence, they can have only limited capacity to influence the selection and design of projects which will ultimately be implemented and administered by them. For example, in the hill districts of Uttar Pradesh (the largest state in India) projects are selected and designed by state government officials who have only a limited consultative relationship with administrators stationed in the districts where the projects are to be implemented. Furthermore, district or local representatives of different state administrative agencies report directly to their superiors at the state capital, by-passing local government. Thus the activities of the different agencies are not always known to, or coordinated with those of, the local or district administrators. This can lead to considerable inefficiency and waste, particularly if the total social profitability of particular projects depends on secondary and tertiary benefits or on complementary investments in sectors under the control of more than one agency or government department.

The following example illustrates the problem. In the above mentioned hill districts overgrazing of pastures causes erosion; considerable effort by soil conservationists and supplies of scarce resources are needed to rebuild the destroyed grazing lands. After expensive rehabilitation the pastures are returned to use and are once again overgrazed by low productivity cattle, the yield from which does not justify the capital cost of soil conservation. Since erosion and conservation come under the control of forestry, while animal husbandry is under that of agriculture, only inter-departmental coordination can ensure that the rebuilding of pastures is coupled with rational pasture utilization through the introduction of high yield stock.

Similar examples abound at all levels of government planning, not only in agriculture, but also in industrial and service sectors. The problem is that in plan disaggregation from national to state, and from state to local levels, both *vertical* and *horizontal* harmonization are required. Vertical disaggregation can be based on agreed-upon uniform investment criteria combined with means for insuring compliance. Horizontal harmonization, on the other hand, is an organizational problem. It can only be resolved if adequate hierarchical relationships and communication channels are created which ensure the flow of information not only vertically, but also horizontally at each level of vertical disaggregation.

Notes

1. See L. Lefeber and M. Datta-Chaudhuri, *Regional Development: Experiences and Prospects in South and South East Asia,* Mouton, The Hague, 1971.
2. See *Report on the Machinery for Planning,* ARC, Government of India, New Delhi, 1968.
3. The Indian states enjoy partial autonomy assured by their right to levy and collect taxes. These consist of sales and commodity taxation as well as the taxation of agricultural incomes. The union, on the other hand, obtains its revenues from non-agricultural personal and business income taxation as well as from international trade and certain types of commodity and wealth taxes. That part of the centrally collected revenue which is not used up on activities and projects directly under the centre's supervision is transferred to the states in the form of central assistance which on the average makes up about 50 per cent of the resources available to the states. The central assistance potentially provides a fiscal means to the union government to exert its influence over the otherwise fiscally autonomous states.
4. See Das Gupta, Marglin and Sen, *Guidelines for Project Evaluation,* UNIDO, Vienna, 1972 and Marglin, *Public Investment Criteria,* MIT Press, Cambridge, Mass. 1967. See also L. Lefeber, "Notes on Integration, Welfare and Project Valuation", *Cuardernos* of the Latin American Institute for Economic and Social Planning, Series II, No. 11, 1970 (original in Spanish, 1969).
5. Here a reminder is in order. If resources are to be regionally redistributed with additional employment creation in mind, the effects on the long-run growth rate of employment must also be considered. In most low income countries there is a close relationship between the rate of employment and consumption; in fact, the rate of employment in the organized industrial, commercial and agricultural sectors is constrained by the capacity for providing wage goods. Thus, increases in the rate of employment which must be accompanied by commensurate increases in consumer good production, must be balanced against the possible adverse change in the capacity to invest due to the transfer of resources from investment to consumer good production. In other words, there is a trade-off between current employment and concomitant consumption on the one hand and growth of output, employment and future consumption on the other hand. See S. A. Marglin, "Industrial Development in a Labor Surplus Economy", mimeo. 1967; L. Lefeber, "Planning in a Surplus Labor Economy", *American Economic Review,* June, 1968.
6. See M. Datta-Chaudhuri, "Regional Planning in India", in *Issues in Re-*

gional Planning, ed. D. Dunham and J. G. M. Hilhorst, Mouton, The Hague, 1971.

7. See Lefeber and Datta-Chaudhuri, *op. cit.* p. 169.

8. *Ibid,* Chapter 9.

9. *Ibid,* Chapter 10.

10. See *Modernizing Indian Agriculture: Report on the IADP (1960-68),* Ministry of Food and Agriculture, Government of India, 1969. The success of the program is particularly difficult to evaluate because of the complicating factors introduced by the three year drought and concomitant abnormal food price increases which affected farmers' motivation to invest and accept risk during the period covered by the report.

11. See Lefeber and Datta-Chaudhuri, *op. cit.,* Chapters 4 and 5.

12. See Lefeber, "Income Distribution and Agricultural Development" in Bhagwati *et al., Development and Planning,* Allen and Unwin, London, 1973.

2

SOCIAL ISSUES IN REGIONAL POLICY AND REGIONAL PLANNING IN ASIA

B. Ganguli *

The trend of economic development in recent years has left us with a sense that, especially in the developing countries, there is a lack of synthesis between economic betterment and the social well-being or general upliftment of the common man. In advanced countries, where the existing social environment was well adapted for development, sufficient inputs of capital investment, coupled with competent policy direction, have generated the expected economic growth. The situation appears, however, to be completely different in the developing countries, where development schemes of a primarily economic nature, such as irrigation projects or construction of dams—though completed successfully in physical terms— have not benefited those who were supposed to be the main beneficiaries.[1] The absence of a suitable organisation and the lack of technical skills and of financial resources, have limited the scope of actual achievement at the human level in these countries. The transmission of benefits was consequently neither smooth nor equitable in most cases—as is evident from the economic and social imbalances with regard to regions and to different sections of the population.

In regional perspective, a development plan has as its objective the attainment of a new regional economy characterized by a different level of welfare and productivity, by new elements in the structure of output, and by a changed pattern of infrastructure. In sociological perspective the objective is seen as a regional society characterized by a different pattern of mobility and social communications, by new elements in social structure, and by changed individual and collective attitudes to development and change.[2] The unified growth of the regional socio-economic structure is not a simple process: it involves optimum utilisation of the natural and human resources and maximisation of the effeciency of labour. The problems of social planning are more complex and at the same time more subtle.

* Town and Country Planning Organisation, New Delhi, India.

It is now generally acknowledged that popular participation in any development project can only help ensure sustained growth and development at both the human and the spatial level. The ultimate goal of any planned development of society is the improvement of the living conditions of the people. The population, in its quantitative dimension and in its qualitative make-up, ethnic composition, and socio-cultural setting (i.e. habits and customs, attitudes and ways of life), exerts significant influence on the overall progress and achievement of economic programmes. If labour is the most important input in an economy, then allocation of a part of the national income to the extension of education, the improvement of public health, and the encouragement of scientific research, has to be looked upon not only as a form of consumption expenditure but also as a form of investment for augmenting the productive and social value of the individuals constituting the society.[3] A better educated worker who has good medical care and the opportunity of making good use of his leisure time will not only be a happier and healthier man but also a more productive worker capable of earning a higher income.[4] Therefore population —seen not simply as a quantity of human mass but also in terms of its qualitative structural dimensions and of its ethnic, social, and cultural attributes—can enable a society to stand the strain of development.

Social Situation

Scientific and technological advancement, industrialisation, urbanisation, and the concentration of affluence in big cities, have shaken the entire social fabric—including the family structure—of the developing countries. The specialised proficiency and skill required to handle modern systems of production, the lack of adequate facilities, and the lack of an appropriate gestation period to build up the common man, have brought about a marked disparity in income distribution, an imbalance in regional development, and an emphasis on appropriate sectoral allocation.

In most developing countries there are striking disparities between regions and unequal opportunities for the masses to participate in the socio-economic development process. One of the most important problems confronting the developing countries stems from the excessive growth of population and the consequent pressure upon resources. The difference between the levels of development of rural and urban areas, massive underemployment and unemployment, and major deficiencies in the institutional facilities and social overheads, are conspicious in these countries. The concentration of industries in some selected areas which absorb only a small proportion of the economically active population, and then mainly people who come from other regions, has left the local population in

298

misery and despair. Massive migrations from rural to urban areas have tended to sharpen the social tension, and to exacerbate maladjustment and social imbalances in urban areas. Social problems such as beggary and destitution, delinquency, crime, youth unrest, etc., are dominating the urban scene, while the vast and largely neglected rural areas tend to stagnate or even to deteriorate, which intensifies the misery, poverty, illiteracy and frustration.

In many developing countries, the population is ethnically highly diversified, consisting of numerous tribes and races who speak different languages, profess different religions, have distinct cultural traits, and are at different levels of transformation and modernisation. In a sense these tribes and races constitute multiple nationalities within one country or region. This is particularly the case in India. The process of regional planning becomes all the more complicated as these diverse groups represent different occupations with different degrees of stability (some of them are nomadic tribes) who are scattered all over the country in small population groups. So any planning in such areas needs to strike a balance between the national and regional interest on the one hand, and the aspirations and expectations of these diverse minority groups on the other. Some of these regions appear, in fact, as Klaassen says, "to be ethnic mosaics rather than a homogeneous territorial base for giving opportunity to different nationalities to regulate their own affairs within the framework of larger national unity."[5] The isolated schemes that have been tried too often have not had much appeal. In many countries the backward communities and tribal populations inhabit the sensitive frontiers. The problems of these people add a new dimension to the demographic structure of the country as a whole.

The steep increase in population acts as a constraint on the process of planning a region. An examination of the demographic trend in these countries leads one to the conclusion that there will probably not be any significant decline in the birth rate in the near future. On the other hand, advancements in medical research have within a few decades brought down the death rate to a level which developed countries took a much longer time to achieve. The proportion of children and youth today comprises almost 60 per cent of the population in these areas.[6] With a fairly constant birth rate and a decline in the infant mortality rate, young people will continue to form a significant proportion of the population in the foreseeable future. Inadequate attention to the needs and problems of children and youth has been one of the major weaknesses of development planning in these countries. The role of youth in modernisation has no doubt been discussed in a general way in many development plans but the objectives have seldom been translated into effective strategies and instruments for modernising society.

299

The trend of urbanisation in many areas reflects a constantly widening gap between the minimum desirable norms of living and the achievable goals. It is not only the smaller cities and towns that suffer from the worst forms of deprivation in terms of utilities, community facilities, and social services: considerable areas of metropolitan cities are in the same plight. The social component of urbanisation has not been integrated properly with the urban development plans but has been assigned a rather perfunctory role.[7] Much attention must be paid to formulating a comprehensive urban and regional development strategy in most of the developing countries.

It is hardly possible, at present, for the benefits of development to be equitably distributed. The better-off farmers in developing countries have succeeded not only in modernising the farming techniques but also in cornering the credit and other institutional facilities extended by the government. Imbalances in agricultural development are also becoming fairly pronounced as a result of the breakthroughs in farming, particularly in areas which have an assured water supply and the facilities required for sustained growth. Small farmers, however, are in the main unable to marshall the resources required for modernising agriculture, in spite of the partial success of land reform measures.

The availability of housing facilities leaves much to be desired, especially with regard to the socially and economically handicapped population. It is estimated[8] that about 50 per cent of the Asian rural population are inadequately housed and that 40 per cent of the urban population are living in slums under subhuman conditions. In India, for example, sample surveys of urban areas showed that 42 per cent of the houses had no latrine, 49 per cent had no safe drinking water supply, 80 per cent were constructed mostly of non-durable materials, and 49 per cent had floor space of less than 200 sq. ft. Surveys conducted in Asian cities have revealed that slum dwelling has a disastrous effect on the individuals and on the communities concerned. The high rate of population growth, the migrations to urban areas, the low levels of productivity and savings, the high and rising cost of land and building materials, and the comparatively low priority given to social housing in national development programmes, may be identified as the key factors which have given rise to many social conflicts and maladjustments in most Asian countries, particularly in urban areas.

However, there is a growing awareness in these countries that steps must be taken to alter the situation. A conscious effort is now being made at the policy formulation stage to include measures which will result in a better distribution of income and of material wealth (especially land), in opportunities for gainful work, and in the possibility of accelerating the formation of human capital.

300

In most of the Asian countries regional development planning and policies have, in the past, constituted an integral part of, though they remained subordinate to, the national development strategy and policies. At the national level, sectoral development priorities prevailed over regional development priorities. Regional authorities, and consequently the planning bodies under their supervision, acted as general transmission points rather than as fully autonomous development policy making units for the regions. Priority was generally given to the continuous and vigorous growth of the national economy as a whole through the development of the agrarian and agro-industrial and industrial base. It has, however, now been realized that the schemes and projects at the national level were not enough to build up the country as a whole and to develop the potentiality of the large population. The priorities of planning at the national level obviously differed from those at the local or regional level.

The social and the economic aspects of planning, which received differential treatment in the earlier approach to planning, are now attracting special attention. In the past, the activities in the social field took the form of social welfare services intended to alleviate the sufferings that had resulted from rapid industrialisation and urbanisation; they did not bring about any positive social change. Recognising that development is an integrated and balanced process in which economic and social factors interact, the ECAFE resolution on economic development stressed "that social progress is no longer regarded as an appendage to economic growth".[9] Important changes in the role played by the state in accelerating the rate of social and economic development have been made in the countries of the ECAFE region, many of whom have incorporated social and economic goals into their constitutions.

The social factors mentioned in the constitutions of the Asian countries—factors which are to be taken into consideration in the formulation of regional development policies—are mainly based on the contentions of the International Development Strategy for the Second United Nations Development Decade as adopted by the General Assembly at its twenty-fifth session:

"As the ultimate purpose of development is to provide increasing opportunities to all people for a better life, it is essential to bring about a more equitable distribution of income and wealth for promoting both social justice and efficiency of production, to raise substantially the level of employment, to achieve a greater degree of income security and to expand and improve facilities for education, health, nutrition, housing and social welfare and to safeguard the

301

environment. Thus qualitative and structural changes in the society must go hand in hand with rapid economic growth, and existing disparities—regional, social, sectoral—should be substantially reduced."

The specific targets to be attained, and the instrumentalities, have been identified in some countries. The current interest in social and economic development testifies to the countries' aspirations for a rapid realisation of their social objectives and goals. In the translation of social and economic development objectives into policies and programmes, and in their integration at different levels, however, much still remains to be done.[10]

It is essential that the developing countries find a solution to the problems posed by the conflicting demands of social justice and economic growth. A considerable proportion of the available resources should be allocated to social justice even if in the short term this will involve some sacrifice in overall essential growth: the long-term results must be considered if the future social structure is to be strengthened and a healthier society built up. The inclusion of such objectives in the policies or plan formulation is not enough on its own. It must be followed up by an im-depth analysis of the social set-up of a given region if the programmes are to be properly implemented in accord with local aspirations.

A question that has often arisen concerns what kind of change is necessary if a country's politico-socio-cultural environment is to adopt the social objectives. It has sometimes been felt [11] that it might be more feasible to change development strategies and modify technology to make them consistent with existing values and institutions than to modify social values to meet technological change. The reasoning was that a nation's politico-socio-economic infrastructure is, in essence, somewhat rigid, and that there may therefore be resistance to the required changes. In a way these changes constitute the price of development, and the developing countries must continually ask themselves whether change is worth the price, whether the ends justify the means.

Most countries in the region will have to adopt more broadbased and positive population policies. These policies will have to include measures not only for the regulation of the rate of population growth but also for its distribution, composition, mobility, deployment, and so on. There are countries which have reported problems in raising the rate of population growth since they are already experiencing a manpower shortage. Although such countries are in a minority, their problems do underscore the fact that population policy has a regulatory and not necessarily a negative function. Population policies will have to be formulated on a much wider basis than hitherto: they will have to concern themselves with the age and sex composition of the population, with the proportion between economic-

302

ally active and dependent sections, with metropolitan mobility, and with migration within and outside the country. The policies should also lead to motivation and successful practice of a kind of family planning that has the consent of Asian families, that is convenient for them, and that they can afford. Eventually, the quality of the population and the standard of living are the factors that will determine the type of contribution that the population will make to national development.

The highest priority should be given to the provision of training and education facilities for the children and the young people—who constitute the most sensitive sector of the economy in these countries. A number of countries have attempted to assess their sectoral development in terms of occupations, skill, and future manpower requirements. Past experience has shown [12] that less emphasis should be placed on classical and academic education, and that the facilities for vocational and technical education should be extended.

When a future expansion of economic activities is being considered, attention must be paid to the location of these activities since it is necessary to absorb the increasing urban population, to eradicate regional imbalances, and to ensure that the local population will be given adequate time and opportunity to adjust to the changing environment in a painless manner. The provision of better working and living conditions, which are essential for social progress, must also be taken into account. National housing policies, for instance, should aim to create conditions that will encourage maximum participation by private cooperative and public agencies in the solution of the housing problem. Special emphasis has to be laid on the provision of social housing for families in low income groups. The short-term objective of national housing policies in the Asian countries should be to arrest further deterioration in the housing situation and to improve the condition of housing in both urban and rural areas; the long-term objective should be to ensure reasonably good housing as per the minimum standards laid down by the national governments. Rural housing policies should be directed towards improving housing conditions in the villages on the basis of aided self-help and as a part of the larger programme of community development and village planning.[13] The construction of simple and sanitary houses, and of community buildings, the improvement of streets, drainage, and the drinking water supply, and the creation of a healthier environment will go a long way towards improving the quality of the labour forces.

Proper utilisation of the existing manpower through appropriate employment opportuntities is posing a serious problem in the developing countries. Even with the best organisational effort, most Asian countries are not able to produce an adequate number of additional jobs in the modern sectors of the economy. Thus, quite apart from the backlog of unemployed people, the surplus manpower transferred from the country-side and even skilled workers in the urban areas are not being absorbed. Measures aimed at the dispersal of industries to backward areas, to remove regional imbalances and initiate a wider participation of labour, are gradually being incorporated into industrial policies in these countries. These policies are, furthermore, becoming oriented to develop agro-industries and also to promote labour-intensive technology to suit their requirements.

There is no doubt that the future development of most of the Asian countries will entail a considerable sacrifice. An important aspect of social policy in all the countries should be the strengthening of the collective will to tolerate austerity. In order to be effective and to ensure that social conditions will not further deteriorate, such austerity measures would have to be directed more to the rich than to the poor. There are large segments of the Asian population whose standard of living is already too low to make further sacrifice possible. The policy directives and implementation in these areas must produce some visible benefits for the masses in the short run or there can be little hope for widespread popular participation in a stable climate of development.

Current Strategies

Approaches to planning are definitely oriented towards the attainment of the objectives that are laid down in a country's planning policy. Realising the urgency of building human resources, the developing countries are now stressing the importance of expanding health services and education facilities and on creating a better environment. It is perhaps too early to expect that investment in "human capital" could have overtaken other capital investments, since capital-output ratio in quantitative terms dominates the entire planning decision making process.

The strategies laid down by the developing countries in pursuance of their planning objectives include integrated programmes of improving social services, such as health, education, housing, family planning, water supply, sanitation, etc., which have an important role to play in the overall amelioration of living conditions. The national programmes of many Asian countries have been built around a consideration of the urgent need to minimise regional imbalances in areas of public consumption. The minimum needs programme in India,[14] for instance, has been formulated to cover major portions of rural development. The prevention and control of major diseases, and the provision of clean drinking water are investments in man which are considered as important as the provision of fertilisers and irrigation projects. Similarly, the development of a system of rural roads is considered important not only because it will result in economic benefits and increasing mobility, but also because it will allow for a wider diffusion of culture.

An analysis of past experience has revealed that attempts to provide for social consumption have failed to have the desired impact partly because the related programmes were not given a high priority in relatively poor states, and partly because decisions regarding individual sectors were taken without considering the need to integrate the facilities that were to be provided. India's programme of minimum needs, as incorporated in the Fifth Five Year Plan, envisages a frontal attack on this problem. The priority areas of social consumption that have been identified in this programme are: elementary education, rural health, nutrition, drinking water, provision of housing, slum improvement, rural roads, and rural electrification. An important feature of this programme is that each scheme included in it is an integral part of a package of facilities. Thus the villages where primary health centres or schools are to be located, are to be provided with water supply facilities, electricity, and link roads. In the past such facilities have, for obvious political reasons, been thinly distributed over a wider area. It is anticipated that the integrated planning and careful implementation of the minimum needs programme, as evolved in the current strategy, will go a long way towards establishing a healthy environment for well-being and growth, particularly in the weaker sections of the society, as well as towards creating a feeling in these sections that they are participating in national development.

As regards education, the consensus appears to be that the planning strategy should not only involve the provision of more schools, or of free primary education. It is extremely important that participation rates, absenteeism, and types of training be adequately considered. Literacy and other skills may be imparted by means other than formal schooling. A mere increase in the proportion of literates may not succeed in improving the quality of labour: vocational training (e.g. agricultural extension work, technical information for workers in industry, etc.) may be much more beneficial even if people remain illiterate. In all forms of education improving attitudes is at least as important as imparting skills.[15]

The emphasis on social progress has necessitated the adoption of new procedures for physical planning, decision making, and the delegation of responsibilities. As a first step in this direction, many of the Asian countries are undertaking a critical appraisal of the operational procedures and functional capabilities of the departmental agencies responsible for the different components of their programmes. The local communities themselves may be able to make valuable contributions to the programmes, in terms of material, financial, and labour inputs. If these resources are to be mobilized, a considerable amount of work will have to be done not only in community organisation but also in making possible a widespread participation of the people in locational decision making. To ensure this, detailed planning will be necessary at the local level (say the district level) for bringing about the physical convergence of different facilities at specific points.

Notes

1. *Social Development in Asia—Retrospect and Prospect,* United Nations (ECAFE, Bangkok, Thailand), February 1971, p. 1.

2. Antoni R. Kukliński, "Prospects of Regional Sociology", p. 6. (Paper submitted to the First Asian Symposium on Regional Planning and National Development, Institute of Development Studies, Mysore, India, 1974, and to the Roundtable Discussion on Social Issues on Regional Policy and Regional Planning, School of International Affairs, Carleton University, Ottawa, Canada, 23rd April 1974.)

3. V. V. Pokshishevski, "Population Geography: Problems of Planned Development of Economic Regions in Developing Countries", in *Economic and Socio-Cultural Dimensions of Regionalisation,* an Indo-USSR Collaborative Study, Census Centenary Monograph No. 7.

4. Leo H. Klaassen, "Growth Poles in Economic Theory and Policy", (Netherlands Economic Institute). Paper submitted in Geneva, March 1969; UNRISD/69/C.69 - GE69-25354.

5. Leo H. Klaassen, *ibid,* p. 8.

6. *Social Development in Asia—Retrospect and Prospect, op. cit.,* p. 28.

7. *Ibid,* p. 45.

8. *Problems of Social Development Planning with special reference to Asia and the Far East,* report of a group of experts for the United Nations Development Programming Techniques, Series no. 4.

9. *Social Development in Asia—Retrospect and Prospect, op. cit.,* p. 21.

10. *Ibid,* p. 26.

11. United Nations *Report on the Symposium on Social Policy and Planning,* Copenhagen, Denmark, 1970. p. 97

12. United Nations *Studies on Social Development in the Middle East,* 1971, p. 21.

13. *Problems of Social Development Planning with special reference to Asia and the Far East, op. cit.,* p. 36.

14. Government of India Planning Commission, *Draft Fifth Five Year Plan: 1974-79,* Vol. I, 1973. Chapter VIII, pp. 87-91.

15. Gunnar Myrdal, *Asian Drama: An Enquiry into the Poverty of Nations,* Twentieth Century Fund, New York, 1968.

3

GROWTH CENTRES AND RURAL DEVELOPMENT IN AFRICA*

D. R. F. Taylor

This chapter represents work in which my association with Dr. Samson Kimani has played a large part. I would like to dedicate this chapter to a colleague and friend whose advice will be sorely missed.

Neither the term "rural development" nor the term "growth centre" is easy to define as both concepts have been used in a variety of different ways by a wide variety of authors. Rural development is generally held to be a holistic concept. The definition used for the purposes of this paper is that accepted by African nations at the Addis Ababa meeting prior to the U.N. Conference on the Environment, and expressed by the Committee on Human Environment in Kenya. Here rural development is defined as ". . . a series of quantitative and qualitative changes occurring among a given rural population and whose converging effects indicate in time a rise in the standard of living and favourable changes in the way of life.[1] Rural development is a much wider concept than agricultural development although the agricultural production base is usually a vital component of any rural development programme.

Growth centre is a much more difficult term to define. A review of the literature reveals that a wide range of terminology exists, e.g. growth point, growing point, growing centre, growth pole etc., and each of these labels is used to describe a series of quite different concepts. Perroux,[2] for example, who introduced the term "growth pole", used it to apply to abstract economic space. Other authors have applied to it to geographical space and have supplemented it with central place theory. Yet others have used the term in relation to organizational space. Darwent[3] noted in 1969 that unless this concept is defined more rigidly it may prove of little use

* This paper was written while the author was a Research Associate of the International Development Research Centre. The support of the Centre is gratefully acknowledged.

for analytical, explanatory, or planning purposes. By 1973, if one is to accept Moseley's arguments, not much theoretical progress had been made: "What is at issue is whether the growth centre is a real entity or a mental construct. Suggested definitions ... contain recurrent themes relating to size, location, functional role, ability to grow, etc., but few authors explain the relative importance of such characteristics. From an extravagant assembly of supposedly interrelated attributes, it is very difficult to single out the irreducible minimum, the sine qua non of the concept."[4] His final conclusion is that "we are still far from a universally acceptable definition of the growth-centre concept, and even further from a generally applicable identification procedure."[5] Moseley points out[6] that if the concept is used in relation to nodes in a variety of spaces such as economic, organizational and geographic, then each dimension needs a separate body of theory. Hermansen,[7] recognising this, has proposed that if the concept is to be useful for planning purposes then a synthetic or integrating approach to existing theory must be used. Such an approach will be attempted in this paper. In addition, an attempt will be made to adapt an urban based theory with a strong industrial component to a rural area and thus to develop a theory and an application of the growth centre concept in rural areas. Inherent in this concept is the idea of concentrated development, and Hansen has provided a useful working definition: "By a "growth centre" or centres is meant a complex consisting of one or more communities or places which, taken together, provide or are likely to provide, a range of cultural, social, employment, trade and service functions for itself and its associated rural hinterland."[8] In the concept as used here both growth and centrality are included, with the former being considered more significant than the latter. The conclusions in this paper are based on a detailed study carried out in Murang'a District, Kenya from May 1972 to September 1973.[9]

Scale

Moseley, in his recent thought-provoking article,[10] raises a number of questions about the definition of growth centres and about attempts to identify such centres empirically.

One important question is that of scale, "... but the relevance of size, much less a suggestion of a relevant hierarchy of sizes, is rarely propounded in the literature."[11] In applying the growth centre concept to rural development, scale is of vital importance. Growth centres can be considered a various scales: there are national growth centres, an example of which in the Kenyan context would be Nairobi; there are regional centres, such as Kisumu; and further down the size scale there are local

308

centres. For the purposes of rural development, it is argued that the local scale is of critical importance and that developmental efforts should be concentrated first at this level. The dichotomy between urban development and rural development is a false one and, rather than concentrating on urban problems or rural problems, emphasis should be placed on the interface between rural and urban sectors. In Kenya the small urban place is the interface between rural and urban sectors and could play a vital role in development.

A basic problem is how to define "a small urban place". There is no easy theoretical answer to this problem as the size and nature of the small places at the interface between rural and urban sectors may vary from country to country as these sectors themselves vary. The definition used here is a functional one which has been formed with Kenyan conditions in mind. In terms of actual population, such places have between 800 and 5000 inhabitants, but the size of the hinterland served is probably more critical than the actual size of the town itself and it is suggested that a population of 30,000 to 80,000 is appropriate.[12] In identifying size, the function of both growth and centrality must be borne in mind. For the viable provision of an adequate package of services a certain minimum size is required. Van Dusseldorp points out that:

> "It is becoming more and more obvious that services catering for rural populations can only operate at their optimum when they provide for a certain minimum number of persons. This minimum numbers of persons (threshold) has a tendency to increase. Enlargement of scale results in the disappearance of many small service centres, or a decline in their function." [13]

In a dynamic situation such as that in Kenya, where population is growing at an estimated 3.3 per cent per annum, the hinterland size suggested is probably the smallest unit which can support an adequate package of basic services which will not be in danger of declining or disappearing over the next twenty years.

From the viewpoint of growth, the significance of size is more difficult to define. In Kenya, the distributive element is held to be particularly important in any developmental activity; consequently, if such activities are provided in too large a hinterland area then the chances of their benefits reaching the maximum number of people are lessened. The degree of accessibility is increased by ensuring that the effective distance most people have to travel to reach such a centre is reduced. This is especially true in rural areas where the principal means of transport is still by walking. The degree of local involvement in growth and developmental activities is also related to size, although the relationship is difficult to test empirically. In too large a community an individual's sense of involvement is lessened:

it is perhaps no accident that in some cities community action groups on a neighbourhood basis are emerging. Community involvement and action is an important element in growth activities. The size suggested is held to be an appropriate one for rural development in Kenya, and is probably applicable to other rural areas in developing nations.

Functions

For the purposes of rural development in developing nations the growth centre concept should be viewed as essentially normative, as a prescription for planning purposes, rather than as positive although, as will be shown later, positive considerations may loom large in the selection of these purposes. The functions such centres should perform include social, economic and service elements; specifically, the stimulation of economic and commercial growth especially in small scale enterprise, the diffusion of innovation (particularly induced innovations), the provision of adequate services for their hinterlands, and the coordination of governmental and local developmental planning. They can also provide residential accommodation and possibly employment for a growing rural population, not all of whom may be able to farm because of scarcity of land.

The particular strategies for the stimulation of economic and commercial growth and the particular types of innovations introduced can vary at different times and in different places. In Kenya, for example, different rural development strategies may be used in different areas. The use of the growth centre as a focal point for such efforts, however, could remain constant. This is not to suggest that the concept is value free —it includes, as outlined here, concentration and planned change—but it does allow a degree of flexibility. Growth centres provide a spatial framework for a developmental strategy which concentrates on a vital contact point between developing rural systems and developing urban systems. This in essence is a spatial development strategy and, as Gould has emphasized so well:

"... with sharper knowledge and understanding, opportunities exist today for spatial planning that will never arise again. Scholarship in this area has direct implications for the rational planning of the basic spatial lattice within which all political, social and economic development will take place in the future ... For the locational decisions of an age that thought mainly in terms of extractive economies may appear far from optimal when new development goals over larger planning horizons, spring from political independence." [14]

310

Service Functions

If the quality of rural life is to be improved then people in the rural areas must be provided with basic services such as health facilities, sanitation, water, power, education and a variety of others. It is obviously advantageous to adopt a package approach and concentrate such services. The amount of capital available for the provision of such services is limited, and concentration allows the most efficient use of capital resources. Ominde *et al.* suggest that concentration in selected centres ensures that "... input of capital resources into the rural areas is used with the maximum possible efficiency and to the greatest possible benefit of the regional economy and the convenience of the local people."[15] The concentration of services in one place also facilitates interaction among them: if all services are concentrated in one centre, a farmer visiting that centre is more likely to use more than one service.

It is in the selection of service centres that the central place theory, with its concept of hierarchy, has much to offer. If, however, the growth centre concept is to be most useful for rural development then the service element must not be allowed to dominate the utilization and selection of such centres. A service element can be added to a growth centre much more easily than a growth element to a service centre. Although service functions are important they must be considered secondary to growth functions.

Van Dusseldorp[16] points out that such centres could provide a residential function. This is not at present very significant in Kenya where most people in the rural areas live on their own land, but it is liable to become more important in the future:

"Stated simply, there will just not be sufficient land for all or even most of the grandsons of today's farmers to become farmers themselves. Some of them may be able to obtain land in resettlement schemes but preliminary studies of soil potential throughout Kenya reveal that the amount of land with surplus population absorption capacity is less than might be imagined, due to the low rainfall, unsuitable soil conditions and other factors, and a large proportion of Kenya's future generations will need to find non-agricultural employment."[17]

In many of Kenya's rural areas population densities are already high and, if current population trends continue, the rural population will double within the next thirty years. Even if the major cities continue to absorb a disproportionate percentage of this increase there will still be population pressure in the rural areas, and the number of landless people will in-

311

crease. The growth centres will have to provide residential accommodation for many of these people.

Growth Functions

Before considering growth functions, the question "growth of what?" must be answered and, as Moseley[18] and others have pointed out, this is an area where growth centre theory is weak and confusing. In rural development, especially in developing nations such as Kenya, it might be useful to view such centres as growth *injection* centres rather than simply as growth centres. This normative concept might help to reduce confusion, and answer to the question "growth of what?" would then vary according to the particular circumstances of the country or area under consideration. The growth centre is then a mechanism for implementing a particular set of policies which may vary in different times and places. This does, however, to some extent beg the question, and as Penouil has pointed out, "one of the most intricate problems a development policy has to solve is that of the choice of activities to be implemented".[19]

Virtually every major source is agreed on the great importance of the diffusion of innovation in rural development. Diffusion theorists emphasize that information flows are always indispensable prerequisites for flows of capital, labour and commodities. Much has been written on the spatial diffusion of innovation, and major contributions have been made by Hägerstrand,[20] Rogers,[21] Berry,[22] Brown[23] and a number of others. Hägerstrand developed an essentially social theory of diffusion which Hermanson has summarized well:

"... diffusion of innovations comprises two processes: the dissemination of information about the innovation and the adoption of the innovation. The first process is largely a function of social communication. The second is a complex process of learning, accepting and decision making. The spread of information takes place through a number of channels that can be classified into two main groups—mass media and interpersonal, of which the latter is contended to be the more important. The pattern of social (interpersonal) communication can be conceived as a network consisting of nodes (sources and receivers) and links (channels). The sources and receivers of information are social actors with definite locations who establish contact with each other for various reasons."[24]

Berry[25] describes the effect of a given innovation as a developing function of time which is also subject to a threshold limitation: a minimum size of region beyond which diffusion will not proceed. Consequently, the lowest levels of welfare are in areas peripheral to small urban centres in the outlying hinterland regions.

There is ample evidence to support the hypothesis that innovation and modernization move from the major urban centres along the transportation routes to smaller urban centres and lastly out into the rural areas. Berry[26] has also argued that a well developed urban hierarchy is essential to this process. The process also suffers from time and distance decay effects. Logan,[27] however, has drawn attention to the fact that a distinction should be made between the acquisition of the material possessions of economic development and the generation of increased productivity. A major aim of rural development is the incorporation of rural inhabitants in the development process. If innovation filters down through a hierarchy with time and distance decay effects then it would seem logical to reduce these effects by introducing innovations at the lowest level or urban centre rather than allowing them to filter down. This of course applies to induced innovations. In the field of rural development the use of the small growth centre as an injection point for innovation is appropriate and could, in fact, be a major growth activity in such centres.

The economic function of such small centres involves trade, marketing, commerce and small scale local industry. These functions are already significant in Kenya and are growing. The enterprises involved, which are essentially small scale, have tended to grow spontaneously and, at least initially, with very little official encouragement. Official encouragement and help to the informal sector is a relatively recent phenomenon and, as the I.L.O. Report[28] points out, greater efforts could be made in this area. The phrase "informal sector" is used here as defined by the I.L.O. who see the sector as being characterized by:

a. Ease of entry
b. Reliance on indigenous resources
c. Family ownership of enterprises
d. Small scale of operation
e. Labour-intensive and adapted technology
f. Skills acquired outside the formal school system
g. Unregulated and competitive markets.[29]

The tendency has been to ignore and underestimate the role of this sector. An important statement of a different opinion is made by the I.L.O.:

". . . the bulk of employment in the informal sector, far from being marginally productive, is economically efficient and profit-making, though small in scale and limited by simple technologies, little capital and lack of links with the other ("formal') sector. Within the latter part of the informal sector are employed a variety of carpenters,

313

masons, tailors and other tradesmen, as well as cooks and taxi drivers, offering virtually the full range of basic skills needed to provide goods and services for a large though often poor section of the population".[30]

Given encouragement, capital, and planning for small scale enterprise, the small urban place could become an important focal point for economic growth. A recent study gives an outline of some of the possibilities in this area.[31]

Some of the advantages of concentrating services in such centres have already been discussed. There are additional advantages in that organizational changes can be made. Nellis[32] has argued that a major problem of rural development in Kenya is the lack of effective coordination both at the centre and in the field at the local level. Sectoral planning, for example, has led to a multiplicity of government agencies with fairly strongly developed vertical linkages but very poorly developed horizontal linkages. Logan argues that "the effectiveness of organizational structures is probably the most critical variable in the whole developmental process."[33] He further comments that, "organization implies the transmittal of developmental impulses and of incentives to which farmers can respond by increasing their productivity; it is the major element in promoting the structural transformation that is the aim of planning policies in developing countries."[34]

Poorly developed horizontal linkages have weakened the effectiveness of transformation in the rural areas as the efforts of various agencies have suffered from lack of coordination. Plans already exist for the establishment of District Development Centres in some of the small urban centres to coordinate rural development in the area. With agencies channelling and coordinating their plans the cumulative effect may well be greater and it should be possible for consideration to be given to the overall impact of different planning elements. Too often in the past innovations have been made in the rural areas which are in themselves advantageous when viewed in isolation, but which have counterproductive effects on other elements of rural life. The use of small growth centres as effective coordinating points will facilitate structural change and increase the possibilities of growth.

Polarized Development

So far it has been assumed that a strategy based on concentration in centres will lead to beneficial spread effects in the hinterland areas. The validity of this assumption can only be tested by applying the strategy,

314

but at the larger urban scale the virtues of a concentrated approach have certainly been challenged. Several authors have criticized the concept of polarization, one of the strongest critics being Lasuén who states that the "... view that economic development necessarily requires spatial polarization is an inaccurate and damaging limitation of the concept."[35] But even Lasuén accepts that "... the early stages of economic development must generate growth points ..."[36] and consequently it can be argued that for rural development a strategy involving growth centres is appropriate.

Hirschmann[37] has argued strongly for spread and trickle down effects and emphasizes that such effects are strongly influenced by the existence of complementarities between the centre and its hinterland. Myrdal,[38] on the other hand, has argued that backwash effects can outweigh spread effects. Both effects are caused by the movement of labour, capital and goods.

There is considerable evidence to show that the structural relationships between the urban system and the rural sector in many developing countries are very weakly developed. Logan[39] postulates that this is due to the fact that spatial systems built up by the colonial governments are not always conducive to rural development since they tend to be geared to "extraction" from the rural areas. Lacoste goes even further: "most towns in the underdeveloped countries are what Mr. Juillard calls 'insular' towns. Some authors have compared them to veritable cysts. These towns have scarely any beneficial effect on the countryside around them ...'[40]

These arguments must also be considered at the scale of growth centres suggested here. There is no use establishing a spatial developmental system which is in fact counterproductive. The key lies in the concept of what Hirschmann calls "complementarities' with the hinterland areas. In the rural development case these should be both economic and social; such linkages are of vital importance. The centres chosen should also be geared to the generative growth functions rather than to the extractive and law enforcement functions typical of colonial times.

Selection and Identification of Centres

If centres are to be chosen primarily as growth centres and are to serve the functions outlined above, what criteria should be used to select them? A detailed empirical study in Kenya[41] has led to the conclusion that growth centres should be chosen on the basis of existing social and economic linkages with the mass of the rural people and that they should build on and complement those elements of the existing pattern which are conducive to rural development. In the study area the existing spatial pattern

315

as reflected by the traditional markets is one which can be built on and there is evidence that similar patterns exist in other parts of Kenya and in other countries. In the application of any growth centre policy the existing spatial pattern should be carefully examined.

This is especially important in countries like Kenya where the existing spatial patterns have been influenced by a variety of factors not all of which have been advantageous to the socio-economic development of the people in the rural areas. The historical development of such patterns often reveals that the colonial networks have little meaning to the people in a social and economic sense and are not the most appropriate choice as growth centres. Identification and utilizing of indices which have a demonstrated meaning for the people in both a social and economic sense is vital. Utilization of these indices of established linkages with the hinterland will ensure the selection of centres with the "complementarities" so important in causing spread and trickle down effects. If the administration and law enforcement element is over-emphasized in the selection of centres, there is a great danger that the centres chosen will perpetuate the exploitive element which Myrdal and others fear. This may mean that capital investment for growth purposes should not be made in some of the existing administrative centres in countries like Kenya.

A number of indicators have been identified, as a result of research in Kenya,[42] by which growth centres for the purposes of rural development can be identified and selected. The most significant of these are:

a)   The relative growth and importance of the informal sector especially in small scale trade, commerce and business;

b)   The relative social attraction and importance of a place; and

c)   The extent of transport and communication linkages with its hinterland and other centres.

Other indicators include the relative wealth of the hinterland area, the relative number of entrepreneurs and the relative degree of community participation in the affairs of a centre. The quantitative weightings and the specific indicators which were used apply to the study area, but the general indicators outlined above are held to have a much wider applicability both in Kenya and in other developing areas, although the relative importance attached to each indicator is likely to vary with particular circumstances. The socio-economic importance of the market, the bar, the teashop, the small shop, and businesses, that was revealed and measured in the Kenya study is probably at least an Africa-wide phenomenon and in all likelihood applies to rural communities in other continents as well.

Perception and Local Involvement

The success or failure of whatever service or growth functions are contemplated will, to a large extent, depend upon the people's acceptance or rejection. In the Kenyan research[43] an attempt was made to measure this by asking people how they perceived the future growth of the centre they identify with. By asking about the kind of new functions they would like to see established and about their membership in various forms of local organizations, it was possible to get a relative indication of their sense of "belonging to" their own community, and of their concern for its welfare. For example, the response of over 6000 individuals as to what they would like to see improved first in their village was as follows:

Communications, Power and Water	34.5%
Health	23.4%
Education	15.6%
Administration and Law Enforcement	11.4%
Industry and Commerce	8.0%
Agriculture and Veterinary Services	7.1%

The importance of local involvement has been well put by Klaassen: ". . . local initiatives could be envisaged as being of such importance that, whatever the growth poles chosen by the central government, room should always be left within the framework of the growth pole theory for the incorporation of such initiatives in the general policy."[44]

Conclusions

This paper has made a case for concentrating on the small urban place as a growth centre or growth injection centre for rural development and has described the functions of such places and the indicators that should be used in the selection of appropriate centres. A case has also been made for making the rural growth centre a central part of rural development strategy and for the adoption of an essentially spatial strategy of rural development. This paper has presented more of a summary than a detailed development of many of the arguments, some of which are more fully elaborated elsewhere.[45] Much further research needs to be done. The concept as applied here, for example, may be valid for settled agricultural areas but has not been tested or applied to nomadic pastoralist areas. Another area for further research lies in the further refinement of *potential* growth indices.

Notes

1. S. H. Ominde, A. N. Ligale, and A. B. Cahusac, "Urbanization and Environment in Kenya", paper prepared for the United Nations Conference on the Human Environment under the direction of the Working Committee on the Human Environment in Kenya, mimeo, Nairobi, 1971, p. 6.
2. François Perroux, "Note sur la notion de pole de croissance", *Economique appliquée,* janvier-juin 1955, pp. 307-320.
3. D. R. Darwent, "Growth Poles and Growth Centres in Regional Planning: A Review", *Environment and Planning,* 1, 1969, pp. 5-32.
4. Malcolm J. Moseley, "Growth centres—a shiboleth", *Area,* Vol. 5, No. 2, 1973, p. 143.
5. *Ibid,* p. 148.
6. *Ibid,* p. 143.
7. T. Hermansen, "Development Poles and Development Centres in National and Regional Development—Elements of a Theoretical Framework", *A Review of the Concepts and Theories of Growth Poles and Growth Centres,* U.N.R.I.S.D./70/C.6, Geneva, 1970.
8. Niles M. Hansen, (ed.), *Growth Centres in Regional Economic Development,* The Free Press, New York, 1972, p. 169.
9. S. M. Kimani and D. R. F. Taylor, *Growth Centres and Rural Development in Kenya,* Maxim Printers, Thika, Kenya, 1973.
10. Malcolm J. Moseley, *op. cit.*
11. *Ibid,* p. 146.
12. The optimum size of a rural planning unit is an interesting question. The average rural commune in China, for example, is 50,000; in India the smallest unit is around 80,000; in Kenya, the Development Plan suggests that rural centres serve around 40,000 people.
13. D. B. W. M. van Dusseldorp, *Planning of Service Centres in Rural Areas of Developing Countries,* Publication 15, *International Institute for Land Reclamation and Improvement,* Wageningen, Netherlands, 1971, p. 12.
14. Peter R. Gould, "Research Strategies for Rural Spatial Planning", *Canadian Journal of African Studies,* Vol. 3, 1, Winter 1969, pp. 282-83.
15. S. H. Ominde *et al, op. cit.,* p. 2.
16. D. B. W. M. van Dusseldorp, *op. cit.*
17. S. H. Ominde *et al, op. cit.,* p. 1-2.
18. Malcolm J. Moseley, *op. cit.*
19. Marc Penouil, "Growth Poles in Underdeveloped Regions and Countries", in A. Kukliński and R. Petrella (eds.), *Growth Poles and Regional Policies,* Mouton Publishers, Paris and The Hague, 1972, p. 130.
20. T. Hägerstrand, *Innovation Diffusion as a Spatial Process,* Chicago University Press, Chicago, 1967.
21. E. M. Rogers, *Modernization Among Peasants; The Impact of Communication,* Holt, Rinehart and Winston, New York, 1969.
22. B. J. L. Berry, "Hierarchical Diffusion; the Basis of Development Filtering and Spread in a System of Growth Centres", in *Man, Space and Environment,* edited by P. W. English and R. C. Mayfield, Oxford University Press,

New York, 1972.

23. L. Brown, *Diffusion Dynamics: A review and revision of the quantitative theory of spatial diffusion of innovations,* Royal University of Lund, Sweden, 1968.

24. T. Hermansen, *op. cit.,* pp. 188-189.

25. B. J. L. Berry, *op. cit.*

26. *Ibid.*

27. M. I. Logan, "The Spatial System and Planning Strategies in Developing Countries", *The Geographical Review,* 62, 2, 1972.

28. International Labour Office, *Employment, Incomes and Equality; A Strategy for Improving Productive Employment in Kenya, Geneva,* 1972.

29. *Ibid,* p. 6.

30. *Ibid,* p. 5.

31. Frank C. Child and Mary E. Kempe (eds.), *Small Scale Enterprise,* Occasional Paper No. 6, Institute for Development Studies, University of Nairobi, 1973.

32. J. R. Nellis, "The Administration of Rural Development in Kenya: Plan Formulation and Implementation in the Special Rural Development Programme", *Issues in African Development,* Canadian Association of African Studies, Ottawa, 1972, pp. 168-182.

33. M. I. Logan, *op. cit.,* p. 229

34. *Ibid,* p. 231.

35. J. R. Lasuén, "On Growth Poles", in Niles M. Hansen (ed.), *op. cit.,* p. 20.

36. *Ibid.*

37. Albert O. Hirschmann, *The Strategy of Economic Development,* Yale University Press, New Haven, 1958.

38. Gunnar Myrdal, *Economic Theory and the Underdeveloped Regions,* G. Duckworth, London, 1957.

39. M. I. Logan, *op. cit.*

40. Yves Lacoste, "The Problems of Urban Networks in the Underdeveloped Countries", *Bulletin Trimestriel,* Secretariat des Missions d'Urbanisme et d'Habitat, Paris, October, 1972, p. 6.

41. S. M. Kimani and D. R. F. Taylor, *op. cit.*

42. *Ibid.*

43. *Ibid.*

44. Leo H. Klaassen, "Growth Poles in Economic Theory and Policy", in *A Review of the Concepts and Theories of Growth Poles and Growth Centres,* U.N.R.I.S.D./70/C., 6, November 1970, p. 141.

45. S. M. Kimani and D. R. F. Taylor, *op. cit.*

4

GROWTH CENTRES IN REGIONAL DEVELOPMENT IN TROPICAL AFRICA

Zygmunt Pióro

Some of the reasons for the failures in development planning experienced in many African countries during the First United Nations Decade of Development have as yet been raised only in limited professional circles and have not been fully recognised by policy makers as intrinsic to the development process.

The most damaging mistake in economic planning is negligence of the space factor when decisions are being made on investment policy and on the allocation of finances for particular projects. A second deficiency of development policies is frequently encountered in the formula "industrial versus agricultural development": both kinds of development are, as René Dumont has said[1], necessary if a country is to keep pace with human needs and the demands of modernisation. In spite of the fact that it is difficult to see how modern agriculture could function without the services of the urban centres where produce is processed, one is often, in connection with settlement policies, further confronted with another formula: "urbanisation versus ruralisation".

Such deficiencies result from a neglect of the role of physical planning. The recommendations of United Nations agencies and of scholars in the field notwithstanding, the importance of regional planning has not yet been properly acknowledged in these countries. (In this respect regional planning differs somewhat from town planning, the value of which has received a certain amount of recognition.)

It has become clear in a number of African countries that the arithmetic of macro-economics and sectoral planning should be supplemented by the geometry of regional considerations. Desicions must be made not only on the quantities of the scarce resources to be allocated for any given purpose but also on where investments should take place. The development policies of African countries during the Second Development Decade are manifesting a growing concern for social and economic development in sub-national areas, i.e. regions and districts. In the determination of national policies, space, distance, and the natural environment are increasingly receiving explicit consideration.

For the purposes of this paper, it is necessary to distinguish three concerns of public policy with regard to the spatial organisation of a national economy and national settlement network:

1. Where the means with which to initiate a programme of sustained development are scarce, a national policy must turn to strategies of spatial selection, i.e. to areas with the potential for the highest marginal returns to the factors of production, or to areas where human productivity is and can continue to be highest in the country;

2. Where economic development occurs unequally across a nation's territory, regional differences in the levels of welfare, and tribal clashes, may become urgent political issues;

3. Where the existing settlement network is dysfunctional with regard to economic efficiency, the people's needs and expectations, and national integration, it is necessary to induce a restructuring of that network through regional planning, which alone is able to combine the exigencies of the natural endowment with population distributions and socio-economic structures.

Its methods of comprehensive analysis of all factors related to development, and its socio-economic and physical programming on the regional level, make regional planning the most reliable basis for policy decisions on these concerns.

Of the host of issues which need to be discussed only one, namely the place and role of growth centres in regional development, will be considered in this paper. This is an issue on which the present author worked in Tanzania in 1966-69.

The aim of this paper is to analyse the historical development of growth centres on an empirical basis, and to define their role and physical place within the national and regional network of settlement.

Growth Centres: The Theoretical Framework

The aim of regional planning is to organise geographical space in such a way that people living in it can develop their natural endowment, both biological and cultural, to its fullest dimensions. Its primordial task is to make the intimate relationship that exists between man, in search of livelihood, and nature, source of that livelihood, more efficient and more rational in terms of human welfare and environmental conservation. To this end, regional planning proposes a definite pattern of land use and settlement system which must be adapted to local geographic, economic, and social conditions.

The habitat of African pastoralists and settled farmers strikingly

322

exemplifies a traditional and spontaneous organisation of space functionally related to different social matrices of human needs, societal organisation, and philosophies. The spatial structure of human activities was
mainly determined by propitious or hostile natural environments and by
tribal cultures.

Colonialism has imposed new political organisations, new economic
systems, new religions, new tools, and new sets of values on the people
of Africa. These innovations, most of which are alien to the traditional
culture and social structure, have resulted in a distortion of the traditional
structure of socio-economic space.[2] The traditional system of socio-
economic relations, with subsistence type production and pre-capitalist
production relations, co-exist uneasily with the colonial expansion of
monetary economy. The result is a dual economy, with concomitant social
disparities, a disruption of tribal cultural and productive harmony, and
a disintegration of social links.

The main task of regional development in tropical Africa must therefore be to restore equilibrium in the spatial organisation of the national
economies between the natural endowment and the new social and
political systems, between the psycho-cultural characteristics of African
people and the new technology and the new worldwide economic links.

In theoretical works on regional development, growth poles and growth
centres are acknowledged as playing a major role. Since African economies
are mainly based on agricultural production, and since the bulk of the
population lives in rural areas, growth centres—or what D. R. F. Taylor
calls "growth injection centres" [3]—will be the focal points of our comprehensive approach to socio-economic development.

The most penetrating, to my knowledge, analysis of the role and conditions of growth centre development in Africa has been made by Marc
Penouil in his paper on "Growth Poles in Underdeveloped Regions and
Countries" [4]. While it is not free of some deficiencies, his standpoint may
be valuable as a starting point for more detailed research and for re-
flections of a positive as well as of a normative nature.

According to Penouil,

> "the growth centre is an agglomeration capable of providing pos-
> sibilities of varied occupations and collective services such as: health,
> educational, cultural, commercial, and industrial services ... This
> idea of growth centre is interesting from the point of view of economic
> policy, because the presence of such centres is indispensable for the
> creation of a milieu in which the growth could spread".[5]

The formation of growth centres depends on many factors: the nature of
growth activities, the natural resources available, the quality of infrastructures, structural elements of society, the level of income in the

323

geographic area, and its physical position with the settlement network. The value of a growth centre can be judged according to its polarisation effects, and these depend largely on the reactions of the milieu to the development stimuli. Several constraints in African milieus have been distinguished by Penouil, who describes how a lack of capital, an abundance of labour, and the possibility of satisfying national needs by the national production, all serve to limit the choice of growth activities. Such limitations lead to a preference for capital saving and labour intensive industries. Under these conditions agriculture can serve as a sufficient source of supplies for the growth industries. The example of the Ivory Coast proves that agricultural development may facilitate the creation of new industries within a very short time.

There are no competitive enterprises within most African countries: the only competition comes from abroad (although it is possible to establish a protective tariff system). In developed countries the size of enterprises is connected with profitability. Penouil writes:

"A medium size enterprise may play, in a given geographic zone, an important role in breaking through the old structural equilibrium. The juxtaposition of medium size units is here even more efficient than the creation of one big size unit only, because of the shortage of markets and because of the danger incurred that one large unit, isolated in the national economy, will not be integrated." [6]

The milieu acts as a powerful brake to development not only because of social structures which are not adapted for innovations, but also because of production structures which are not diversified and do not permit the creation of complementary relationships. This is an argument for accepting a model of growth centres of a limited effect to permit the concentration of financial, cultural, and technical conditions for later development.

In an underdeveloped economy, the main obstacle standing in the way of a mechanism of polarisation is the existence, within the structure of socio-economic space, of a vast non-monetary economic sector which is largely self-reliant. Illiteracy, a scarcity of qualified labour, and the existence of a cultural milieu as yet unaccustomed to rational organisation of production and to scientific and objective measures, are further obstacles that are very difficult to overcome. The problem, according to Penouil, "is not to adjust the structures, to correct them, but to replace one form of society by another".[7] And if Penouil is right when he asserts that growth poles allow the type of new society required for economic progress to be created only within a limited area, then why not develop many growth centres, each surrounded by a polarised zone within which new production forms in each sector of the economy can be diffused? The

324

action of growth centres on innovation is one of the best ways to spread progress across a whole society.

The transformation of African societies depends, in other words, not only on the growth of production in industry and in agriculture, but also on the polarising effects of growth centres which are capable of diffusing innovations in work organisation and in ways of life only to their own hinterlands.

Agriculture and Industry in Tropical Africa

African agriculture, because of the variety of conditions determining it, is extremely heterogeneous. Soils, rainfall, altitude, and other aspects of the natural environment are highly diversified, often over very limited areas. With a small number of exceptions, the physical milieu is generally not conducive to successful and remunerative crop and animal husbandry. As René Dumount says, "The soils in Africa form a patchwork of very varied quality, but on the whole they are inferior to those in tropical South America".[8] For the most part the soils in tropical Africa are, contrary to popular belief, very poor. Rainfall is generally so scanty or so erratic that farming and herding is hazardous, and occasionally so intense that erosion is a real obstacle to agricultural development.[9] In addition, pests and diseases inflict great damage in some areas.

On to this physical mosaic is superimposed an equally diverse social and cultural matrix: there are hundreds of distinct societies with different patterns of values, motivations, systems of land use, and levels of modernisation. No less important is the fact that the rural population is very densely settled in the relatively few areas with most favourable agricultural environments. In P. McLoughlin's words [10], "Virtually all of intertropical Africa's good agricultural land is thus heavily crowded, with most of the region's land area sparsely settled because of adverse physical conditions which inhibit successful agriculture".

The experience of many generations taught the African farmer to adapt his techniques of cultivation to the limitations of his environment. The widely prevailing system of shifting cultivation, for example, facilitated the rapid regeneration of plant growth. Under the impact of colonial administration African farmers have, however, become sedentary, and permanent cultivation has been developed in and around villages, while the land farther from the village is still subjected to shifting cultivation.

Subsistence production in African agriculture has been assessed [11] as accounting for as much as 70% of the land and 60% of the labour. The most important factor acting in favour of continued food self-sufficiency on the farm is security. The remoteness of many areas from markets, and

325

poor and costly communications, reinforce the desire to be independent of the market for food supplies. Thus African farmers are caught in a vicious circle, for the inadequacies of the market prevent them from raising their output through specialisation, while their own desire for security inhibits the growth of the market.

This subsistence economy also involves land, one of the principal factors of production. Land is not bought and sold in the market; it is primarily a source of security and a guarantee of basic livelihood. E. H. Jacoby describes land tenure tribal systems in African countries in this way:

> "These traditional tenure systems guarantee a high measure of security to the man on the land, but function at the same time as a bulwark against any changes in the customary standards of life and work . . . Prevailing tenure conditions in large parts of Africa are one of the greatest obstacles in the way of agricultural development. As long as their population balance was more or less stable, the African peasants enjoyed a relatively high degree of economic and social security. But under the pressure of outside forces, the customary institutional framework began to disintegrate and this gradually increased the need for an alternative tenure system. The impact of Western legal and economic concepts isolated time-honoured values and even brought into clear relief how unrealistic these were, without, however, making a positive contribution to the cultural and social life of the people. The role of land as a regulating device for the routine of tribal life was gradually reduced, and with it the traditional values, taboos, and attitudes. This released impulses and propensities that hitherto had been safely channelled and controlled by the tribal society." [12]

Over time the traditional ways of using the land, whether for cultivation or for grazing, have undergone considerable modification. Production and trade have developed significantly. Yet in many ways the nature and extent of the changes have fallen short of expectations: "Innovations", says de Wilde, "have added to African agriculture, but they have not generally transformed it".[13]

One of the reasons for this disequilibrium is the lack of a comprehensive approach to development policy and planning and, in particular, the lack of integration between agriculture and industry and a negligence of spatial considerations.

One of the most noticeable features of the economies of the African countries is the small contribution made by industry to the GDP. Recent (1968) estimates for the African countries as a group show that the contribution of the manufacturing industries to the GDP was only 10.6%.[14] This global figure hides the considerable differences that exist between

326

different countries: in Zaïre, for example, the percentage is 18.9 and in Ghana it is 17, while it is only 2.1 in Mauritania and 2.4 in Gambia. In most countries the industralisation process has been characterised none-theless by a steady increase in the manufacturing sector's contribution to GDP—during the period 1960-1967 the average annual growth rate for the whole of Africa was 7.3% [15]—but the rate of growth of manufacturing output has generally not been fast enough to satisfy the growing demand for manufactured goods. As a result these countries had to import a greater quantity of such goods from the developed countries in the 60's than they did in the 50's.[16]

In many countries in tropical Africa the growth of manufacturing output fell short, not only of demand, but also of the targets that had been set in official economic development plans. As has been pointed out, one of the main reasons for the failure to put economic plans into effect is that the objectives set for the industrialisation programme were not integrated with those set for the development of other sectors of the economy.

Industrialisation and the development of agriculture are not alternative goals of development policy, but complementary and mutually supporting processes. An imbalance between the growth of agriculture and the growth of industry has unfortunate consequences for the growth of the economy as a whole. The slow growth of agricultural production in many African countries has acted as an obstacle in the way of faster industrialisation, and inadequate development of the industrial sector has influenced the slow rate of growth of the agricultural sector. An expanding agricultural sector requires steadily increasing supplies for agricultural machinery, tools, storage facilities, pesticides and fertilizers. The local production of these goods can form an important element in the emerging industrial sector.

The relationship between the industrialisation programme and the construction industry is equally important. The construction industry in the African countries is one of the fastest growing sectors of the economy, but a shortage of building materials has held up progress in many countries.

Natural resources extraction contributed 6.2% to the GDP of the African countries in 1963; the figure for North America was only 1.5%, for Western Europe 1.8% at the same time. The development policies in Africa are therefore now oriented towards building up the processing capacity to meet the growing demand from the domestic market and from the markets of other developing countries and, above all, to enable them to process a greater quantity of primary commodities that are at present exported to the developed countries in an unprocessed or only partly processed form.

The pattern of sectoral distribution that has evolved in the industrial

327

sector in African countries is strongly differentiated from country to country. Recent estimates suggest that the African countries produce about two-thirds of the manufactured consumer goods they need, and about one-fifth of the capital goods. The heavy manufacturing industries contribute between 20% and 30% of their total manufacturing output. Of the light industries, the most important in these countries are food processing and textiles, both of which have been growing in the last decade at an average rate of 4% to 5% per year.

There are many other issues in industrial development that are important in connection with regional development policies, but the length limitations of this paper do not allow us to do anything more than mention these: import substitution and export-oriented patterns of industrialisation, the elimination of structural unemployment, the distribution of income and wealth, the spatial distribution of economic development, etc.

One of the fundamental issues of economic and social development in the African countries must, however, be considered more thoroughly. This is the spatial integration of all aspects of development in a settlement network.

Three Phases of Settlement Development

An examination of the historical process of human settlement in tropical Africa allows us to distinguish, grosso modo, at least three phases of spatial organisation of human activities and habitats: organic-tribal, alienated-colonial, and integrated (i.e. on the way to integration)—independent.

The people of these countries organised their habitat quite satisfactorily in pre-colonial times around the exigencies of the natural environment and the tribal socio-cultural systems, with the help of rudimentary techniques of food production. The pattern of settlement was determined by geographical and social conditions: people settled in places where the environment was safer and healthier and where there was a possibility of leading a better life. Nomads, hunters, and pastoralists followed their routes in intimate connection with nature, and farmers settled predominantly in a nucleated pattern of farmsteads. Major villages grew up among small dispersed settlement units, and these were the seats of tribal chiefs and centres of trade and social ceremonies. The spatial concentration of administrative, commercial, religious and societal activities made these the primary points of growth, and the tribal authority and justice, wisdom and magic power that emanated from such centres strengthened social bonds, fostered social participation, and maintained a balance between the

328

people's needs and production in their hinterlands. The outer world had practically no influence on these centres.

In the colonial period a new administration, a new technology and economy, a different social order, and alien values and patterns of behaviour drastically changed the spatial structure of African economies as well as the settlement pattern. The location of plantations became oriented towards ports and transportation routes, and roads and railways were built connecting harbours with mines and plantations. Parallel with the exploitation of resources and the development of plantations along the transportation routes, new centres of local authority and basic services were established. While African people's farmsteads were still scattered, the alienated mining and plantations settlements provided the basis for colonial semiurban concentration and small-scale industrialisation. The export oriented agriculture demanded processing industries—e.g. sisal decortication plants, cotton ginneries, four mills, meat canneries, etc.—and these were conveniently situated in localities where there already was some concentration. Marketing facilities, the concentration of services, employment opportunities, and an increasing demand for food in these towns stimulated the growth of agricultural production, income increases, and some structural socio-economic changes in surrounding rural communities.

These focal points of development attracted immigrants. The phenomenon of polarisation played a major role in the functioning of colonial economies. Native agriculture had only to a small extent been involved in cash production and modernisation, and the export oriented colonial economy located along the roads left huge areas unaffected by the polarisation impulses of the growth centres. Once these became properly established, however, their influence began to be felt in the concentration of population and in the capital and social infrastructure, to the detriment of the peripheral areas that remained largely unchanged. The dual society and the dual economy in tropical Africa have been paralleled by a dual network of settlement.

The independent African countries are now striving for a new polarized equilibrium in the spatial organisation of the national economies. Regional planning development policies are increasingly taking the space factor and concentration effects into consideration. One of the major policy issues is the transformation of the poorly integrated and badly functioning settlement systems. Agricultural and fishery produce frequently rots because of the lack of local markets and transport facilities; and poor employment opportunities cause young people to abandon villages and small towns. The primary aim of independent governments in these countries is, therefore, to integrate the two settlement systems and create one which will be functional with regard to geographical conditions and modern technology,

329

and to social and political objectives, and that at the same time will be conducive to economic growth and social progress.

The fact that 80%-90% of the population in most African countries live in rural areas and that agricultural production contributes 70%-80% to the GDP and is largely governed by the principle of self-reliance, has led to an emphasis, in planned re-structuring of settlement patterns, on rural areas where agricultural extension work and local industry can afford a sufficient basis for growth centres. The exigencies of modern agriculture, combined with the growing demand for better standards of living, are making imperative the development of a network of growth centres to cover the whole national territory, but a host of factors are militating against their uniform distribution. The Tanzanian exercise of "district optimisation" will provide us with an example of one of the many ways in which it is possible to find rational models of settlement patterns functional with regard to the whole set of local conditions.

The Selection of Areas for Growth Activities:
A Model for an Integrated Settlement Network

What is called the "district optimisation" procedure was adopted in Tanzania to meet the need for a rational methodology of the spatio-functional analysis of organic factors of development.[17] The aim of this empirical and normative exercise was to define areas on the country's mainland territory where, thanks to natural endowment, available economic and technical infrastructures, and favourable human factors, a limited input would be able to secure the highest returns.

District areas within the national space economy were graded according to a number of factors and indices of growth:
    a.   the index of agricultural marketed produce;
    b.   the area of good soil for agricultural production;
    c.   the amount of reliable rainfall;
    d.   average maximal temperature;
    e.   population density;
    f.   the index of all-weather roads;
    g.   access to ports and railway stations;
    h.   the index of GDP.

The exercise has shown that enormous differences exist between districts in terms of the factors analysed, and has made it possible to identify four relatively homogeneous groups of districts from the point of view of their development potentials with regard to:
    a.   industrial development;

b. intensive agricultural development;
c. extensive agricultural development;
d. a freezing, for the time being, of development activities except tourism in particular areas.

The variety of development potentials on Tanzanian mainland territory excluded the possibility of finding one single model of settlement network. A specific settlement pattern was accordingly proposed for each area of definite potential capacity.

Central place and polarisation theories permitted the assumption that the level of concentration should be adapted to the size of the area, to the number of people likely to be living in the future sphere of influence of the growth centre, to the type of economic activities, and to the organisational set-up of administration. The size of settlement units is then a function of the scale and type of production and of the number of people living in their hinterlands. Such factors determine the hierarchy of settlement units. The hierarchy of settlement units for all four categories of homogeneous areas in the Tanzanian mainland was proposed according to Spearman's correlation coefficient.

National level integration was effected by means of a set of definite devices:
a. a moderate concentration of all development factors;
b. a reduction of the number of existing hierarchy of settlement units;
c. a denser allocation of rural growth centres; and
d. a fostering of development belts along transportation routes internally connected with a sufficient number of outlets to neighbouring countries.

For the areas of industrial potential a three-tiered settlement pattern was designed: village—major rural centre—district town. Basic service facilities located in concentrated villages are to characterise minor rural centres; major rural centres serving some 30,000 people will attract some small scale processing industries, as will modern agriculture in the area; a district town is to concentrate industries, public administration, and a well-developed system of services and transportation, and will, as a result of the diffusion of development impulses, create a polarised zone.

Areas of high agricultural development potential may be divided into two categories according to different levels of population density. For areas of low population density, where human settlements are far apart from one another and there are large areas suitable for land reclamation for cattle breeding or large scale farming, a two-tiered settlement hierarchy is proposed: rural centres of some 2,500-3,000 inhabitants, and district towns. The distance between these is not to exceed 30-50 km.

331

For areas of higher population density, where the existing network of settlement and its hierarchy is overcomplicated, this two-tiered model would surely act as an impediment to improving farming and ranching and to the efficiency of service facilities. Large scale farming of the "ujamaa" type demands a district administration that corresponds more closely to the production units. Therefore a four-tiered hierarchy is necessary for these areas: villages, minor rural centres, major rural towns, and subregional centres. These last, which will be characterised by large scale industries, higher economic organisation, a higher level of service facilities and of storage facilities, will perform the functions of Mosher's Progressive Rural Structure model, combining:

"1. district (wholesale) markets for farm produce and for farm supplies and equipment;
2. regional agricultural research;
3. district extension administration;
4. district banks;
5. district roads and communication";[18]

and assorted processing industries and social infrastructure.

In areas of medium agricultural potential, where only minor extension projects are envisaged, the existing settlement network would be slightly changed by the selective concentration of indispensable service facilities and technical infrastructure in larger villages and towns.

The existing settlement system in areas of low agricultural potential is not likely to be changed in the immediate future; no economic intervention is planned in these very sparsely populated and climatically hostile areas. The natural endowment of some of these may result in an expansion of tourist facilities, which would create job opportunities for the local people and a concomitant change in living conditions.

In our search for a definition of the functional place of growth centres in regional development in some of the African countries, the above presentation of both empirical and normative approaches, which has been facilitated by the central place theory and by the growth centres theory, can help us to see how to move rationally from empirical observation to the normative proposals characteristic of the regional planning procedure.

Notes

1. R. Dumont, *False Start in Africa,* Sphere Books Ltd., Londen 1968, p. 85.
2. Cf. M. Rósciszewski, "Organisation and Typology of Socio-Economic Space in Third World Countries", *Norsk. Geogr. Tidaskr.,* 28, 1974, pp. 41-52.
3. D. R. F. Taylor, "Growth Centres and Rural Development in Africa", in this volume.

4. Marc Penouil, "Growth Poles in Underdeveloped Regions and Countries" in *Growth Poles and Regional Policies,* edited by A. Kukliński and R. Petrella, Mouton, Paris and The Hague, 1972, pp. 120-131.

5. *Ibid.*

6. *Ibid.*

7. *Ibid.*

8. R. Dumont, *op. cit.,* p. 94.

9. Cf. J. de Wilde and others, *Experiences with Agricultural Development in Tropical Africa,* The Johns Hopkins Press, Baltimore 1967, p. 15.

10. P. McLoughlin, *Some Conclusions from the World Bank Study of African Agricultural Productivity,* Bloomington, Indiana, 1966.

11. J. de Wilde *et al., op. cit.,* p. 25.

12. E. H. Jacoby, *Man and Land: The Fundamental Issue in Development,* Deutsch, London, 1971, p. 319.

13. *Loc. cit.*

14. United Nations *Survey of Economic Conditions in Africa, 1960-1964,* New York 1968.

15. Commission on International Development of the World Bank, *Partners in Development,* New York, 1969.

16. UNIDO, *General Issues of Industrial Policy,* New York, 1969.

17. Z. Pióro, *The Spatial Structure of the Tanzanian Economy,* Ministry of Lands, Settlement and Water Development, Dar-es-Salaam, 1969.

18. A. T. Mosher, *Creating a Progressive Rural Structure,* New York, 1969, p. 14.

Selected Bibliography

Afryka w Statystyce (Africa in Statistics), Centre of African Studies, University of Warsaw, Warsaw, 1974.

Alajew, E. B., *Regionalnoje Planirovanije v Razvivajuscichsja Stranach* (Regional Planning in Developing Countries), USSR Academy of Sciences, Moscow, 1973.

Dobrska, Z., "Trudnosci procesu industrializacji w krajach afrykanskich" (Difficulties in the Processes of Industrialisation in African Countries), *Ekonomista* (Warsaw), 1, 1970.

de Wilde, J., *et al., Experiences with Agricultural Development in Tropical Africa,* The Johns Hopkins Press, Baltimore, 1967.

Dumont, R., *False Start in Africa,* Sphere Books Ltd., London, 1968.

Dumont, R., *Développement Agricole Africain,* Presses Univ. de France, Paris, 1965.

Friedman, J., "A General Theory of Polarised Development", mimeo. paper, Santiago, Chile, 1967.

Jacoby, E. H., *Man and Land, The Fundamental Issue in Development,* Deutsch, London, 1971.

Johnson, E. A. J., *The Organisation of Space in Developing Countries,* Cambridge, 1970.

Kukliński, A. R., "Poles de Croissance et Centres de Croissance en Matière de la Politique et du Planification Régionale", in *Poles de Développement et Centres de Croissance dans le Développement Régional*, Dunod, Paris, 1970.

McLoughlin, P., *Some Conclusions from the World Bank Study of African Agricultural Productivity*, Bloomington, Indiana, 1966.

Mosher, A. T., *Creating a Progressive Rural Structure*, Agricultural Development Council, Inc., New York, 1969.

Penouil, M., "Growth Poles in Underdeveloped Regions and Countries" in A.R. Kukliński and R. Petrella (eds.), *Growth Poles and Regional Policies*, Mouton, Paris and The Hague, 1972.

Perroux, F., *L'Economie du XXè Siècle*, Presses Univ. de France, Paris, 1964.

Pióro, Z., *The Spatial Structure of the Tanzanian Economy*, Ministry of Lands, Settlement and Water Development, Dar-es-Salaam, 1969.

Pióro, Z., "Growth Poles and Growth Centres Theory as Applied to Settlement Development in Tanzania", in A. Kukliński, (ed.) *Growth Poles and Growth Centres in Regional Planning*, Mouton, Paris and The Hague, 1972.

Pióro, Z., "Polarised Structure of the Tanzanian Economy", *Africana Bulletin* (Warsaw) nr. 18, 1974.

Stöhr, W. B., "Regional Planning as a Necessary Tool for the Comprehensive Development of a Country", United Nations *Interregional Symposium on Training of Planners for Comprehensive Regional Development*, Warsaw, 1971.

Taylor, D. R. F., "Growth Centres and Rural Development in Africa", in this volume.

UNIDO, *General Issues of Industrial Policy*, New York, 1969.

UNIDO, *Report on the Interregional Seminar on the Industry Location and Regional Development*, New York, 1969.

334

5

REGIONAL PLANNING AND THE EMPLOYMENT CHALLENGE IN UNDERDEVELOPED COUNTRIES*

Víctor Grosman **

There seems to be enough historical evidence to show that the so called "developmentalist approach" has completely failed. The countries of Latin America are a good case in point. As a result of the world wide crisis of the thirties and the Second World War, these countries adopted their present developmentalist approach by fostering an internally oriented growth pattern of extensive industrialization aimed at import substitution. Hitherto the growth pattern had been largely externally oriented: the exportation of raw materials had provided the necessary foreign exchange to import the required manufactured goods.

While the developmentalist approach did result in considerable economic growth in the countries involved, it has failed because at the same time it resulted in social and regional disequilibria, increasing marginalisation, unemployment and underemployment for the majority of the people, increasing income disparities, and narrowing domestic markets. In short, it produced all the mechanisms leading to massive frustration.

It is becoming very clear that there is an urgent need for a new strategy that will enable us to eliminate social and regional disequilibria in the underdeveloped countries. Thus these days we frequently hear people advocating the necessity of sacrificing a certain amount of economic development in order to get more social development, i.e. better living conditions for the people.

In the case of Mexico, it is well known and publicly admitted that here

---

* Paper submitted to the "First Asian Symposium on Regional Planning and National Development", Institute of Development Studies, University of Mysore, India, 1 to 4 July, 1974.

** The author was PREALC Regional Representative for Central America and Panama. (PREALC is the ILO Regional Employment Programme for Latin America and the Caribbean). The opinions expressed are his own and do not necessarily reflect the official views of the organisation with whom he is presently engaged (FAO Senior Economic Adviser, Brasilia, Brazil).

there are twenty million people (approximately 40% of the population) with a marginal or subsistence standard of living; that it is necessary to create a minimum of 600,000 new jobs per year just to absorb the new-comers to the labour force, not to mention the already existent (1970) half-million unemployed. And in Brazil it has been estimated that at least one million new jobs will have to be created annually just to keep pace with the natural growth of the labour force.

Admittedly, labour-intensive programmes are often undertaken in these countries, in an attempt to create employment for the local labour force, particularly in rural areas (which in Mexico, for example, account for two thirds of the total unemployment). Road and building construction programmes are good cases in point. The magnitude and cumulative nature of the unemployment problems, however, require more drastic and integral solutions: the problems will not be solved by merely taking isolated measures, no matter how large or how positive these may be.

The rapid population growth and the frequent and substantial rural-to-urban migrations in underdeveloped countries present a tremendous challenge to those who are making an effort to provide the people with well paying job opportunities and more humane living conditions. Low educational and training standards further seriously hamper absorption of the labour force in productive activities. It is quite often the case that an important mass of unemployed and underemployed people exists at the same time as an increasing need for, and shortage of, qualified personnel. This need is usually satisfied by using skilled workers in the big metropolitan centres. Thus there is a continuous flow of commerce, capital and people from backward regions to the more developed ones, and this exacerbates regional disparities in income levels and growth rates.

The unchecked importation of capital-intensive and labour-saving technologies—without the necessary adaptation to the relative availability of resources in each region—aggravates the situation. Two types of circumstances can be responsible for such a phenomenon in the underdeveloped countries. The first is a lack of systematic and coordinated efforts to adapt technology to the real needs of the backward areas; and the second is a lack of governmental and other public policies that explicitly and significantly favour the full utilisation of the labour force and a more equitable regional distribution of the benefits derived from dynamic economic growth.

The various policies involved—monetary and fiscal, public investments, foreign trade, taxation, social welfare, labour, and so on—have never in fact been integrated into a comprehensive development policy in which explicit employment and regional equality goals are clearly defined. The current argument against such a policy is that advanced labour and social security legislation have increased the cost of manpower while, at the same

336

time, tax and credit policies and the customs duties exemptions for the importation of machinery and equipment, have lessened the real cost of capital, thus stimulating and strengthening the use of high capital density and labour-saving technologies.

If the exorbitant social costs of a dynamic growth process (marginalisation and frustration of the majority of the people, regional inequalities, unemployment and underemployment, narrowness of the domestic market and its consequent monopolistic structure due to the inequitable income distribution) are to be avoided, it is absolutely essential to formulate and implement an integral development policy with explicit consideration of regional equality and employment objectives. A national-regional or inter-regional approach must be adopted if we really want and expect to overcome the unfortunate side-effects of rapid growth.

In an attempt to catch up with the "revolution of aspirations" of their peoples, the underdeveloped countries have, as we stated above, fostered a strong industrialisation policy aiming at import substitution. However, the narrowness of the internal markets, the need to take advantage of external and internal economies, the indivisible character of infrastructure investments, the severe competition faced by local industries from similar products coming from other areas, and the protectionist fiscal and marketing policies, have resulted in an increasing industrial concentration in the big urban centres, inefficiency, high costs of production, low competitiveness, small manpower absorption and idle plant capacity. The picture gets even worse if we add the low qualification levels of the labour force in those countries vis-à-vis an increasing demand for more specialised and sophisticated personnel for a dynamic industrial sector.

The rural sector is, of course, also crucial in underdeveloped countries. Any income and employment increases will bring about increases in the demand for foodstuffs. The high proportion of the population engaged in agriculture, with its low productivity and low salaries, tends however to perpetuate the inequitable regional and personal income distribution, and the narrowness of the domestic markets. Thus the rural sector constitutes a serious barrier for the expansion of the industrial sector.

The lack of a national-regional planning system is clearly reflected in the rural sector. Quite often efforts are made to lower the seasonal unemployment levels, to organise the peasants in cooperatives so that burdens would be lessened and unproductive individualism minimized, to provide them with fertilizers, selected seeds, small-scale irrigation, credit, etc. Such measures may have some effect in the short-run and they are certainly better than nothing. They clearly do not constitute the long-run solution of the problem, however, since they do not touch on the land tenure and land use systems which are the main obstacles to development in these countries. As they stand, these systems seriously hinder an in-

337

crease of productivity and a more substantial absorption of manpower in better paying jobs. It is often the case in Latin America that a change in land use—even with the same technology—would allow for the full employment of at least three times the number of those presently under-employed in rural areas. These aspects, therefore, need to be considered within the framework of an integral development plan and not merely through stopgap or band-aid actions and programmes.

An inter-regional development strategy with explicit regional equality and employment goals should coordinate and integrate many actions, policies and programmes. Let us briefly list what are, as far as the underdeveloped countries are concerned, the most important of these:

1. Continual massive personnel training should be implemented at all levels. Such training should fully utilise the existing facilities and infrastructure.

2. Strong and substantive support should be given to research and experimental programs leading to and speeding up the adaptation of technologies imported from the more advanced countries to the needs and resources available. It is worthwhile emphasizing here that when there is considerable unemployment, total output can be increased not only by raising the productivity per worker, but also by employing more people.

3. Fiscal policy measures (incentives, taxes, credits, etc.) should be implemented in order to encourage a more intensive use of manpower and to enable restoration of the equilibrium between the real costs of labour and capital, taking into account the relative scarcity of the latter as compared with the more ample supply of the former in backward areas.

4. There should be a dynamization of personnel recruitment services in order to establish more effective communication channels between those people looking for and those offering jobs. If such services are to be operative, they must, of course, be supported by adequate information systems regarding the qualifications needed, offered and requested.

5. Solutions must be found to the problems of latifundios (large estates usually held by absentee owners) and of excessive fragmentation of hold-ings in rural areas. The organisation of the small land-owners in more efficient productive units should be considered, and they should be given credit facilities, technical assistance and training.

6. Small industry and handicraft development should be encouraged not only in order to fully utilise the local natural and human resources, but also in order to improve rural living conditions, thereby arresting the prevalent rural-to-urban migrations and the consequent increasing urban marginalisation.

7. There should be an effective policy of industrial decentralisation through fiscal incentives, industrial parks, creation of infrastructure in less developed zones, credit, and technical assistance. Small and medium sized

as well as large-scale industry should be considered here.

8. The industrial sector should be supported—by means of fiscal incentives, technical information, credit and marketing facilities, regular supply of raw materials, etc.—in order to more fully utilise existing idle capacity. Employment could thus be significantly increased in the short run, without considerable additional capitalisation.

9. All types of special programs should be encouraged that would allow the backward regions to fully benefit from their existing resources and potentialities and natural comparative advantages. Tourism, in particular, is a good example.

In summary, the dynamic efforts now being made by the underdeveloped countries, and the substantive amounts of capital that they are investing through various plans, programmes and development projects, do not guarantee the full and rational utilisation of their human resources; nor do they guarantee regional equality. The rate of growth of expectations created by industries and public investments in urban areas, for example, is significantly higher than the real possibilities of productive absorption of the increasing labour force migrating from the country to the urban centres. Unfortunately, that trend is not being reversed, that is, the frustrated migrant is not returning at the same speed to his rural area, and thus the army of the urban marginalised people is constantly growing. The need to fully integrate inter-regional planning with employment planning has become strikingly apparent and can hardly be over-emphasized.

6

REGIONAL PLANNING AND RURAL DEVELOPMENT IN LATIN AMERICA

Harold A. Wood

Before embarking on any discussion of regional planning, it is desirable to specify whether one is concerned with planning *in* regions or *by* and *for* regions, because the processes are rather different. In many countries, power is retained in a central office, and decisions on regional allocations of activities and resources are made with little or no reference to opinion elsewhere in the country. In other cases, under some over-all constraints, planning groups within the regions are given considerable autonomy in the identification of their principal problems and in the definition and execution of development programs. For the purpose of the present discussion, the latter approach is considered to be the more appropriate, for three reasons.

Firstly, if regional "development" is to become self-sustaining, it must involve considerable local human creativity and not merely high levels of consumption. The diffusion of man's innovative capacity is therefore more urgent than the diffusion of material goods or technology.[1] And it is useless to try to promote innovative ideas among the people of a region unless they are able to use these new initiatives in meaningful ways.

Secondly, rural areas have been discriminated against so consistently in the past that, unless special measures are taken to ensure some rural autonomy, traditional urban-oriented planning approaches will probably be adopted almost unconsciously. It is noteworthy that the introductions to many regional plans state almost casually that their main purpose is to curb excessive migration to urban centres or to ensure the adequate production of food and other raw materials which supply the cities and are exported in exchange for the countless imported items which the cities need. Usually the actual welfare of the rural dwellers is the least of the planner's concerns, unless and until, by their migrations or their demands, they begin to raise difficulties for the urban population. This kind of discrimination must not be allowed to persist.

Thirdly, development planning which ignores regional participation has, by and large, not worked. Particularly notable has been the failure of growth pole strategies to create true regional development. The problem, of course, is that no one has worked out the complex mechanisms by which development impulses are transmitted from the pole to the region, or, in other words, the mechanisms which integrate the region while preserving the relative interests of all parties involved in the integration process. If any single bottleneck exists in the movement towards development in the so-called developing countries, it lies exactly here, between the town and the country. The policies of the past, based on purely urban interests, are proving increasingly inadequate, and it is necessary now to allow the rural areas their rightful share in the shaping of new, more equitable approaches to the solution of national problems.

For these reasons, it is the thesis of this paper that regional planning must take as its primary objectives (1) the satisfaction of regional needs, as defined by the inhabitants of the region, and (2) the involvement of these inhabitants in all phases of the development process.

To illustrate the validity of this thesis, we shall briefly examine three cases of purported rural development. One is a typical example of land reform; the second involves attempts to create integrated agricultural colonies; and the third aims to improve conditions in an area of spontaneous pioneer colonization.

The first example comes from the Pacific Coast of Guatemala, an agricultural region with extremely high potential due to its humid climate, fertile soils, and ready access to national and international markets. Expropriated private properties have here been subdivided into parcels of about 20 hectares in size, the area judged necessary to provide a decent living for a rural family, and each parcel has been turned over to a farmer. Under the prevailing ecological conditions, however, a farmer working by hand cannot, even with the help of his family, cultivate more than about one-seventh of the parcel. He is invariably too poor to buy machinery, and is unable to raise money by mortgaging his land since the terms of his tenure preclude the scale or subdivision of the holding. So he continues to work manually, and, so as not to leave most of the land idle, brings in six other families as sharecroppers, demanding of each a rental payment of one half of the crop. Thus the owner of the parcel is comparatively well off, and the land is intensely cultivated. It would be easy to produce statistics proving that the entire program has had very beneficial results. But, of course, any apparent success is based on the fact that six sevenths of the population of the area live in dire poverty, each surviving on half the production of a mere three hectares of land. Only because of their deprivation does the new landowner realize an adequate income.

The second case is that of northeast Brazil, where agricultural colonization has been carried out in a more organized and controlled fashion.[2] Most of the parcels are about 10 hectares in size, this being an amount which might reasonably be worked by a single family in this region of mediocre soil and subhumid climate. Each lot is provided with various facilities, including road access, a dwelling, simple tools, and some livestock. Community facilities include a meeting place, processing machinery for local crops, mechanical equipment, technical supervision, etc. It all sounds eminently reasonable and even generous. Yet the very nature of the plan gives rise to two interrelated problems so far-reaching that life in the colonies is little better than life in other areas where none of these improvements have been made.

The first problem is that of payment for the land and the facilities. Each of the colonies is financed by some sponsoring body which has made a considerable investment in the project and which wants to recoup its capital so that it can repeat the process elsewhere. Each colony has a group of administrators who, in order to guarantee adequate production on each holding and to collect the periodic payments of the colonists, bring direct or indirect pressures to bear on the farmers to ensure that they produce the commodities which have been selected as the most suitable or profitable. The colonist thus has little freedom of choice and fails to develop the sense of responsibility and the initiative he will need as an independent operator: dependence and class distinctions are built into the system.

The system fails not only at the level of human development, however, but also in the very area of production for which it was designated. It has invariably proven impossible for the average colonist to produce enough under these conditions to cover the cost of the land and improvements, and the salaries of a relatively well-paid administrative and technical staff, while still having enough left over for his own subsistence. The annual property payments average $390, and the minimum acceptable family requirements for food and clothing would cost about $1500 per year, yet the actual average gross income per family ranges from $1007 to only $506.[3] Nor is an over-prediction of the productivity of the land the only defect in the operation. One finds, in fact, a negative correlation between family income and the degree of central supervision. The most successful colonies have been the ones which provide assistance with marketing, but give the farmers the greatest amount of freedom in choosing what, when, and where they will plant.

Yet the third case study demonstrates that the absence of demands on the rural people does not in itself guarantee success. Here our example is the Program to Assist Spontaneous Colonization which was carried out on the Pacific Coast of Ecuador from 1965-1969.[4] At first glance, this project appears to be exactly what the local people needed. The settlers

343

who had moved spontaneously into this empty area of great agricultural promise were to be provided with titles to their land, a community organization based on a cooperative system, roads, schools, medical care, other social services, agricultural experimental centres, and loans to cover new houses and agricultural improvements.

Despite the expenditure of approximately $1500 for each family in the area, the present attitude of these people is more one of disillusion than satisfaction. While the legalization of land holdings has, on the whole, been quite successful and the provision of credit has permitted an increase in land clearings and the purchase of more livestock, other aspects of the program have been partial or complete failures. Medical and other social services have been abandoned; the agricultural stations have closed; the road system was only partially completed and, with the termination of the project, deterioration rapidly set in; the housing program never got off the ground; and the cooperative system created as many problems as it solved.

It is particularly revealing to compare the performance of farmers inside and outside the project area. For this purpose, we may identify three zones: zone A is outside the project area, and in general is much less accessible, but has similar physical conditions; zone B is inside the project area, but is not reached by road; zone C, inside the project area, is adjacent to a major highway.

For these three areas, the gross income per hectare of cleared land is still $111, $116 and $90, while income per day's work in each is $3.49, $2.65 and $2.36 respectively. It is true that landowners have larger incomes in the project area—gross incomes, including the value of food produced and consumed by the farm family, are $1050, $1389 and $1864 respectively for the three zones—but the higher incomes are only obtained by the use of hired hands paid at a rate of no more than $300 per year. In the three zones, the number of days of non-family labour employed on the farm are respectively 0, 116, and 586.

The poor performance of the Ecuadorean project serves to support our thesis at two levels. At the national level, many aspects of the program failed because they were introduced from outside the country and were never integrated with national policies. Thus roads were built, but no provision was made to ensure that their maintenance would be handled by the Ministry of Public Works. Similarly, clinics were established, but they were not taken over by the Ministry of Public Health when the project ended, and were abandoned. Bypassing these Ministries during the planning and execution of the project may have saved some time, but the long term results were decidedly negative.

Yet, if it can be a mistake not to pursue development programs using existing institutional machinery which, despite some defects, has a measure of continuity, it is also counterproductive to establish such programs without the involvement of the local people. For even if many things are done correctly, a few key errors may spoil the whole scheme. In the case being examined, the provision of titles to land, medical care, and investment capital were actually all elements which the local population would have supported. The failure of the housing program did not really bother anyone, and could easily have been predicted: it was unreasonable to expect poor people to borrow money for the construction of small concrete houses when the dwellings they could build themselves using local materials, at little or no capital expense, were in many ways more comfortable and better adapted to prevailing climatic conditions. Even deficiencies in the road construction program were not very serious since farmers living off the highway routinely fed their crops to hogs, cattle or chickens, animals of sufficient value to warrant a trip of several miles over forest trails. Of more importance was the fact that agricultural advice was generally spurned, that facilities were abandoned, and that the community centres failed to function properly. These resulted largely from the adoption of 50 hectares as the standard farm size, which meant that settlement was too dispersed. With lots so large, most farm residences were too far from the schools in the community centres for the children to walk back and forth each day. To cope with this problem, the farmers were provided with small building lots in the community centre where they could build second homes to be occupied throughout the week by the mother and the school age children, while the father spent his time alone, or with his older sons, on the farm. This arrangement is no more appealing to an Ecuadorean family than it would be to a North American.

Another disadvantage of the large farm is that it encourages a latifundio-type economy in which most of the work is done by peons. This perpetuates the socio-economic inequalities which a land reform program is supposed to eliminate or at least reduce.

If, then, we can admit—and to do so is to take a long step forward in rural development—that the planner should try to provide what the rural people believe they want, rather than what he, the planner, thinks they ought to have, the question arises, "What do the people want?" Surprisingly, we find very few serious attempts to obtain objective answers to this question, but a survey of a sample of the rural population in the lower Guayas Basin in Ecuador produced results which seem to have the ring of truth: in descending order, the expressed desires of the people were health, education, land, and "honour"; money came only in fifth place. There is here a lesson which all planners need to learn.

This is, however, only part of the lesson. There exists a further complication—one which, in the opinion of the writer, is one of the most critical of all—namely, the virtual impossibility at the present time of

345

arriving at a rural consensus. It can be utterly frustrating to reason that rural development depends on providing what rural people want, if there are irreconcilable disagreements in their definition of these wants. And, despite the results of the survey mentioned above, deep disagreements as to development objectives are almost universal.

The problem is that rural society in Latin America normally comprises three classes: (a) the "latifundistas", or owners of large estates, most of whom live off their properties for most of the year and depend on hired labour; (b) the small farmers who, with the help of their families, work on parcels of about the size needed for their subsistence; and (c) the landless peons who either move about the country finding work wherever they can or attach themselves to individual estates where they receive reasonably regular employment and a small plot on which to build a hut, but relatively low wages.

These three classes have values and objectives which appear to be so divergent that in many areas it is felt that the only path to rural harmony is through the elimination of one class (usually the latifundistas) or even two (the latifundistas and the peons).

We do not intend to argue that some reform of land holdings is not necessary or desirable. The largest estates are frequently poorly run and could well be broken up. Moreover, the landless workers often live in shameful conditions, and constitute a socially disruptive element. Nevertheless, there are distinct advantages in the existence of a spatial mixture of small, medium, and large properties. On the one hand, the small operators provide a flexible labour force, able to work on large estates during periods of peak activity and to fill in the quieter parts of the year with labour on their own holdings. The large operators, on the other hand, provide the advantages of advanced technology for production and transportation, an organized marketing system, and the opportunity of local employment paid for in cash. To preserve these not inconsiderable benefits, some mix of farm sizes should be retained provided that such a mix can be made to coexist with a measure of social justice. Or, to put it another way, land reform could be much less drastic and disruptive than it usually is if there were some way of eliminating the class exploitation which is so widespread in Latin America, and which lies at the root of the rural tensions and disagreements. The question is so important that we shall look in some detail at three of the principal forms of such exploitation.

First, we find a financial exploitation which is, in fact, promoted by most government agricultural development policies. Normally, funds set aside for this purpose go mainly to the major producers of export crops; it can in fact almost be stated as a general law that large commercial farms always operate on credit, using funds borrowed from official in-

346

stitutions at rates of interest which are always low and, in countries with monetary inflation, even negative. The personal capital of the large land owners, including the income from their subsidized agricultural activities, tends to be invested in other sectors of the economy, especially in industry and in urban housing, where earnings of the order of 30% per year are commonly obtained. Alternatively, money may be loaned at usurious interest rates to the small farmers who, for lack of a proper title to their land or because they are poor, cannot obtain loans from governmental agencies. Thus, either through the high rates of interest they pay on loans, or through the taxes they pay to the government, the small farmers are subsidizing the large operators. This is an enormous injustice, which demands rectification.

Secondly, the small producer is consistently exploited in the marketing of his produce, due to his vulnerable position vis-à-vis the large producers or the middle-men. For example, export contracts at official prices are normally held only by large producers. When they are unable to fill their quotas from their own operations, they will buy from the small farmers, but at much lower prices. Similarly, the middle-men regularly make extravagant profits as they buy from the farmer and sell to urban markets: mark-ups of 500% are more the rule than the exception, particularly in the case of vegetables and other products which are not easily stored. In fact, local businessmen commonly make similar profits on food which never even moves out of the area, by buying from the farmers at harvest time at depressed prices, storing the produce, and reselling at a handsome profit during periods of scarcity. The farmers are unable to hold back their crops because they are desperately in need of money and because, even for relatively durable commodities such as corn and beans, it is difficult for the small farmer to construct or purchase storage facilities which are safe against rats, weevils, mould, etc. It is commonplace for a farmer who sold his corn for 1 cent a kilo at harvest time to have to buy it back ten months later at 5 cents.

Of course, against this kind of exploitation the small farmer has some defences. He may turn away completely from the production of export crops, or he may concentrate on the raising of livestock, for which the prices are more stable. But the adoption of such measures frequently reduces the overall productivity of the land.

The third type of exploitation of the small farmer is in his land tenure. The lack of an adequate system for the survey and registry of rural properties usually makes it extremely difficult for a small farmer to obtain secure title to his land. All too often, a company or a well-placed individual will manage to obtain legal possession of an extensive tract of land which is already partially or even completely occupied by small farmers who are then forced to vacate. This kind of exploitation is not so common as the other two, but when it does occur it results in much bitterness.

What should now be noted about these three forms of exploitation is that they all have their roots in the legal system or in the organization of trade. It is a question not so much of class prejudices, which are only changed slowly and gradually, but of regulations which are subject to modification. It should therefore be possible to achieve a marked reduction in the occurrence of these abuses by relatively simple means. And, with more equal access to the income produced by farm labour, one may be cautiously optimistic about the emergence among all rural classes of a desire for cooperation and a readiness to agree on the development goals which should be pursued. Among these goals we should expect to find a maximization of production per hectare and per day's work, an objective which is presently very seldom adopted by planners. Also, it would be essential to assign to the region some specific role in the national development plan.

It is a paradox of so-called "regional planning" that the spatial units designated "regions" are commonly used more for the collection and analysis of data than as functional units. Where no regional function is clearly defined, the region will either lack an overall plan or have a general "Development Program" which may be totally uncoordinated with the national plan and with the development plans of adjacent areas. In either case, the proper integration of the region within a spatial model of national development will be difficult or impossible. It is therefore necessary that the actual and potential contribution of the rural region to the national well-being be spelled out as comprehensively as possible. Then the contribution of the nation to the region should be of roughly equivalent value if the region is not to be discriminated against. This concept is undoubtedly a complex one, and would represent something of a revolution in planning procedure, yet it is precisely the lack of equitable regional treatment which produces the hyperurbanization and similar spatial imbalances which trouble so much of Latin America.

In summary, regional planning for rural development in Latin America could be greatly expedited through the fulfilment of the following objectives:

a. The provision of adequate rural social services, particularly in the fields of health, education, drinking water, and electricity;

b. Some control of property sizes so as to ensure that the family farm is the most common type of holding, but without necessarily eliminating the large estates completely;

c. The creation of an equitable system for the marketing and storage of farm products;

d. The establishment of a system of supervised credit, under which loans can be made with little risk even to poor families without secure title to their land;

e. The adoption of an efficient system for the registration and transfer of land holdings;

f. The development of improved varieties of plants and breeds of animals, provided that their production and use are consistent with local ecological and socio-economic conditions;

g. The creation of a technology especially suited to the tropical family farm. Particularly necessary are machines which can work efficiently on the sloping land which must so often be cultivated in the tropics;

h. The installation of small agro-industries, which will help in the preservation of stable prices for farm products, provide employment during periods of agricultural inactivity, and bring greater diversity of opportunity to the rural areas; and

i. The provision of access roads. These appear last on the list, not because they are unimportant but because they do not necessarily have beneficial effects on regional development; under certain circumstances they can lead to rural depopulation and to an excessive dependence upon metropolitan regions.

Once these steps are taken, the principal obstacles to rural development will have been removed, and it will then be appropriate to proceed with the formulation of a development plan, as suggested in the following outline.

General Composition of a Rural Regional Development Plan

A. Diagnosis of the position of the region with respect to the nation as a whole; preparation of input-output tables, giving a monetary value to each of the following contributions made to the nation by the region:
   a. products of all kinds, including water and energy
   b. human resources (emigration)
   c. conservation of resources for the future
   d. recreation facilities
   e. strategic values
Subsequent determination of what the contribution of the nation should be to the region, at least in the following items:
   a. products of all kinds
   b. funds for development

B. Determination of the region's potential populations, taking the following into consideration:
   a. natural resources
   b. land use

c. the level of industrialization

d. the desired ratio between the number of persons engaged in primary and secondary activities and the number engaged in tertiary and quaternary activities

C. Determination of regional population policies:
 a. level and type of emigration to be promoted
 b. level and type of immigration to be promoted

D. Determination of national and regional social development policies:
 a. definition of the basic level of social services to be provided throughout the nation
 b. determination of a system of priorities for the allocation of services which go beyond the basic level

E. Determination of regional economic policies:
 a. the type of production to be encouraged
 b. the level of technology to be encouraged
 c. the system of storage and marketing to be established
 d. the system of credit and financial assistance to be established

F. Determination of regional policies with respect to land tenure:
 a. system of land tenure to be encouraged
 b. system of land taxation to be established
 c. identification of appropriate property sizes
 d. survey and registration of properties

G. Determination of policies with respect to the provision of infrastructure:
 a. Social—organization of local groups to participate in the planning process
 b. Industrial—establishing industries based on regional resources or producing for a regional market
 c. Urban—creation of a network of urban places suitable for the provision of social and economic services
 d. Transportation—creation of a suitable network of roads

When analyses of these kinds have been carried out, and when the indicated set of interlocking development policies have been established, it should be possible to define the specific programs and projects which will make genuine rural development a reality not only in Latin America but throughout the world.

Notes

1. For a good analysis of the theory relating development to the diffusion of innovations, see Lasuén, J. R., "Urbanizacion y Desarrollo: una hipotesis sobre la integracion de las Concentraciones Sectoriales y las Aglomeraciones Geograficas" in *Avaliacao Do Planejamento para o Desenvolvimento Salvador-Bahia, Brasil 1970,* Publicacion de la Sociedade Brasiliera de Planejamento, pp. 344-405.

2. Darnel, B. W., *Land Settlement in Northeast Brazil: A Study of Seven Projects,* Ph. D. Thesis, McMaster University, 1973.

3. Income figures include the value of food produced and consumed by the family. Excluded is the income of Japanese settlers on one of the colonies. Average income for the Japanese families is $3552.

4. Wood, H. A., "Spontaneous Agricultural Colonization in Ecuador", *Annals of the Association of American Geographers,* 1972, pp. 599-617.

7

POLARIZATION, DEVELOPMENT, AND INTEGRATION

José Luis Coraggio **

The role played by various general social theories and by their corresponding strategies in Latin America has been the subject of many valuable studies in recent times.

The "dominant ideology" is conceived not as a homogenous body, but as an ideological system articulated in cores inserted in the different social practices. This is particularly so in the theoretical practice of what are called the social sciences.

In order to make out the ideological elements in a discourse which is allegedly scientific, it is necessary to refer to the ideological systems themselves. The analysis of ideological processes should, however, take the study of specific ideological formations as its point of departure, showing their origin, progress and diffusion within a specific field, as well as their junction with complementary formations inserted in apparently different problem areas. Furthermore, a better understanding of this process may seem impossible without simultaneous research on the processes of the material structures with which these ideological formations are linked.

One of the effects of the ideological process is the success of certain concepts. Such success can be manifested in the lavish (if not always accurate) utilization of the terminology associated with these concepts, or in the decision of important official agencies to support activities (congresses, research, etc.) along the new lines, or in various other ways.

If the concepts are to continue being successful, one of the factors that will come into play is the ability of the ideology to maintain the domination structures.

In our specific field, i.e. economies and planning, an increasing amount

* Published in *Revista de la Integración,* INTAL, Buenos Aires, Nr. 13, May 1973.
** Economist and head researcher of the Center for Urban and Regional Studies of the Torcuato Di Tella Institute, Buenos Aires.

of attention is being paid to spatial and regional problems in Latin America. The publication of new journals, the abundance of conferences and courses, as well as a proliferation of specialized research and planning organizations testify to this growing interest. The contributions of what is called the Theory of Growth Poles, which is related to these spatial and regional problems, deserves special attention.

A mechanistic speculation claims that this growing interest is due to a worsening of regional problems, a process which would have effects on theoretical practices. Another hypothesis attributes it to an internal process of theoretical practice, that is, to some sort of flowering of ideas that can finally be impressed on the decision-makers in the academic world or in the planning agencies.

There may be elements of truth in both hypotheses, but even if that is the case (and one would have to prove that "regional problems" were not more severe in former periods, or that theoretical progress has been really significant with respect to the classical outlook), it is, in our view, not sufficient.

In this sense, and bearing in mind that we are dealing with speculations, the following hypotheses could be stated:

1) A characteristic of the predominant ideological configurations in the Latin American economy over the last decades has been a building up of a fetish about the "external sector", to which is ascribed the power of "generating" a sizeable portion of the evils in our social structures.

2) This characteristic, together with a static view of the balance of payments, has produced a sequence of economic strategies for development which (although they are neither identical nor simultaneous in all countries) correspond to the real predominant sequence: export of raw materials; import substitution in a growing degree of complexity; and exports of finished goods.

3) The strategy of growth poles is efficiently integrated in the second and mainly in the third stage of the sequence.

4) Very schematically, the international mobilization of capital through large corporations, and through institutions linked to their interests, has as its direct or indirect objective the obtaining of differential rates of benefit.

5) This differential of benefit is increasingly associated with the establishment of production plants in areas of plentiful labor force with differential wages, and/or scarce raw materials (or else whose usual sources have escaped the control of corporations and of the states associated with these corporations).

6) The planning of the development of backward areas on the basis of the existence of unused resources is efficiently integrated with the necessary trend of international capital. If it is not politically feasible or

economically convenient to extract and directly export these raw materials, the trend is conveniently labelled a "national" strategy of "non-traditional" exports.

If these were not merely hypotheses, but rather a correct characterization of real processes and trends, one could better understand the growing success of the regional issue and its main strategic component. Moreover, one could foresee that the increasing convergence between economic-political and ideological processes would, for some time, permit this conception to play a prominent role in the economic ideology, replacing the outworn strategy of import substitution.

The foregoing is intended only to place this study in a broader context in order to assess its many limitations, while at the same time clarifying its meaning. Our objective has only been to point out certain elements of recent contributions to the regional issue which are in some cases directly, in others indirectly, linked to the dominant ideological system. In this sense, this paper, along with an earlier one which was centered on the work of F. Perroux,[1] should be viewed as a starting point for a further, more detailed, elaboration in depth.

As a basis for discussion, I have selected three papers that were presented for the first time or circulated at the International Seminar on Regional and Urban Planning in Latin America, which was held in April, 1972, at Viña del Mar, Chile, under the auspices of ILPES and ILDIS.[2] These papers have the advantage of exemplifying the above mentioned problems in a relatively unveiled form; at the same time, they represent one line of development of regional planning in Latin America.

It should be made clear that we do not intend to invalidate the regional approach, nor to diminish the importance of the problems of unequal spatial development. What we do intend, is to pose questions on the functionality of certain ways of approaching the problem, ways that maintain and further conditions which are incompatible with the solution of problems they allegedly want to solve. We do not want to deny that these works have contributed to the "recognition" of actual aspects of the problem—although we might stress that in some of the research, particularly that which has attempted to continue and develop directions opened up by F. Perroux, the negative elements seem to have made more progress than the positive.

Growth Poles as an Alternative Policy in the Latin American Countries

For Pedrao, the present economic structure of Latin American countries —resulting from the superimposition of an import substitution process on patterns of agricultural or mining monoproduction—determines market

355

perspectives, with regard to which resources are assigned either to investment for production of commodities or to overhead investment. The pattern of economic occupation of the territory in turn influences national trends of exploitation of natural resources, the employment structure, and the opportunity cost of capital among regions, thus limiting the possibilities of outlining a strategy for regional development.

Starting from these conditioning factors, Pedrao proposes the application of criteria of macroeconomic efficiency in order to exploit available resources and, on that basis, the programming of a system of poles.[3] This implies an "orientation" with respect to the two main components of the process underway within the present structure: a) import substitution and the succeeding economic centralization, and b) urbanization or spatial concentration of population and activities.

This is an overall normative proposal with respect to spatial-sectorial planning, whose essential characteristics are as follows:

i) It strongly depends on the present structure and particularly on the profile of internal and external demands, and their location;[4]

ii) It proposes a spatial-sectorial organization to satisfy such demands according to efficiency criteria internalizing external economies and diseconomies;

iii) It anticipates (non-specified) beneficial effects of polarization,[5] only to be achieved if: a) there is an end to protectionism (which would reduce the possible impact of polarization by creating monopolistic conditions); b) there is a massive concentration of capital and technology in the new sectors (leading propulsive industries); and c) the traditional exporting sector is also included among investment plans. The reasons for this last condition are, firstly, that empirical observations show that an impulse in the industrial sector does not ensure its spreading to the agricultural sector; and secondly that the modern sector depends on the traditional one—through mechanisms of international trade—given the difficulty for the former to place its commodities in the international market.

iv) It stresses that the specification of an overall prescription in each country must, as its point of departure, consider not only geographical peculiarities and the use of space, but also limitations in the power of decision allowed by the existing political structure and social organization. Moreover, Pedrao points out that "in Latin America the structure of fixed assets and the pattern of territorial accumulation of capital has been conditioned . . . to a great extent, by decisions adopted by the firms—and often by firms whose decision center is located in other countries".[6]

356

The central scheme on which, in our view, Boisier's work is based, is as follows:

The theory of growth poles has been elaborated regarding actual processes in developed European countries. The application of such a theory to that realm produces a strategy for development which cannot be transferred directly to underdeveloped countries which have different situations. This poses ideological problems. Nonetheless the theory does contain certain propositions of universal scope (presumably in the field of praxeology) which, if applied to our countries, would produce a strategy without ideological connotations. Within such a belief, Boisier elaborates his proposal.

Boisier states that his strategy constitutes a "spatial modernization" tool for developing economies, and in his introduction promises that he will present a new approach to their "political" aspects. He also notes that a strategy must "include sociological aspects of the process of change . . . removing in this way the exceedingly economic and technological orientation of the theory of polarized development".

When trying to explain why certain strategies of polarized development in Latin America have produced "the creation of real poles of underdevelopment", Boisier lists some possible causes commonly forwarded (insufficient lapse of time; lack of complementarities, scattering of resources), but he also points out some conceptual errors caused by a lack of adaptation of the theory to the Latin American context. The principal of the errors he mentions are (a) that functional (stressed in Europe) and geographical aspects (which should be relatively stressed in Latin America) are not considered simultaneously; and (b) there is a point-by-point, rather than an areal conception of the strategy.[7]

As far as his proposal goes, the main difference between developed and developing countries lies, for Boisier, in that the developed countries have an urban network which secures the effects of territorial spreading of polarization (a fact that explains the emphasis placed by European scholars on the functional aspects of the strategy) whereas this it not so in the developing countries which require an explicit consideration of the urbanization process and of its relationships with polarization and industrialization.

For a better interpretation of Boisier's proposal, it should be useful to note some of his basic definitions:

a) *Development:* "a qualitative as well as quantitative process of economic and social change, of lasting character";

b) "This process of change can be adequately viewed as a permanent and sequential process of *decision making* by participating agents (govern-

357

ment, individuals, firms, social groups, etc.)";

c) *Planning:* "a technique destined to change the actual process of decision making into a rational one. As such, it is a neutral concept from the ethical and political point of view".[8]

His strategy consists of a decision process composed of nine complementary stages.[9]

The length of this paper does not allow of a detailed criticism of these stages; we will therefore confine ourselves to a description of what is essential in the proposal.[10] In any case, Boisier does not discuss or explicitly specify his objective (cf. his definition of "development"). An internal evaluation of his strategy is thus impossible, since a strategy is not linearly determined by the real situation to which it is applied.

It is, however, possible to ask how political and sociological elements are involved in his proposal. The answer lies perhaps in the claim that in the first stage the "local class groups [sic] (producers, trade unions, merchants)" should be consulted. Or perhaps in what is described as the prerequisite for a successful experience, namely that a region exhibit ". . . a social structure and social leaders capable of perceiving the new opportunities generated by the polarization process as well as of understanding and utilizing innovations. In other words, the social structure of the subsystem must be linked more to modern values than to traditional ones; it has to be a structure favorable to change". Or perhaps again in the premise (the implication of which, in order to be effective, he does not explain) that says: ". . . the process of polarized industrialization cannot exclude and marginalize, as is the case in a majority of present industrialization processes in Latin America. On the contrary, it should mean the massive incorporation of the population into the benefits of progress." Yet in the observation that in order to achieve a better distribution of regional rent, he writes, ". . . at the same time it will be necessary to modify some ownership structures in the region".

Even if for Boisier "undoubtedly the process of modernization and change in a developing society is more strongly linked to political variables than to economic or technical variables . . .", in our view *politics* does not appear explicitly in his work.

With regard to the "sociological" aspects, although he admits that his proposal is "not essentially a strategy of social development . . .", he indicates that its application must be conducive to transformations which ". . . simultaneously affect the spatial, economic and social structures of the area under study". What are social transformations for Boisier? ". . . the social *modernization* of the area through the introduction of urban ways of life (even in the rural environment), through the creation of employment opportunities in the secondary and tertiary sector, and mainly through a greater social mobility consequent to an increase of income".

358

Moreover, Boisier ascribes to his strategy the characteristic of being independently applicable (although he recognizes its discrete nature) at regional as well as at national and international levels. However, these levels may not be completely independent. For example, applied at a regional level, his strategy requires that: ". . . the growth center should be adequately located in the national (or international) web of growth centers. This makes them more receptive to innovations . . ."

Even so, the theory of growth poles does not imply for Boisier the presence of multinational enterprises in a scheme of polarized development, since this is a matter of strategy. (He does not explain whether in *his* strategy they are implicit or not).

Urbanization and Development: The Temporal Interaction between Geographical and Sectorial Clusters

Lasuén equates the development process with the generation and adoption of innovations, but assumes that the generation of innovations is an international process. So, "nations may develop to a greater or lesser extent relative to others by the more or less rapid adoption of innovations brought forward internationally". National urban policies, however, are supposedly "less conditioned by the world urban patterns and can be considered autonomous and creative".

Thus, his general frame is one in which: "an international phenomenon (the development process) affects countries according to the way in which national phenomena (the national urbanization process) react to it". The essential "agent" of development is "technological and managerial change". According to Lasuén, it seems irrelevant for the Latin American countries to ask in what countries these innovations are generated. We should concentrate on explaining how innovations are diffused among countries, and on understanding how to adapt conditions for the adoption of innovations, not on how to innovate.[11]

In short, Lasuén believes that ". . . the scope of national development processes of most countries is limited to the question of the best and fastest way of adapting the economy to the international process of innovations". In this sense, urbanization policies should be directed to ". . . change all sorts of organizational traits of activities in geographical clusters and between them. This calls for a revision of the different types of habits, customs, institutions, labor and business practices, administrative and legal rules, political participation and decision-making schemes". In addition, he proposes to centre these policies of organizational change around the corporations, with as much reference to their internal structures as to inter-entrepreneurial relations.

359

Lasuén attempts to explain "how the traits of geographical use condition the generation, diffusion and adoption of innovations and how the characteristics of the innovation process, when they are adopted, influence the future use of geographical space".

Centering on the process of diffusion and adoption, for the above mentioned reasons, he distinguishes between innovations in consumption and innovations in production, concluding that in developed countries both tend to a pattern which he calls "an oil-stain" within a hierarchical urban structure.

It is important to stress that the significance he ascribes to sectorial and geographical clusters is general and functional: "it ranges from the very small to the very large, from the simple to the complex, because the mechanism explaining them is functionally the same". Thus, the international polarization process can be reproduced not only at national and regional levels, but also at the local level, taking into account the scale of their effects.

For Lasuén "most innovation adoptions are the result of import substitution policies, desired or undesired, but imposed by balance of payments difficulties". He affirms the importance of functions and not of instruments. In that sense, the process of innovation adoption will produce a natural trend towards the reproduction of the preexisting spatial pattern. Thus, the alternatives open to our countries are a dual economy on the one hand, and a homogeneous, but backward economy on the other.

Considering the conditions of rapid worldwide technological change that face our countries, Lasuén describes his proposal of organizational change for the firms as the development of a process of *centralization of capital* ("assuming it will not end in monopoly or diseconomies"). National boundaries are, however, too narrow to allow the process of adopting innovations to attain the speed required to close the technological and managerial gap. The only solution, according to Lasuén, is to "override national boundaries and plan the necessary multinational firms for continental areas". He himself anticipates the possible consequences when he remembers that "as everybody is aware, the only really multinational firms in the (European) Common Market, are the subsidiaries of the large multi-product, multi-plant American conglomerates".

In order to complete the perception of Lasuén's thought, it may be useful to comment on some of the concepts used in another of his papers.[12] This is a proposal for a decision process destined to determine a possible growth strategy in the Amazon region. The suggested procedure for determining a "function of social preference" involves consulting the "informed élites" of Brazil and of the Amazon region, and *explicitly* disregards the alternative of taking into account the whole population, since "the planning process requires the identification of values which are really current in the country, i.e. those which actually weigh and will operate on future actions". On the other hand, this strategy would be a result of "the possible sphere of action", defined as the set of objectives and measures for which a maximum degree of consensus among different élites could be gathered.

The Implicit Content of the Proposal

Although it cannot be maintained that the above mentioned works are similar in all respects, there are certain explicit coincidences and other easily recognizable ones, which allow us to analyze them as a single conception. *Thus, we will deal now with the proposition that the polarization strategy constitutes an advisable alternative for the development of Latin American countries.* In this discussion we will refer to these three authors in general, but to none in particular (except to differentiate between their proposals) since the resulting conception is more important than personal convictions.

The concept of national development. Whether implicitly or explicitly, development is identified by these authors with modernization. In general terms, the concept of development refers not only to technology, but also to institutions, habits, social practices, etc. At the sectorial and spatial level it is in turn identified with industrialization and urbanization.

Thus, underdevelopment is conceived as the absence of characteristics attributed to the present so-called developed nations. The ideal line of a traditional-modern continuum avoids any explanation of underdevelopment. This scheme is applied among countries, as well as internally to each national space.

Diffusion as a basic component of the strategy. From this concept of underdevelopment it follows, as stated by S. Bodenheimer [13], that "if the aim is to stimulate and repeat in Latin America the successful development of the United States and Europe, the problems of social and political development may be minimised in the attempt to discover those mechanisms which facilitate the transfer of Western institutions and attitudes to the Latin American traditional milieu, and to defeat any resistance to such a transfer". The diffusion theory tries to play the role of the theory of change, assuming not only that progress in our countries will be achieved by adopting the advances of modern countries, but also that they are in favour of, and even need, our modernization. [14]

Therefore, since the "obstacles" to development are to be found in traditional environments, diffusion will be promoted by effecting certain changes that will prepare the ground for modern ways.

At the functional-sectorial level, this appears as a proposal to stimulate the reorganization of existing enterpreneurial structures, as if indeed the

361

present national firms could change their internal structures and become the large future conglomerates, and not be merely displaced or absorbed by foreign "modern" corporations.

At the spatial level, the diffusion theory suggests the need for an efficient organization or urban structures to further the rapid adoption of innovations generated by the sectorial-geographical polarization.

It is interesting to note here a difference between the work of Boisier and Pedrao on the one hand, and that of Lasuén on the other: the former emphasize geographical reorganization while the latter stresses functional reorganization for a better diffusion. Furthermore, Boisier practically maintains that the relevant difference between the so-called developed and developing countries is the absence in the developing countries of an appropriate network for diffusion of modern ways; Lasuén, meanwhile, stresses as a difference the incapacity of these countries to generate their own innovations.[15]

The international system. In broad lines, the system of "Western" countries is viewed as basically harmonious. For Pedrao and Lasuén, the process of national and international diffusion should be as open as possible since every "artificial" obstacle would diminish the beneficial effects of polarization. Thus, for them, national protectionism acts negatively in that it checks international diffusion and creates internal situations of monopoly which in turn reduce the effects of polarization within each country.[16]

It is not necessary to detail the real terms of international trade, since they are reflected in numerous international conferences on the subject. It is necessary, however, to point out that modernization and the proposed mechanisms refer not only to production, but also to consumption innovations. This is of overall importance because these are not independent: they constitute, rather, two complementary components of dependency.

It should be noted that the process of import substitution is taken as a fact and that its origin is implicitly or explicitly attributed to "problems in the balance of payments".[17] In this way, the analysis of the causes of the structural crisis in our countries and of the reasons why there does not seem to be a solution within the current system of relations, is replaced by the analysis of an accounting mechanism.[18]

There is a particular reluctance to examine the internal contradictions of this modernization proposal.

Boisier does not describe his proposal for international relations, although he mentions the need for "internalizing" measures, but it is clear that the so-called modernization is not restricted to buying modern products in the international market, but necessarily implies a process of intensification of dependency. In other words, market relations do not exhaust, nor are they independent from, socio-political relations which, in addition, have a clear dominance structure. One can hardly accept Lasuén's neo-classic view that technology is a product that can be bought in a competitive international market. Neither can it be assumed—within the dominant framework in Latin America—that it is possible to delineate an internal demand profile free from imported cultural patterns—which clearly are a complement of technological dependence.

Internal structures. The point of departure is the immersion of the proposed "strategy" in the social and political structures existing in each country. In no way are these structures challenged: at most, they are presented as due for modernization. It could, however, be asked if the launching of such a strategy does not imply a direct change in the present structures. Our answer is negative.

In the first place, the State only appears superficially in the discussed works, always as an ideal State, practically apart from any real power structure: the managing State, the State that consults various interest groups, and so on.

It is, furthermore, assumed that a neutral bureaucracy exists, playing the role of rationalizer and consulting the élites about their objectives. This does not prevent the inclusion, in this type of consultation, of some interest groups that do not directly hold power—the state needs a certain degree of consensus for its policies.[19]

As a consequence, the application of the strategy as such would not bring about changes in the predominant political structures.

In the second place, what are called "social transformations" do not deserve that name. It is even possible that the implementation of the proposal would have quite the opposite effect.

The unity of economic and social aspects in the proposal may be illustrated through the model of industrial development which is contained in it, and through its application to the specific context of the Latin American countries.

According to recent studies by ILPES and ECLA, 40% of Latin America's population (100 million inhabitants) has a per capita income of less than $159 million, and generates less than 6% of total demand in the manufacturing industry. On the other hand, 5% of the population has a per capita income of more than $2,200 and generates more than 50% of the demand for commodities. This demand is in turn characterized by its high level of diversification, suitable to the above mentioned level of income, and this means there is a very small market for each line of production.

As Norberto González has noted,[20] the style of growth implied by this structure "does not provide enough opportunity for productive employment of the labor force, allows the survival of great backwardness in agriculture, is based on the dynamics of a very small number of manufacturing sectors with insufficient capacity to spread over the rest of the economy, and therefore is conducive to a certain income distribution which is not only highly unequal, but also a cause of social and economic segregation. This in turn results in the marginality of those groups with less income with regard to labor and consumption markets. In this way, the circle is closed and the unfavourable characteristics are perpetuated".

If the present structure of internal demand (reflecting, among other things, a certain social structure) is taken as a point of departure, and if the modernization process is centered on the substitution process of imports included in that demand, then the selected industries will be essentially predetermined and will tend to maintain the basic characteristics of the present social structure.[21]

Modernization implies the adoption of more advanced techniques, whose characteristics of scale and factors proportion contribute to the perpetuation and even the worsening of the already noted growth model.

But modernization also implies the diffusion of cultural patterns of the "modern" countries, so here we can observe another complementary effect. The small social groups which constitute the core of demand for products of the pioneering industries are continually driven to adopt consumption innovations, and this implies a growing diversification and fragmentation of the market. Moreover, in the case of new products, it is difficult to talk about "selection" of techniques, since usually technique and product are developed simultaneously. This strengthens even more the model of industrial growth and, in the application of this strategy, limits the possibilities of change in the social structures.

The economic and technical orientations of the proposal. The main problems of development have, of course, an economic basis. All three authors, however, support the idea that it is possible to outline a development strategy solely in terms of economic considerations, and thus they effectively limit themselves to approaching the problem only from the realm of economics.

This approach is based on a rather generalized assumption, with two main difficulties. One is the real impossibility of composing a strategy of development through "economic engineering" alone. In our view, a strategy for development must be stated in an integral manner: it must, in particular, include political terms—which is quite different from just *mentioning* social or political factors or variables. The second problem with that kind of strategy is that it will, because of the above mentioned impossibility, necessarily be stained by ideological elements.

An evaluation of this proposal, beyond individual differences of each author, must lead us to consider up to what point and under what conditions a manipulation of spatial and functional configurations tending towards the creation of a polarized structure, may contribute to accelerating development in the Latin American countries.

In our view, what is essential in the polarization of an economic structure is not spatial concentration, but rather the particular pattern of relations between its elements. Spatial aspects cannot, when we are speaking of social processes, precede "functional" aspects.

Furthermore, at least in the "Western world", *polarization is a worldwide historical phenomenon,* composed of the configuration of a domination system, where poles override national boundaries and advance towards the construction of a world economy (which is different from an "international" economy). These poles generate negative and positive effects in their hinterlands, in terms of the usual indicators. Inasmuch as they induce technological progress and the emergence of new activities, they also destroy pre-existing forms of production. They activate certain potential resources as well as destroying or disregarding resources previously considered valuable. Man is just another resource and his fate is not expressly featured in the objective-functions of conflicting poles. Nonetheless the idea prevails that the net result will be the growth of "relevant" indicators.

It is characteristic of this process that activity be continuously concentrated through an expansion of the poles' cores and through the incorporation of other related elements into the system. This leads to a situation in which a limited number of monopolistic clusters control the type and extent of structural change in the capitalist system as a whole.

Once this is realized, the proposition of a polarization strategy for national development can be based on one of two lines of thought.

The first could be called the "pure" theory of polarization. Essentially, this consists in abstracting certain "polarization mechanisms" observed in the course of a historical process, and in deductions derived from economic theory, pretending not only that it is feasible to reproduce them at will, but further that they can be adapted to any spatial level: continental, national, regional, or local.

In our view, this repeats the same mistake of those who look for a universal, a-historical mechanism that can be equally applied to different systems and periods—a mechanism that is in fact construed on the basis of the actual functioning of the worldwide capitalist system in its last stage. It is assumed, for example, that the polarization of activities in the realm of a region or a nation (with corresponding functional and even

365

spatial concentration) will allow a growth of "relevant" indicators, similar to that shown at world level. (We do not intend to discuss here the meaning of such indicators). Thus, the strategy consists in triggering off a concentration process leading to the formation of a system of national or regional poles which supposedly will activate the whole system through polarization mechanisms.

It is important to note that the "willful" element of this proposal consists only in giving the initial push which—assuming the policy is adequate—would create conditions that would enable the process of polarized development to get under way. Once the required structural situation is settled, the process would have its own dynamics, so it would not be necessary to plan the effects of induction and feedback proper. Indeed, this saving of planning efforts is one of the elements on which the defence of this strategy is centered.[22]

However, in the actual context of our countries, the proposal usually results not in the achievement of an internal transformation of structures, but rather in an acceleration of the rate of growth of indicators—with the backing of the large, already existing world poles.

In short, "national polarization" results in national space being opened up for branches from the world poles, which thus broaden their hinterland without actually "locating" in the national space. Since the centre of the world pole determines the policy to be followed by these branches, national dependency becomes deeper even if some indicators may grow.

It is, however, not only a question of decisional structures. For example, the adoption of current techniques from the system of poles in countries with an effective narrow market leads to an extremely unequal income distribution, to the formation of "internal" monopolistic situations, and to a production and employment structure which feeds back the distortions in the economic and social structure.

As a consequence, *"national polarization" ends up as a technical, political and cultural integration of national space dependent on the world capitalist system and its internal and external connotations.*

The other line of thought consists in freely admitting that the proposed strategy for development in underdeveloped countries involves adjusting to the world system of poles through the creation of favorable conditions for the establishment of a part of the productive apparatus in the national space. This idea is sustained by F. Perroux who explicitly denies the possibility that our countries may have "the privilege of defining their own law of development".[23]

However, in order to avoid the possibility that the new "locations" might become enclaves, he suggests we should couple our internal system with the propulsive core so as to internalize the effects of diffusion.

As we can see, the difference between these two lines of thought is only

366

formal: the former—in spite of certain seemingly neutral mechanisms—leads to what the latter openly claims as the only possible way to escape from the relative stagnation of our indicators.

Now that we have explained what in our view a relevant process of polarization at this stage really means for our countries, we will consider the following question; to what degree is this proposal conducive to the stated objectives? Here we repeat directly what Perroux himself proposes as a distinction:[24] while *"growth"* supposedly means "a sustained rise of the dimension indicator in an economic set (for example, gross product)"—and it can happen of course that "the real state of populations be rather independent of the national product and of real average income"—the concept of *"development"* implies "the set of social and mental changes by which the production apparatus is linked to the population, so that the latter may attain the ability to use that apparatus in order to obtain a satisfactory rate of growth, and *so that the productive apparatus yield services for the population and not be alien to it"*. And Perroux adds: "this dialectic between productive apparatus and population, *which is essential for development, allows us to show the basic difference* between a growth pole and a development pole".

As noted in our discussion of the way in which the proposal views internal structures it is clear that in the majority of Latin American countries the productive apparatus is meant to serve not the population as a whole but only certain social groups.

As long as the present social and political structures are taken as given all changes in the economic structure effected by means of polarization development will be of minor importance or will collide with those structural limits whose defence will curb the process.

In short, and in Perroux's own words, *social development poles must not be mistaken for the development of poles.* It seems as if our probable case could be the latter. It is not surprising therefore that "polarization" is another way of approaching "integration", since both tend towards a greater profitability of industrial poles.

Is the Proposal of Polarization and Integration an Alternative for Development in Latin America?

If an awareness of the world polarization process and its characteristic trends is set aside, it is easy to show the "need" for unifying national markets in regions of adequate size. This is usually presented as, technically speaking, the only way out for national development. This means, however, that other alternatives, possible from a technical point of view, have been disregarded. If we conclude, for example, that due to the

367

fragmentation of national markets the unification of the Latin American market is necessary if we are to reach efficient levels of production, then we are accepting as immutable the demand structure—and therefore the internal social structure and external cultural dependency.[25]

Polarization, like integration, is presented by some authors as an option that, if implemented, would lead to social development in Latin America.

It is our contention that within the present socio-political structure, polarization as well as the tendency towards the unification of markets, far from being an alternative which we many adopt or not, is a clear trend of the world capitalist system, a trend that is influencing the countries of Latin America in a particular way.[26]

Seen in this light, it does not seem feasible that the system of dominant poles may allow of a different growth model for the Latin American region.

Therefore, *within the system,* the real choice is as follows: either we accept this trend and adapt our countries in such a way that the process may be accelerated, or else we submit to a relative stagnation of indicators. Under no circumstances will the decision lead directly to a significant social development.[27]

Recognizing the problems posed by having to make such a choice, authors like Perroux propose a strategy of accepting the domination structure and its polarized way of growth, but in order to bridge the gap between *development* and national *growth,* they add two conditions: 1) that the external coupling be not directly and unilaterally with the hegemonic elements of the world system, but rather with subdominant elements, which would have a certain autonomy;[28] 2) that the internal structures be transformed in order to achieve an internal coupling to the poles.

While it is possible to speculate with the conflicting interests of different world poles, the proposal contained in the first of these two points does not really offer a safeguard—especially since, in the European space, important attempts to pose an alternative to the American absorption of firms in the industries have failed.

As far as the second point is concerned—and here we are within the general context of Perroux's works—it could be assumed that the "internal coupling" is characterized by putting the productive apparatus at the service of the *whole* population.

If the meaning of this internal coupling is not clearly stated—and Perroux does not make his meaning clear—the proposition may seem acceptable.

The "division of labor" proposed by Perroux—the poles provide the propulsive unit (external coupling), while the élites of underdeveloped countries deal with the organization of their society in such a way as to achieve development and avoid their becoming enclaves (internal coupling)—

368

is, however, clearly not feasible, since *the linkages are not independent*.

In the first place, the existence of an overall plan under the direction of the state is, according to Perroux, a condition sine qua non for internal coupling. Although Perroux never defines what his concept of the State is, it seems clear that he sees it as a political apparatus involved with the predominant economic interests. So, taking into consideration that within the present structures a national planning process will lack effectiveness if the dominant "oligopoly of oligopolies" (Merhav) does not participate, we question the scope of the objectives of such an overall plan.

The conditions required for world poles to develop their branches in backward countries restrict the possibilities of drastically changing the internal situation through cooperation between such countries. Such conditions therefore restrict the possibilities of allowing the productive apparatus to serve the population. In Latin America there is clear evidence that the slightest reformist attempt to change the "internal" structures immediately affects "external" interests and provokes a negative reaction. This reaction can take the form of "internal" efforts to modify the internal structures again or else it can take the form of external pressure, the effect of which is not limited to the enterprises that are directly concerned.

We have examined the limitations of the polarization approach as an alternative for development policies—limitations which are due to its economism: there is more to the problem than the purely economic aspects. In connection with this and in order to evaluate the political meaning of polarization, it will be useful to analyse the expected distribution of benefits of such a process on various social groups. As can be seen in recent papers from ILPES and CEPAL, a polarization process within the existing institutional framework leads to the acceleration of growth in a subsystem oriented to the demands of a small privileged proportion of the Latin American population, without positively changing the perspectives of the workers and peasants, while the proportion of people "marginal" to the system is increased. In this context, the question whether the usual indicators are growing or not seems rather irrelevant, and the question of political action will have to receive the consideration it deserves.

Concluding Considerations

It is necessary now to discuss the scope of these critical formulations. They are primarily directed at those who openly claim that a strategy of polarization and dependent integration is equivalent to a development policy for Latin America. Our criticism is, however, also meant for those who are helping to sustain this proposal by seemingly dissociating the technical from the socio-political aspects of their professional activity.

369

In our judgement, this latter situation is more critical since, whether intentionally or not, it coincides functionally with the former, but without defining its approach to social relations. Thus a correct evaluation of the proposal is bypassed.[29]

Our criticism of this proposal may be summarized thus: while talking about development, it is in fact recommending a strategy of modernization which will exacerbate the conditions of underdevelopment. The main points leading us to reject the proposal as a false alternative are, briefly, the following:

a) The basic goal is either inadequately stated or else identified with modernization or other concepts, the meaning of which must be clarified in the discussion;

b) The terms "strategy" or "policy" for development are used, dismissing any explicit statement on the political meaning of the proposal;

c) Even when the effective objectives and the social and political implications of the proposal can be determined, its feasibility depends upon a series of hardly acceptable assumptions, among which may be pointed out: i) That there seems to be no structural unity between economic, social and political phenomena; therefore, a strategy aiming at social objectives can be reduced to purely economic terms, to which socio-political considerations are *added on* later; ii) That international relations seem situated in a harmonious context, and thus the unity of development and underdevelopment is ignored; iii) That the State is an autonomous element in the social system; and iv) That polarization mechanisms can be reproduced independently at any level.

These characteristics of the proposal, which lead us to reject it, may be due either to the ideological position of the proposal's defendants or alternatively to the absence of a theory of social change which would allow scientific work on the subject.

In the light of this evaluation the reader is entitled to ask if then everything related to polarization is "polluted", if there is nothing that can be rescued, adapted or used in a neutral way.

We believe that there are two critical approaches to the theory of growth poles that deserve to be discussed in the future. One is represented by, for example, Kosta Mihailovic [30] who has tried to salvage the dialectical logic underlying the original version of the theory, charging it with the mission of helping us ". . . emerge from the labyrinth of the countless relations between variables and their mutual interaction, and select a combination of variables which performs the most radical changes in a given regional structure". For Mihailovic, the concept of development pole includes "social and institutional, in addition to economic factors, whose decisive importance in the forming of the structure is not thereby diminished".

370

In our case, without implying an opposition to this proposition, we think that it is neither necessary nor convenient to depart from the present state of things in the theory of regional development.

It is clear, for example, that dialectical logic cannot be attributed to such a theory.

Our contention is that there are useful elements in some of the writings on the subject pertaining to what could be called "economic engineering". Taking into account the differences, what can be salvaged is something grossly equivalent to the input-output coefficients. No one would deny their usefulness in the planning processes, but neither would anyone say that the input-output model constitutes a strategy for industrial growth.

Instead, we believe that a theory of regional development (at the subnational or supranational level) must be based on a theory of social change. As Mihailovic says: "the problems involved in choosing methods of regional development have remained unsolved because a solution has been sought for them which would avoid the need to destroy one and create another socio-economic structure".

Notes

1. J. L. Coraggio: "Hacia una revisión de la Teoría de los Polos de Desarrollo", *EURE,* Vol. II, No. 4, 1972, and "Towards a revision of the growth pole theory" in *Viertel Jahres Berichte,* 53, September 1973.

2. Pedrao, F.: "Los Polos de Desarrollo como alternativa de Política en los Países Latinoamericanos" (Paper presented at the International Seminar on City and Regional Planning in Latin America, Viña del Mar, April, 1972).
Boisier, Sergio: "Industrialización, urbanización, polarización: hacia un enfoque unificado" (Presented at the same Seminar and published by *EURE,* Vol. II, No. 5, 1972).
Lasuén, J. R.: "Urbanization and Development. The temporal interaction between geographical and sectoral clusters" (Paper originally presented at the Conference on Growth Poles: Hypotheses and Policies, organized by the Universidad Autónoma de Madrid and the Institute for Social Development Research, United Nations, in Madrid, September, 1970).

3. Although Pedrao does not explicitly say so, his concept of pole seems parallel to that of growth centre, as defined by Boisier, i.e., emphasizing geographical aspects.

4. To verify this statement, see F. Pedrao: "Problemas prioritarios regionales y urbanos de América Latina" (Paper presented at the United Nations' Seminar in Quito, Ecuador, September, 1971).

5. This is sometimes defined as the "economic phenomenon by which the external economies arising from the temporal, spatial and sectoral concentration of investments in a certain geographical place are taken advantage of" or else as the "formation and expansion of growth poles".

6. See *op. cit.* in footnote 2.

7. A further cause listed by Boisier is what he calls the "political dysfunctionality" of the strategy. Judging by his explanation, this does not seem very different from what is commonly meant by incompatibility between national and regional objectives, taking into account the priority of the former.

8. S. Boisier: "Polos de Desarrollo: hipótesis y políticas en América Latina" (mimeographed paper for the Institute of Social Development Research, United Nations, March, 1971).

9. These are: 1) identification of industrial activities; 2) identification of the urban system; 3) identification of footloose processes: 4) analysis and evaluation of comparative advantages of urban components: 5) allocation of industrial processes to urban components; 6) selection of systematizing actions; 7) selection of internalizing actions; 8) physical and financial programming; 9) control and evaluation of the strategy.

10. For our view on this type of "neutral" approach, see J. L. Coraggio: "Towards a revision of the growth pole theory", *op. cit.*

11. More details of the conception sustained by Lasuén can be found in J. R. Lasuén: "Tecnología y desarrollo. Reflexiones sobre el caso de América Latina" in: *La ciudad y la región para el desarrollo,* edited by Julio César Funes, Venezuela, CAP, 1972.

12. J. R. Lasuén and others: "Una aproximación a la planificación regional a largo plazo" (Mimeographed, circulated among participants of the Seminar held in Viña del Mar).

13. Susanne J. Bodenheimer: "La ideología del desarrollismo: paradigma supletorio de las ciencias políticas norte-americanas para estudios latinamericanos" in: *Desarrollo Económico,* April-June, 1970, Vol. 37.

14. It is important to point out that the idea of domination, which—although limited to an empirical assertion and not developed to its last consequences—is central to Perroux's original enunciation of the theory of polarization, has been disregarded in recent works on this subject, and particularly in those mentioned in the present paper. Undoubtedly, the relationship between the dominant and dominated creates discomfort in a conception that ignores the unity of development and underdevelopment.

15. In this sense see: J. R. Lasuén: "Tecnología y desarrollo . . ." *op. cit.*

16. This desire to achieve the performance of a competitive system (expressly mentioned by Pedrao) can only be understood for the world market, because the actual functioning of modern technology impairs the possibility of greater competition in each country or, if this were feasible, would seriously affect the accumulation capacity. In that case, once our countries are opened up to international competition, it is uncertain whether the positive effects of polarization will still increase; they may even disappear in some instances because fiscal and tariff disparities often favour foreign capital which locates—under a mixed or pure form—part of its productive apparatus in our countries.

17. Analyses on the meaning of balance of payment accounts and their implications can be found for example in: F. Perroux, *La coexistencia pacífica,* FCE, 1952; and O. Barsky and others: "Las corporaciones imperialistas en América Latina", C.T.I., Rosario, 1971.

18. It is illuminating to watch the desperation of attempts at finding a "way out" when the exercise is based on available quantitative data and carried out under the assumption that the structural limits of the current system of relationships may not be surpassed. In connection with this, see: CEPAL "Aspectos básicos de la estrategia del desarrollo en América Latina", 1970 (E/CN. 12/851) where in the long run, everything is seen to depend on a voluntary concession on the part of dominant countries in international relations.

19. Boisier claims his strategy does not require a particular balance of forces between the public and private sectors. Apart from the fact that the political structure is not necessarily correlated with that balance, it is obvious that if his strategy is applied within the framework of current political structures in Latin America, it will hardly provoke any substantial changes in them.

20. N. González: "Planteamientos sobre el desarrollo económico de América Latina " in *Revista de la SIAP,* 1970, Vol. IV, No. 15.

21. In this sense it is quite irrelevant whether the imports of consumption goods are substituted for imports of the machines producing them, or else that a posteriori these imports are substituted by machines to produce machines, etc. On this subject see Mair Merhav, *Technological Dependence, Monopoly and Growth,* Pergamon Press, Oxford and New York, 1969.

22. This differs from Boisier's approach, who seems to propose an overall planning of the whole polarized structure, and whose proposal therefore is more static and unreal in the actual Latin American context.

23. See F. Perroux: "Les investissements multinationaux et l'analyse des poles de développement et des poles d'integration" in *Tiers Monde,* April-June, 1968, Volume IX, 34.

24. See F. Perroux, *ibid.*

25. It is possible to think perhaps in terms of the standardization of a much less diversified production regulated by needs and not by the accumulation requirements of oligopolies provided there is a different income distribution.

26. It is interesting to remember what Perroux himself said in *La coexistencia pacífica,* on the subject of integration policies among the weaker countries: ". . . if the integration policy is not wanted by the nodal country, there is a chance that it will, whether openly or not, confront the obstacles raised by the same . . . if integration is wanted by the nodal country, it will further it by means of commerce between governments and long-run credits to a certain country or, to some growth pole as a whole, the prosperity of which reflects immediately in the recipient country and later spreads to others".

27. On the other hand, it is doubtful if, even accepting an alignment in this trend, such a dependent growth model could be generalized in Latin America.

28. Perroux points out "the hidden discriminations which in Latin America act in favor of the United States" and maintains that "the relative autonomy of the European Six is a basic condition of cooperation, tending to favor the relative autonomy of Latin American nations. If the European Six were deprived of their own political will and the means to implement it, they would only be intermediaries, one more screen" ("Les investissements multinationaux . . .").

29. This statement may serve to explain the apparent confusion of levels

in the specialized literature. It is not surprising that, starting with the analysis of regional development problem, one ends up talking about international relations, or then when trying to concentrate on the economic analysis one finishes by mentioning social and political factors. When a municipal council mobilizes certain interest groups in its hinterland, pushing national agencies to use certain tools of economic policy to further the location of an industrial complex, hoping that the direct and indirect effects will activate the zonal economy; or when it is claimed that it is necessary to organize a polarized structure in order to achieve a better growth of the system of regions and discussions are started with the intellectual élites and interest groups at the national, regional and local levels as to what industries can be located in each centre, etc., these are not neutral propositions with respect to the internal social and political structures or to the position of the country in the world system. The reason for this is that such proposals derive their significance from their inevitable insertion in the social context within whose limits they will eventually be implemented.

30. See K. Mihailovič: "The dynamics of structural changes as a context for the growth pole theory" (Paper presented at the Conference on Growth Poles: Hypothesis and Policies, Madrid, 1972).

8

THE "UNIFIED APPROACH" TO DEVELOPMENT PLANNING AT THE REGIONAL LEVEL:

THE CASE OF PAHANG TENGGARA

Benjamin Higgins

1. *Origin of the "Unified Approach" Project*

The "unified approach" project has been one of the major activities of the United Nations Research Institute for Social Development (UNRISD) in recent years. It originated in Resolution 1494 (XLVIII) of the Economic and Social Council, which was adopted on May 26, 1970 and endorsed by the General Assembly in Resolution 2681 (XXV) of December 11, 1970. These resolutions, in turn, were prompted by the Report of an Expert Group on Social Policy and Planning in National Development which met in Stockholm in September 1969. The movement for the adoption of the "unified approach" has its roots mainly in the disappointment that was felt with the results of the First Development Decade and in the fear that unless there was a substantial change in approach, the Second Development Decade (DDII) might merely repeat the frustrating experience of the first one. Levels of unemployment and underemployment might rise in the less developed countries as a whole. The drift to the cities might continue without sufficient expansion in the industrial sector to provide all comers with urban occupations productive enough to provide them with a living. The transfer of poverty, unemployment, underemployment and low productivity from village to city would continue. Yet at the same time population pressure on the land was not likely to diminish: it would indeed probably increase as absolute numbers in the agricultural sectors would continue to grow. In many of the developing countries, it was expected that small modernizing minorities would prosper, while the conditions of the low income majorities would improve much too slowly —particularly in the context of growing income disparities—to provide a basic sense of satisfaction.

The "unified approach" is an attempt to re-examine the problem of development as a total societal process in the context of developing countries as they exist today. It is an effort to improve, first of all, the basic concepts and analyses of development, and to suggest means of improving planning methodology in accordance with these improved concepts and analyses. One essential concern of the approach is the means whereby a country can determine the "style" or pattern of development most appropriate to its own values and circumstances. Another is the assurance of wider participation of all major groups of the society in the process of development and in its benefits, without retarding or stopping the process. All developing countries are vitally concerned, not only with raising general levels of production and consumption, but also with the distribution of increased incomes among social groups and regions, with reducing unemployment, with health and education, and with improving the physical and cultural environment.

As pointed out in an UNRISD paper, there is no single definition of "unified approach". Four ways in which it may be conceived are:

(i) As an attempt at a more comprehensive appraisal of the prerequisites for and of the consequences of economic development.

(ii) As an effort to construct bridges between the various sectors of governmental activity and planning.

(iii) As a correspondence between knowledge and action (or theory and practice).

(iv) The fourth interpretation of a "unified approach" focuses on the content of development in its relations to the values of human well-being and equity. This assumes that acceptable development styles and policies must meet the criterion of enhancing the capacity of a society to function over the long term for the well-being of all its members. Under this interpretation, development policy and planning must continually strive to reconcile and promote simultaneously a number of objectives that are not easily compatible, at least in the short term, including increases in production per capita, redistribution of incomes and consumption in the direction of greater equity, social structural change and wider popular participation in decision-making, and protection of the human environment in the interest of future generations.

While the first interpretation may seem more manageable in terms of planning experiences and availability of information, the UNRISD team has considered it less promising that the fourth, which tries to identify the actual content of development as a system of interactions which is susceptible to modification by policies which incorporate objectives, techniques of diagnosis, and instruments of action with "development" treated as a complex feedback system.

376

2. The Unified Approach at the Regional Level

During 1971 and 1972 the present writer was a member of both the UNRISD "unified approach" team and of a team engaged by the Malaysian Government to undertake a major regional planning project, Pahang Tenggara. It seemed a good opportunity to test the unified approach at the regional level. The idea was enthusiastically adopted by the writer's colleagues, and ultimately also received the support of the Malaysian Government.

In terms of budget, area, potential population, and potential regional income, the Pahang Tenggara project is the biggest regional development project so far undertaken by the Malaysian Government. The region is capable of absorbing some 600,000 immigrants—more than the present population of the entire State of Pahang—at per capita incomes that can remain close to the national average throughout the expansion period. The project was financed by a "soft" loan from the Canadian International Development Corporation and was carried out by a team of some 50 professionals.

The "Objective Function"

The team decided early in its operation to adopt a "unified approach" that would combine social, economic, and environmental considerations. In deciding on an "objective function" (or "welfare function") the team was guided by the project document on the Scope of Work, by the New Economic Policy (NEP) and by the Second Malaysian Plan. The NEP gives top priority to the reduction of economic and social disparities between Malays and non-Malays. The Malay population, about 45% of the total, is relatively poor, largely confined to the land or engaged in the government service. Industry, trade and finance are dominated by the Chinese (35% of the population) and, to a lesser extent, by Indians. It was expected that the great majority of the immigrants into the region would be Malays. Thus the higher the level of welfare generated by the development of the region, the greater would be the contribution made by the project to the reduction of gaps between Malays and other Malaysians. After some thought and discussion, the team decided to treat this objective as an overriding consideration affecting all decisions regarding development of the region, rather than as a factor in evaluating individual strategies, sectors, or projects. This decision left the team with four major objectives as components of the "welfare function" to guide it in planning for the region:

Objective one: to maximize the growth of per capita income over the planning period (while at the same time improving its distribution, particularly as between Malays and non-Malays);

Objective two: to maximize the reduction of unemployment over the planning period (with particular emphasis on creating employment opportunities for Malays);

Objective three: to maximize the contribution to the ecological harmony of the region (physical environment);

Objective four: to maximize the contribution to the cultural enrichment of the people living in the region (cultural environment).

These objectives were not regarded as mutually exclusive. On the contrary, it was assumed that all four must be given some weight in any acceptable development plan for the region. However, the team experimented with different weighting systems, giving each objective priority in turn, in order to determine how, and by how much, the outcome differs according to which objective is given top priority. The Malaysian Government was thus able to decide which result it preferred. The final system of weighting, in other words, was determined by the Government. In the course of the exercise, which involved fairly continuous discussion with the Economic Planning Unit (EPU) and the Steering Committee set up by the Government, it became possible to exclude some patterns of development as clearly inferior in terms of national objectives. Consequently, only two alternative strategies of development were presented to the Government for a final choice. One of these gives greater weight to employment, the other to income and cultural enrichment. There was a sharp conflict between the strategy (sectoral mix) that would maximize employment, and the strategy (sectoral mix) that would maximize income and cultural enrichment. No significant differences appeared with respect to impact on the physical environment.

The Income Objective

Theoretically there is much to be said for using a single concept of "income" as the sole criterion for ranking projects and designing development programmes. The concept in question is known as the social rate of return, and requires the incorporation of all objectives into national income at appropriate "shadow" prices. For example, a bias towards increasing employment can be built into the definition of social rate of return by using a shadow price for labour below the market price. Similarly, ecological harmony, and an enriched social and cultural life can be included in the concept of social return to investment by attaching a positive shadow price to each of these objectives and considering them as part of national income. If ecological harmony and enriched cultural life also raise productivity (as in the case of education and public health), this factor, too, can be included in the estimate of such returns. The "social return to investment"

378

concept has the advantage of providing a single measure of cost/benefit ratios for all projects and groups of projects and so of permitting the selection of an "optimum" pattern of development.

There were, however, certain disadvantages in applying this single rate of return for the purposes of the Pahang Tenggara project. For one thing, the "Scope of Work" required the team to present figures of present net worth of projects from a strictly market point of view. In short, it was asked to rank projects in terms of profitability, among other things, with a view to isolating "bankable" projects. Profitability, however, is not a satisfactory measure of contribution to income, either private or social. Indeed, in terms of the Government's stated objectives, it was possible that some high-yield projects would be undesirable, generating more profits for non-Malays than wages and salaries for Malays. In measuring profitability wages are treated as costs; obviously they must also be considered as income. Accordingly, projects were ranked in terms of average wage rates paid as well as of private rates of return (profitability). Moreover, given the importance attached by the Government to employment, and given the fact that not all the readers of the final report would be trained planners, it was unlikely that the Government would be satisfied with a single measure of returns in which the impact on employment was hidden by the system of shadow prices. The same was true of the impact on ecology or on the transition to a more rewarding social structure. These statements applied with even more force because of the lack of quantification of the Government's own welfare function when the project was launched. The submission of two to four alternative strategies had the advantage of assisting (and in effect requiring the Government to define its welfare function more precisely.

At the same time it was recognized that neither profitability at market prices nor wage rates, or even both together, gives a satisfactory approximation to the measure of contribution to "income", in the sense of *social* return to investment, with employment and the other objectives (ecology, culture) taken out of "income" for separate consideration. There seemed no escape, therefore, from measuring social return on all components except employment, ecology and transition, by using appropriate shadow prices where market prices were unacceptable excluding impact on employment and on the physical and cultural environment from the concept of "income".

The team decided to measure "income" in three ways: present net value per acre; internal rate of return; and value added per man year. Since neither capital nor labour were expected to be scarce for the region greatest weight tended to be given to the present net value per acre.

None of these three measures of income gives the information needed to determine the net impact of individual projects, or even of the whole levelopment programme, on the *distribution* of national income among various social groups. Peasants who migrate from Kelantan or Trengganu (the poor states to the north) to rubber or oil palm developments in Pahang Tenggara may be better off than they were on their small rice farms, but they may not be better off than they would be if they had gone elsewhere, and they may simply be replaced by other people on the paddy farms. Moreover, it is clear that the pattern of settlement, the form of organization, the mix of public and private enterprise, and the nature of the administration of projects will all have a major impact on the outcome in terms of income distribution. It was for such reasons as these that it was decided to deal with the problem of income distribution separately, rather than attempting to utilize redistribution of income as a fifth objective in the welfare function. This decision did not mean that the high priority attached by the Government to improved income distribution was ignored, but simply that this highly complex issue could not be dealt with in the same way as the other four objectives.

Employment

Employment is the most straightforward of the four objectives. It could be measured in terms of employment-creation per unit of investment (M$). It was decided not to attempt to weight employment by level of skill, for the following reasons. Differences in skills would be reflected in value added per man year, and would therefore be taken into account under the "income" heading. Moreover, as explained below, differences in skill also entered into the measure of cultural enrichment. Finally, since the social objective was really to reduce unemployment, which was concentrated among unskilled and semi-skilled members of the labour force (including high school leavers with little or no work experience), it was not desirable when considering employment as such, to attach higher weight to the creation of high-skill employment than to that of middle- or low-skill employment.

Ecological Harmony

The development of a largely empty region involves clearing land for human settlement—in other words, a violent disturbance of the region's ecology. It was clear that the plan must take account of the ecological impact of alternative patterns of development. Carelessness in this respect could destroy large tracts of land, kill fish and wildlife, and pollute air and water. If the projects or programmes were poorly meshed with the existing ecological pattern, they might prevent an optimum utilization of the resource potential over time. On the other hand, the development of

380

the region offered opportunities to improve the ecology. The most obvious instances of such improvement would be flood control and irrigation. On the positive side, therefore, there was not only the possibility of designing a development programme that would mesh with the ecological pattern in a neutral fashion, but also a possibility of using existing natural processes in such a way as to improve the ecological balance.

There were two ways of measuring the impact on ecology. One was to use a "dummy variable": perhaps to score a sector or project "2" if it brought about great improvement in the ecology, "1" if it brought about some improvement, "0" if it caused no change, "—1", if it caused some deterioration, and "—2" if it brought about much deterioration. The other way was to measure the costs of preventing any deterioration in the ecology (preventing stream pollution, for example) and to measure the costs and benefits of improvements in the environment (through flood control and irrigation schemes, for example).

Cultural Enrichment

Sir Arthur Lewis, speaking of the theory of economic change, says that the difference between men and pigs is not that men are necessarily happier than pigs, but that they lead richer and more varied lives, in the sense that the range of opportunities and choices open to them is much wider. Development is largely a matter of broadening this range and a regional development plan accordingly must take account of the impact of alternative development strategies on the diversity of economic activities, available services, and choices provided by various patterns of daily life, including leisure-time pursuits. The more "complex" the social structure, the greater will be the number of permutations and combinations available to the population in choosing a way of life.

It is clear that there is a close correlation between the sophistication and diversity of daily life and the degree of urbanization. Indeed, the availability of a wide range of opportunities and choices is well summarized by the single word "urbane". A simple approach to the concept of cultural enrichment, therefore, would be to use the impact of projects and programmes on the degree of urbanization as a proxy variable. However, the team did not wish to rule out entirely the possibility that a high degree of urbanization might prove impracticable for the region, whereas a relatively satisfactory pattern of social and cultural life might be created in a structure of small towns and villages. An alternative measure might therefore be the amount of employment created in "rare" services (education, research, professions, recreational and cultural activities) and in administrative, scientific and technical activities in industry. It was decided to use both measures of "benefits".

381

A smooth transition to the new and richer way of life was also considered to be important. Here, it is not merely a question of creating a more complex, diversified, and sophisticated mode of life but also of designing institutions to facilitate the movement from one socio-cultural pattern to a new one. The "cultural enrichment" concept includes not only the broadened range of activities and institutions which permit greater choice and diversification in daily life, but also the institutional framework to achieve this higher level of complexity and to smoothen the transition. Some of these "institutions for transition" may be relatively familiar— schools, community centres, recreation facilities—but others may be new. In any case, the cost of the "hardware" and "software" needed to create the institutions for transition must be estimated and included in the cost of development programmes.

3. *The Priority Formula*

Given the four objectives, together with the proposed measures for each, a flexible priority formula can be constructed in which major weight can be given to each of the four objectives in turn and the resulting patterns of development programmes compared. The basic idea is that strategies, sectors and projects are ranked in order of priority by classifying them in terms of their contribution to each of the four objectives.

Let "Y" stand for income, "N" for employment, "E" for impact on the ecology and "T" for the smooth transition to an enriched social and cultural life. "R" is rate of return to capital, "W" average wage rate, "C" costs, "U" urbanization (population in centres having more than 10,000 people, for example) and "S" employment created in rare (quaternary) services and administrative, technical and scientific activities. "D" is a dummy variable and "Q" the capital per job. One might then have something like this:

| | Y | | N | E | | T | |
Rank	R	W	Q	D	C	U	S
A	20%	3000	1000	2	—10%	60%	60%
B	15-20%	2500-2900	1000-1900	1	0%	40-60%	40-60%
C	10-14%	2000-2400	2000-2900	0	0-10%	20-39%	20-39%
D	5-9%	1500-1900	3000-4000	—1	11-15%	10-19%	10-19%
E	0-5%	1500	4000	—2	>15%	10%	16%

The "Q" figures above are in US dollars, and are based on a study made some time ago by ECAFE which showed an average capital-job ratio for the whole Asian region of $2500. Wage rates are based on the average industrial wage of M$ 2,000 per year in 1967. There is no real basis for the "cost of offsetting ecological damage" figures, presented here as a percentage of total development costs, but the figure for "A" category projects in this concept is negative to allow for cases of net contribution to ecological improvement.

The Floor

The above scheme is designed to reject projects that rank lower than "E" by each criterion. It would be possible, however, to define a "floor" for each concept more precisely. For example, one could decide that projects yielding less than the national average income in agriculture, or involving a capital-job ratio above the national average would be rejected. The question needs further thought and discussion. For one thing, complementarities must be taken into account. Some low-priority projects may have to be included because they are necessary complements to high-priority projects. The extent of such complementarities will obviously depend on how "project" is defined. It would be possible to define a "project" as one basic economic activity plus all related economic activities, whether in the private or in the public sector.

Establishing Priorities

When the rankings by each criterion have been established, one can proceed to determine priorities, giving superior weight to each of the four concepts in turn. The weighting is done by selecting the patterns of rankings that are considered "superior" in terms of each concept. Patterns similar to the following then emerge:

Priority	Income Objective				Employment Objective				Ecological Objective				Cultural Objective			
	Y	N	E	T	Y	N	E	T	Y	N	E	T	Y	N	E	T
1	A	A	A	A	A	A	A	A	A	A	A	A	A	A	A	A
2	A	A	A	B	A	A	A	B	A	A	A	B	A	A	B	A
3	A	A	B	B	B	A	B	B	B	A	A	B	B	A	B	A
4	A	B	B	B	B	A	B	B	B	B	A	B	B	B	B	A
5	A	B	B	C	B	A	B	C	B	B	A	C	B	B	C	A
6	A	B	C	C	B	A	C	C	C	B	A	C	C	B	C	A

If a government is not clear about its ranking of objectives, the planners can try every possible ordering; with four objectives, there would be twelve possible rankings of objectives, and accordingly, twelve possible development programmes. In choosing a development programme, the government is implicitly ranking objectives. However, if a government is reasonably clear with respect to the weighting of objectives, and is aware of the implications for choice of projects of their ranking of objectives, the number of trial rankings can be reduced. It should be noted that when any of the four objectives is being given top priority, only projects classified as "A" on that concept are retained, and that, whatever concept is being applied, "AAAA" projects are always retained.

4. *Infrastructure*

The team also decided in principle to use the "Tinbergen shortcut" with respect to infrastructure. That is, the formula was applied to directly productive enterprises only. Requirements for infrastructure were derived through a form of input-output matrix. However, where strong complementarities exist among directly productive enterprises themselves, some input-output analysis must be conducted for these enterprises as well. Infrastructure costs can then be allocated among various directly productive enterprises.

After considerable discussion, the team decided to define "project" in a straightforward fashion, i.e., as directly productive enterprise on a scale large enough to be efficient and small enough for unified decision making. Thus a "project" might be an entire FLDA settlement scheme involving, say, 20,000 acres of oil palm or rubber; it might be 50 acres of livestock production; or one forestry complex having 70,000 acres of forest with a sawmill and a plywood factory. It was also agreed that infrastructure needed solely because of a particular project (an example would be access roads from main highways) should be attributed to the project; that costs of infrastructure required to take care of a growing population (schools, hospitals) should not be attributed to individual projects; and that, if the costs of meeting the needs of a growing population are higher (or lower) in Pahang Tenggara than they would be if the population stayed where it now is, the marginal costs (positive and negative) should be taken into account.

5. *Health, Education, and Settlement Patterns*

There were at least ten special features of the future situation in Pahang Tenggara which called for a tailor-made approach to the planning of public health, education, and other social services for the region.

1. *An abnormal age distribution.* FLDA projects tend to favour set-

tlers aged between 25 and 40, and private estate companies and forestry complexes are likely to prefer workers in a similar age bracket. Accordingly, mortality rates, morbidity rates, and crude fertility rates will all be askew. Similarly, the age distribution of children in the region will be askew (and platykurtic) in the early years of the project, and are likely to remain so for many years. Thus both health and education requirements will be different from those prevailing in parts of the country which have been settled for some time.

2. *Abnormally high rates of population growth.* For the same reason, the rates of population growth will be abnormally high. Because of the concentration of female immigrants of child-bearing age, crude fertility rates will be unusually high. Because of the relative youth of the initial population and the probability that health services are likely to be above average, crude mortality rates will be relatively low and the natural rates of population growth will consequently be above average. When net migration to the region is added to the high rates of natural population growth, the over-all population growth rates will be very high. The pressure to extend health, education, and other social services will accordingly be severe.

3. *An abnormal distribution of educational achievement.* It is likely that the educational status of migrants will also be abnormal. FLDA tends to reject illiterate people, and the private estates and forestry complexes will tend to do the same. On the other hand, few of the migrants are likely to have high levels of education. In short, the initial population is likely to cluster around the median level of education, with both the lowest and the highest levels of education being under-represented.

4. *An abnormal distribution of need-achievement.* The team's sociological studies, together with past experience in certain schemes, suggest that the immigrants to settlement schemes are neither the most ambitious nor the least ambitious members of the population. The most ambitious migrants from existing villages (or those with the highest levels of need-achievement, to use a more precise psychological term) tend to go to the cities. Those with the lowest levels of need-achievement tend to remain in the kampongs. This tendency is aggravated by the age distribution of settlers: people under 25 are more attracted by the cities; people over 40 are reluctant to leave their kampons. Thus there will be a concentration in the region of people with middle levels of need-achievement. This fact has implications not only for the training of adults, but also—since children tend to derive their level of need-achievement from that of their parents—for the education of the children in the region.

5. *An abnormal distribution of health problems.* The incidence of various maladies varies from one part of the country to another, and is also affected by age, income, distributional and other factors. The settlers

will tend to bring into the region the health problems peculiar to their areas of origin and to their age, income, and level of education. Moreover, there is a relationship between health and the physical environment and, in particular, between health and ecological disturbance. Thus Pahang Tenggara is likely to have a peculiar pattern of health problems.

6. *Racial distribution.* It is also expected that Malay settlers will be the predominant element. This fact has implications with regard to educational demands, habits relating to health and, above all, recreation facilities and other amenities which together constitute an environment considered to be desirable by that population element.

7. *An abnormal occupational structure and an abnormal rate of structural change.* In the early years of the region's development, the concentration of employment in the primary sector will be much higher here than in the country as a whole. On the other hand, the rate of structural change, in the form of relative growth of employment in manufacturing and services, will be higher than the average for the country as a whole, as will the relative rates of urban growth in percentage terms. The phasing over time of employment opportunities and of income generation on settlements is quite different from that in other parts of the country. Consequently, requirements for specific types of vocational training and the capacity of the population to pay for future training have a pattern quite different from that of established centres of population.

8. *Limited choice of occupation within the region and progressive widening of choice as urban centres grow.* In the early years of the region's development, there will be a narrow range of employment opportunities. As time passes and the manufacturing and services sectors expand, however, with a related urbanization of the region, the scope of potential employment will broaden. Some of the better-trained and more ambitious settlers, and a larger proportion of their children, will wish to move from primary sector employment to employment in manufacturing or services. The educational system should be designed to facilitate such movement. On the other hand, some members of the younger generation may prefer to remain on the land, whether they move into new settlement schemes or take over the farms of their parents. The educational system should, therefore, also provide the option of agricultural training for these children. As shown earlier, the complexity of the occupational structure increases as various thresholds of city size are passed. The educational system should be designed to take account of this increasing complexity of the occupational structure by providing a widening range of options to students.

9. *An abnormally mixed community.* In the past the pattern of FLDA settlement has been to select settlers from various parts of the country and re-establish them in a new settlement, rather than endeavouring to move the whole kampong (as has been done, for example, in some of the

386

Indonesian "transmigration" schemes). The labour force on private estates and on forestry complexes may also be more mixed than is typical of the kampong. Whether or not this policy is the appropriate one (and the project has not made studies which would make it possible to say with any certainty whether it is the best policy or not), it is clear that this approach creates social problems of a particular kind. These problems have implications for the design of the education system and of recreational and other facilities.

10. *Absence of any existing social infrastructure.* Obviously, an empty region lacks schools, hospitals and recreation facilities. This fact presents both a problem and an opportunity: a problem in that the need to expand the social infrastructure at an extraordinarily rapid rate will strain the capacity of the economy and of the society; and an opportunity since the fact that educational, health, agricultural and recreational facilities must be built up from scratch means that they can be tailor-made for the needs of the region.

Need for Tailor-made Planning Techniques

Given the special nature of the health, education, recreation and other social services required in the region, the approach to planning such services in the region must clearly be tailor-made. The standard approach to this kind of planning in macro-economic and macro-social terms is of limited use in the special context of development of Pahang Tenggara.

6. *Malay Participation*

When the project concluded it was—contrary to initial impressions—thought possible that developing Pahang Tenggara by settling a predominantly Malay population on the land could make a contribution to the Government's top priority development goal: increased participation of Malays in higher-income occupations, and consequent reduction of economic and social gaps between Malays and other Malaysians. The team's last projections indicated that, with the most efficient management available, with the application of the most advanced techniques, with the reorganization and mechanization which these techniques make possible, and with a gradual increase in the number of acres per man, value added per man-year could be close to the national average, both in 1973 and over the next twenty years, on rubber or oil palm estates and in forestry complexes. Some of the possibilities for diversified agriculture looked even more promising.

Some questions still remain, however. Firstly, the foregoing conclusion

387

implies that the gap in productivity and income between unemployment or traditional agriculture, on the one hand, and rubber, oil palm and forestry complexes, on the other, is wider than the gap between well-run settlement schemes and urban occupations in manufacturing and services. Present indications are that moving people from unemployment or traditional agriculture to settlement schemes can reduce the economic and social disparities between the settlers and the urban population, but the question merits further study.

Secondly, the net effect on economic disparities obviously depends a good deal on how the income generated in settlement schemes is distributed. Even when value added per man-year approaches the national average on settlement schemes, if half of the value added goes to owners and managers, and the owners and managers are non-Malay, income disparities between Malays and other Malaysians may be enhanced rather than alleviated.

Finally, social disparities are not the same thing as economic disparities. Settlement schemes may well reduce income gaps without reducing social gaps if the life of the settlers remains more circumscribed than the life of people living in urban centres. To turn Malays from poor peasants into "kulaks" (prosperous small farmers) is not enough to eliminate the social disparities between Malays and others. The social disparities can be eliminated only by bringing Malays into the high-income urban occupations.

Settlement Patterns

The extent to which the problems of health, education and other social services can be solved, and the extent to which gaps between Malays and others can be reduced through the development of the region, depends largely on the patterns of settlement adopted. Both the range of occupations open to settlers and the quality of public services that can be reasonably provided tend to improve with size of settlement. The team recommended a pattern of settlement that concentrates the population in centres of 5,000 to 20,000—and preferably of 10,000 to 20,000—linked to two major regional centres, at least one with a population of over 50,000, to provide a wide choice of occupations to settlers, and to permit the installation of an educational system (and of other social services) which would enable the settlers to take advantage of this wide range of employment opportunities. Such a pattern would also reduce the costs of public services, more than offsetting the extra transport costs involved.

If Malay settlers and their children are to be given opportunities for moving into the managerial, technical, and scientific occupations associated with development of the region, two requirements must be met: there must

388

be a system of identifying settlers and children who have the capacity to benefit from specialized training and to perform effectively in high-level posts after being trained; and there must be facilities for education and training to prepare qualified persons for managerial, technical and scientific posts in the primary sector itself and in manufacturing and services. Essentially, these requirements boil down to early establishment of both adult education and secondary school facilities which can provide training in the pertinent agricultural, commercial and technical fields. The larger the settlements, the brighter the prospects for providing such facilities.

The Urban Hierarchy

Having decided to recommend a highly urbanized pattern of settlement, the team was confronted with the question of how the cities of the region could best be fitted into the national urban hierarchy. There was evidence that the urban structure of Malaysia was following "Lasuén's law": the structure was moving ever closer to the simplest version of the "rank-size rule" and, as development took place, was becoming more rigid both in terms of approximation to the rule and in terms of ranks of individual cities (see Chart 1).[1] Moreover, the team's studies had shown that with regard both to manufacturing activity and to services, there are in Malaysia, as in most advanced countries, distinct thresholds of city-size. In short, it appeared that it would be difficult either to change the urban structure, or to attract high-productivity manufacturing and services to cities smaller than those where they were normally found. At the same time, some government decisions (regarding a new east-west highway in the north, the Kuala Lumpur-Seremban highway, etc.) had been made, and some other events (such as the exhaustion of certain mines and forests) were taking place that would tend to alter the urban structure. The team again adopted a "two-pronged approach" to determine an appropriate urban structure for the region. First of all, the urban structure of Malaysia as a whole was projected to 1990, and the urban centres of the region were fitted into this hierarchy on the basis of a case-by-case study of prospects of other cities. Then, starting from the present, the primary, secondary, and tertiary employment of each sub-region for each Plan period to 1990 was determined in terms of land use for each sub-region of Pahang Tenggara. On the basis of these projections, coupled with an analysis of geographical and topographical considerations, a probable urban structure for each sub-region was arrived at. The main centres in this projected structure were Bukit Ridan in the heart of the region, with a population of about 120,000 in 1990, and Lubok Baru towards the south with about 40,000 people in that year. Reaching these population levels will require an active policy on the part of the government, favouring these two new towns over possible rivals in the same size category which, for various reasons, have grown slowly over the last two decades. The new towns could be encouraged to grow by providing incentives for certain government activities (an agricultural college at the secondary school level, a teachers training institute, etc.).

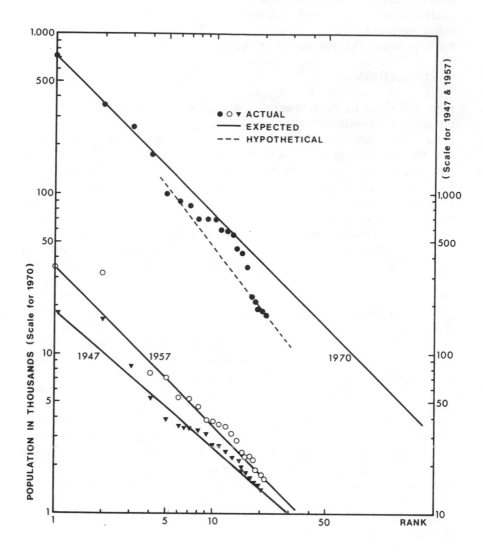

Chart 1. Urban Structure: Actual and Expected 1947, 1957 and 1970

390

Some results

To no one's surprise, the technical and economic studies combined indicated that the best use for most of the land was for rubber, oil palm, and forestry complexes. Smaller scale projects for cattle, tea, and sago were also included in the masterplan. Table 1 shows the results of the analysis with respect to income and employment for "representative firms" in the fields of rubber, oil palm, and forestry. As is readily apparent from the table, a clearcut conflict appeared between maximization of income (on any of the three measures used) and maximization of employment. In terms of employment per 1,000 acres in year ten, rubber was clearly best and forestry complexes clearly worst. However, the time-pattern of employment creation was quite different for rubber and oil palm: rubber requires considerable labour for planting, and then very little for the next seven years while the trees mature; oil palm needs intensive application of labour throughout the first five years. Since the government was clearly more interested in employment-creation during the next ten years than in employment-creation ten years hence, we applied the same discount factor to employment as we did to income. When that was done, oil palm emerged as slightly superior to rubber for employment. In terms of the four major objectives, our ultimate rankings were as follows:

	Objectives			
Strategies:	N	Y	C	E
Maximize rubber	B	D	D	C
Maximize oil palm	A	C	C	C
Maximize forestry	C	B	B	A
Maximize forestry plus incentives for manufacturing	D	A	A	B

The government's task of choosing among strategies, given these results of our study, was facilitated by technical considerations. Some land was suitable for one of the four uses and not for others. The final plan therefore ended up with a judicious blend of all four strategies, with a different mix of the four main types of economic activity in each sub-region.

Conclusions

Planning for Pahang Tenggara was "integrated" or "unified" in at least four senses: the team itself was multi-disciplinary, including economists,

Table 1. Macro Cost Effectiveness Matrix

	Internal Rate of Return			Net Present Value			Value Added Year 20			Employment per 1,000 Acres Year 10		
	Worst	Best	Probable	Worst	Best	Probable	Worst	Best	Probable	Worst	Best	Probable
Oil palm	8.3[1]	17.0[2]	15%[3]	−$186	$1,103	$686	$7,024[8]	$9,552[9]	$8,500[10]	60[13]	67[14]	65[15]
Rubber	10.4[4]	16.0[5]	13.0[6]	69	1,287	511[7]	5,461	8,590[11]	7,000[12]	96[16]	146[17]	146[18]
Forestry	30.0[19]	34.5[20]	32			677[20]			30,711[21]			8

1. Class III soils; present high-yield seeds.
2. Experimental seed.
3. Best minus 1 standard deviation.
4. Present clones, no stimulant, limited soils.
5. Experimental clones, best soils, stimulants.
6. As in "3". With limited soils, new clones, stimulants, IRR = 14.3% ± 2.5.
7. As in "3". With limited soils, new clones, stimulants, NVP = $854 ± 608.
8. Present varieties.
9. Present varieties, new methods.
10. Average.
11. With mechanization, stimulated present clones, best soils.
12. Average.
13. Present varieties.
14. Future varieties.
15. Guess.
16. Present clones new techniques, Class 1 & 2 soils.
17. Present methods, present clones, limited soils.
18. Employment year 5:

	Worst	Best	Probable
Oil Palm	84	92	96
Rubber	36	66	60

19. Bukit Ibam.
20. Lesong.
21. Lesong; $18,675 at year 10, assumed increase of 5.1% per year.

other social scientists, physical planners, and technicians of various sorts; the "objective function" included social as well as economic goals, and efforts were made to deal with interactions among them; interactions among urban growth, patterns of regional development, and ultimate impact on national economic development were the core of the analytical process; and the planning included three or, with the creation of the Pahang Tenggara Development Authority, four levels of government.

The present writer has no doubt that the resulting plan was considerably more effective than it would have been if any of these aspects of unification had been neglected. It should be reported in conclusion, however, that our experiment with unified planning at the regional level revealed very clearly the gaps in our knowledge as to how such planning should be done. For such interdisciplinary efforts to be successful, there must be enough *common* knowledge and enough overlap of techniques and methods to permit useful dialogue and effective collaboration. There must be binding mortar as well as solid bricks if the structure is to be solid. The Pahang Tenggara project was unusually fortunate in this respect, and the success of the operation sprang largely from the fact that economists, physical planners, agricultural experts, and foresters *were* able to talk to each other. But communications were not always easy, and it sometimes required conscious effort to transcend the traditional bounds of one's own discipline. Economists feel more comfortable when they stick to something like the "two-gaps analysis" (gap between savings and investment requirements, gap between foreign exchange earnings and foreign exchange requirements) or input-output analysis. These may not be of much use in the preparation of a development plan but a competent economist is fairly safe from attack on technical grounds within his own framework if he sticks to such things, because these are the things he has been taught to do. The same may be true of the physical planner who sticks to design, or of the sociologist who sticks to family structure, relations among social groups, etc. But it is precisely at the interstices between disciplines that expert knowledge becomes most important.

The deficiencies were most apparent with respect to the environmental objectives. No professional ecologist had been requested by the government, and so there was none on the team and as a result our judgements with respect to ecological impact were perhaps more amateurisch than others. But what kind of "ecologist" could have done the job properly? We needed someone who not only knew what ecological impacts might be, but who could also apply his knowledge within a framework of unified planning. There was no question of leaving the whole area under jungle to avoid some possible damage to the environment (although the plan did include some forest and wild life reserves): it was a matter of sophisticated cost-effectiveness analysis with the environmental impact included as a

393

strategic element.

In short, more unified planning, whether at the regional or at the national level, requires more unified training. No "Manual of Unified Planning" yet exists. It is doubtful whether any one person could write one, and even an interdisciplinary team might not succeed unless all members had some experience with interdisciplinary operations in the field. A truly unified approach to the training of regional planners, and teaching materials for the purpose, are likely to emerge slowly from the analytical reporting of field experience. It is for this reason that the story of Pahang Tenggara has seemed worth telling.

POSTSCRIPT

During 1973 and 1974 the author was invited back to Malaysia to work with the Economic Planning Unit on problems of urban and regional development related to the preparation of the Third Malaysia Plan. This mission gave me the opportunity to visit the region of Pahang Tenggara, together with other regions where plans were being prepared or implemented. On the whole these visits were gratifying. The EPU has recognized the need to plan the entire urban structure as a system of development poles and growth centres in order to assure the desired pattern of regional and national development. The Johore Tenggara Development Authority, as well as the Pahang Tenggara Development Authority, has adopted the type of urban structure recommended by the Pahang Tenggara team: a small number of good-sized cities, with one large and one middle-sized city, in place of the scattered villages of the earlier FLDA settlement schemes; holdings of 14 acres per family instead of 8 or 10; and provision for increasing the size of the holdings as time goes by. In Pahang Tenggara itself, some 200,000 acres have been cleared and planted, Bukit Ibam is a thriving town, the site for Bukit Ridan is cleared and construction has begun, the north-south highway is well on the way to completion, two large forestry factories are operating, and a prefabricated housing plant is busy turning out houses for the region with materials and labour from the region.

The strategy of developing the region from the north to the south, so as to maximize spread effects to the northeast, has been retained; and a new study has been launched of Kuantan as a potential development pole for the east coast. A deepwater port is under construction at Kuantan.

Yet the execution of the plan is far behind schedule, and the east-west road from Bukit Ibam to the coast has fallen into such a state of disrepair as to be virtually unusable; if not improved soon even the truckers will abandon it and it will revert to jungle. What went wrong?

Basically, the mistake made by the team was to prepare the plan on the assumption that the land itself was the only really scarce factor of production. True, during the final review stage the team did try to impress on the Malaysian government the enormity of the managerial problem of executing a $1 billion project, and the overwhelming need for managerial, engineering, scientific technical, and detailed planning skills (for working drawings, city plans, etc.) in the implementation phase. But that was a bit late, and during the plan preparation itself we assumed essentially that all resources *other* than the land needed to implement the plan would be forthcoming from either the public or the private sector. Such has proved not to be the case. The demands on government for scarce skills have been more than can be met from domestic sources, and the government has wished to become independent of foreign resources, both human and financial. In short, while we made more effort than our predecessors to relate our planning to what was going on in other regions and on the national scene, we did not go far enough in this direction. We should have ascertained, through studies and discussions with government, what the supply of scarce *human* resources was likely to be, *before* the plan was cast in final form. We can therefore learn from the shortcomings, as well as from the success, of the Pahang Tenggara project. One cannot plan effectively for any region in isolation. The plans must always be put into the context of the national economy, with full cognizance of inter-regional and inter-urban flows; and potential supplies of all scarce resources must be carefully estimated.

Note

1. J. R. Lasuén, "On Growth Poles" *Urban Studies*, June 1969.

IV

INTERNATIONAL

TEN YEARS' EFFORT IN PROMOTING REGIONAL DEVELOPMENT
A Review of the Progress of the United Nations Programme of Research and Training in Regional Development

Gerald Wen *

The United Nations Programme of Research and Training in Regional Development has undergone considerable reorientation since its inception nearly a decade ago. The programme was established at a time when the rate of growth was still generally being regarded as essentially synonymous with development and when investment efficiency and productivity were the major concern of all development plans. More recently, there has been a growing recognition that growth alone is not the answer to development, and that efficiency must be balanced with equity considerations if development is to achieve its ultimate goal of human well-being and a better quality of life for all.

When the United Nations programme was first established, regional socio-economic development was still a novel approach to achieving balanced economic and social development by focussing on sub-national and national space, and only a few isolated examples were identified for study purposes. Today, a growing number of developing countries in all major areas of the world have adopted or are adopting the regional approach as a national development strategy. Along with this changing situation, the role of the UN programme has changed from that of promoting and pioneering the concept and the approach 10 years ago to that of monitoring progress, updating concepts and methodologies, and providing channels and facilities for the interchange of knowledge and experience in this field. Also reflecting the global interest in regional development is the greater number of United Nations units interested in the various aspects of regional development. The research and training programme, which is

* The author of this paper is the Chief of the Institutional Development and Popular Participation Section, formerly known as the Regional and Community Development Section, of the United Nations. The Section has been responsible for servicing the UN Programme for Research and Training in Regional Development since its inception. The views contained in the paper are those of the author and do not represent the views of the Organization.

serviced by the Social Development Division, represents only part of the total United Nations activities in support of member governments' development efforts.

After nearly a decade of promotional work, over fifty national, multi-national, and international institutions are now linked with the United Nations to form a global network for the sharing of knowledge and for mutual support; technical support is being provided to a number of national research and training programmes; a series of studies and training material are being prepared and distributed for global adaptation; and a plan is underway for developing a system of "Correspondence Seminars" through which the programme could share with the key officials of developing countries the up-to-date concepts and methodologies on the integrated approach to development at local and intermediate levels.

In the present paper, an attempt will be made to give a summary account of the scope and purpose of the programme and of the progress it has made to date, as well as some indication of its future trends and prospects.

1. The Purpose of the Programme and Some Initial Explorations

According to the original resolution of the Economic and Social Council which established the programme, the aim of the programme was "to promote modernization" of town and country and, through improved patterns of human settlements and through programmes of planned social and economic adjustment, to minimize the undesirable effects of excessive concentrations of people and activities.[1] The programme was to be concerned primarily with the social and demographic aspects of regional development in the broad context of urbanization and national development. Under the auspices of the programme, a number of developing (sub-national) regions reflecting different stages of development were to be selected for research and training purposes.

As a part of the selection process, preparatory visits by teams of experts on the social, economic, and physical aspects of planning were under-taken to eleven developing regions during 1966 and 1967.[2] These preparatory visits resulted in several institutions being established or brought into relationship with the programme.[3] Certain other programmes visited were followed up by direct assistance under the United Nations Development Programme. These included Lerma (in Mexico), Sudene (in Brazil), Asswan (in Egypt) and Wadi Jizzan (in Saudi Arabia).

While the observations and recommendations of the missions were directed to specific programmes visited, some general conclusions could be drawn from them. It was observed that development efforts of a regional character had generally been confined to a natural resource such as water, timber or minerals; or to a strategic location of industrial enterprises; or to plans for the physical location of economic facilities and public works; or to metropolitan regions. While such efforts could provide the stimuli for elaborate multi-sectoral development plans and programmes, progress in that direction had been slow. This appeared to be due partly to the dearth of trained personnel who were able to undertake the various surveys and analyses needed to relate data in a particular field to those in other fields and to integrate sectoral plans into a broader framework of regional socio-economic development. It was also evident from the observations of the preparatory visits that while a number of detailed economic studies and projects had been undertaken in many of the projects, there were many gaps in research and surveys in the social aspects of regional development. Demographic studies of the people directly affected by regional development, analytic studies related to location of population and services, the process of settlement, the problem of controlling migration, and social problems connected with nomadic groups, had almost invariably been given secondary importance or had been dealt with in an incomplete fashion.[4]

It was also the consensus of these missions that the growing interest, on the part of governments, in regional development as an instrument to modernize their economies and to bring about a more equitable distribution of income in the various regions, had led to an acute awareness of the need for training personnel with integrative skills who are able to relate their particular specialities to other needs and problems in the region.

While this series of observatory missions was being conducted, the United Nations Research Institute for Social Development in Geneva was in 1967, as a part of the programme, initiating a series of studies to inquire into the experiences in regional development in various parts of the world and to focus particularly on such topics as the regional disaggregation of national policies and plans, the role of growth poles and growth centres, regional information systems, and regional sociology. These studies enabled the countries to benefit fully from the experiences of others and they also pointed out a number of gaps in which both conceptual and applied studies were required.

Benefitting from the findings of the exploratory missions and the results of the UNRISD studies, the Economic and Social Council in 1971 further defined regional development as a potential instrument for integrated social and economic development within a country, particularly to:

"(a) Induce rapid structural change and social reform, especially to achieve a broader distribution of returns from development among less privileged groups in society;

(b) Increase popular participation in setting development goals and in developmental decision-making and organizational processes;

(c) Create more effective institutional and administrative arrangements and operational approaches to carry out development plans;

(d) Achieve a better distribution of population and human activities and settlement through a more effective integration of urban and rural development;

(e) Include environmental considerations more effectively in development programmes." [5]

With the purpose of regional development thus defined, the Council also set the stage for the establishment of a global network of centres and for a more intensified effort in mobilizing and utilizing available resources to strengthen the capacity of member countries in adopting regional development as a strategy for achieving national goals.

2. *The Scope of the Programme and Summary of Progress Made to Date*

Building upon the exploratory activities mentioned in the previous section and influenced by the demand from the member countries on the one hand and inadequacy of resources on the other, the programme has undergone a considerable evolution during the past 10 years. The scope of the programme, as it emerged, can be covered under four headings: (1) promotion of a global network of centres, (2) convening of international conferences and symposia, (3) preparation of research and training material, and (4) assistance in the training of personnel.

Because of the internal administrative constraints, the resources that have been made available from the regular United Nations budget are not commensurate with the importance the governing organs attached to the programme. Fortunately, some extrabudgetary resources were made available for this programme from several governments and this permitted the establishment of a modest staff at headquarters to provide central services for the programme, the establishment of a Research and Training Centre for Asia and the Pacific, and the provision of certain limited advisory services to strengthen the training and research capacities of member countries. Moreover, collaboration of such United Nations institutions as UNRISD and the regional planning institutes in Santiago, Chile and Dakar, Senegal, and such Secretariat units as the Centre for Housing, Building and Planning, the Centre for Development Planning, Projections and Policies, and the Public Administration Division also assisted the Social Development Division in discharging its responsibilities for the programme.

A Global Network of Centres

The original scheme as established by the series of ECOSOC resolutions envisioned a limited number of multinational and international centres to serve the programme's research and training needs. During the early stage of the programme, one international centre was established under direct management of the United Nations and two previously existing centres were brought into relationship with the programme and their training activities in regional development extended. Due to financial limitations, the effort of the United Nations programme to promote additional international centres and to support existing ones had only limited success. In the meantime, as the national interest in regional development grew, the number of national institutes for research and training in this field also increased and some of them were prepared to service neighbouring countries while others were in need of outside support. In order to ensure that the programme meets the demand of this changing situation, the concept of a network needed to be revised and a more open system needed to be adopted by including in it a large number of national and international institutions engaged in or intending to undertake research and training in regional development. With this decentralized, open network, the programme was better able to monitor the supply and demand of international assistance, to facilitate the sharing of knowledge and mutual interest between countries and institutions. On this basis, over fifty institutions representing all major areas of the world are now included in the programme to form a global network. While the majority of these are national centres, a number of them do perform some international functions.

The first centre directly operated under the UN programme is the United Nations Centre for Research and Training in Regional Development (UNCRD) in Nagoya, Japan. It was officially established in 1971 with financial support from the Japanese Government, after a three-year trial period when it was known as Chubu Centre. It was felt that the dramatic progress in the Chubu region in industrialization and urbanization during the post-war period offered an excellent example of how growth and development can be accelerated with concentrated effort. On the other hand, the difference in the current levels of development between Japan and the majority of other Asian countries has also meant that the Centre needs to reach out to the other countries to gather current experience (such as the case studies being conducted in the Philippines and India) and occasionally to borrow expertise from other institutions (such as the Rehovot Centre in conducting courses in rural development).

The Centre's functions cover four areas: training, research, information exchange and advisory service. During the first years, the activities of the

Centre had been mainly centered on the first two areas.[6] There is currently a proposal for a "unified input package programme" to enable the Centre to effectively transfer useful knowledge and skills in regional development planning by combining all four functions into one "package". The project envisages three phases:

(1) data collection and research work in a selected region and the preparation by the Centre staff and research fellows of a syllabus for training;

(2) conducting of research and training courses for the local regional development personnel to take place partly at UNCRD and to stay mainly in the selected region; and

(3) actual formulation of a development plan for the region with the combined effort of the training local personnel and the UNCRD staff.

This package is to be applied in a concentrated manner in a selected region of a country for a year's duration. The Jogyakarta region in Indonesia has been proposed, beginning in mid-1975, to test out the idea.

Two well established centres have been brought into the UN programme and have performed certain international functions. They are the Settlement Study Centre in Rehovot, Israel and the Institute of Social Studies in The Hague, The Netherlands. Their contribution has been mainly on training and, to a lesser degree, in research, which is to be discussed in the later sections of this report. The UN has provided short-term lecturers and consultants to these training courses and has, in certain cases, provided fellowships. Both centres have participated actively in the various conferences sponsored by the programme and have undertaken the training of personnel in the UN-assisted projects.

The regional institutes for development in Santiago (ILPES) and in Dakar (IDEP) have organized a number of training courses and seminars on social and other aspects of regional planning and have collaborated in the preparation of teaching materials for circulation within the programme.

In addition, the network includes training and research institutions in countries of three principal developing continents. These include Algeria, Arab Republic of Egypt, Cameroon, Ivory Coast, and Nigeria in Africa; India, Indonesia, Iran, Philippines and Pakistan, in Asia; and, in Latin America, Argentina, Brazil, Chile, Mexico and Venezuela. Of these, the Centro Nacional de Capacitación e Investigación Aplicada para el Desarrollo Regional y Local (CIADEC) in Maracqy, Venezuela and the Centre for Research and Training in Regional Planning at the Plan and Budget Organization in Teheran, Iran were established with direct assistance from the UN programme and have expressed an interest in performing international functions. Two others, the Institute of Development Studies at the University of Mysore in India and the Department of Geography at the University of Ibadan in Nigeria have collaborated in the convening of continental conferences in Asia and Africa respectively.

In the industrialized parts of the world, a number of competent institutions in Europe, the USSR, and North America have collaborated in the programme and have indicated interest in supporting training and research efforts in developing countries under the UN umbrella. In Europe these include: The Economic Institute of Belgrade University in Yugoslavia, The European Research Institute for Regional and Urban Planning in the Netherlands, the Committee for Space Economy and Regional Planning of the Polish Academy of Sciences in Poland, the Institute "Mens en Ruimte" in Belgium, the Akademie für Raumforschung und Landesplanung in the Federal Republic of Germany, the German Development Institute in Berlin, and the Academy of Sciences of the Soviet Union; and in North America the Universities of Pennsylvania and of Pittsburgh and Cornell University, the Special Programme for Urban and Regional Studies of Developing Areas at MIT in Cambrdige, Massachusetts, the School of Architecture and Urban Planning at the University of California in Los Angeles, and numerous universities and research institutes in Canada. Contacts are also maintained with relevant institutions in Czechoslovakia, Denmark, France, Ireland, Italy, Spain, Sweden, Switzerland and the United Kingdom.

To support this global network of centres and the programme as a whole, certain basic services are provided from the headquarters. These services range from collection and dissemination of substantive information relevant to regional development, to the development of teaching materials appropriate for the kind of training envisaged in the UN programme, publicizing more widely the purposes and policies of the programme, and mobilizing and channelling international support to the programme. Using mainly the extrabudgetary funds available to the UN programme, an interdisciplinary professional group has been assembled to attend to the tasks of establishing a continuous relationship with institutions and other entities engaged in regional development planning, to collect information on literature pertaining to regional development, and to analyze, assemble, and issue it in forms that will be useful for teaching and training purposes.

Some of the more significant results of those activities which were widely circulated include a Thesaurus of Key Terms and numerous bibliographies on various aspects of regional planning and development. More extensive work related to research and the preparation of training material is reported in the following sections of this paper.

Two general publications have given the programme considerable publicity: one is a brochure setting out the background to the UN programme, its objectives, the policies guiding the programme, as well as other relevant information concerning the programme; and the second is in the form of an "executive briefing paper" which attempts to clarify the concept of regional planning and development, its relationship to other planning activities, problems and issues connected with the regional approach, and the kind of expertise required for it. Information on the UN programme of research and training is also given, together with a selected bibliography. This paper has been considered useful for policy makers and high government officials to provide them with an orientation to regional planning, development, and implementation. It has also been used as teaching material in many training courses which are organized by centres participating in the programme, and for this purpose it has been translated into several languages.

Convening of International Conferences and Symposia

Another function of the programme aimed at stimulating the flow of knowledge and experiences, assessing needs and the progress made, and promoting international co-operation is the convening of international conferences and symposia. Three significant global meetings concerned with training and research took place in Warsaw, Stockholm and Nagoya during the years 1971 and 1972. The Warsaw conference,[7] which was attended by representatives of 20 countries, discussed approaches to regional planning, clarified essential training elements and, in particular, assessed the training needs of developing countries engaged or interested in regional planning. The Stockholm conference,[8] which was attended by European institutions engaged in training for regional development, followed up on action proposals arising of the Warsaw deliberations by considering the role of European institutions in meeting the training needs of the developing countries. The Nagoya conference,[9] attended by directors of over twenty national and international institutions interested in training and research in regional development, provided an opportunity for the participating institutions to compare experiences and to discuss co-operation and concerted action. The spirit generated by the centres represented in Nagoya (the "Nagoya Club") has been reflected in the inter-institutional collaboration which followed and which provided a solid base of constituents for the United Nations programme.

The Nagoya conference was particularly significant from the point of view of the programma's development, because it was the first international conference which moved from generalities into the specifics of the problems and approaches to training and research in regional development. The conference conclusions represent the sum of the experiences and felt needs of those who constitute the network for international exchange and co-operation, and they thus provide a solid basis for the programme's future directions. Moreover, the club spirit which was generated in the conference has since been reflected in the continued cooperation and good will of the participating centres towards the United Nations' global efforts in promoting regional development. The spirit of the "Nagoya Club" has prevailed in all subsequent efforts towards international co-operation either on a bilateral or on a multilateral basis among the centres. The fact that the staff of the Centre was involved in the conference proceedings was also a factor which has influenced the direction of the Nagoya Centre's work programme towards meeting the needs of the countries it serves.

Some of the findings and recommendations of the conference are reflected in the discussion on research and training that follows. The conference's major conclusions of a more general character were:

1. In view of the general acceptance of regional approach as a development strategy, there is a need to broaden the concept and scope of the UN network of centres for research and training, a point which was referred to in the previous section of this paper;

2. The role of the individual international centres in the network with regard to in-service training and action-oriented research was emphasized and elaborated upon as was the corresponding need for expansion of the supporting role of international centres and the programme's central service, including formation and documentation exchange;

3. Training and research should be closely related. The UN programme should devote itself primarily to supporting in-service training activities, designed to prepare persons concerned to perform various functions in the regional development process. The need to link such training with existing academic institutions was also emphasized;

4. The conference endorsed as the criteria for major research investigations those aspects which were stressed in the UN resolution that established the programme, namely, structural change and social reform, popular participation, effective institutional arrangements, improved patterns of settlements, and production and environmental factors. The research projects of the centres should be concentrated on policy and action-oriented research. It should further place emphasis on the methodological aspects of planned development processes;

5. The conference urged the United Nations to accord higher priority to this programme and resource allocation for regional development, and appeal for additional governmental and non-governmental contribution in kind and in service in support of the programme; and

6. The centres of the UN network should meet periodically, in order to promote joint research and training activtities and mutual support among the centres.

These global conferences envisaged a series of conferences in the continental regions as a follow up in order to bring the discussion to a more practical level among the countries under similar material and social conditions and at similar stages of development. Such regional conferences took place in Latin America,[10] Africa,[11] and Asia,[12] and although under different sponsorship, they all related themselves to the UN effort in promoting regional development. There was considerable interchange of participants between the different global regional conferences and each was built upon the findings and conclusions of the previous ones.

At the most recent conference, the Mysore Symposium, considerable emphasis was laid on the social goals of development, rural orientation to planning and a grass-root approach to decision-making and to implementation. Some of the major conclusions were:

1. Emphasis should be laid on the incorporation of development goals and strategies which lead to improvement of the quality of life, especially of those who have been by-passed by earlier efforts directed to economic growth alone;

2. In a multi-level framework, the social components of planning will receive their due attention at the lower and intermediate levels, ensuring people's participation on the one hand and, on the other, creating the necessary social capital for the future development of the local, regional and national economy;

3. While the interregional allocation of investable resources has to be based on cost and benefit considerations, the present tendency to neglect the social cost and benefits from development projects has led to increased areal disparities in development;

4. The present urbanization processes in many countries are not conducive to integrated rural-urban development. There is a need for a policy of decentralized urbanization;

5. The concepts of growth poles and growth centres need to be appropriately modified and adapted to meet the various national situations in order to make it possible for a hierarchy to be developed so that the spatial economy may be both vertically and horizontally integrated;

6. The grass-root approach to regional planning is essential in order to bring home the benefits of development to every citizen and to effectively mobilize people's participation in the planning and development process. Along with this approach is the need to integrate local plans into areal and regional plans; and

7. Population policies should be treated as integral parts of national, regional and local development policies. These should cover the control of population growth rates as well as the spatial distribution of population.[13]

Research Activities

Reference was made earlier to the contribution made by the United Nations Research Institute for Social Development (UNRISD) in Geneva to the initial research aspect of the programme during the period 1967-1970. The Institute contributed immensely both in substance and in volume to a better understanding of the basic concepts of regional development as an approach to integrating social, economic, and administrative aspects within the framework of multi-level planning. Five broad areas were indentified for the research activity, namely:

1. A worldwide study of regional development: experiences and prospects;
2. The role of growth poles and growth centres in regional development;
3. Information systems for regional development;
4. Regional sociology; and
5. Regional disaggregation of national policies and plans.

As a result of this research programme, the UNRISD-MOUTON Regional Planning Series was established in 1971. This series will incorporate ten volumes with the following publication schedule:[14]

(1) *Regional Development: Experiences and Prospects in South and Southeast Asia,* 1971.

(2) *Regional Development: Experiences and Prospects in the United States of America,* 1971.

(3) *Regional Development: Experiences and Prospects in Latin America,* 1974.

(4) *Regional Development: Experiences and Prospects in Eastern Europe,* 1972.

(5) *Growth Poles and Growth Centres in Regional Planning,* 1972.

(6) *Regional Information and Regional Planning,* 1974.

(7) *Social and Institutional Dimension of Regional Development,* to be published in 1975.

(8) *Regional Disaggregation of National Policies and Plans,* 1974.

(9) *Growth Poles and Growth Centres as Instruments of Modernization in Developing Countries,* to be published in 1975.

(10) *Urban-Regional Development in South America—A Process of Diffusion and Integration,* 1974.

Other studies, which were published as UNRISD staff reports, include country studies on growth poles and growth centres, on information systems, and on the social aspects of regional development.

With the completion of UNRISD's series of studies on regional development, research initiated by the UN programme has followed new directions. At headquarters level, priority is being given to research connected with the preparation of teaching materials that could be adapted to national and multinational training programmes. Particular emphasis is being placed on the social dimensions of regional development since these were the major concern of the UN governing organs which established the programme and are a subject whose vital importance has been repeatedly emphasized at international meetings. Research in this area falls mainly into the following categories:

1) *Approach and methodology of intra-regional planning.* Separate readers of selected available literature supplemented by original contributions are being prepared for Latin America, Africa, and Asia. The reader for Latin America has already been completed with the co-operation of ILPES in Santiago. The reader for Africa is expected to be completed during the latter part of 1974 with the help of IDEP in Dakar and the University of Ibadan. A similar reader for Asia is being planned as part of the Nagoya Centre's research work. Preparation of these readers represents the first stage of a worldwide scheme for preparation of training materials in regional development. Succeeding stages will include the preparation of textbooks and handbooks for regional development practitioners and of a series of technical reports which will summarize results of major problem-oriented research projects being undertaken around the world;

2) *Social dimensions of regional development.* A review of available literature in this area has been completed with the selection of reading materials to be published in 1974. The reader covers social-demographic issues such as urban and rural migration and settlement patterns; socio-economic issues such as rural development and industrialization, employment and income distribution; and socio-political issues such as power and administrative structure and popular participation. It also includes some methodological considerations concerning the integration of social aspects in the regional planning process from policy formulation to plan formulation, implementation, and evaluation;

3) *Administrative aspects of regional development.* A study has been prepared by the Public Administration Division of the UN Secretariat and will be published during the latter part of 1975. The study is based upon reports prepared by specialists in regional administration in fifteen countries representing Africa, Asia, Latin America and the Middle East, and focusses upon the central issues and practical problems of organization and execution of sub-national developmental activities;

4) *Integrated development for predominantly rural regions.* This study, which is in an advanced stage of execution, draws upon existing national experiences in achieving integrated development in regions which are predominantly rural in character and where agricultural production is the main economic activity. The interdependence of rural and urban sectors in such regions is being covered, as is the interaction of economic, social and spatial factors in improving the totality of living and working conditions of rurally based populations;

5) *Popular participation in development.* A study has been com-

410

pleted [15] on the concept of, and on approaches to, popular participation as a means of accelerating the achievement of national development goals. This will be followed by a more systematic assessment of national experiences in citizens' involvement in policy decision-making and programme implementation. Attention will be given in these studies to promotional techniques and to requisite institutional arrangements to make citizens' participation more effective; and

6) *Systematic monitoring and evaluation of the impact of developmental programmes on the intended beneficiaries.* A system for assessing and monitoring the impact of developmental programmes on their intended beneficiaries has been developed and is currently tested through a number of field projects. Several case materials have already been prepared to form the basis of a manual for field-level personnel.

In addition, the UNCRD in Nagoya has also engaged in some research work based on the experience in Japan and on other selected Asian experiences. Four areas have been identified for in depth studies, and work on the first two has been started. These four areas are:

a. The role of urban centres in attaining desirable population distribution in the context of rapid urbanization;

b. The role of governments in the development processes;

c. The problem of environment in regional development;

d. Utilization of economic concepts and tools for regional development planning.

On the whole, the trend in research work being carried out within the programme has gradually shifted from propagating the need for a regional approach to development to developing methodologies and instrumentalities for analysis, planning, and implementation at the regional level. With the wide acceptance of multi-level development planning as a national policy, the need to advocate *why* has been supplanted by the crucial necessity of outlining *how* this policy can be carried out effectively.

Aside from the research work carried out by the UN units themselves, the programme also promotes research work in developing countries, particularly through the network of centres, and is instrumental in disseminating and facilitating the exchange of research results. The programme benefits considerably from research activities undertaken by the centres in developing countries. While monitoring such research activities, efforts have been made to inspire new research projects in gap areas which are most relevant for the developing countries. This emphasizes the importance of the documentation and information exchange service of the programme which, inter alia, circulates bibliographies and then prepares abstracts, as well as disseminating original documents and research results. International seminars and conferences are another means of circulating research results, and the UN programme has done much in this respect.

Training Activities

The training of personnel was recognized at the outset as the most important means of strengthening the governments' capacity to implement regional development policies and was, therefore, made the centre of the programme's activities when it was established by ECOSOC. The shortage of trained personnel for planning and implementing integrated development policies and programmes at regional and local levels was also emphasized by the series of exploratory missions and international conferences that followed.

The contribution of the UN programme in this regard has been mainly in assisting national programmes of in-service and mid-career training, and in preparing training materials for general adaptation. Conduct of longer term professional and degree-programmes training has been left to academic institutions, and the UN-operated and assisted training programmes have focussed on medium- or short-term training activities. While longer periods of training would permit more extensive coverage, the need to attract senior officials made it necessary to adopt shorter periods of specific training activities since governments are not usually able to spare these officials for longer periods. Thus, the main courses of the Nagoya Centre have been set at four months, with seminars dealing with special subjects lasting for three to four weeks each. In a similar fashion, most of the ECLA/ILPES annual courses on regional development last for three months and the intensive regional development training courses of CIADEC are of six weeks' duration.

For those who can afford a longer period of training and wish to enhance their careers as planners, administrators, trainers, or researchers, the one-year course in comprehensive development planning at the Rehovot Centre and the nine-month diploma course in regional development at the ISS offer realistic options. In addition to training provided by the international centres, the programme also provides a limited amount of direct assistance in support of a number of national training efforts.

During the past two years, assistance in training design, curriculum development, and project formulation has been rendered to, i.e. Iran, Pakistan, the Philippines, Brazil, India and Venezuela. This effort in the first two of these countries resulted in the initiation of a comprehensive project for UNDP assistance of in-service training. Thus the programme serves as a catalyst in bringing about projects for more sustained support from the richer resources of UNDP. One drawback of such an arrangement is that once the project becomes a UNDP project, it is operated under a different set of rules and policies and these do not necessarily carry through a global strategy such as that enunciated by the ECOSOC resolution on regional development.

412

Attempts were made during the early part of the programme to organize training activities within the context of on-going regional development projects assisted by UNDP. This effort was confronted with more constraint than was anticipated due to the need for often protracted negotiations with the host government, the executing agencies, and the project personnel.

Limited progress has, however, been made in this regard, through the international centres. The Nagoya Centre, for example, organized a six-week special course for the Korean personnel working in the UNDP-assisted project in regional physical planning. The Rehovot Centre provided training opportunities for the personnel involved in the UNDP Northern Thailand regional development project.

With its limited resources, the programme has been seeking a more efficient means through which the most current concepts and approaches can reach the largest number of those who could influence national development policies. For this purpose, a "correspondence seminar" on comprehensive development in local and intermediate levels has been designed to begin in 1975 and to be repeated in the following years if resources permit. This seminar will focus on critical issues involved in promoting comprehensive development at local and intermediate levels, and will synthesize the latest approaches and methodologies employed in meeting them. The seminar will consist of a series of six correspondence sessions at one month intervals, with a concluding workshop during the seventh month. Topics to be covered by these sessions are:

1. Introduction to comprehensive development at local and intermediate levels;

2. The social dimensions, including social goals and planning targets, key elements in social change and social indicators;

3. Concept and approach to comprehensive development in predominantly rural areas;

4. Social institutions and popular participation;

5. Implementation of development policies and plans at local and intermediate levels; and

6. Introduction to methods of analysis, planning, and evaluation.

The reading materials for the above subjects were organized by the programme staff and drew heavily upon the collective knowledge and experiences of the United Nations system; these were tested by a group of experts, some representing the prospective recipients of such training, at a seminar which met in West Berlin at the invitation of the German Foundation for International Development in July 1974. The materials prepared for this purpose were generally endorsed by the group which also made a number of practical suggestions for improvement. It is expected that as a result of the correspondence seminars, a number of training activities

413

will be organized by those developing countries which did not have such training until now, and in which the need for training for comprehensive local and intermediate level development is strongly felt.

3. *Trends and Prospects*

As was stated earlier in the paper, the basic concern of the UN governing organs which established the programme was the mitigation of human problems arising out of various measures which have been taken by member countries to modernize their economies through industrialization and agricultural improvements, and which often result in overconcentration of population and industry in a few metropolitan centres and in neglect and deterioration of the countryside. It was felt that a better spatial distribution of population and human activities would ensure a more equitable distribution of the benefits of development to the masses of population, and substantially assist in raising their standards of living and in improving their quality of life.

Today, after ten years of promotion work, the social goals of development have received near universal acceptance, and regionalization of development has been adopted by an increasing number of countries which are now turning their attention to a grass-root approach and to the problems of rural poverty. Some of these recent trends are reviewed below.

Adoption of the Regional Approach as a National Development Strategy

An overriding trend which we have witnessed during the past few years is the recognition by an increasing number of countries of the regional approach as a national development strategy. Earlier examples of regional development, including those assisted by the United Nations, were mainly concerned with special problem regions such as the metropolitan regions of Bombay, Singapore or Lagos; river basin regions such as the Gal Oya of Sri Lanka, Lerma in Mexico, or Euphrates in Syria; the potentially resource-rich regions of Nabouk Valley in Malaysia or Ciudad Guayana in Venezuela; and the frontier regions of Northeast Brazil or of North Togo. More recently, an increasing number of countries such as Chile, Peru, Venezuela, Iran, the Philippines, Tanzania and Zambia, have adopted regionalization as a policy for social and economic development of the entire country.

The interest in developing the whole country by areas or by regions stems from several sources. Those concerned with national planning have found it useful, for implementation purposes, to break the area to be covered by the plan down into smaller and more manageable units. At the same time, those concerned with community development at the local level were

414

finding it valuable to work with units that are somewhat larger and more viable than the village or the small local community. And in addition, those concerned with urban planning are increasingly aware that the problems of rapid urbanization have their roots in the conditions of rural areas and that solutions to these problems lie partly in the development of rural areas. Thus, attention is turned to a regional approach which recognizes the interdependence of urban and rural development.

Along with the interest in nationwide regional development comes progress towards the multi-sectoral approach to development. As has been observed in the past, economists tend to dominate planning at the national level, the engineers and architects at the regional level, and the social and community development workers at the local level. The integration of national and local level development through the introduction of intermediate levels has helped to bring about an integration of the various disciplines which hitherto have each made important contributions at the respective levels.[16] Simultaneously, the regional approach to national development has brought to light the crucial issues of economic versus political subdivision of the countries and the need to establish corresponding administrative hierarchies which would be able to organize and coordinate development activities. The solutions adopted vary from country to country according to the existing decision-making system, the sociocultural structures inherited from the past, and, last but not least, the size and geographical characteristics of the countries.

Emphasis on Predominantly Rural Regions

While some of the earlier regional development problems also dealt with certain rural problems, these were not stressed. The main approach to regional development was dominated by physical planners and their experience in urban planning, and by economic planners whose main concern was the disaggregation of national plans and allocation of national resources. The adoption of a nation-wide regional development strategy has directed more attention to rural development on an area basis. This is not difficult to understand when one remembers the predominantly rural character of the developing world. Hence, an area approach to integrated rural development has been made an important element of the national development strategy, for example, in Pakistan, Peru, Sudan and Tanzania.

Since agriculture is the main occupation in a rural society, requisites and facilities for agricultural production naturally occupy an important place in programmes for rural regions. On the other hand, as has been proven in a number of countries, an increase in production does not on its own guarantee a solution to the problems of rural mass poverty which plague all the developing countries. Simultaneous attention needs, therefore, to be

415

directed to the other interrelated problems, and these include over-population, under-employment, poor health, and lack of education. An attack on all these problems would require services and activities both of an agricultural and of a non-agricultural nature. The former include marketing, credit and extension services; the latter deal with rural industrialization, public works, community development, public health and in- and out-of-school education. Particularly important among all these measures is the introduction of agrarian reform to ensure that farmers receive their rightful share of the increased production.

It is essential that measures designed to increase production, such as the introduction of a high-yielding variety of crops, do not discriminate against the small farmers, thus further widening the gap between the rich and the poor in a rural society. Similarly, in order to avoid a worsening of the unemployment situation, capital-intensive production methods should not be introduced in a densely populated region. The types of agrarian reform, land settlement, agricultural and non-agricultural projects that are initiated should depend on the geographic and climatic conditions of the region, on the density of the population, and on the prevailing pattern of agriculture. The development of urban centres in the predominantly rural regions should be consistent with the need for distribution of employment opportunities and social services as well as for meeting the supply and marketing needs of the adjoining rural community. In this respect, recent work on the growth centre approach, which has attempted to correct certain of the weaknesses inherent in earlier formulations, is particularly relevant.[17]

Focus on the Social Implications of Development

In contrast to the situation a decade ago, the social goal of development, which may be essentially described as a concern for the well-being of the members of society as reflected in equity and quality of life, has found general acceptance in statements of governmental policy. To translate such a lofty purpose into specific programmes and plans requires greater and more detailed knowledge of the key social issues in regional development, including population structure and dynamics, the social aspects of settlement structure, the organization of industrialization and urbanization processes, agrarian reform and rural development, employment patterns and income distribution levels, and the role of growth centres in the diffusion of new technology. It also requires institutional arrangements to promote popular participation in developmental decision-making, implementation, and evaluation. All of these are factors which have to be taken into account in the formulation of regional strategies, in the implementation of regional programmes, and in assessing the impact of these programmes.

416

The three above-mentioned interrelated trends and concepts in regional development have important implications with respect to the regional planning process and methodology. This cannot be otherwise, because regional planning, when broadly defined, is nothing other than a particular way of designing a strategy, formulating policies and reaching decisions pertaining to the very phenomenon of regional development. One can single out at least three major implications of the above trends and concepts for regional planning so defined.

(a) *Regional planning should be comprehensive.* This requirement takes two directions: firstly, regional plans (or strategies, policies or programmes) based on sound economic, social and physical (technical) considerations should cover all relevant sectors of the regional economy and spheres bearing on the well-being of the population. The emphasis here is not so much on the scope of the coverage as on the co-ordinated planning of interrelated key phenomena. A case in point is planning for rural areas, which has to include, besides the agricultural sector, the commercial, industrial, educational and social services sectors. Secondly, comprehensiveness of regional planning has a temporal meaning. Recent trends and concepts in this field make it imperative to plan not only long-term development processes (say, of 15-25 years' duration) during which restructuring of a regional economy can be accomplished, but also short-term operational actions which bear on the present state of the economy and levels of living of the population. One could even argue that operational regional planning is more important because it is only through a series of short-term plans that the long-term plans can be implemented. Naturally, short-term regional plans differ from long-term ones in character, scope and methods of implementation.

(b) *Regional planning should be decentralized.* While it is possible to prepare regional development plans for individual regions of the country at the centre, this approach is costly and has many serious deficiencies. The preparation of a good regional plan requires a vast amount of data and information which often cannot be assembled at the centre. Furthermore, qualitative information is difficult to transmit from the region to the centre. Therefore, the closer the regional planning unit to the area covered by the plan, the easier and less costly the collection of necessary information.

However difficult the above problem is, it will, with the development of modern information techniques, gradually be overcome or at least reduced. But other, more profound, factors justifying decentralization will remain or even, in the course of time, grow in importance. These are all connected with popular participation in development. For obvious reasons, this participation will be more effective if people not only share in the execution of development plans but also participate in the decision-making process. As regional planning is the most comprehensive form of decision-making pertaining to an area's development, this means, in other words, popular participation in the planning process.

In order to give people an opportunity to participate in the planning process, it is necessary to designate planning fields in which the regional authorities would be free to make their own decisions according to the needs and desires of the inhabitants. Such decisions have, naturally, to stay within the scope of the locally available resources, supplemented by funds from the national budget. These decentralized planning fields can have a differentiated scope according to circumstances in a particular country. Generally, they will refer to those sectors of the regional economy and services which influence the social aspects of development, i.e., education, health services, social welfare programmes, communal facilities, etc. A maximum possible decentralization of regional planning is in the interests of good planning and successful implementation. This calls for no important policy change for countries that already have a certain degree of local autonomy in development (such as the various republics in Yugoslavia and the communes in China). For countries which are traditionally unitary in nature, special measures to decentralize the planning process are required such as those which have recently been applied in Iran and the Philippines.

On the other hand, one must bear in mind that not all development decisions can be decentralized. There is a vast area of economic decisions which have to be made at the centre, in order to safeguard the proper overall development of the country, particularly in connexion with its international trade and balance of payments situation. Besides, with growing economies of scale, particularly in industry, and a consequent increase in the optimum size of production units, there is a constant shrinkage of production for local needs: local markets gradually change into national and even international ones. Any major policy decisions pertaining to production for such markets have to be formulated in the centre.

In order to secure a harmonious development of centrally and decentrally guided spheres of the regional economy, it is necessary in the planning process to develop mutual information procedures and coordination techniques of planning and to work out methods for the overall guidance of the decentralized spheres of planning from the centre without impairing the formers' autonomy. It is also crucial to clearly define the dividing line between the centralized and decentralized spheres of planning in order to avoid an overlapping of activities.

(c) *Planning at the local level should be integrated with regional planning.* If regional planning is to accommodate the recent trends and concepts of development, it has to acquire a new dimension: it has to be disaggregated into local planning processes. This is the implication particularly of the emphasis on social aspects and on the development of rural areas, with an active participation of local population. The local dimension can have a beneficial influence on the quality of regional plans, especially if they are worked out in a top-downwards planning process (disaggregation of national plans), and consequently on their implementation. Conversely, local planning activities will, through close ties to regional planning, acquire the much-needed development dimensions which were lacking in the traditional welfare approaches to community development.

There are several ways of integrating local planning with regional planning. All should aim at merging planning from above and from below in one integrated process: the one cannot properly fulfill its task without the support of the other. The integration of both approaches to planning should commence at the very first stage of planning activities, i.e. at the analytical stage. This can be achieved primarily through the development of an information system to transmit a speedy and comprehensive knowledge of existing situations at the regional and national levels in both directions. Particular emphasis should be put on the elaboration of social indicators to measure the achieved level of living and specify further needs in this respect.

At the planning stage, close links between local and regional planning can be provided through a proper specification of locational policies and mutual information on particular locational decisions. An effort should also be made to formulate at the regional level other parameters relevant to development through which local authorities could be guided in taking their autonomous development decisions (within the decentralized sphere). Finally, during the implementation stage, the links between local and regional planning will be strongest if based on a systematic evaluation of the achieved results. Such evaluation, which far exceeds the customary collection of statistical data and pays particular attention to qualitative information, is worth the rather extensive efforts it requires if it is closely tied to the decision-making process. Consistent with decision-making at local and regional levels, the systematic evaluation should also be performed on these two levels. Local and regional authorities will have to co-operate closely in this matter if there is to be speedy and proper feedback on the effects of planning.

Changes in regional planning in the above three directions require a proper institutional setting at the regional and also at the local level. Regardless of the specific administrative set-up, there is a need at these levels for units which would be able to co-ordinate development plans and programmes of individual sectors, maintain links with regional and central planning authorities, and advise policy-makers and administrators about concrete development decisions. Recent examples of efforts to establish such units can be found in India (at the district level), Malaysia, and Senegal. In addition to their traditional functions, the local and regional planning units have a relatively new and difficult function: that of promoting popular participation in development. This requires special abilities and skills on the part of regional development workers who, in addition to mastering the techniques of planning, have to be knowledgeable about group dynamics, possess the art of persuasion, acquire relevant organizational skills, etc. These are skills traditionally not expected from regional planners. In the new situation the term regional planner acquires new meaning: he has to be an action-oriented development worker.

In summary, the new trends in nationwide coverage of regional development, in extending comprehensive development activities to rural areas, in focussing attention on social implications, and in promoting broad-based popular participation in development, all present new challenges to the various disciplines which contribute to regional socioeconomic development concepts and methodology. New approaches and techniques need to be developed. Progress needs to be closely monitored and periodically assessed. A wider circle of policy makers, administrators, planners, and practitioners needs to be trained. Such development is unprecedented. Nations can benefit from each other's experience in this undertaking by pooling and sharing their newly acquired knowledge. It is in this area of facilitating such an exchange of knowledge and experience that the UN Research and Training Programme will be orienting future work. The global network of centres and professional contacts that have been built up over the years should continue to be expanded and lines of communication strengthened.

Notes

1. Resolution 1086 C (XXXIX) of the Economic and Social Council of the United Nations (ECOSOC).
2. The following preparatory missions were made: to Asswan, Egypt in October 1966; to Awash, Ethiopia in October and November 1966; to Wadi Jizzan, Eastern and Western Provinces, Saudi Arabia in December 1966; to Ghab and Euphrates, Syria in December 1966; to East Pakistan in January 1967; to Chubu, Japan in January 1967; to Gal Oya, Sri Lanka in February and March 1967; to Lakhish and Upper Galilee, Israel in May 1967; to Oaxaca and Lerma, Mexico in June 1967; to Arica and Conoile in Chile in June and July 1967; to San Francisco Valley project, Brazil in July 1967; to Poland, Czechoslovakia and Yugoslavia in November 1967; and to Italy and the Netherlands from November to December 1967.
3. They were: The Settlement Study Centre in Rehovot, Israel; the Institute of Social Studies in the Hague; and the United Nations Research and Training Centre for Regional Development in Nagoya, Japan.

4. The reports of these preparatory visits which include specific recommendations were published in the document, "Selected Experiences in Regional Development", UN Publication, Sales No. 70.IV.14.

5. ECOSOC Resolution 1582 (L).

6. UNCRD's activities in training and research will be discussed later in this paper.

7. Interregional Symposium on Training of Planners for Comprehensive Regional Development, Warsaw, June 1971. The report of the Symposium was published as an internal document of the UN.

8. Symposium on European Co-operation in Training Regional Planners from Developing Countries, Stockholm, September 1971. The report of the Symposium was published as a UN document, SOA/ESDP/1971/4.

9. Interregional Workship for Directors of Centres Engaged in Research and Training in Regional Development, Nagoya, November 1972. The report of the workshop is pending publication by the United Nations.

10. Interregional Seminar on Regional Development Planning, Quito, Ecuador, September-October 1971, organized by the UN Centre for Development Planning, Projections and Policies, as the sixth in a series of seminars on development planning. Besides regional planning in Latin America, the Seminar dealt also with other continental regions of the world.

11. International Conference on Regional Planning and National Development in Tropical Africa, University of Ibadan, Nigeria, March 1972.

12. Asian Symposium on Regional Planning and National Development, sponsored by the Institute of Development Studies of the University of Mysore, India, July 1974.

13. Report of the First Asian Symposium on Regional Planning and National Development to be published by the Institute of Development Studies, University of Mysore.

14. Outside the UNRISD-MOUTON Regional Planning Series, the following volumes were published: (1) T. Hagerstrand and A. R. Kukliński (eds.), "Information Systems for Regional Development—A Seminar", General Papers, *Lund Studies in Geography*, Ser. B. Human Geography, No. 37; and (2) A. R. Kukliński and R. Petrella (eds.), *Growth Poles and Regional Policies*, European Co-ordination Centre, Vol. III in the Publication Series of the Vienna Centre with Mouton, 1972.

15. To be published as a UN publication during 1974.

16. This was recently stressed at a meeting of a group of experts on integration of economic and physical planning, New York, 10-14 September 1973, organized by the Centre for Housing, Building and Planning, in co-operation with the Centre for Development Planning, Projections and Policies and the Social Development Division, United Nations (report in preparation).

17. See, for example, A. R. Kukliński (ed.), *Growth Poles and Growth Centres in Regional Planning*, Mouton, Paris and The Hague, 1972; and R. P. Misra, *Growth Poles and Growth Centres in Urban and Regional Planning in India*, Institute of Development Studies, University of Mysore, Development Studies Number 8, June 30, 1971.

2

INTERNATIONAL COOPERATION IN THE FIELD OF REGIONAL POLICIES

Niles M. Hansen

In the postwar period a great deal of progress has been made in multinational regional cooperation, but as yet there is relatively little to show for this: few concrete measures have actually been implemented in intranational regional policies as a result of international cooperation efforts. This stems in large measure from the fact that multinational institutions have been created to settle disputes among nations, whereas disputes among subnational regional units must find some degree of resolution within the national framework.

It has properly been argued by A. J. Brown that "Regional economics starts from the existence of grievances that are identified with particular parts of the country, and from conflicts of economic interest between the predominant parts at least of different regional communities".[1] Whether or not this is true of regional economics as a discipline, it is true of regional policy. Although the redress of regional grievances is often presented as being consistent with economic efficiency from a national viewpoint, the more fundamental issue is likely to be equity. In all of the Western nations with whose regional policies I am familiar, these policies have, in varying degrees, been responses to demands from regions with relatively low per capita income and/or high unemployment that "something be done". These regions tend to fall into one of two categories. The first are rural areas characterized by relatively low-productivity agricultural employment, or by surplus labour that has been released from agriculture as a result of technological advance (mechanization, chemical fertilizers, etc.) but is unable to find other local employment opportunities. The second are older industrial regions with an overdependence on declining sectors. In addition, it is often argued that the largest metropolitan area of a country is too big or too crowded, and that policies to direct population and economic activity to other regions would benefit the whole country. This argument is perhaps heard less frequently now than it was a few years ago because more attention is now being paid to the rational management of bigness, but the literature on city size is still marked by considerable rhetoric on all sides. In any case, the demands of those who feel they have been wronged have led governments toward an increasing tendency to attempt to alter the spatial allocation of resources in favour of patterns deemed more desirable than those that would result from market forces in the prevailing institutional setting.

It may be noted that there is, of course, no necessary reason why a region should look to its own national government for its own ultimate self-interest. The reason why regions nearly always do so at present is because of the economic and political power vested in the nation-state. When the inhabitants of a region believe that the nation-state is not responsive to their needs, they may be more likely to seek international co-operation and perhaps eventual international integration. The relatively ardent "Europeanism" of the Belgians is no doubt explained in part by the inability of the Belgian state to cope with the grievances of the Flemish regions on the one hand, and the Walloon regions on the other. Belgian Law Professor François Perin, who heads the separatist Walloon Party, reflects the sentiment of many Belgians and other Europeans when he maintains that Europe cannot cohere without regionalism:

> The base of Europe must be the region, where people feel that they can influence their destinies. The top is Europe. It is the nation-state in the middle that is bankrupt. The state is losing power to Europe on top and to the regions below. The old centralized state of Napoleon is too distant from people.[2]

Many border regions also have unique characteristics which transcend narrow attachments to any one national perspective. Consider, for example, the case of Alsace-Lorraine:

> Isolated, this region appears to be distinct and different from other parts of France. The feeling of inferiority toward the Germans in industrial and technical matters, notable in France, does not exist in Alsace-Lorraine.
>
> In addition, the inhabitants show little distrust concerning the intentions of the Germany of tomorrow, which no longer arouses fear. The people of the region speak German, work with Germans and for German companies, think they understand them, and according to a great number of the French who were questioned, do not feel condescending toward Germans.
>
> Above all French, they have appreciated certain aspects of German culture, which they have kept and assimilated. In a sense, and because of the events of the last two wars, they are super-French . . .
>
> In these regions physically close to Germany the people feel remote

from Paris. Thus Alsace and Lorraine present characteristics at once insular and alpine, recalling the situation of Turin in Italy.[3]

While it may seem apparent that the many European border regions whose situations are not unlike that of Alsace and Lorraine might be particularly receptive to international co-operation in regional policies, there is of course no necessary reason why a region with grievances against the nation-state should seek such cooperation. Regions in nations whose dimensions are continental may seek autonomy as separate nations more than international cooperation in regional matters. The situation of Quebec—and, some might add, of British Columbia—in Canada is a case in point. In any event, while it is evident that policy-related research and practice must be oriented toward the historical, social, and institutional perspectives of particular nations, it should not be forgotten that this orientation is also relevant when regions are being considered.

Although regional policies tend to be the result of political pressures, this does not mean that efficiency considerations should be or are neglected. As Cameron points out, there are two possible meanings of efficiency in this perspective:

> The first is concerned with questions of how to devise regional policies which maximise the growth in real G.N.P., probably with a long-term perspective in mind. The second is concerned with using public resources and public policies in such a way that the goals of regional policy are achieved efficiently. This might imply a rule of minimum social costs for the achievement of a given "quantum' of regional goals.[4]

Of course, however complicated equity versus efficiency questions may be in the framework of national regional policies, they are even more so in an international context. It is precisely such issues that are, at this writing, impeding implementation of the European Community's proposed Regional Development Fund. The problem of who, on balance, is subsidizing whom is made even more difficult by the fact that national policies that were not designed specifically as regional policies may nonetheless have important differential regional consequences. Agricultural policy in the United States has contributed heavily to a process whereby some forty million people have been transferred from rural farm areas to cities and suburbs during the past three decades. On the other hand, in countries such as France and Western Germany direct and indirect agricultural subsidies have served to keep more people in rural farm areas than would have been the case if market forces had alone been operative. Similarly, subsidies to the shipbuilding sector in the United Kingdom have served to prop up employment in the industrial centres of western Scotland. The

425

complex interplay and feedback among regional policies and other policies will no doubt continue to be an impediment to international cooperation in the field of regional policies.

International cooperation is also made difficult by the fact that regional policies are often motivated in large part by peculiarly national desires to decentralize decision-making with respect to regional and local problems and the means needed to solve them. The nature and importance of this issue are very largely conditioned by the institutions and administrative structure of each nation. France, for example, has a highly centralized system of government, and most decisions that have significant consequences for the respective regions are made wholly or in part in Paris. Despite a great deal of rhetoric surrounding the importance of the twenty-one planning regions into which the country has been divided, the regions have not, in fact, been given the fiscal capacity to be more independent. Italy has recently made some progress in this respect, but it is too early to evaluate the consequences. On the other hand, regional planning is in fact decentralized in West Germany because of its federal structure of government. A federal structure does not, however, necessarily guarantee decentralized decision-making authority. In the United States the national government has acquired increasing control and influence over regional matters, though the Nixon administration has tried to reverse this process by substituting revenue sharing with state and local governments for categorical grant programs. It should also be noted that some regions with strongly held grievances about real or alleged neglect want funds from the central government but prefer to be their own masters in other respects, even at the cost of some degree of economic disadvantage. These regions often have large concentrations of national minority groups, e.g. the French in Canada, the Basques and Catalans in Spain, and Indians in the United States.

Despite the difficulties that have been pointed out, there are a number of reasons why it would be at least potentially fruitful for nations to cooperate in the area of regional policies. For the most part these are less grandiose than schemes to create a Europe of the Regions (it is nevertheless worth noting that this possibility has been taken seriously even at the highest levels in France. Michel Debré has written that "To create large regions strongly independent of central power—is this not to prepare an "integrated" Europe, where the idea of France would have only a folkloric character since the nation would be "disintegrated"?").[5]

In the first place it is extremely useful to exchange information on how regional data sets are gathered and organized, and on techniques for applying economic and other social science theory and methods to the analysis of regional and urban processes and problems. Certainly the activities of the Regional Science Association, the Association de Science

Régionale de Langue Française, and other international professional groups have proven valuable in this regard. But few would argue that the possibilities for such exchanges have been fully exploited.

A related area where international cooperation would be mutually beneficial is research on how academic and professional work is, or can be, linked with potential users of data and methods, and especially those users who are decision-makers or persons in a position to influence decisions. In the United States, for example, research funds from the Economic Development Administration virtually created and sustained regional economics programs in a considerable number of major American universities. Despite this effort, agency officials have continually complained that scholarly research has been of little use to them in making their policy and program decisions. Has this been because agency officials are too interested in the political aspects of their work or because they have not made a genuine effort to make use of research results and their implications? Or has the research really been devoid of policy relevance? Such shortcomings have no doubt existed on both sides, yet it seems likely that a major fault—perhaps the major fault—has been a lack of any systematic mechanism for linking research and decision-making. This is, of course, a general problem in governments and institutions of all sorts. Nevertheless, if perfection will remain elusive there is substantial room for feasible improvements. Foreign experience may provide useful insights in this regard. After all, the Swedish government regularly works closely with scholars on regional and urban policy matters, and the Royal Commissions have had a decided influence on similar policies in the United Kingdom. This is not to say that the formal or informal arrangements of one country are readily transferable to other countries; but they may, with appropriate modifications, provide serviceable notions for reform.

Unfortunately, it is far easier to make a case in principle for international cooperation than it is to delineate precise mechanisms for such cooperation. Exchanges among scholars and professional persons are often difficult enough within countries; though the situation varies among countries, the feudalism of research institutes is notorious.

Similarly, when a foreigner studies regional policies in another country his open-mindedness may be a virtue, but too often a lack of preconceptions may indicate intellectual fuzziness rather than an opportunity for the positive application of a different perspective. How many times have legislators and senior civil servants concerned with regional policies received foreigners with questionnaires which reflect no real understanding of local problems or institutions? Good intentions are no more a guarantee of success in international cooperation than they are in other aspects of life.

How then should international communication on regional matters be fostered? Should people be brought together in a systematic manner? If so, what networks should be used? Who, and which disciplines or organizations, should be involved? Should cooperation be highly structured and directed? Or is it best to take a relatively laissez-faire approach, with maybe an occasional organized conference thrown in? After all, a certain amount of disorder and luck does not always lead to bad results. (Serendipity has, or should have, a place of honour in the history of whatever progress man has made.)

It would be difficult if not foolish to attempt to respond to these questions with blanket generalizations, but reasonable choices can be made if the objectives of cooperation are defined with some precision. One of the most common pitfalls in collaborative research is to draw up at the beginning a set of goals to be achieved. I recently directed a comparative study (1974) of public policy and regional development in nine Western nations. At the conclusion of my summary it was suggested that the clearest generalization that could be drawn from the diverse national experiences was that what is most needed from all those people who are concerned with regional policies is not hasty selection of general goals, but rather a better elucidation of what the problems really are. After a year and a half of collaboration, none of the eight colleagues who worked with me on the study questioned this finding, and a number expressed strong agreement.

International exchanges which are solely concerned with the advance of tools and techniques can at the outset benefit from the widest possible range of participants. In this area the community of scholars is truly international, even though national institutions and policies may influence to some extent the direction of theoretical work. Given that resources to support such exchanges are severely limited, it might seem appropriate to devote most of them to translating key contributions and giving them wide circulation. The main reason why this simple expedient is not used more often may be that those who hold the relevant purse strings are more interested—as are their colleagues—in the touristic externalities that accrue from international meetings. A case can, on the other hand, be made for such meetings when we consider the long time lags that occur between the initial formulation of new concepts and methods and their eventual publication, not to mention translation.

A stronger case can be made for the need for face-to-face contacts when policy issues are the major concern. An understanding of historical, social, and institutional differences and the ways in which they condition and are conditioned by regional research demands considerable direct communication.

It is particularly important for the organizer of an international conference on regional policies to be clear in advance about what he wishes

428

to accomplish. This may seem a trivial observation, yet again and again one finds that the papers presented at international meetings do not seem to have any common thread. Variety may be the spice of life, but in international regional policy exchanges it rarely results in a product which is of real usefulness to all of the various participants.

One approach to organizing a meaningful exchange would be for the host country representative to decide what he really wants to learn from other countries' experience. He must decide if he is primarily interested in intra-urban problems, rural development, systems of cities and their relations with hinterland areas, institutional mechanisms for implementing regional policies, or some other issue.

Once a focus has been established it is equally important to select the appropriate participants. There is always a great temptation to invite persons who have become familiar through established networks. As often as not, however, they will discuss their latest research whether or not it is directly relevant to the theme of the meeting. The person with the freshest insights into the problem at hand is frequently not the easiest person to identify in advance. In a related vein, if the host country organizes a conference to learn from foreign experience about how to deal with its own problems more effectively, it is advisable to invite foreign scholars or officials, as the case may be, who are at least somewhat familiar with the host country and its regional problems. Otherwise the information imparted is likely to be irrelevant.

There are other situations where the purpose of international co-operation is not focused on the problems of one country, but on the common problems of the participants. Contrary to what many of my colleagues may feel, I believe that such cooperation should, at least initially, take place among countries with relatively homogeneous problems and institutions. If the Western industrial nations, the Socialist bloc countries, and similar groups of countries cannot cooperate effectively *within* their own contexts, why should they be expected to learn more from countries with quite different characteristics? The question is not one of impeding communication between nations with widely differing official values and institutions, but rather one of proceeding in stages: first make progress where it should be relatively easy to achieve, and then put more emphasis on the more difficult tasks that would be involved in meetings between East and West or between the industrial and the developing countries.

Perhaps the best place to begin international regional policy exchanges is with broadly regional considerations rather than specifically urban or specifically rural development issues, though these orientations might be subsumed in varying degrees. If the purpose of the conference is for one country to learn from the experience of the others—which is likely to be the situation when the financial support comes from a single country—then the host country should define the agenda. On the other hand, when funding comes from a group of countries, a foundation, or an international agency, the participants will expect to discuss problems of mutual interest rather than those of any one country. This kind of meeting runs the risk of lacking the focus of a meeting addressed to the carefully defined problems facing one country. It is therefore highly desirable that the group members identify at the outset the policy issues that are of significant interest in all or most of the countries represented. This task is by no means as easy as it may appear. Before meeting again, the participants should have a period of from six to eight months to prepare comparable papers covering such issues as the following: (1) description of general regional tendencies, (2) policy issues and goals, (3) regional development policies and tools for their implementation, (4) evaluation of policies, and (5) indications of likely future directions of regional policy. The drafts of these papers should be circulated among the participants (and among interested parties within the respective countries) for comment and then revised to conform to the mutual expectations of the group before a second meeting is held. If these preliminary steps are taken, the results of the second meeting should prove valuable to all of the participants. Moreover, the foundations will then exist for the participants to proceed to the discussion of more specific issues (e.g. the management of intra-urban problems) following similar procedures, or for possible meetings involving a broader range of nations (e.g. East-West discussions).

Given that many nations have now been actively involved with regional policies for two decades or even longer, it would seem that the time has come for the creation of more permanent and systematic means for international cooperation on regional issues. Whether or not this will happen may depend initially on the benevolence of international agencies or international-minded foundations. These should, however, not be expected to maintain such support ad infinitum—only long enough to demonstrate to the countries involved whether or not it is in their mutual interest to sustain a long run program.

Notes

1. A. J. Brown, *The Framework of Regional Economics in the United Kingdom,* Cambridge University Press, London 1972, p. 1.
2. In *Time* Magazine, March 18, 1974, p. 28.
3. Délégation à l'Aménagement du territoire et à l'action régionale, *Survol de la France,* travaux et recherches de prospective No. 29, La Documentation Française, Paris, 1972, p. 98.

430

4.   G. Cameron, "Regional Economic Policy in the U.K.", in Niles M. Hansen (ed.), *Public Policy and Regional Economic Development in Nine Western Countries,* Ballinger, Cambridge, Mass., 1974, p. 67.

5.   M. Debré, *Au service de la nation,* Stock, Paris 1963, p. 237.

3

THE SPATIAL DIMENSION IN POLICY AND PLANNING

Antoni R. Kukliński

Policy, Planning and the Society of the Future

Socio-economic policy and planning is a phenomenon of the twentieth century. During the last fifty years different societies have, for different reasons, come to the same conclusion, namely that the invisible hand is no longer an acceptable solution for the development of society and the economy. Each country has, of course, its own way of questioning the wisdom of the invisible hand and of promoting some sort of policy and planning, if not in the sphere of facts, then at least in the sphere of declarations.

While stressing the importance of specific conditions that are characteristic of each country, we should nonetheless not overlook the crucial phenomena which have, in a universal or semi-universal way, influenced the ideological substance of policy and planning around the world. I think the following four phenomena should be mentioned:

1. The development in the socialist countries of a new theory and practice of socio-economic policy and planning;

2. The development of new socio-economic policies in the western countries as a response to the great depression of the Thirties, which exposed the weaknesses of the invisible hand;

3. The development in the developing countries of an anti-colonial ideology which stresses the necessity of social and economic transformations; and

4. The *quo vadis* discussions of the year 2,000 and, in most countries, attempts to develop new visions of the society of the future.

In a world wide perspective there is a growing dissatisfaction with past performance and a growing role for socio-economic policies and plans. The scale and intensity of this dissatisfaction is, however, highly differentiated both in time and in space. We will not, in this paper, be reviewing the broad spectrum of diagnostic features and motivations in this

433

field; rather we will limit ourselves to outlining the basic difference between the kind of dissatisfaction that is voiced by those who fundamentally approve of the status quo and the kind that is voiced by those who fundamentally object to the status quo. Dissatisfaction of the first type is represented by the idea of improvement: the state of the society and the economy is here viewed as fundamentally good, but some disturbing phenomena make improvement necessary. The second type of dissatisfaction leads to quite different conclusions: the state of the society and the economy is fundamentally bad and thus very radical structural changes are viewed as necessary. In practical terms we in most cases find a mix of these two types of dissatisfaction. In policy and planning terms, the first type of dissatisfaction is reflected in the promotion of incremental change, the second in the promotion of structural change. The comparative evaluation of different systems of socio-economic policy and planning should look into the mutual relation between the expression of these two types of dissatisfaction and the promotion of these two types of change.

The Ideological Substance of Policy and Planning

Three elements of the ideological substance of policy and planning should be mentioned in this context:

1. The system of values, preferences and priorities prevailing in the given country. The most important problem here is the distinction between egalitarian and anti-egalitarian values, preferences and priorities;

2. The process by which the goals for the future are selected and transformed into planning objectives. The most important items here are the trade-offs between economic, social and environmental goals and objectives and among long and short term goals and objectives; and

3. The social and individual motivations of the human beings in the society and their dedication to the given set of values and goals.

J. Ziolkowski's point is well taken:

Within the scope of—let us call it so—the sociology of planning, the first and fundamental requirement is to analyze the factors which determine the "ideology" of the planner and consequently influence the preparation of the plan. Planning, like every other form of intellectual work, is socially conditioned. This has been generally recognized since Marx's time. Penetration to the motivations behind planning activity, to all the evaluating judgments, preferences and prejudices, states of consciousness—or lack of them—with respect to the social results of planning decisions, has a considerable importance for the understanding of the nature and course of the processes

434

caused by it.

It would also be important to investigate the factors causing deviation from the plan in the course of its implementation. For the carrying out of the plan depends on the actions, interests and conceptions of different human groups and even individuals. Behind every element of the plan there are some social forces which can accelerate or check, modify, or even completely nullify its implementation as an integral, logical whole.[1]

The Intellectual Equipment of Policy and Planning

Improvement and structural change in the society and the economy are very complicated phenomena. The problems in this field cannot be solved without proper intellectual equipment, three elements of which should be mentioned:

1. The explicative and predicative power of the theoretical framework. Each policy and planning activity is explicitly or implicitly built into a theoretical framework which should be adequate in relation to the objective reality of the given country;

2. The conceptual clarity in the formulation of policy and plans is, in most cases, a consequence of the high or low quality of the theoretical framework. In any situation, however, it is important to test if the scope and meaning of different concepts used in policies and planning are well defined.

3. The operational efficiency of methods, models and instruments applied in policy and planning. It is important to select a proper level of technical sophistication of these methods and models in order to avoid a situation in which comprehensive models are applied to simple problems and vice versa.

The evaluation of the intellectual equipment of policy and planning should always be related to the ideological structure of these activities. The history of Regional Science associations has demonstrated that attempts to isolate the intellectual equipment from the ideological substance generate an ivory tower atmosphere in which research activities lose practical meaning and social motivation.

Information Systems for Policy and Planning

No policy and planning system can function without a continuous supply of adequate information. The past two decades have been especially fruitful in the creation of different channels of mutual interrelations be-

435

tween the information and the planning systems.

The development of new approaches to policy and planning and the growing scope of these activities have created a demand for new types of information. The methodological, technological, and managerial progress in all activities related to the collection, processing and distribution of information has created new perspectives for the development of the intellectual equipment of policy and planning. Rapid progress has recently been made in this field. However, the gap between the possibilities of technical and intellectual excellence and the everyday practice is, in many countries, very wide and in some cases even growing.

The Institutional Pattern in the Field of Policy and Planning

The institutional framework of policies and planning is expanding very rapidly, at least in quantitative terms. This quantitative growth is not always associated with positive qualitative changes, which are much more difficult to effect than quantitative changes. A comparative review of institutions responsible for policy and planning in different countries will reveal an astonishing number of inefficient administrative and managerial solutions. It would be wrong, however, to restrict the comparison purely to technical managerial considerations. Well organized institutions may sometimes achieve only a very limited success or create only a fictitious impression that something is going on in the field of policy and planning. Good organization is definitely one of the necessary conditions for the development of policy and planning, but it is not a sufficient condition. The efficiency of policy and planning institutions is more dependent on ideological motivation, and on the political will to change the reality, than on technical managerial excellence.

The Integration of Policy and Planning Systems

The trend towards the integration of policy and planning systems can be observed in numerous countries around the world. However, the universality of this trend should not be over-estimated. The integrative forces sometimes encounter disintegrative forces which, in a given place at a given time, are able to arrest or even reverse the trend towards integration of the policy and planning systems. The problem of integration must therefore be seen in a broad historical and dynamic perspective: integration is a long term process involving extremely complex mechanisms of change. Four channels of integration of the policy and planning systems may be mentioned here:

436

1. the ideological channel
2. the intellectual channel
3. the information channel
4. the institutional channel

1. The Ideological Channel

The integrated policy and planning ideology is a fundamental condition for the development of an integrated policy and planning system. In all planning activities in a given country some common denominators should be accepted.

Naturally, it is extremely difficult to achieve this state of affairs in practical terms. In all policy and planning systems there will be differences in the interpretation of fundamental goals, in the application of basic criteria, and in the individual and collective motivations. This is an extremely delicate matter: a planning system without internal differences of opinions and approaches is a dead system, as, however, is also a planning system without the minimum amount of consensus and common denominators. Any discussion concerning the integration of the policy and planning system should therefore take, as a starting point, the integration of the policy and planning ideology and total conditions of the political, economic and social environment in which the policy and planning system is functioning. If in a given country different pressures and interest groups are guiding the activity of different policy and planning agencies, then there is little hope for integration of the system.

2. The Intellectual Channel

The attitudes and the behaviour of the academic community is an important factor in increasing the chances of integration or disintegration of the intellectual equipment applied in policy and planning. In the traditions of academic communities around the world the power of differences is stronger than the power of similarities, and attempts to promote integrated research on policy and planning are thus not always particularly successful. The distinction between interdisciplinary and meta-disciplinary approaches as presented by W. Alonso is pertinent in this context:

> My point in brief is that especially in the hard social sciences but also in the soft ones there has begun to develop a meta-disciplinary competence that rests in particular individuals, and that this provides a better model for the incorporation of the social sciences into the planning process than does the idea of an inter-disciplinary team. The

437

key difference is that members of a meta-disciplinary team share a common ground, while members of an inter-disciplinary team are brought together because of their diversity. If my basic point is granted, the urgent need is to develop a means of producing greater numbers of individuals with such competence to meet the demands of the work that must be done, and to do everything possible to advance these meta-disciplines.[2]

There is no doubt that we need, very urgently, to develop meta-disciplinary research activities on the integration of the intellectual equipment of policy and planning.

3. The Information Channel

An integrated policy and planning system is creating a demand for, and is a product of, an integrated system of information. The integration of policy planning and information systems can be seen in conceptual, in historical, and in geographic perspective. In other words, the information flows circulating in the system must be related to the same concepts, time horizons, and geographical units. In recent years rapid technological progress has been made in this field. The modern technology can be used as an instrument for the integration of policy, planning, and information systems. The technical solutions are, however, not able to eliminate barriers that may exist in the flow of information between the different institutions responsible for policy and planning. A tendency for some institutions to build up their own restricted information domains which are not accessible to other units of the system is a disintegrative force inside the system. The Minister's integrative declarations have very little value if his staff is not transmitting to other governmental offices the information necessary for their activity. The information channel is a very sensitive test of the real conditions for the integration of the policy and planning system.

4. The Institutional Channel

The institutional channel operates in two ways:

1. through direct links of an administrative character among the different policy and planning units of one central agency. From this point of view, the perfect administrative integration of the policy and planning system is achieved when the whole system is organized as one institution; and

2. through various types of formal and informal coordination of the activities of the policy and planning agencies. In practice, different com-

binations of direct administrative links and various types of formal and informal coordination are developed and applied. This well-known problem of the relative merits of centralization and decentralization in the organization of the policy and planning system is complicated in that no one can any longer assume that a high level of centralization automatically means a high level of integration of the policy and planning system. The policy and planning experience of different countries is indicating that an integrated policy and planning system can, and even should, absorb both centralized and decentralized administrative and managerial solutions. The centralized solutions safeguard the coherence of the system while the decentralized solutions guard its elasticity. It is true that a planning system cannot exist without a minimum amount of central guidance, but it is equally true that each unit in the planning system must have a minimum amount of autonomy in order to be a creative participant of the planning process. In any well functioning system a balance is kept between the power of the central guidance and the relative autonomy of the different units.

This approach to the integration of policy and planning systems is much broader than the conventional considerations which restrict integration of the operation of the institutional channel. The efficiency of the institutional channel has, in the present writer's opinion, very little power of its own: the power it has is a function of the integrative forces which operate via the ideological, intellectual and information channels.

The Explicit Spatial Dimension in Policy Planning

The dimension of space was incorporated relatively late into the system of policy and planning in which the global and sectoral dimensions hold a much stronger position. However, in the last decades it has been almost universally recognized that no efficient system of policy and planning can disregard the spatial dimension in the development of the society of economy. This spatial dimension is different in different countries. Nonetheless, we would probably agree that three types of policy and planning activities are most essential in this field, namely:
  a) Regional policy and planning
  b) Urban policy and planning
  c) Environmental policy and planning.
  In recent years the role of regional, urban, and environmental policies has been constantly growing. We could say that these three interrelated activities have emerged as a sui generis subsystem within the general system of policy and planning. A comparative review of this subsystem could

439

concentrate firstly on the joint features shared by regional, urban, and environmental policies, and secondly on the differentia specifica among regional, urban, and environmental policies.

1. The Joint Features

The common ground shared by regional, urban, and environmental policies can be described as follows:

a) These policies relate to the spatial dimension in the development of a given society;

b) In these policies the long term goals and objectives should have a determining influence on medium or short term decisions and choices;

c) These policies are multi-dimensional and face the necessity of integrating the different approaches in this field. Perhaps the most important issue here is the integration of economic, social and ecological approaches; and

d) These policies deal with particularly complicated issues where at the diagnostic stage the relation between causes and effects is not always easily discernible. The same can be said of the relation between means and ends in the stage of policy design implementation and evaluation.

2. The Differentia Specifica

a) *The differences in the scope of these policies.* Three domains in the scope of these policies can be distinguished: (i) a domain which is common to regional, urban and environmental policies; (ii) a domain which is common to two of these three policies; and (iii) a domain which is the exclusive concern of one of these three policies. A substantial review of the scope of regional, urban, and environmental policies in different countries would indicate that this distinction has a universal character. The relative size of the three domains and their hierarchical interrelation will however be different in different countries.

b) *The differences in the intellectual structure of these policies.* In each country, regional, urban, and environmental policies are introduced in a particular historical sequence. Each of these policies is initiated under particular conditions and circumstances which contribute to the establishment of some dominating elements in the intellectual structure of the given policy. So it might happen that in the formative years regional policies were dominated by macro-economic approaches, urban policies by considerations of technical design, and environmental policies by the philosophy of the protection of nature.

Although each of these policies later accepts the multidimensional approach, the original impact of the dominating factor in the formative

440

years remains an important element in the explanation of the differences in the intellectual structure of regional, urban, and environmental policies in a given country.

c) *The differences in the institutional patterns.* In the international comparisons in this field we should discuss not only the similarities and differences related to the technical problems of government organization and management, but also, most importantly, the political and ideological motivation which is the driving force behind the activities of different institutions responsible for regional, urban, and environmental policies in a given country. In this broad framework we can discuss the interrelations between the ideological substance of regional, urban, and environmental policies, the intellectual structure of those policies, and the institutional patterns. As a rule, the different institutions will try to develop a clear delimitation around their activities. This is justified to a certain extent since each institution must guard its identity. However, this search for identity, if it is driven too far, can be detrimental and act as a disintegrative force within the totality of the system.

The Implicit Spatial Dimension in Policy and Planning

The development of regional, urban, and environmental policy and planning activities has been described in this paper as the explicit spatial dimension in policy and planning. This explicit dimension is very important but not sufficient either for the explanation of the past or for planning for the future. We have to take into account that all global and sectoral policies and plans have spatial implications which sometimes have a stronger impact on the spatial pattern of human activity than do explicit regional, urban and environmental policies and plans. There is no doubt that sectoral policies related to industry, agriculture or transportation have a strong spatial impact. The same applies to social policies in the field of health, culture and education. Therefore, it is necessary always to take into account the implicit spatial dimension incorporated into the global and sectoral policies and plans. This is a very complicated topic since the implicit dimension is often very fluid and difficult to pinpoint. It is not an accident that the implicit dimension is mentioned very seldom in explanations of the past and in plans for the future. The performance in both situations will remain very imperfect unless the implicit and explicit dimensions are fully integrated both in the analytical and in the planning stages.

441

This dilemma can be formulated as follows: will the society of the future develop new spatial patterns for its activity or will it only reinforce the patterns created in the past? John Friedman presents a simple and clear answer to this fundamental question:

> A rudimentary pattern of urbanization and regional development will tend to maintain itself. Such a pattern may be established quite early in a country's history. Subsequent flows of controlling decisions, innovation diffusion, migration, and economic location will tend to reinforce this pattern so that, whatever happens, the future will look very much like the past.[3]

It is true that spatial patterns demonstrate a remarkable degree of stability. It is also true that the attempts to introduce structural changes into those patterns via different social and economic policies can claim only a limited amcunt of success. I am convinced, however, that it is wrong to accept the experience of the past as an unavoidable verdict for the future. In a world wide perspective there is a growing dissatisfaction with the performance of the past, and various societies are looking for new models for the society of the future. Naturally, one could argue that new functional structures of the society will be accommodated by old spatial patterns. But this accommodation is not a conflict-free process, and in at least some cases the new functional structures must generate new regional patterns. If policy and planning is really an innovative activity then a much more radical assumption should be accepted. The new spatial pattern should accelerate the emergence of new social and functional structures.

The Research Priorities

Each of the three policy fields discussed in this paper is at present represented by different research institutions which, since differences are as a rule a stronger force in research activities than are similarities, are dedicated to different intellectual and professional traditions. Therefore, it is necessary to promote some research activities both in individual countries and in international organizations which will develop the integrated approach to regional, urban, and environmental policies. Let me mention a few research projects which could be established and implemented in this field.

1. A world wide review of regional, urban, and environmental policy and planning activities implemented in the past and anticipated for the future. Perhaps the period from 1950 tot 2000 would be an appropriate

time horizon for this study;

2. The ideological substance of regional, urban, and environmenta¹ policies; the values, goals, and priorities in this field; the tradeoffs between long- and short-term goals and objectives; and the individual and collective motivations of persons involved in different activities related to regional, urban, and environmental policies;

3. The intellectual equipment of regional, urban, and environmental policies: a review of theories, concepts, models, methods, and instruments applied in this field;

4. The information systems for regional, urban, and environmental policies: a review of experiences and prospects in this field taking into account the methodological, technological, and managerial aspects of this problem;

5. The institutional patterns developed for the formulation and implementation of regional, urban, and environmental policies; the ideological and technical problems involved in the process of institution building in this field; and

6. The systems of training and education as related to the issues involved in regional, urban, and environmental policy and planning activities.

These six research projects could be integrated into an efficient programme supported by a group of national and international institutions involved in different activities in the field of regional, urban, and environmental policies and planning.

Notes

1. J. Ziolkowski, *Socjologia i planowanie spoleczne* (Sociology and Regional Planning), Panstwowe Wydawnictwo Naukowe, Warsaw, 1972, pp. 193-194.

2. W. Alonso, "Beyond the Inter-Disciplinary Approach to Planning", Working Paper No. 90, Center for Planning and Development Research, University of California, Berkeley, 1969, p. 10.

3. John Friedman, as quoted by Alan R. Pred, "The Growth and Development of Systems of Cities in Advanced Economies", *Lund Studies in Geography*, Series B, Human Geography, 38, Lund, 1973, p. 47.

CONCLUDING REMARKS

This volume is a follow-up to a series of special seminars on Regional Development and Planning in World-Wide Perspective which I had the privilege to direct at the Norman Paterson School of International Affairs at Carleton University in the spring of 1974. The twenty-eight papers collected in this volume provide a fairly comprehensive view of regional development and planning as practised in different parts of the world.

It is an open question to what extent the papers in the three main sections, on the Western countries, the Eastern countries, and the Developing countries, are really representative in their coverage of the salient problems, issues, approaches, and solutions. That coverage seems to me to be quite good in the case of the Western and Eastern countries, in which the policy and planning approaches based on the predominant application of indicative (in the Western countries) or imperative (in the Eastern countries) instruments are presented rather well.[1]

The materials on the Developing countries are very interesting and informative but, since the differences among the developing countries are too big and the problems too complicated, this section is somewhat less representative than the other two.

In the intellectual organization of the book we can thus find some weaknesses generated by the problems of presenting in one volume a comprehensive analysis of regional development and planning in world-wide perspective, and the title of the volume is accordingly more modest than the somewhat ambitious title of the seminar series. The expression "Regional Development and Planning: International Perspectives" does not suggest a full world coverage, but rather a broad international review of experiences in this field. In my opinion this review could stimulate discussion of three important topics, broached particularly in the final "International" section of the volume:

1. The scope and limits of universal approaches to regional development and planning;

2. The international transfer of experiences in the field of regional development and planning; and

3. International cooperation in the field of regional development and planning.

445

1. The Scope and Limits of Universal Approaches to Regional Development and Planning

The content of this volume might create the impression that the problems and approaches to regional development and planning are similar in all parts of the world. There are indeed certain similarities, and these have two sources, the first of which can be associated with the common features of the technological elements in the spatial patterns. In the relation of human activity to space we can find some parameters which are like the coefficients in the input-output analysis. These coefficients are determined by technical and balance laws of the spatial patterns[2] and are universal to the extent that the given type of technology is universal. The universal features of technological elements in the spatial patterns are especially evident if similar patterns are being developed in countries with different socio-economic systems and similar environmental conditions. The vast Arctic territories are a good example of this situation.

The second source of similarities is associated with the techniques applied in analytical and planning procedures. Quantitative techniques particularly have a strong dimension of universalism and act as integrating forces in regional studies carried out around the world. The activities of the Regional Science Association are a good example of this intellectual attitude.

The selection of technological solutions and of planning techniques is, however, a social process determined by the values, preferences and priorities prevailing within a given economic and social system and within a given country. So the ideological substance of regional development and planning[3] is a powerful countervailing force in relation to the harmonious universal attitude. In this volume the best formulation of ideological problems is presented by José Luis Coraggio, who expresses his dissatisfaction not only with the planning theories applied in Latin America but also with the political and social structures that dominate in that part of the world. Coraggio makes the following methodological suggestion:

> In order to make out the ideological elements in a discourse which is allegedly scientific, it is necessary to refer to the ideological systems themselves. The analysis of ideological processes should, however, take the study of specific ideological formations as its point of departure, showing their origin, progress and diffusion within a specific field, as well as their junction with complementary formations inserted in apparently different problem areas. Furthermore, a better understanding of this process may seem impossible without simultaneous research on the processes of the material structures with which these ideological formations are linked.[4]

446

The proposal to take the study of specific ideological formations as point of departure is an implicit challenge to the atmosphere of harmonious universality created by technological and technoplannistic considerations. Any comparative analysis of regional development and planning should take into account both the universal and the non-universal problems and attitudes. A worthwhile comparison can be made from this point of view of the papers on the Western, Eastern, and Developing countries presented in this volume.

2. *The International Transfer of Experiences*
   in the Field of Regional Development and Planning

The publication of a volume incorporating contributions by more than thirty authors representing almost all parts of the world can be expected to provide an interesting set of analyses and of tentative answers to fundamental questions of regional development and planning. This volume can also, however, be viewed in a more practical framework of the international transfer of experiences in the field. We are assuming that international meetings and publications are as a rule good vehicles for this transfer, not only in terms of methods and theoretical insights but also in terms of policy and planning solutions and instruments.

I think that the content of this book can be used in an explicit examination of this topic. Let us have a critical look at the intellectual and operational anatomy and mechanisms in the international transfer of experiences in the field of regional development and planning. Let us ask ourselves what the necessary and sufficient conditions are that must be fulfilled in order to make possible the transfer of experiences from one country to another; how the channels for such a transfer can be improved; and how the barriers in this endeavour can be diminished. Let us, in other words, ask ourselves how we can avoid the kind of situation described by Louis Lefeber and Mrinal Datta-Chaudhuri in the following way:

> Since regional development shows a tendency toward urban agglomeration, regional planners of backward regions have a particularly difficult problem to deal with. One type of effort to attract small and middle scale industrial entrepreneurs to such regions is the industrial estates programme widely used in various parts of Southeast Asia.
>
> The basic question is why a region is backward. It was thought that a simple answer emerged from the pre-war success of the Trading Estates Programme in Britain. If the forces of agglomeration in the developed centres are due to economies of scale and indivisibilities in the industrial infra-structure then the proper policy for inducing

447

new industries to move to the backward areas is (a) to build in the backward area an integrated complex of factory sheds complete with the various overhead facilities, (b) to offer financial incentives in the form of tax concessions, subsidies, etc., to the incoming entrepreneurs.

Several Southeast Asian countries imitated the British programme by building up what came to be known as industrial estates. A selective survey largely based on the experiences of two countries, India and Singapore, brings out the following observations: (a) the industrial estates have, in general, been more successful in the already in-dustrialised urban centres, than in the rural or semi-urban areas, and (b) in the choice of product and of the technique of production, the successful estate entrepreneurs have, in general, chosen rather so-phisticated products with higher capital-intensity than had been anti-cipated by the government sponsors.

... The British example was misleading. The backward areas in Britain were unutilized locations of a geographically small and highly industrialised country. In the opposite case of a large underdeveloped country the dispersal of industries to rural or semi-urban areas, even if economically justifiable, would obviously require much stronger incentives than those provided under these schemes.[5]

This was an example of a transfer of an individual institution and planning instrument from a developed into a developing country. This is probably the most important problem in the transfer considerations. The developing countries are absorbing different experiences of the developed countries. In this context the popularity of growth poles and growth centre policies in the developing countries is significant, and the papers by Taylor and Pióro in this volume are attempts to adapt this concept to the African reality. The importance of initiating growth pole policies in the developing countries has been well expressed by Akin Mabogunje:

> The growth pole concept offers developing countries a possibility of thinking of development in specific locational or spatial terms. By doing this, it forces their gaze slightly away from the national ac-counting view of their developmental performance to more concrete concern with spatial structural transformation in different parts of the country. As a strategy for development, it calls attention more directly to natural resource development as well as to welfare aspects of economic advancement both for the urban and the rural population.
>
> Yet, in spite of these, it is clear that as a concept it still requires clearer definition to give it a greater focus and incisiveness. This is nowhere more important than in attempts to use it in dealing with developmental problems of developing countries. As a planning strategy, it runs grave risks that in the absence of supporting institu-

tions and relevant policies, its best efforts may be frustrated. What these institutions need to be is, however, not always clear nor can one have a pre-determined set of policies to suit conditions in every country. This element of experimenting is however part of the strength of the strategy since it implies a constant aliveness and imaginative concern with the problems of development. For Nigeria, there can be no doubt that the adoption of a growth pole strategy will move development planning away from the futile regional or state conflicts and obsession with political balancing. It should move to a level where part of the country could see where it relates to other parts in an integrated economy striding forward to greater achievements.[6]

While concentrating attention on the technical substance of the growth pole hypothesis we should not forget the controversial issue related to the ideological substance of this theory. It is worthwhile, in this context, to quote a few lines from another challenging paper written by Coraggio:

> Even the mildest review of the "prescriptions for development through the establishment of growth poles" leaves an uneasy feeling of dissatisfaction: a feeling that the essential components of the proposal are being subtracted from the analysis, i.e. the components concerned with the real functioning conditions of a system of regions operating within a framework of dependent capitalism.
>
> The methodological validity of the analysis and its corresponding strategy are therefore questioned. Are they not an attempt to apply to our [Latin American] countries a theory eleborated on the basis of different factual situations, more specifically those of the dominant countries? Is it not also true that only the mechanistic elements of this theory are selected, proceeding next to their superficial adaptation to hazardous conditions, and that the essential content is left aside?
>
> Finally, is this strategy of development poles not an ideological screen concealing the real process of increasing integration of our spaces to the dominant system?[7]

I will not try to propose a solution to the controversial issue of the interrelation between the ideological and technical substance of the growth pole theory. There is no doubt, however, that the transfer of experiences in the field of regional development and planning cannot be reduced to its technical dimensions. Moreover, we have to note that the attitude of the developing countries toward the experiences of the developed countries is changing very deeply. In the developing countries new original policy and planning ideologies are emerging,[8] which reflect the real needs of the developing economies and societies in Asia, Africa, and Latin America. This active attitude will create new conditions for the transfer of experiences

449

in the field. Uncritical imitation will decline, and instead the developing countries will examine the experiences of the Western and Eastern countries critically in order to find solutions that are really applicable to their own needs. Depending on the socio-economic system prevailing in the given developing country the preference will be allocated to indicative or to imperative planning instruments. Naturally the most important element in the new policy and planning ideologies emerging in the developing countries will be represented by the generalization of their own experiences.

The growing intellectual sovereignty of the developing countries can be observed in the proceedings of the international conferences on regional development and planning which have recently been held in Latin America,[9] Asia,[10] and Africa.[11]

3. *International Cooperation in the Field of Regional Development and Planning*

In the last twenty years different schemes and programmes of international cooperation in the field of regional development and planning have been developed and implemented. I will not try to present a full and comprehensive review of these activities here; this should be done through a special publication on this topic. Here it is sufficient to discuss a few characteristic cases.

Case 1: The Regional Science Association

The Regional Science Association, created in 1954 in Detroit, Michigan, has a very distinguished record in promoting international cooperation in the field of new analytical and planning techniques. Its meetings and publications have contributed enormously to the perfection of the technical apparatus applied in regional studies in most countries of the world. The extraordinary intellectual capacity and the apostolic spirit of Walter Isard were instrumental in the rapid diffusion of the ideas of the Association on a well-nigh global scale. After the first decade of very successful expansion, however, the progress of the RSA slowed down to such an extent that it is now in a state of stagnation. The experience of the Association is an important indicator that international cooperation in the field of regional development and planning cannot be reduced only to the technical substance of this activity. The discussions of models and methods not incorporated into the authentic reality of socio-political processes and planning activities have a limited appeal. We originally planned to print a comprehensive review of the successes and failures of the RSA in this

450

volume, but unfortunately it was impossible to get such a paper in the time available. We will therefore have to await another occasion for the presentation of this interesting and important issue.

Case 2: The United Nations Research Institute for Social Development

A programme of research and planning was implemented over the period 1967-1971 at UNRISD in Geneva [12] as a conscious effort to build an approach to international cooperation in the field of regional development and planning which would offer an alternative to the model developed by the Regional Science Association. The essence of the UNRISD approach to cooperation is a comparative analysis of the experiences of different countries and continents in regional development and planning, and of the problems and solutions in this field, built into the framework of specific systems of policy and planning. The techniques and models of regional analysis are considered in this context as of secondary importance, subordinated to the leading problems emerging from the objective reality and the solution of these problems via proper instruments of policy and planning. The programme consisted mainly of the following projects: [13]

1. A world-wide study of experiences and prospects in regional development;

2. The role of growth poles and growth centres in regional development;

3. Information systems for regional development;

4. Regional Sociology; and

5. Regional disaggregation of national policies and plans.

The studies and the materials developed in the framework of this Geneva programme are published in the UNRISD-MOUTON *Regional Planning* series. Six volumes of this series are already available, and the remaining four will be published in the years 1975-76.

Different evaluations of the Geneva programme and of the UNRISD-MOUTON series of volumes have already been published in Poland, [14] France, [15] the Soviet Union, [16] and the United States. [17]

Case 3: An International Institute for Regional Studies: A Proposal

The experience of the Geneva programme and a review of the world situation in the field of regional development and planning induced me to prepare a Memorandum concerning the establishment of an International Institute for Regional Studies. Although this Memorandum was formulated in 1971 the ideas and proposals incorporated in it are still valid and ready for implementation, and it seems appropriate to quote the following text from it here:

451

Recently I had conversations with Louis Lefeber and Mrinal Datta-Chaudhuri. We came to the conclusion that efforts should be made to set up an international institute for regional studies, which would be a logical central point in the network of institutions promoting regional development and planning. The institute could perform three functions: 1. research; 2. training; and 3. expertise.

The research programme could concentrate on topics which are crucial for regional development and planning. My experience here in Geneva has shown that there are many such topics and that valid results can be obtained which are accepted in both developing and developed countries of the East and the West.

Training activities in the institute would be advisable, perhaps concentrating on training at the highest level. For example, university professors in economics, geography, sociology, statistics, urban planning, and so on, who would like to start new departments for regional planning in the developing countries could spend some time in the institute participating in high level seminars and discussions.

Lastly, but of no less importance, the institute could be a place for briefing experts who would be assuming responsibilities in the promotion of regional planning. Frankly, the present practice in the briefing of experts by international agencies is rather a bureaucratic ceremony than a substantial preparation of the expert. The briefing function should be associated with the debriefing of experts returning from developing countries. At present there is no place in the world which could perform a function of sui generis data bank, accumulating the field experience of the past so that the new experts would not start from the beginning to discover once more what has already been discovered by his professional colleagues.

I am sure than an interaction of research, training and expertise would be a special inducement for the development of such an institute.

My paper in this volume on the spatial dimension in policy and planning should be treated as a follow-up and as an extension to this Memorandum. The research priorities proposed in this paper are built around two fundamental assumptions:

1. That the spatial dimension in policy and planning is represented by three interrelated activities:
   a. regional policy and planning;
   b. urban policy and planning; and
   c. environmental policy and planning.

In this way regional policies and planning are built into a broader framework of a subsystem in the general system of policy and planning; and

2. That the ideological and technical substance of policy and planning should be seen in a new perspective of comparative studies which are not trying to avoid the difficult and controversial problems emerging in our field.

* *
*

The concluding remarks presented here do not follow the conventional recipe for the preparation of such texts. This is not a more or less skilful summary of the content of the volume, but rather a set of impressions designed to suggest to the critical reader some topics which may be examined using the materials of the volume as a starting point. It is, in other words, an invitation to an intellectual adventure in the field of regional development and planning. However, a modest hope is expressed that this volume will stimulate not only some intellectual adventures but also some practical actions which will improve the pattern of international cooperation in the field. *Quod felix faustum fortunatumque sit.*

Jablonna, January 1975   Antoni R. Kukliński

Notes

1. A comprehensive analysis of the approaches to regional planning in the socialist and capitalist countries is presented in Antoni R. Kukliński, "Macro-regional Planning in the Developed Countries", in A. Kukliński and R. Petrella, eds., *Growth Poles and Regional Policies,* Mouton, Paris and The Hague, 1972, pp. 213-235.

2. Oskar Lange has written on the scope of technical and balance laws of production as follows: "The laws with the widest application in history are those arising from the production process—the technical and balance laws of production. The most general of these laws are universal in character, which means that they are valid at all stages of social development in which production is a conscious and purposive human activity—i.e. beginning with the appearance of mankind. A general technical and balance law of production of this kind arises from the very existence of certain necessary technical and balance relationships in the production process". Oskar Lange, *Political Economy,* Vol. 1, Pergamon Press, New York, 1963, p. 64.

3. The definition of the ideological substance of policy and planning is presented in this volume by Antoni R. Kukliński in "The Spatial Dimension in Policy and Planning".

4. José Luis Coraggio, "Polarization, Development, and Integration" in this volume.

5. Louis Lefeber and Mrinal Datta-Chaudhuri, *Regional Development: Experiences and Prospects in South and Southeast Asia*, UNRISD-MOUTON Regional Planning series, Vol. 1, Mouton, Paris and The Hague, 1972, p. 16.

6. Akin Mabogunje, *Growth Poles and Growth Centres in Regional Development in Nigeria*, UNRISD, Geneva, 1972, p. 79.

7. José Luis Coraggio, "Toward a Revision of the Growth Pole Theory", p. 14 of a manuscript that is a partially revised version of a paper with the same title published in *Eure* (Santiago, Chile), Vol. 11, No. 4, March 1972.

8. See Gunnar Myrdal, *Asian Drama*, Vol. 11, Chapter 15, "The Spread and Impact of the Ideology of Planning", Penguin Books, Harmondsworth, Middlesex, 1968, pp. 709-740; and A. Lukaszewicz, "Poverty and Development", *Economica Polonia*, No. 1, 1974, pp. 95-119.

9. ILPES-ILDIS, "Planificación regional y urbana en América Latina", Siglo XXI, editore, Mexico, España, Argentina, 1974.

10. See the proceedings of the Asian Seminar on Regional Planning and National Development sponsored by the Institute of Development Studies at the University of Mysore, India, July 1974.

11. See the proceedings of an International Conference on Regional Planning and National Development in Tropical Africa, University of Ibadan, Nigeria, March 1972.

12. The Geneva programme was part of a wider United Nations effort outlined in Gerald Wen's paper in this volume.

13. See Antoni R. Kukliński, "The UNRISD Research Programme on Regional Development" in Antoni R. Kukliński and R. Petrella, eds., *op. cit.*, pp. 239-245.

14. *Bulletin of the Committee of Space Economy and Regional Planning of the Polish Academy of Sciences*, No. 64, Warsaw 1971.

15. Christiane de Ribet-Petersen, "Quelques Recherches Récentes sur les Poles de Croissance et les Poles de Développement", *Mondes en Développement*, No. 3, 1973, pp. 127-140.

16. L. N. Karpov, G. W. Sdasiuk, G. N. Utkin, "Problemy regionalnogo razwitija i planirowanija za rubiezom—Analiz serii mezdunarodnych publikacii pod obszczej redakcief dr. A. Kuklinskogo", in *Ekonomiczesko-geograficzeskije problemy formirowanija tieritorialno-proizwodstwiennych kompleksow Sibirii*, IV, edited by M. K. Bandman, Novosibirsk, 1972, pp. 41-72.

17. Michael E. Conroy, "The United Nations Research Series on Regional Development, A Review Article", *Growth and Change, A Journal of Regional Development*, January 1974, pp. 47-50.

NOTES ON THE CONTRIBUTORS

M. K. Bandman is Chief of the Laboratory of the Institute of Economics and Industrial Engineering of the Siberian Department of the Academy of Sciences of the U.S.S.R. in Novosibirsk. His main fields of specialization are the location of productive forces in Siberia and spatial systems modelling. The author of a number of publications on regional economics and the applications of quantitative methods in regional planning studies, Dr. Bandman has also edited a collection entitled *Modelling the Formation of Spatial Production Complexes* (1971), and a series of six volumes on the *Economic-Geographic Problems of the Formation of Siberian Spatial Production Complexes*. He is an associate member of the IGU Working Group on Industrial Geography.

Thomas N. Brewis is Professor of Economics at Carleton University, and a former Director of the School of Commerce. He is the author of a number of studies on various aspects of Canadian economic policy. During the past decade he has devoted particular attention to regional problems and the policies to which these have given rise. He is currently engaged in an examination of the recommendations and policies of the European Community designed to improve the economic situation in the less favoured regions of the member countries. Dr. Brewis is a member of the Canadian Council on Rural Development.

José Luis Coraggio is Professor of Spatial Economics and Micro-economics at the Universidad Nacional de Buenos Aires and Head Researcher at the Centro de Estudios Urbanos y Regionales. He was previously (1971-72) Dean of the Department of Economics of the Universidad Nacional del Sur in Argentina. Professor Coraggio has published several works, both in Spanish and in English, on regional issues in Latin America, among them: *Equidad Eficiencia y Conflicto entre Regiones* (1969); *Diseño de Normas para la Elaboración de Planes Regionales en Argentina* (1970); *Metropolitan Areas and National Development: A Long Term Perspective* (1970); jointly with G. Geisse; and *Centralización y Concentración en la Configuración Espacial Argentina* (1971).

John H. Cumberland, who earned his Master's degree and his Ph. D. in economics from Harvard, is currently Professor of Economics at the University of Maryland. He has served as advisor to numerous local, national, and international organizations in the field of regional and urban environmental management. He is the author of *Regional Development Experiences and Prospects in the United States of America,* as well as of other books and papers on development and the environment.

Anthony C. Fisher is Associate Professor of Economics and Research Associate at the Bureau of Business and Economic Research at the University of Maryland. Micro-theory, public economics, and natural resources and environment are his main fields of interest, and his major publications include *The Evaluation of Benefits from Pollution Abatement,* a study prepared for the U.S. Environmental Protection Agency in 1972; and *The Economics of Natural Environments: Studies in the Valuations of Commodity and Amenity Resources* (1975), written jointly with J. Krutilla. He is at present a consultant for Resources for the Future, Inc., and a member of the National Academy of Sciences Committee on Assessment of Demand for Outdoor Recreation Resources and Ionizing Radiation in the Environment.

B. Ganguli, one-time Research Officer and currently Sociologist for the Government of India's Town and Country Planning Organization, has been concerned with the social aspects of urban and regional development for more than a decade. Dr. Ganguli has participated in several international seminars, among them the International Geographical Congress held in Delhi in 1968, where she highlighted the social problems associated with the development of the South-East resource region in India. She has also been actively involved in special courses conducted by the Indian National Buildings Organization and the United Nations Regional Housing Centre for ECAFE on the sociological aspects of housing.

Alexandr G. Granberg is head of the department of optimization of territorial systems in the Institute of Economics and Industrial Engineering of the Siberian Department of the USSR Academy of Sciences in Novosibirsk. He also teaches at Novosibirsk State University, where he is head of the department of the application of mathematical models in economy and planning. Dr. Granberg's research has mainly been devoted to the modelling of the regional and national economy, and to the methods of elaborating programmes of economic development, and he has published several papers in Russian on these subjects.

456

Victor Grosman is currently FAO Senior Economic Adviser in Brasilia. Previously PREALC Regional Representative for Central America and Panama, he is a former Professor of Economics and Director of the Department of Economics at the University of Concepción. Chile. He conducted an *Economic Survey of the Concepción Region* (in two volumes, 1964/65), and is the author of many papers and surveys on regional planning and development. In 1967-69 Dr. Grosman was United Nations Economic Advisor to the Brazilian Government, and in 1970 he was a staff member of the United Nations Research Institute for Social Development in Geneva. He was ILO Senior Advisor on Manpower Planning and Development in Plan Lerma (Mexico, 1971-1973), and has participated in numerous international meetings and seminars in various parts of the world.

Bohdan Gruchman is Associate Professor at the Institute for Planning and Regional Analysis and Head of the Centre for Applied Economic Research at the School of Economics in Poznan, Poland. He holds a Ph.D. degree in economics. At one time he was Head of the Development Planning Division of the Regional Planning Board, Poznan, and a member of a United Nations' planning team in Libya (1967-69). Dr. Gruchman has written two books (in Polish) on *Industrial Development of the Poznan Region* (1964), and on *Agglomerative and Deglomerative Factors of Industrial Location in a Planned Economy* (1967), as well as a number of papers on methodology of national and regional planning, industrial location, regional consumption, income savings, and market analysis.

Niles M. Hansen, Professor of Economics and Director, Center for Economic Development, University of Texas (Austin), is on the editorial boards of *Growth and Change, Regional and Urban Economics,* and the *Review of Regional Studies.* Apart from numerous papers and articles he is the author of a number of books: *French Regional Planning* (1968); *France in the Modern World* (1969); *Rural Poverty and the Urban Crisis: A Strategy for Regional Development* (1970); *Intermediate-Size Cities as Growth Centers* (1971); *Location Preferences, Migration and Regional Growth* (1973); and *The Future of Nonmetropolitan America* (1973). He has also edited volumes on *Growth Centers and Regional Development* (1970), and on *Public Policy and Regional Economic Development: The Experience of Nine Western Countries* (1974).

Benjamin Higgins is Professor of Economics and Vice-Dean of Research for the Faculty of Social Sciences at the University of Ottawa. He was Advisor on Urban and Regional Planning for the Government of

457

Malaysia (EPU) in 1973-74, and Senior Economic Advisor for the Pahang Tenggara Regional Plan in 1970-71. From 1971 to 1974 Dr. Higgins was Senior Consultant for the UNRISD Project on the "Unified Approach" to Development Planning. His many other responsibilities have included directing the Resources for the Future Project on Economic Prospects for the U.S. Southwest (University of Texas 1961-67), chairing the Special Task Force for the Montreal International Airport (1968-69), acting as Senior Consultant for the Conference of Asian Planners, ECAFE (Bangkok, 1971-) and, most recently, directing a government and University of Ottawa joint project on the Economic and Social Development of Eastern Ontario and acting as Economic Consultant for the CIDA project on Regional Planning for Haiti. Among his numerous publications are books on *Economic Development; Problem, Principles, Policies* (1968), *Technical Assistance and the Economic Development of Greece* (jointly with A. Maddison, 1965), and *A Regional Planning Approach to the Problems of Bi-Culturalism* (Report to the Royal Commission on Bilingualism and Biculturalism, 1966).

Bruno Jobert has, since 1967, been affiliated with the Centre de Recherche sur l'Administration Economique et l'Amènagement du Territoire de l'Institut d'Etudes Politiques de Grenoble in France. His principal interests include urban planning, urban growth, and social planning.

David G. Khodzhaev teaches at the State University of Moscow and is involved in work on Gosplan SSSR. His main interests are the development of urban settlements and the problems of controlling urban growth, subjects on which he has published various papers in Russian.

Boris Sergeivitch Khorev is Chairman of the Department of the Socio-Demographic Problems of Settlement at the Centre for the Study of Population Problems at Moscow State University. He has specialized and has published several studies in the fields of the distribution of industrial power, economic geography, and demography.

Briitta Koskiaho is Associate Professor of Social Policy in the Faculty of Social Sciences at the University of Tampere in Finland. She has published studies on "Level of living and industrialization" (1969), "Environmental policy" (1972), "Basic questions of environmental policy" (1974) and on "The housing question and satisfaction of needs" (1974).

Antoni R. Kukliński is Professor at the Centre for African Studies at the University of Warsaw, Deputy Editor of the *Polish Geographical Re-*

view, and Chairman of the Polish Economic Society's Commission on International Cooperation. From 1967 to 1971 he was Programme Director on Regional Development for UNRISD in Geneva, and he is Editor of the UNRISD-Mouton series of books on *Regional Planning*. His other publications include *Criteria for Location of Industrial Plans: Changes and Problems* (New York, 1967), and *Contributions to Regional Planning and Development* (University of Mysore, 1971). Dr. Kukliński has also written numerous papers on environmental policies, on regional development and planning, and on the integration of regional, urban, and environmental policies.

Louis Lefeber has held teaching positions at Harvard, M.I.T., and Stanford, and is currently F.C. Hecht Professor of International Economics at Brandeis University and Professor of Economics at York University (on leave). His publications include monographs on planning and development as well as articles in professional journals and contributions to volumes of essays. He has frequently been consultant to various United Nations agencies, the Panamerican Union, and governments of various developing countries in Asia, Latin America, and Africa. He was also Ford Research Fellow as well as visiting scholar at the Institute of Economic Growth, Delhi University, and at other academic institutions.

Jurij M. Pavlov is Vice-Chairman of the Council for Studying the Productive Forces and Vice-Chairman of the Council for International Scientific Relations in Regional Studies attached to the Presidium of the Academy of Sciences of the USSR in Moscow. Dr. Pavlov has specialized in scientific research on the regional economics of the Soviet Union and of other countries, and has published several monographs and papers in Russian on such subjects as the regional policies of capitalist countries, theoretical problems of regional economics, and governmental intrusion into territorial development processes.

Poul Ove Pedersen is Associate Professor in Regional Science at the Technical University of Denmark in Copenhagen. In 1967-69 Dr. Pedersen was Visiting Professor at the Center for Urban and Regional Studies (CIDU) at the Catholic University of Santiago, Chile, and prior to that he was employed in a public planning commission and as a private consultant in Denmark. He has published *Models of population structure and development in metropolitan areas—especially with regard to Greater Copenhagen* (in Danish, 1967); *Urban-Regional Development in South America—a process of diffusion and integration* (1974); and several articles on urban and regional development and on

459

innovation diffusion. Lately he has been working on the problems of rural industrial development and on rural public transport.

Zygmunt Pióro is Head of Ecology and Economics of the Settlement Division at the Institute of Town Planning and Architecture in Warsaw, and Associate Professor, Deputy Director, and Head of the Regional Planning Section of the African Studies Centre at the University of Warsaw. He also lectures on Physical Planning for the Post-diploma Course at Warsaw Technical University. In 1966-69 Dr. Pióro was U.N. expert in physical planning in Tanzania, where he carried out research on town and regional planning. His publications include a book on *Human Ecology and Town Planning* (1962) and a contribution to the UNRISD series of studies on *Regional Planning* (1972), as well as several articles published in various journals in Poland and elsewhere.

Vadim V. Pokshishevski is a member of the Institute of Ethnography of the Academy of Sciences of the USSR in Moscow, and has previously published papers in Russian journals such as *Sovietskaya Etnografija* on ethnic problems in cities of the USSR.

D. Michael Ray is Professor of Geography at Carleton University, Ottawa. Most of his teaching and research has been on economic geography and quantitative methods, particularly industrial location and economic development in Canada. He has undertaken research programmes for a number of Canadian government agencies including the Agricultural and Rural Development Administration, the Royal Commission on Bilingualism and Biculturalism and the Privy Council Task Force on the Structure of Industry, and since 1968 he has served on the Commission on Quantitative Methods of the International Geographical Union. Among his major publications are three monographs: *Market Potential and Economic Shadow: A Quantitative Analysis of Industrial Locations in Southern Ontario* (1965); *Regional Aspects of Foreign Ownership in Canada* (1967); and *Dimensions of Canadian Regionalism* (1971). A new book, *The Geography of Economic Systems*, written jointly with Brian J. L. Berry and Edgar C. Conkling, is now being published.

Harry W. Richardson, Professor of Regional and Urban Economics at the University of Pittsburgh, previously held posts at the Universities of Aberdeen, Newcastle-upon-Tyne, and Kent at Canterbury in the United Kingdom. He is Technical Consultant for the United Nations and OECD, and the author of twelve books (including *Regional Economics, Elements of Regional Economics, Urban Economics, Regional Growth*

460

Theory, Input-Output and Regional Economics, The Economics of Urban Size, and *Regional Policy and Planning in Spain)* and of more than fifty papers.

Fernando Fernández Rodriguez is Professor of the Institute of Economic Studies in Madrid and lecturer in Economics at the University of Madrid. For several years he was Head of Regional Development Studies in the Ministry of Economic Development, and in this capacity was the Spanish representative on the Committees on Regional Policy of various international organizations. At the present time he is Economic Advisor of the Banco de Bilbao, one of the leading Spanish banks. Dr. Fernández Rodriguez has written several books assessing the Spanish policy of designating Special Areas of Development, and is the principal author of the chapters on regional development in the three Economic and Social Development Plans. He has also published numerous papers in Spanish journals.

Zygmunt Rybicki is Rector of the University of Warsaw, where he is also Professor of Law. He is President of the Committee of Law of the Polish Academy of Sciences, Vice-President of the General Council of Science, Higher Education, and Technology, and President of the Society for the Dissemination of Knowledge. Among the most important of Dr. Rybicki's publications are *The Council of Workers' Delegates in Poland 1918-19* (1962), *The Structure and Functioning of People's Councils in the Polish People's Republic* (1965), *The System of Local Government in Poland* (1971), and *Economic Administrations of European Countries of the Council for Mutual Economic Assistance* (1974).

Kazimierz Secomski, First Deputy Chairman of the Planning Commission of the Council of Ministers in Poland, is Professor of Economics and Head of the Department of Economic and Regional Policy in the Central School of Planning and Statistics in Warsaw. A member of the Polish Academy of Sciences, and of the Board of the Academy, Professor Secomski is especially involved in the activities of three committees of the Academy: he is President of the Committee of Economic Sciences, Vice-President of the Committee for Space Economy and Regional Planning, and Vice-President of the Committee for Research and Prognoses Poland 2000. For many years he was Deputy Chairman of the Polish Economic Society, of which he was a founding member, and he has been President of the Central Board of the Society since 1968. Professor Secomski has published many books and papers in Poland on the problems of investment policy, on the rational distribution of

461

productive forces, on perspective planning, and on economic and social policies.

D. R. F. Taylor is Professor of the Geography Department and of the Norman Paterson School of International Affairs at Carleton University. He spent five years in Kenya as an Education Officer with the Kenya Government, during which time he was involved in field research in Kikuyuland, and he has since been actively involved in research in Africa. Dr. Taylor recently completed an eighteen month joint research project with the University of Nairobi on growth centres, and the results of this study have been published in *Growth Centres and Rural Development in Kenya,* written with S. M. Kimani (1973). Other recent publications include "Spatial Aspects of Kenya's Rural Development Strategy" (1974), "The Role of the Smaller Urban Place in Development: The Case of Kenya" (1974), and "Spatial Organization and Rural Development" (1975).

Rainer Thoss is Professor of Regional Economics and Director of the Institute for Settlement and Housing at the Westfälischen Wilhelms-Universität Münster. He is President of the German speaking section of the Regional Science Association, a member of the Council of Advisors on Regional Policy of the Federal Republic of Germany, of the German Academy for City and Regional Planning, and of the Academy for Regional Science and Regional Planning. He has published many papers in Germany on various subjects related to regional problems.

Paul Y. Villeneuve has been Assistant Professor of Geography at Laval University in Quebec City since 1971. Articles on "Urban Ethnic Accumulation: A Functional Report" (1972) and on "Un paradigme pour l'étude de l'organisation spatiale des sociétés" (1972) are among his publications. A new paper, "Invention, Diffusion, and Allometry: A Study of the Growth and Form of the Pulp and Paper Industry in Central Canada", written jointly with D. Michael Ray and R. Roberge, is now being published. He is currently preparing a monograph on Post-War Urban Growth in the Province of Quebec.

Gerald L. Wen is currently Chief of the Institutional Development and Popular Participation Section (formerly known as the Regional and Community Development Section) of the United Nations Department of Economic and Social Affairs. In this capacity he has been in charge of the United Nations programme on research and training in regional development since its inception in 1963. He has contributed numerous works published by the United Nations in the field of regional development, rural development, and community development. (The United Nations regulations prohibit the attribution of authorship of its publications to individual staff members.) In the course of his service to the United Nations, Mr. Wen has been designated by the Secretary-General to represent the organisation in a number of meetings of the specialised agencies and other technical conferences, and he has participated in a number of evaluation and consultant missions in Mexico, Egypt, China, and elsewhere, for the United Nations Development Programme and the World Food Programme projects. He acted as Deputy Executive-Secretary of the World Conference on Land Reform in Rome in 1966, and was Director of the Global Workshop of Directors of Regional Development Centres in Nagoya, Japan, in 1972.

Harold A. Wood is Professor of Geography at McMaster University, where he has taught since 1950. He led various field surveys for the Government of Canada in 1951-53 and worked for the Organization of American States in 1965-66 as an expert in land use. Founding Chairman of the Ontario Cooperative Program in Latin American and Caribbean Studies in 1969, he was also Director of the Inter-American Planning Society 1968-72 and President of the Regional Geography Committee of the Pan American Institute of Geography and History from 1965 to 1973. He is currently President of this Institute's Commission on Geography. His publications include *Northern Haiti, Land, Land Use and Settlement, The United States and Latin America,* and numerous articles in various journals. In addition he was editor of *Documentación del I Seminario sobre Regionalización* and of *Documentación del II Seminario sobre Regionalización,* both of which have been published by the Pan American Institute of Geography and History.